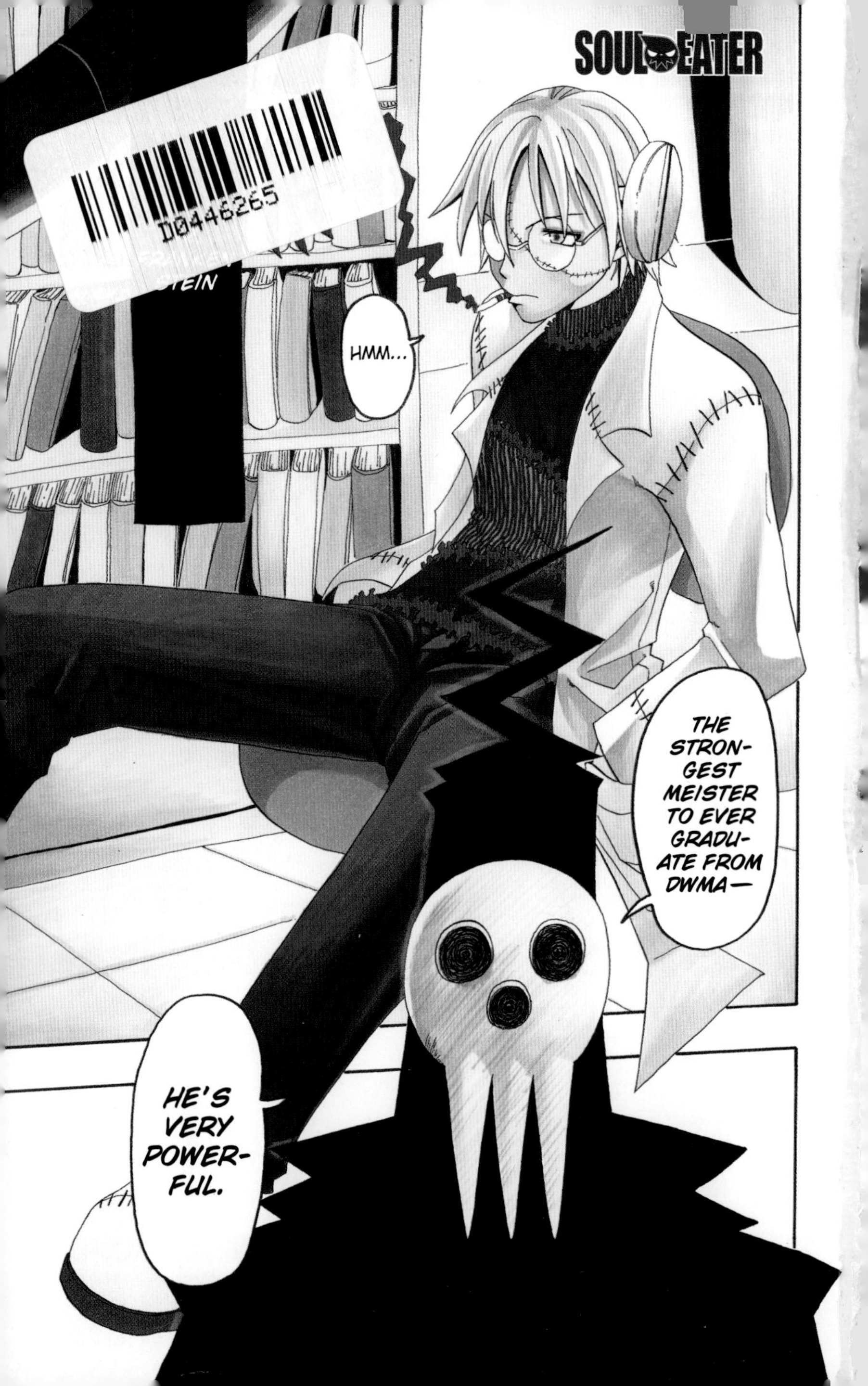
SOUL EATER
HMM...
THE STRONGEST MEISTER TO EVER GRADUATE FROM DWMA—
HE'S VERY POWERFUL.

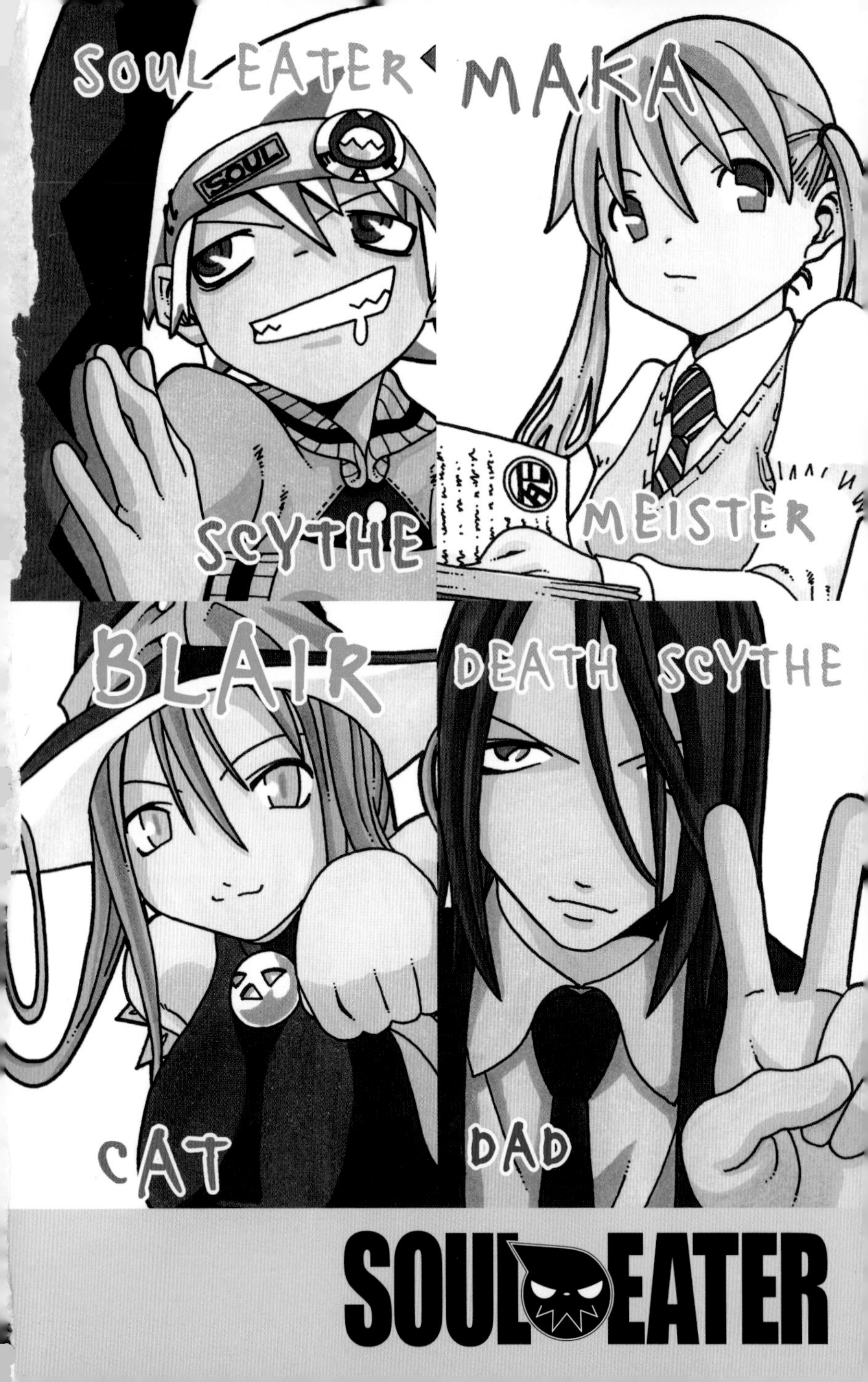
MAKA
MEISTER
SOUL EATER
SOUL
SCYTHE
DEATH SCYTHE
DAD
BLAIR
CAT

SOUL EATER

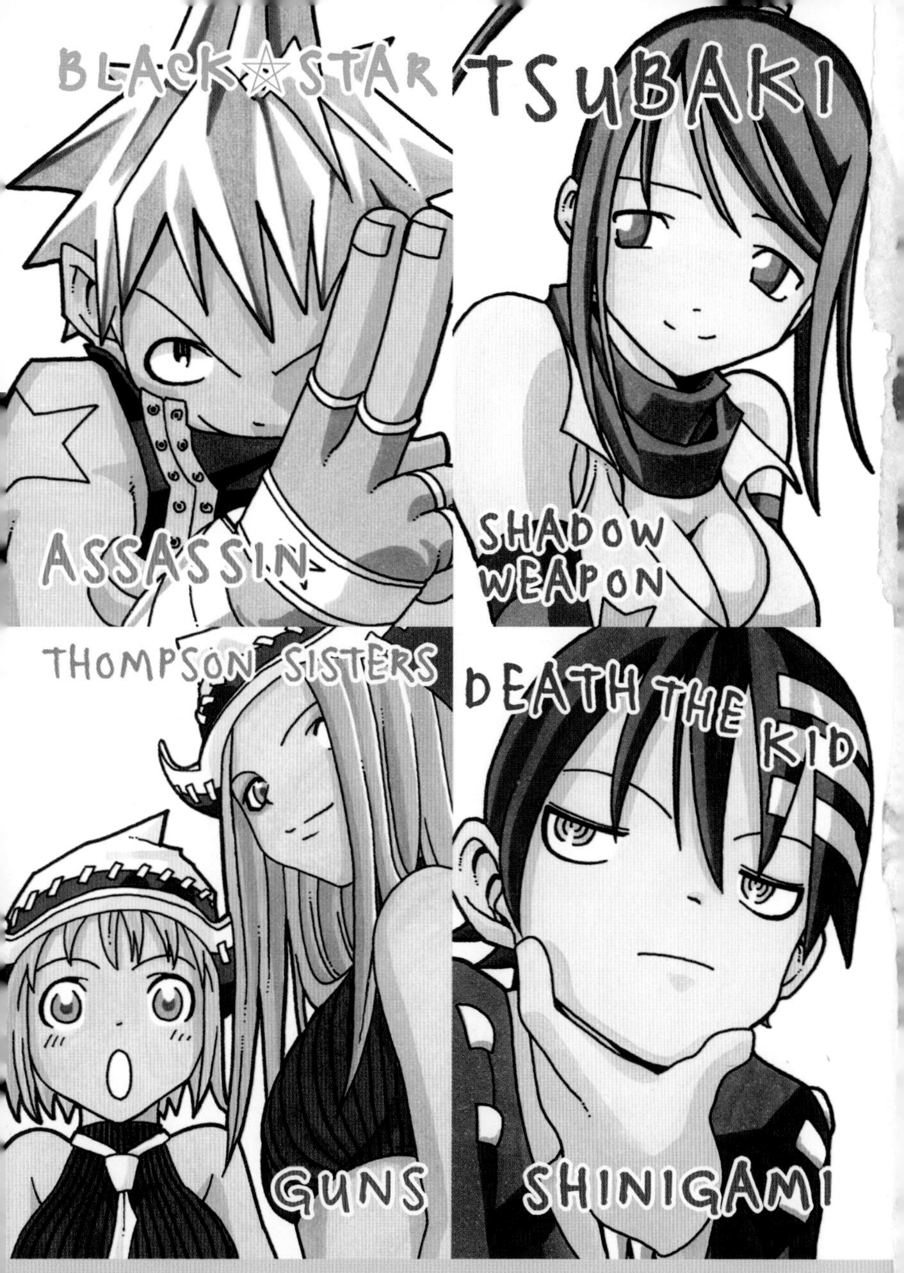
TSUBAKI
SHADOW WEAPON
BLACK☆STAR
ASSASSIN
DEATH THE KID
SHINIGAMI
THOMPSON SISTERS
GUNS

CHAPTER 2: REMEDIAL LESSON (PART 2)

ATSUSHI OHKUBO

SOUL EATER 2

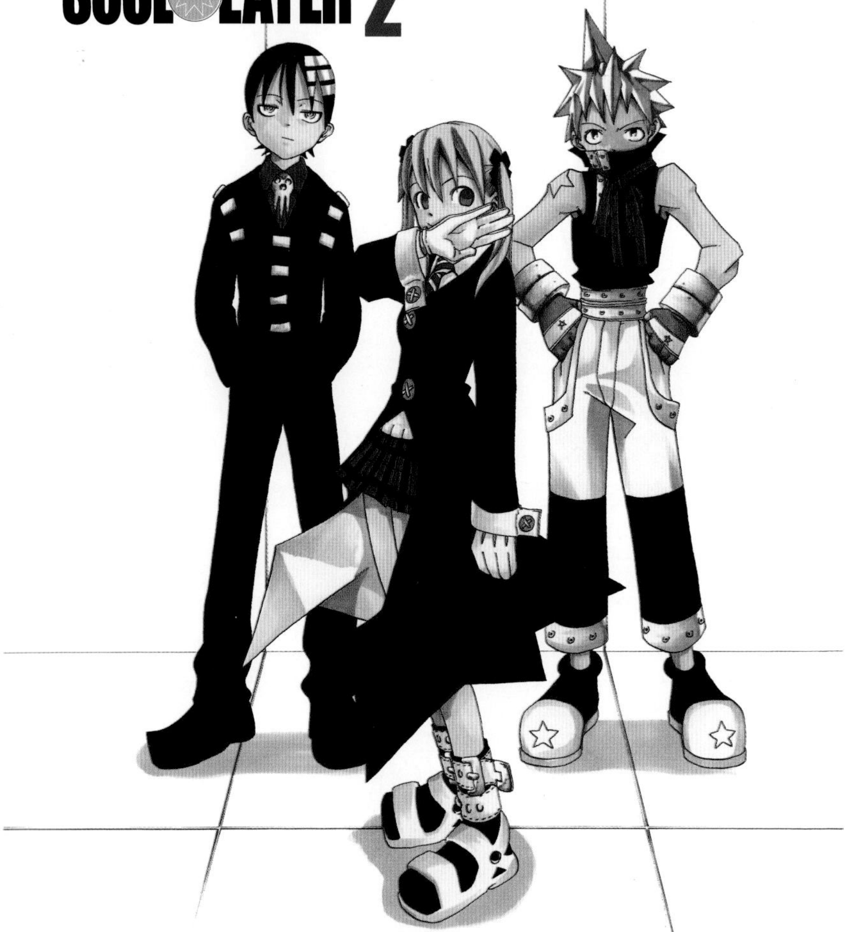

CONTENTS

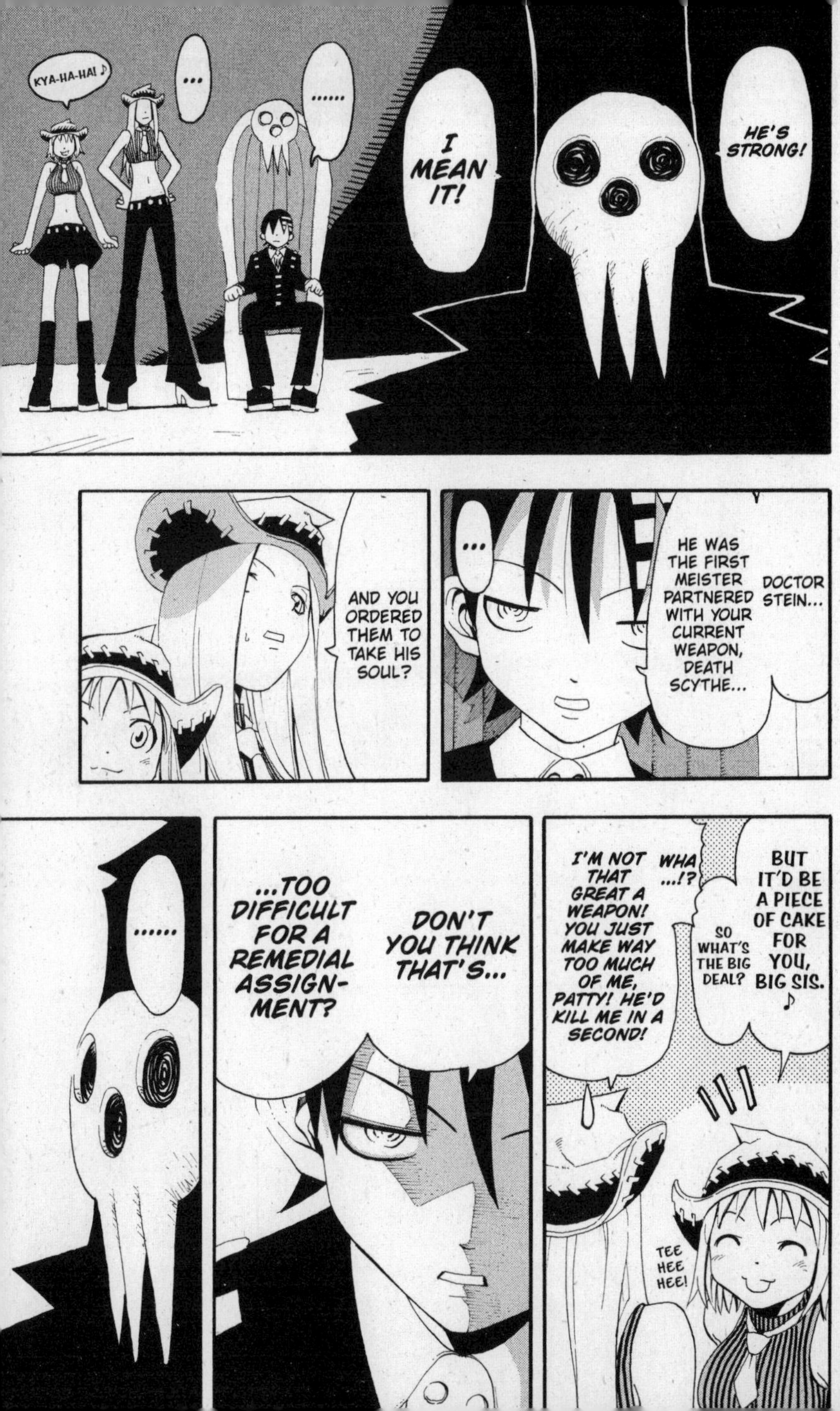
HE'S STRONG!
I MEAN IT!
......
...
KYA-HA-HA! ♪
DOCTOR STEIN...
HE WAS THE FIRST MEISTER PARTNERED WITH YOUR CURRENT WEAPON, DEATH SCYTHE...
...
AND YOU ORDERED THEM TO TAKE HIS SOUL?
BUT IT'D BE A PIECE OF CAKE FOR YOU, BIG SIS. ♪
SO WHAT'S THE BIG DEAL?
WHA ...!?
I'M NOT THAT GREAT A WEAPON! YOU JUST MAKE WAY TOO MUCH OF ME, PATTY! HE'D KILL ME IN A SECOND!
TEE HEE HEE!
DON'T YOU THINK THAT'S...
...TOO DIFFICULT FOR A REMEDIAL ASSIGNMENT?
......

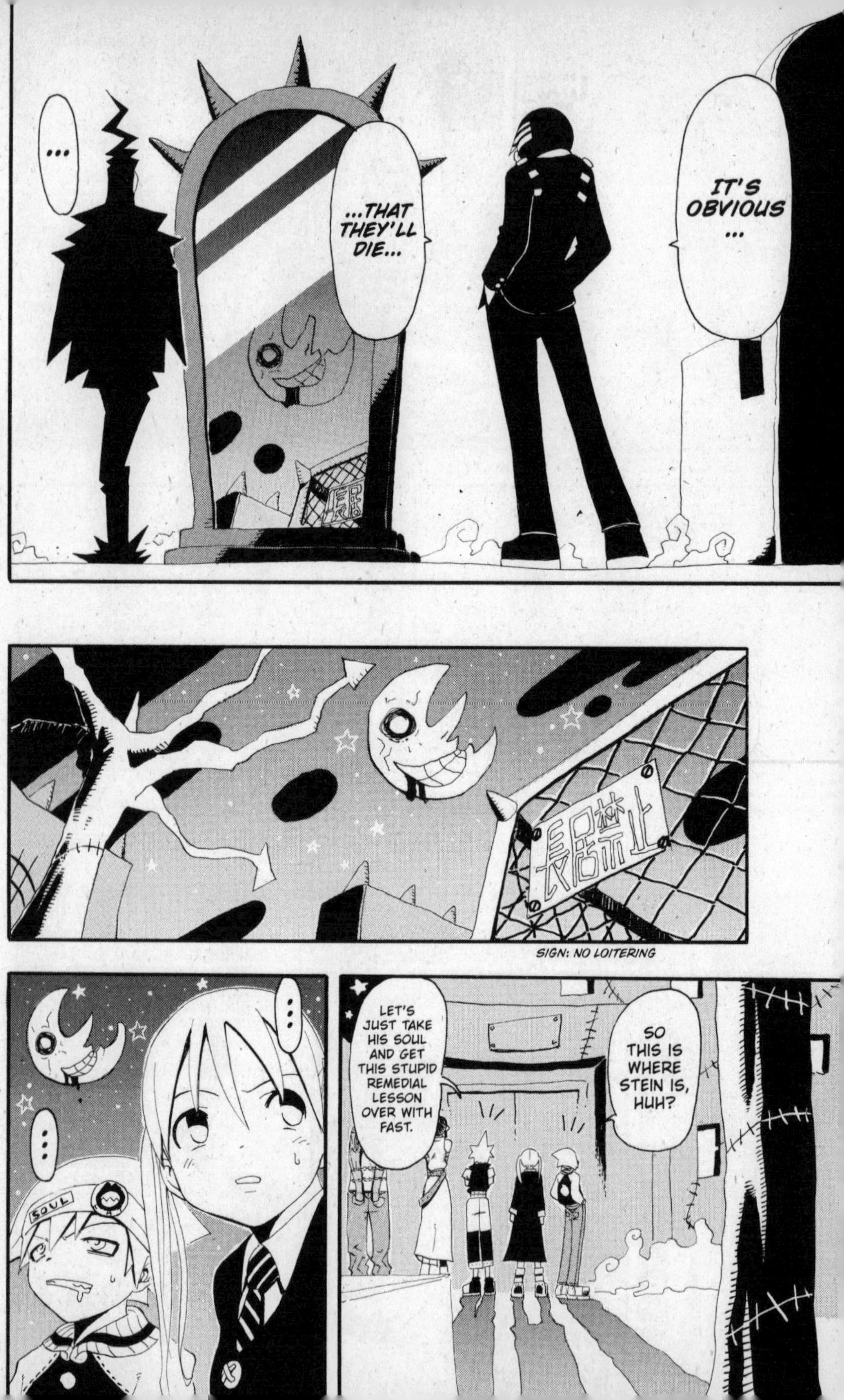
IT'S OBVIOUS ...
...THAT THEY'LL DIE...
...
長居禁止
SIGN: NO LOITERING
SO THIS IS WHERE STEIN IS, HUH?
LET'S JUST TAKE HIS SOUL AND GET THIS STUPID REMEDIAL LESSON OVER WITH FAST.
...
...
SOUL

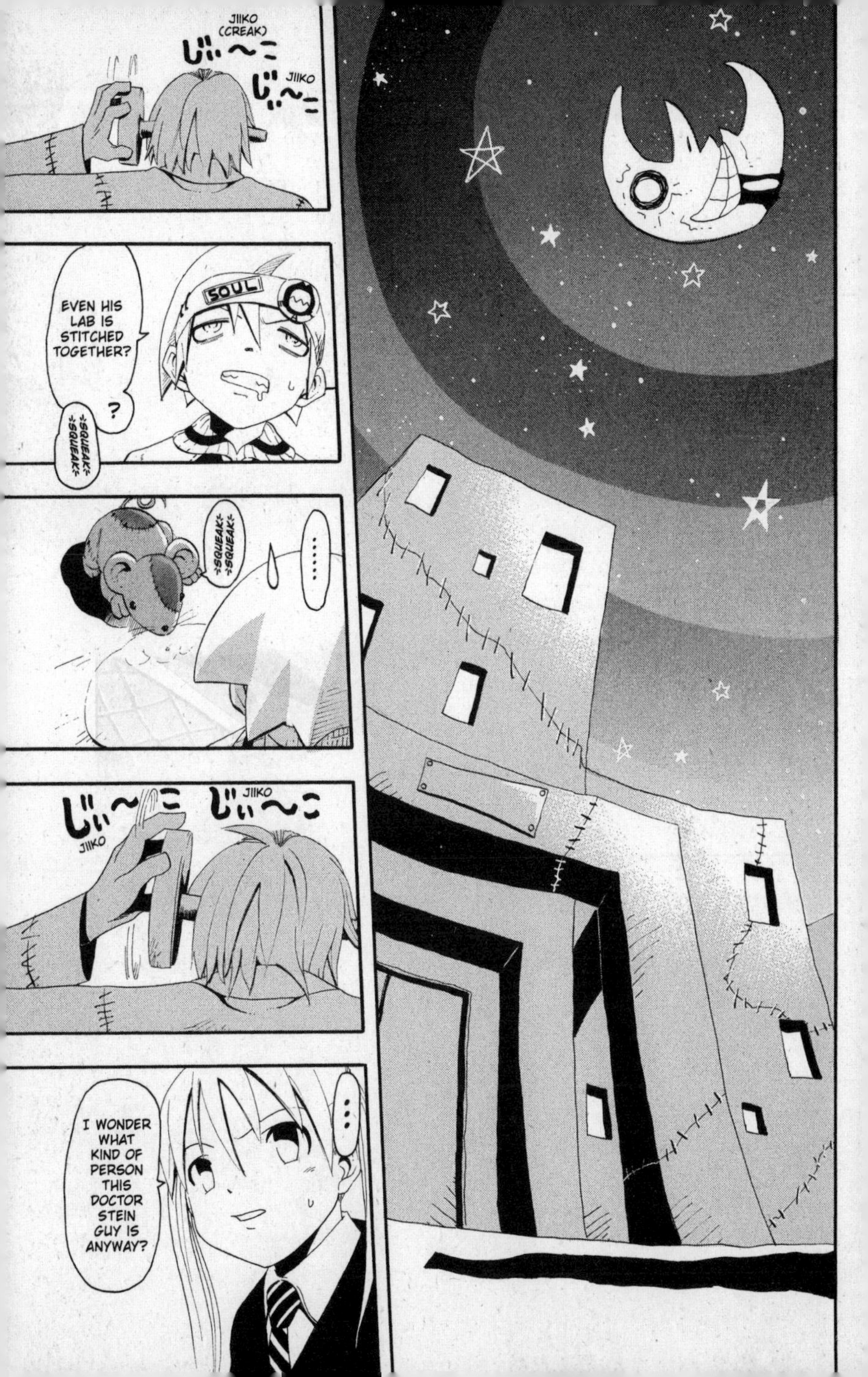
JIIKO (CREAK)
じぃ〜こ
JIIKO
じぃ〜こ
EVEN HIS LAB IS STITCHED TOGETHER?
?
SQUEAK SQUEAK
SQUEAK SQUEAK
......
JIIKO
じぃ〜こ
じぃ〜こ
JIIKO
...
I WONDER WHAT KIND OF PERSON THIS DOCTOR STEIN GUY IS ANYWAY?

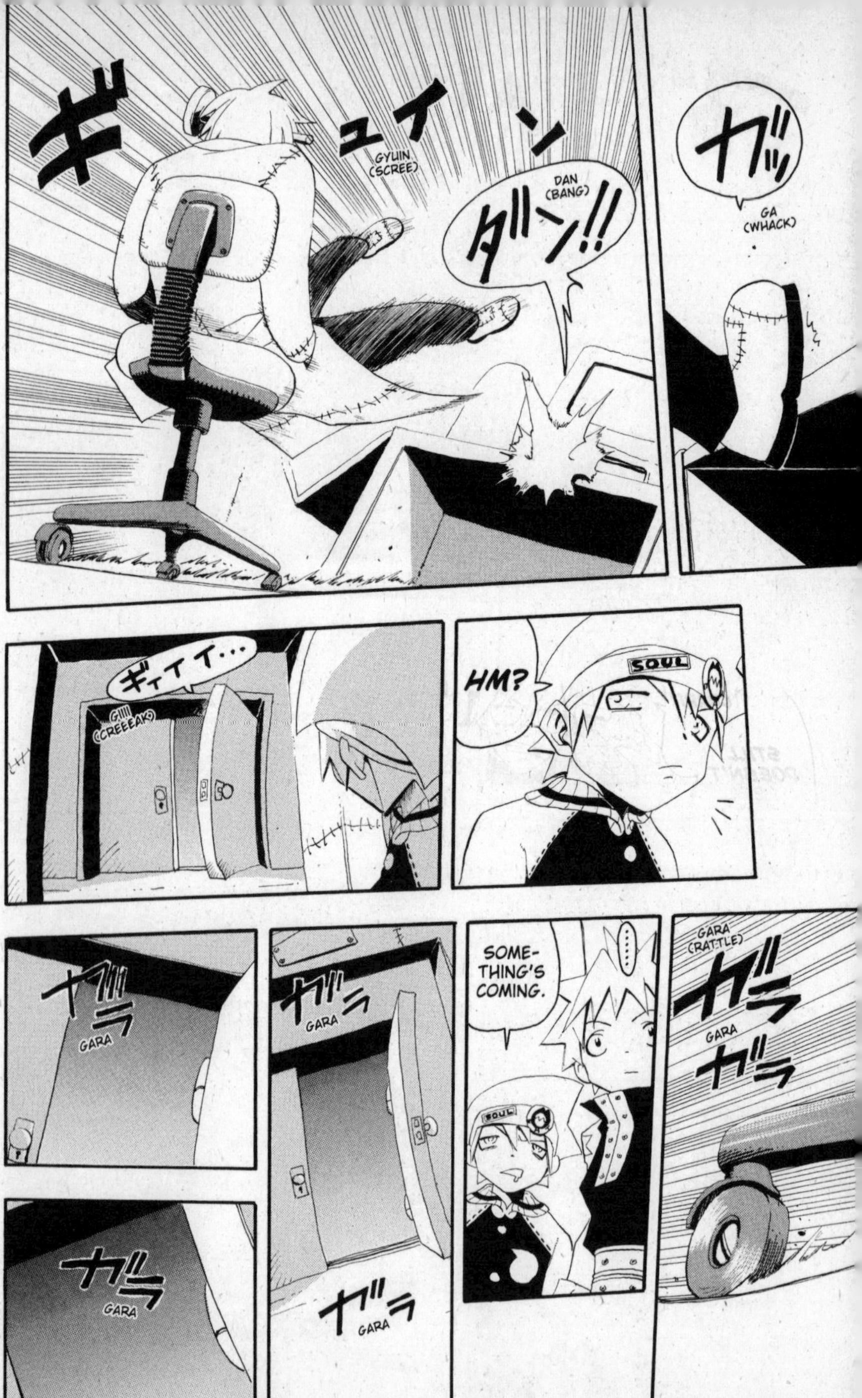

ガッ
GA (WHACK)
ギュイン
GYUIN (SCREE)
ダン!!
DAN (BANG)
HM?
ギィイイ…
GIIII (CREEEAK)
GARA (RATTLE)
ガラ
GARA
ガラ
……
SOMETHING'S COMING.
ガラ
GARA
ガラ
GARA
ガラ
GARA
ガラ
GARA

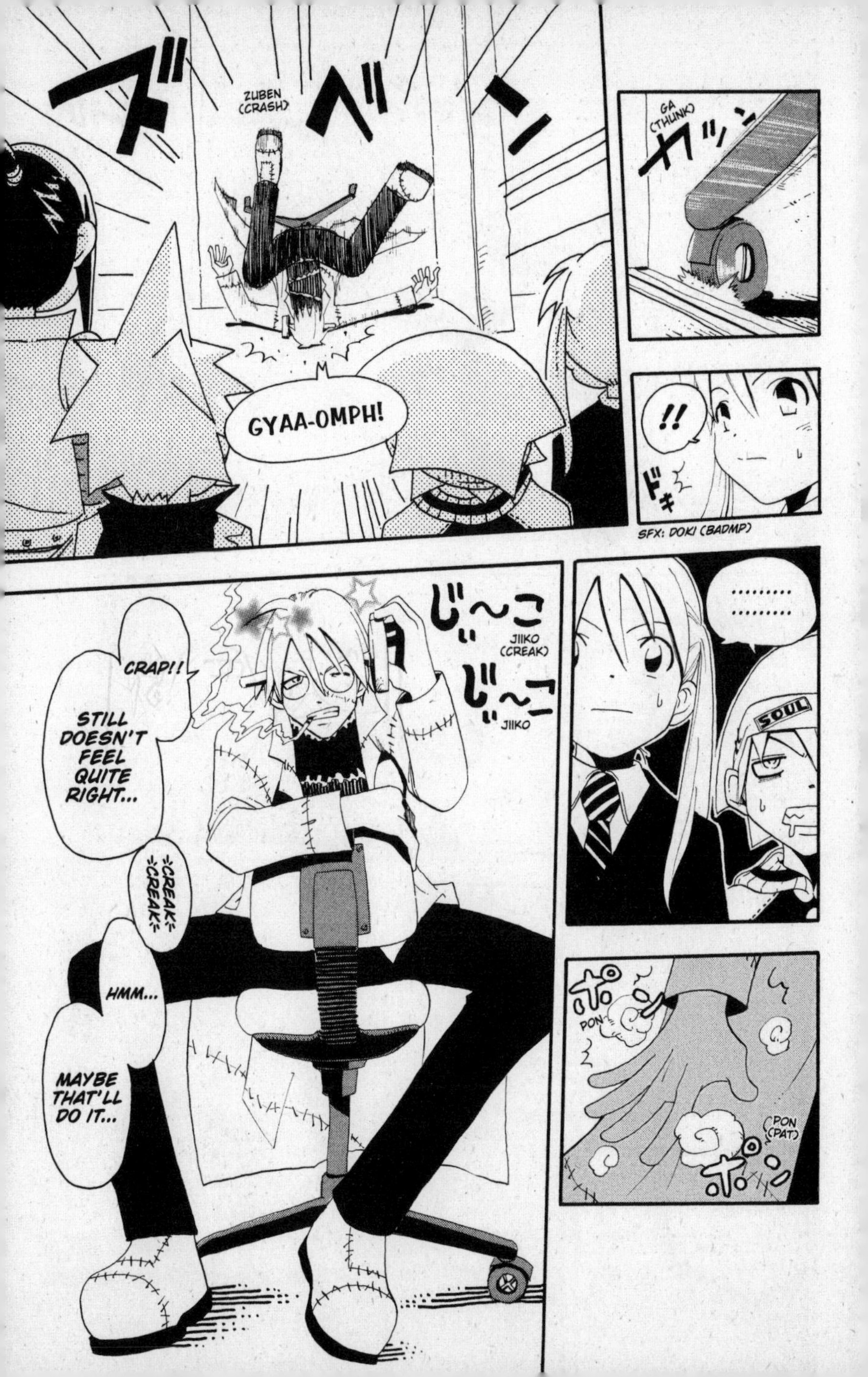
GA (THUNK)
!!
SFX: DOKI (BADMP)
ZUBEN (CRASH)
GYAA-OMPH!
....
....
PON
PON (PAT)
JIIKO (CREAK)
JIIKO
CRAP!!
STILL DOESN'T FEEL QUITE RIGHT...
CREAK CREAK
HMM...
MAYBE THAT'LL DO IT...

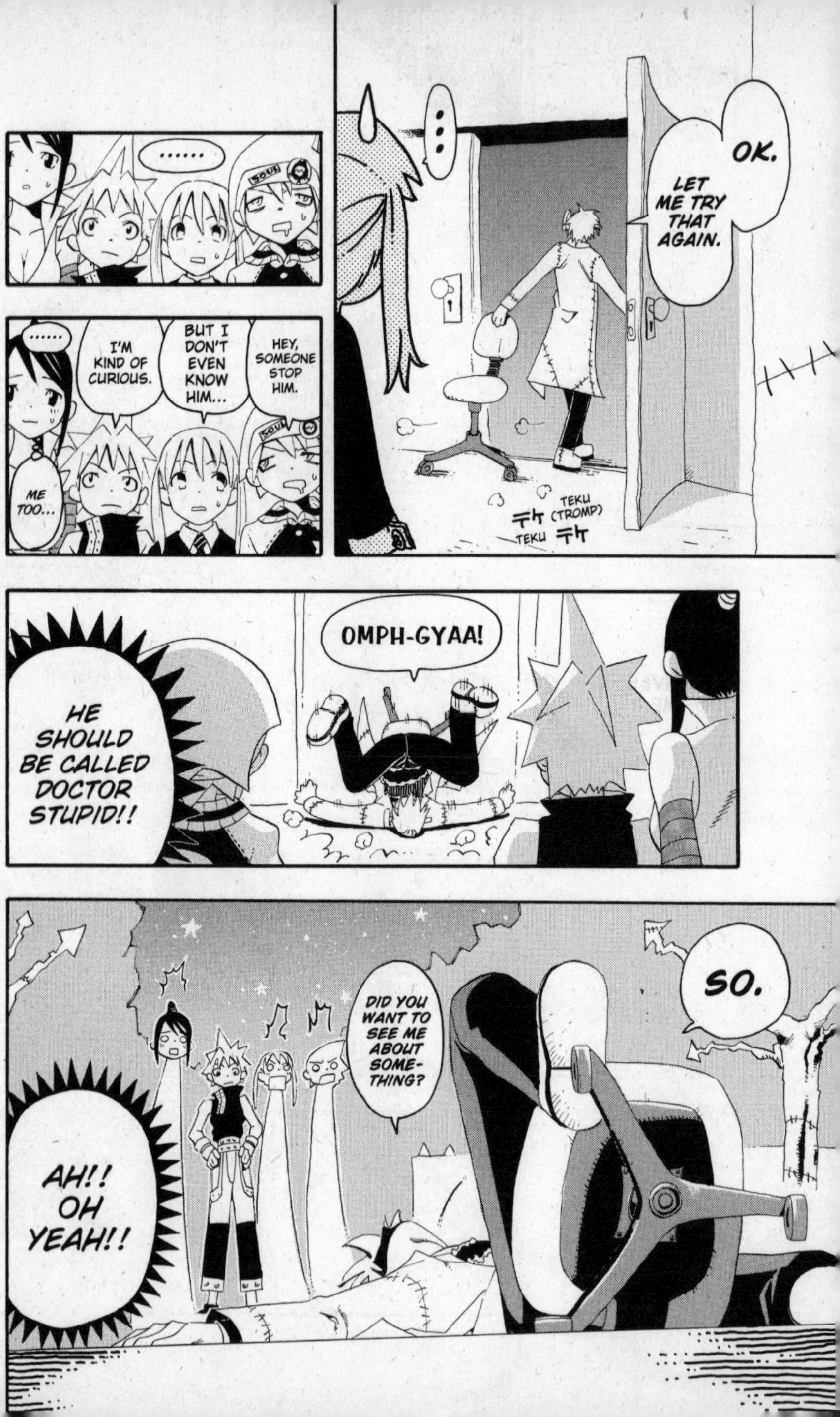
...
OK.
LET ME TRY THAT AGAIN.
テク TEKU (TROMP)
TEKU テク
....
HEY, SOMEONE STOP HIM.
BUT I DON'T EVEN KNOW HIM...
I'M KIND OF CURIOUS.
....
ME TOO...
OMPH-GYAA!
HE SHOULD BE CALLED DOCTOR STUPID!!
SO.
DID YOU WANT TO SEE ME ABOUT SOME-THING?
AH!! OH YEAH!!

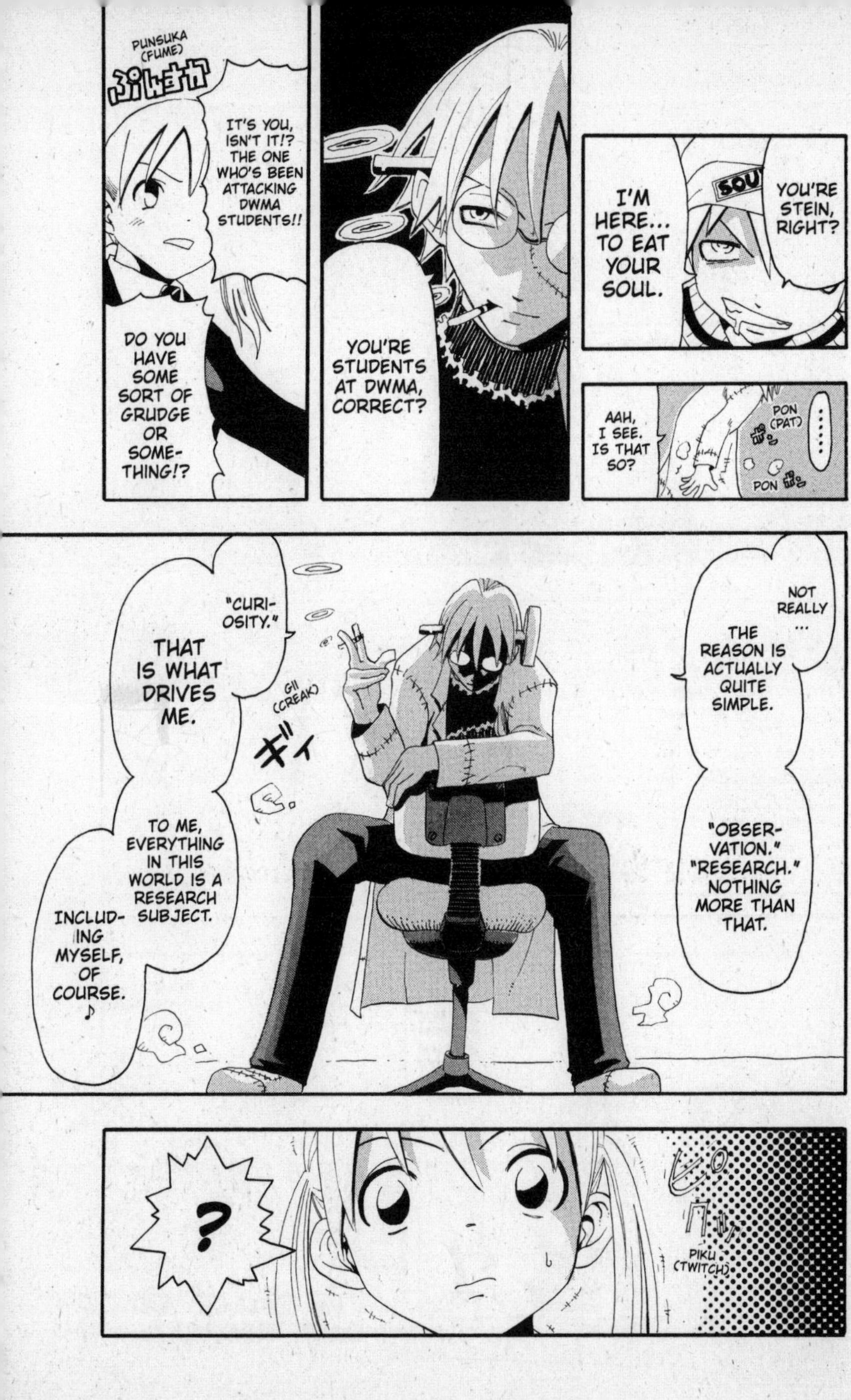
YOU'RE STEIN, RIGHT?
I'M HERE... TO EAT YOUR SOUL.
......
PON (PAT)
PON
AAH, I SEE. IS THAT SO?
YOU'RE STUDENTS AT DWMA, CORRECT?
PUNSUKA (FUME)
ぷんすか
IT'S YOU, ISN'T IT!? THE ONE WHO'S BEEN ATTACKING DWMA STUDENTS!!
DO YOU HAVE SOME SORT OF GRUDGE OR SOME-THING!?
NOT REALLY... THE REASON IS ACTUALLY QUITE SIMPLE.
"OBSER-VATION." "RESEARCH." NOTHING MORE THAN THAT.
"CURI-OSITY."
THAT IS WHAT DRIVES ME.
GII (CREAK)
ギィ
TO ME, EVERYTHING IN THIS WORLD IS A RESEARCH SUBJECT.
INCLUD-ING MYSELF, OF COURSE. ♪
ピクッ
PIKU (TWITCH)
?

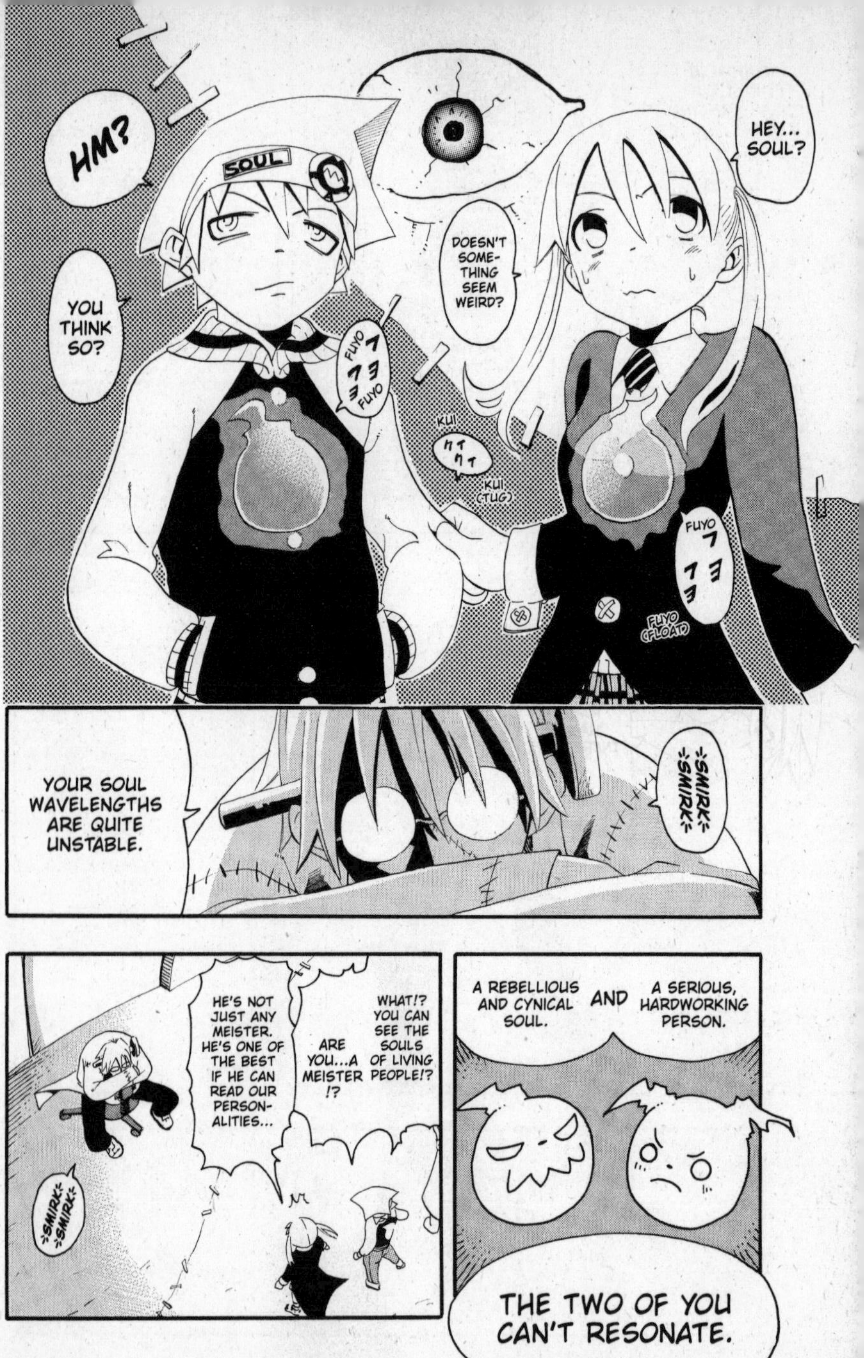
HEY... SOUL?
DOESN'T SOMETHING SEEM WEIRD?
FUYO FUYO (FLOAT)
KUI KUI (TUG)
FUYO FUYO
HM?
YOU THINK SO?
SMIRK SMIRK
YOUR SOUL WAVELENGTHS ARE QUITE UNSTABLE.
A REBELLIOUS AND CYNICAL SOUL.
AND
A SERIOUS, HARDWORKING PERSON.
THE TWO OF YOU CAN'T RESONATE.
WHAT!? YOU CAN SEE THE SOULS OF LIVING PEOPLE!?
ARE YOU...A MEISTER!?
HE'S NOT JUST ANY MEISTER. HE'S ONE OF THE BEST IF HE CAN READ OUR PERSONALITIES...
SMIRK SMIRK

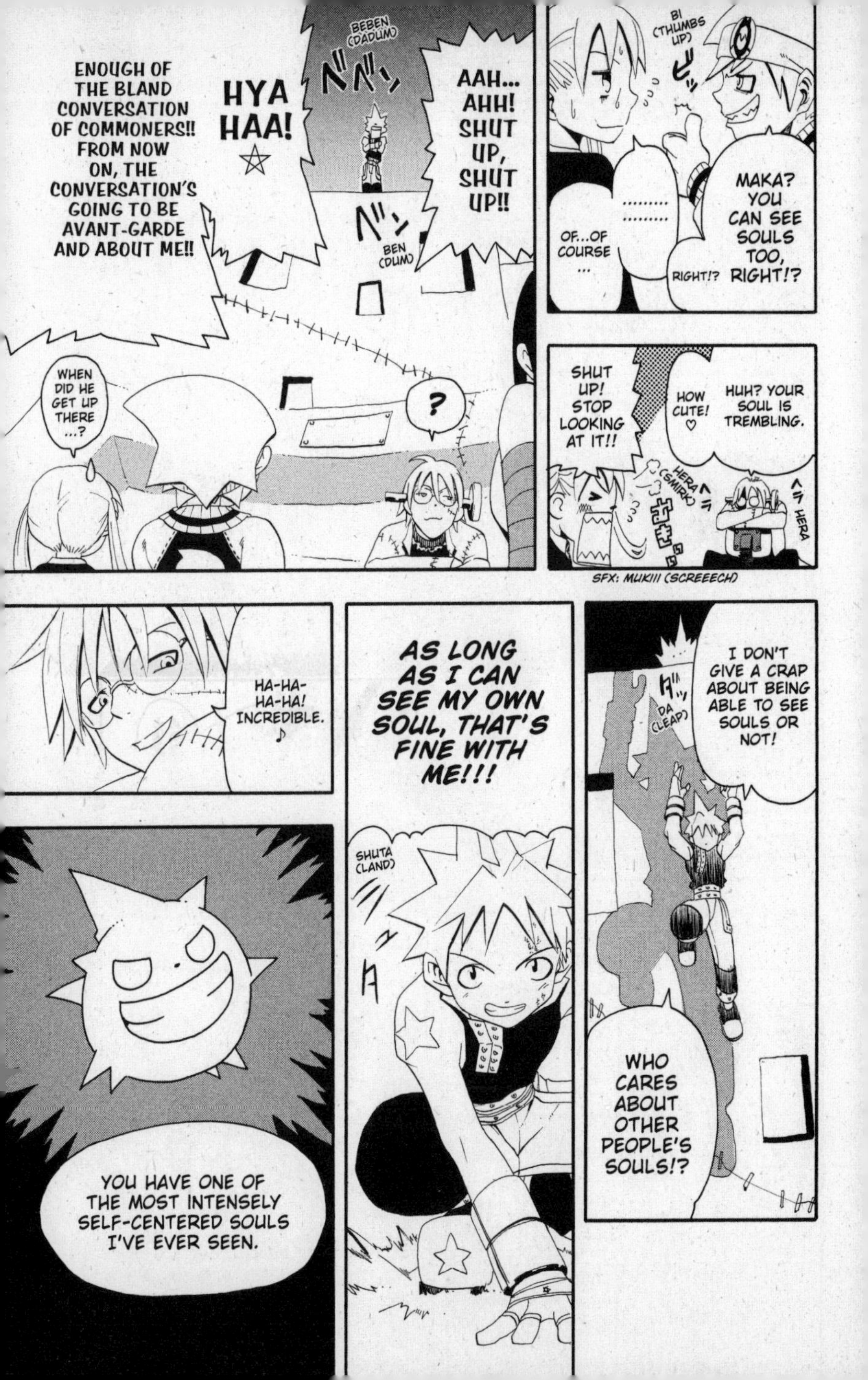
BI (THUMBS UP)
MAKA? YOU CAN SEE SOULS TOO, RIGHT!?
RIGHT!?
………
OF...OF COURSE ...
HUH? YOUR SOUL IS TREMBLING.
HOW CUTE! ♡
SHUT UP! STOP LOOKING AT IT!!
HERA (SMIRK)
HERA
SFX: MUKIII (SCREEECH)
BEBEN (DADUM)
AAH... AHH! SHUT UP, SHUT UP!!
HYA HAA! ☆
ENOUGH OF THE BLAND CONVERSATION OF COMMONERS!! FROM NOW ON, THE CONVERSATION'S GOING TO BE AVANT-GARDE AND ABOUT ME!!
BEN (DUM)
?
WHEN DID HE GET UP THERE ...?
I DON'T GIVE A CRAP ABOUT BEING ABLE TO SEE SOULS OR NOT!
DA (LEAP)
WHO CARES ABOUT OTHER PEOPLE'S SOULS!?
AS LONG AS I CAN SEE MY OWN SOUL, THAT'S FINE WITH ME!!!
SHUTA (LAND)
HA-HA-HA-HA! INCREDIBLE. ♪
YOU HAVE ONE OF THE MOST INTENSELY SELF-CENTERED SOULS I'VE EVER SEEN.

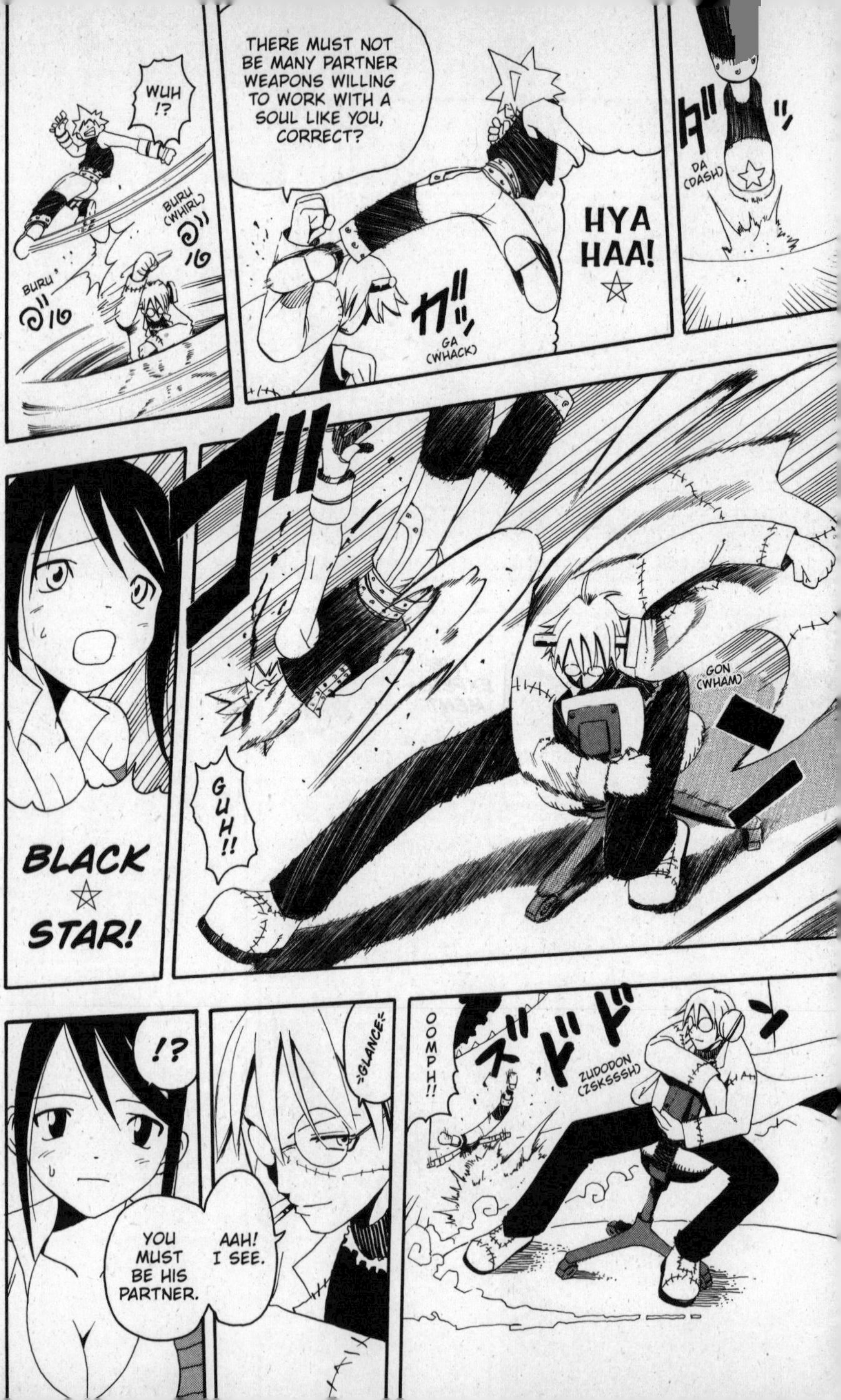

ダ
DA (DASH)
HYA HAA! ☆
THERE MUST NOT BE MANY PARTNER WEAPONS WILLING TO WORK WITH A SOUL LIKE YOU, CORRECT?
ガ
GA (WHACK)
WUH !?
BURU (WHIRL)
BURU
GON (WHAM)
GUH!!
BLACK ☆ STAR!
ズドド
ZUDODON (ZSKSSSH)
OOMPH!!
GLANCE
AAH! I SEE.
!?
YOU MUST BE HIS PARTNER.

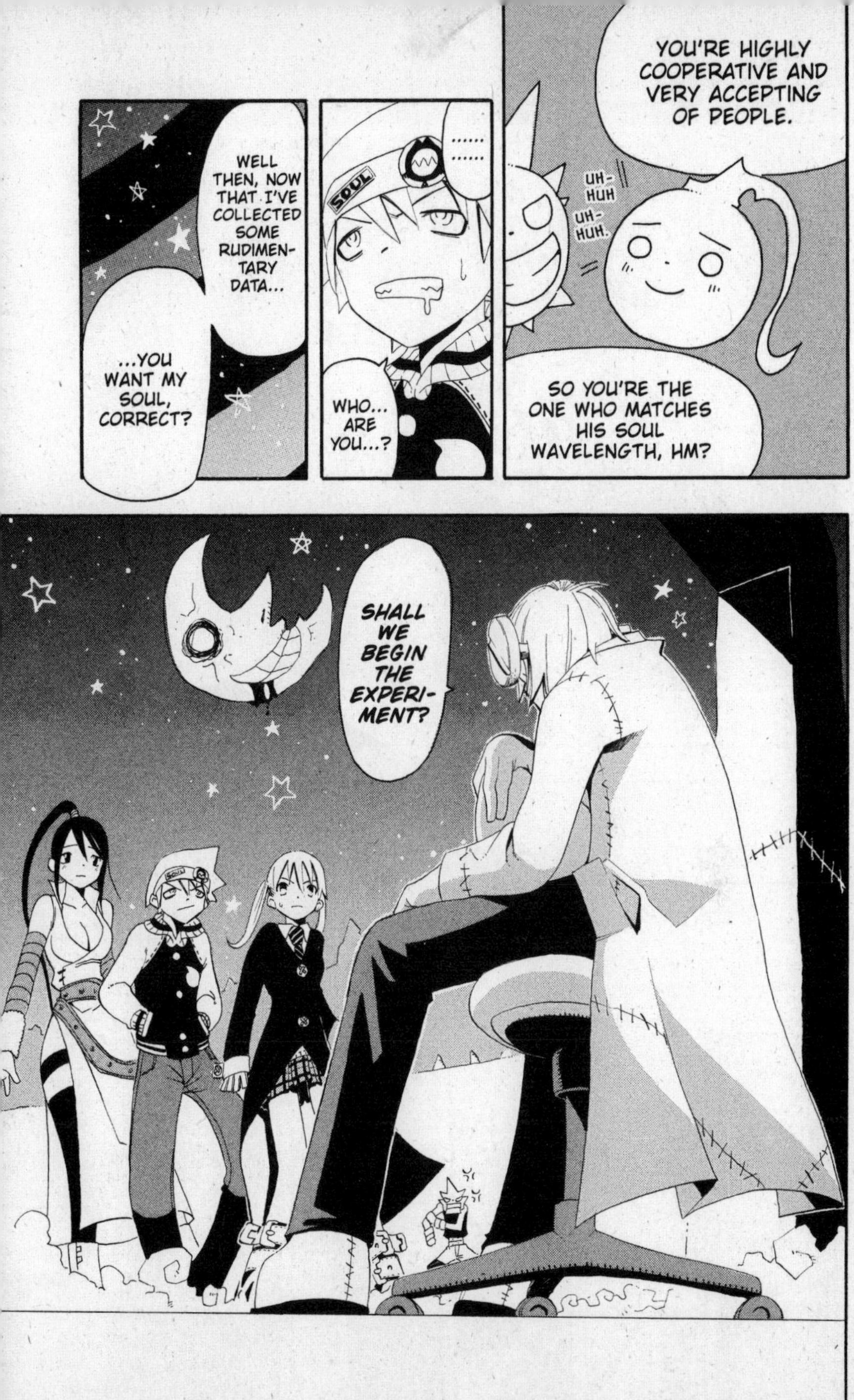
YOU'RE HIGHLY COOPERATIVE AND VERY ACCEPTING OF PEOPLE.
UH-HUH
UH-HUH.
SO YOU'RE THE ONE WHO MATCHES HIS SOUL WAVELENGTH, HM?
......
......
WHO... ARE YOU...?
WELL THEN, NOW THAT I'VE COLLECTED SOME RUDIMENTARY DATA...
...YOU WANT MY SOUL, CORRECT?
SHALL WE BEGIN THE EXPERIMENT?

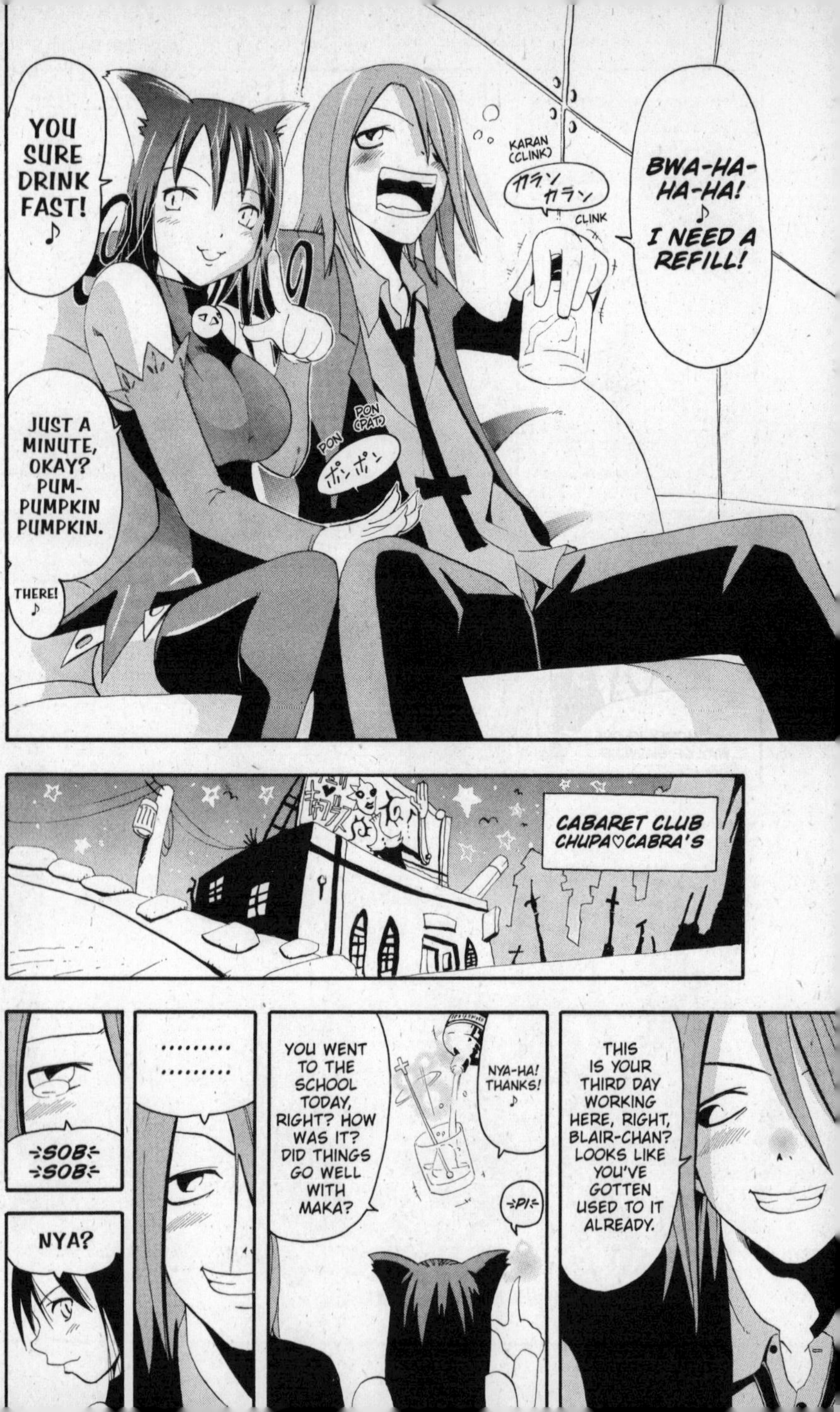
BWA-HA-HA-HA! ♪ I NEED A REFILL!
KARAN (CLINK)
カランカラン
CLINK
YOU SURE DRINK FAST! ♪
PON (PAT)
ポンポン
PON
JUST A MINUTE, OKAY? PUM-PUMPKIN PUMPKIN.
THERE! ♪
CABARET CLUB CHUPA♡CABRA'S
THIS IS YOUR THIRD DAY WORKING HERE, RIGHT, BLAIR-CHAN? LOOKS LIKE YOU'VE GOTTEN USED TO IT ALREADY.
NYA-HA! THANKS! ♪
YOU WENT TO THE SCHOOL TODAY, RIGHT? HOW WAS IT? DID THINGS GO WELL WITH MAKA?
PI
....
....
SOB SOB
NYA?

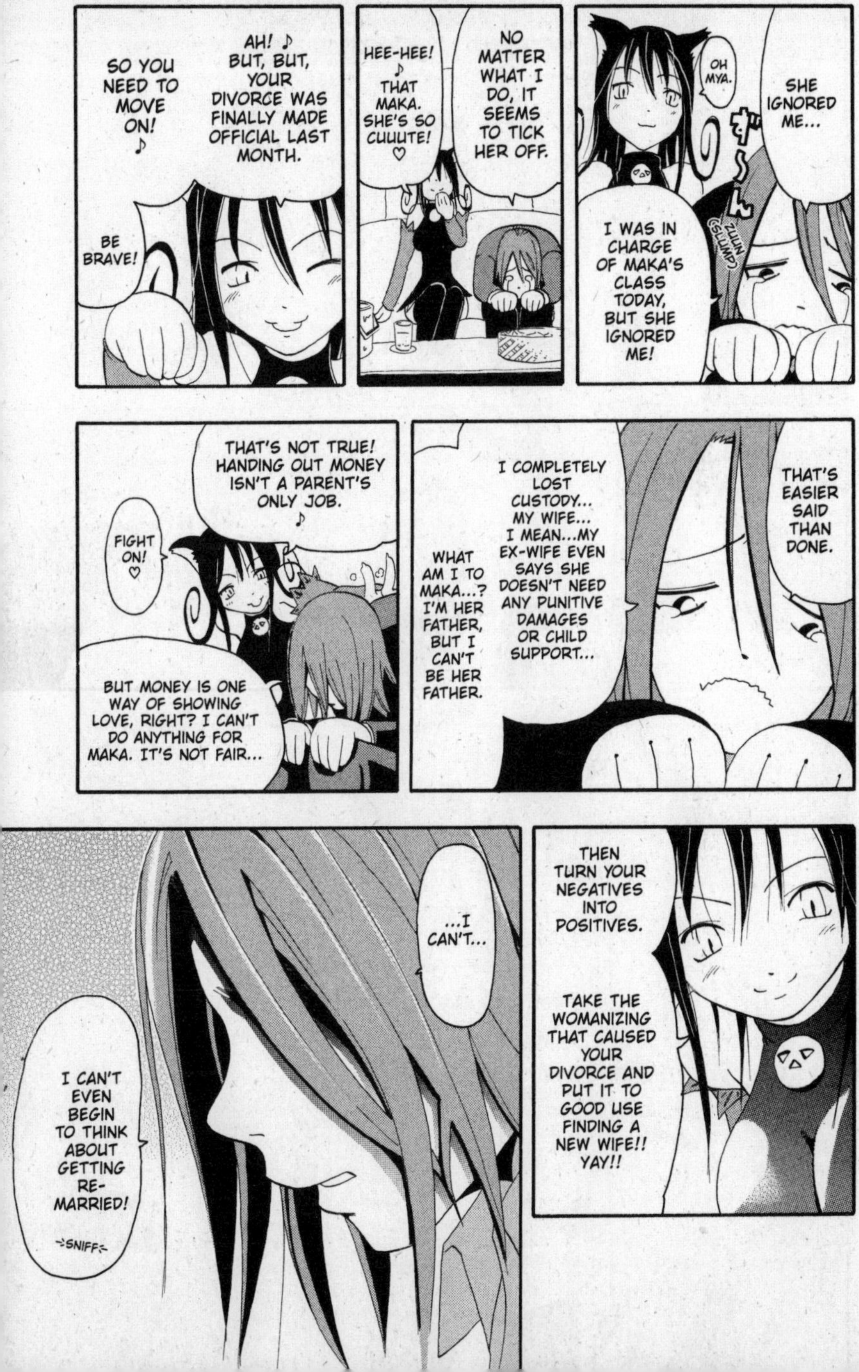
SHE IGNORED ME...
OH MYA.
ZUUN (SLUMP)
I WAS IN CHARGE OF MAKA'S CLASS TODAY, BUT SHE IGNORED ME!
NO MATTER WHAT I DO, IT SEEMS TO TICK HER OFF.
HEE-HEE! ♪ THAT MAKA. SHE'S SO CUUUTE! ♡
AH! ♪ BUT, BUT, YOUR DIVORCE WAS FINALLY MADE OFFICIAL LAST MONTH.
SO YOU NEED TO MOVE ON! ♪
BE BRAVE!
THAT'S EASIER SAID THAN DONE.
I COMPLETELY LOST CUSTODY... MY WIFE... I MEAN...MY EX-WIFE EVEN SAYS SHE DOESN'T NEED ANY PUNITIVE DAMAGES OR CHILD SUPPORT...
WHAT AM I TO MAKA...? I'M HER FATHER, BUT I CAN'T BE HER FATHER.
THAT'S NOT TRUE! HANDING OUT MONEY ISN'T A PARENT'S ONLY JOB. ♪
FIGHT ON! ♡
BUT MONEY IS ONE WAY OF SHOWING LOVE, RIGHT? I CAN'T DO ANYTHING FOR MAKA. IT'S NOT FAIR...
THEN TURN YOUR NEGATIVES INTO POSITIVES.
TAKE THE WOMANIZING THAT CAUSED YOUR DIVORCE AND PUT IT TO GOOD USE FINDING A NEW WIFE!! YAY!!
...I CAN'T...
I CAN'T EVEN BEGIN TO THINK ABOUT GETTING RE-MARRIED!
SNIFF

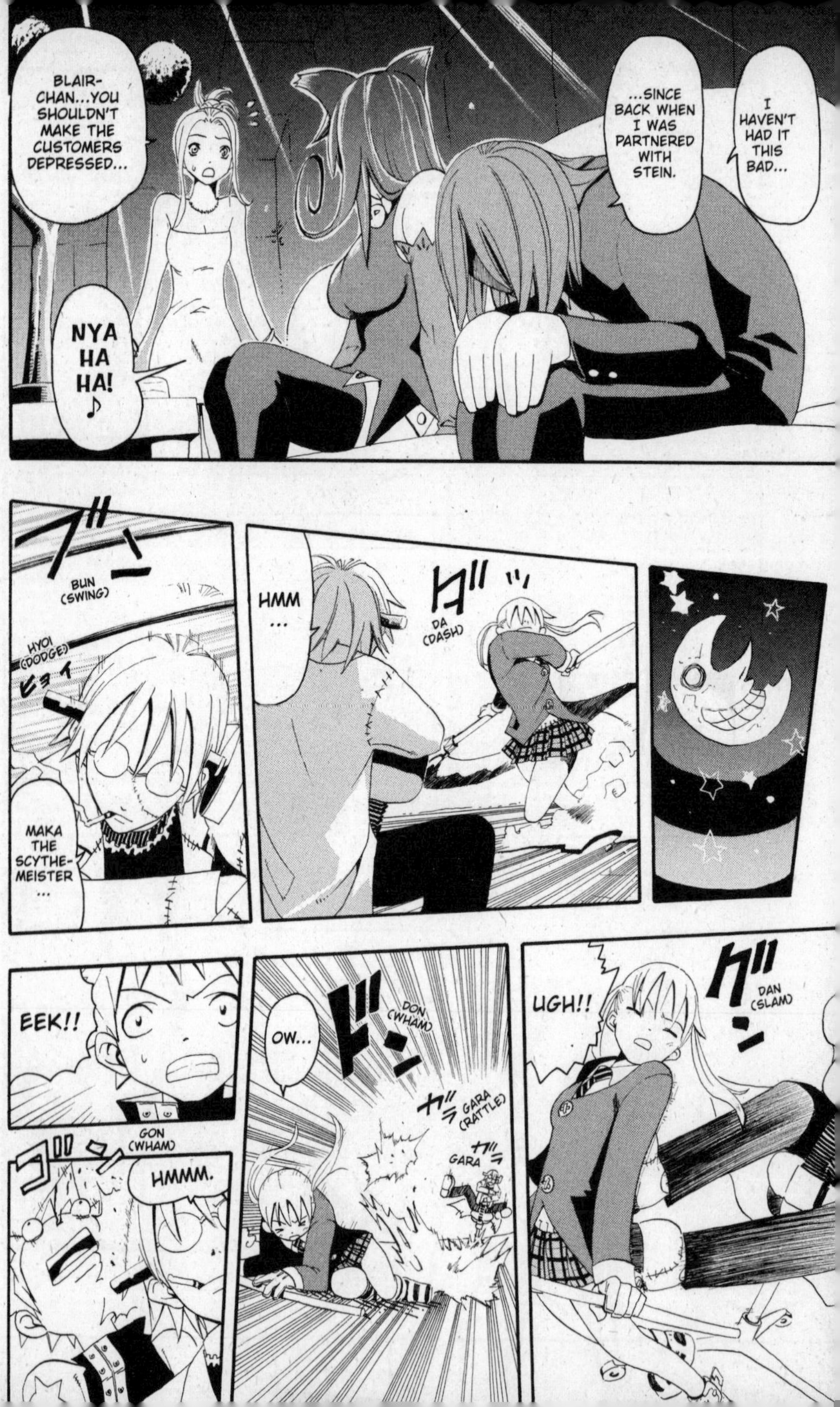
I HAVEN'T HAD IT THIS BAD...
...SINCE BACK WHEN I WAS PARTNERED WITH STEIN.
BLAIR-CHAN...YOU SHOULDN'T MAKE THE CUSTOMERS DEPRESSED...
NYA HA HA! ♪
DA (DASH)
HMM...
BUN (SWING)
HYOI (DODGE)
MAKA THE SCYTHE-MEISTER...
DAN (SLAM)
UGH!!
DON (WHAM)
OW...
GARA (RATTLE)
GARA
EEK!!
GON (WHAM)
HMMM.

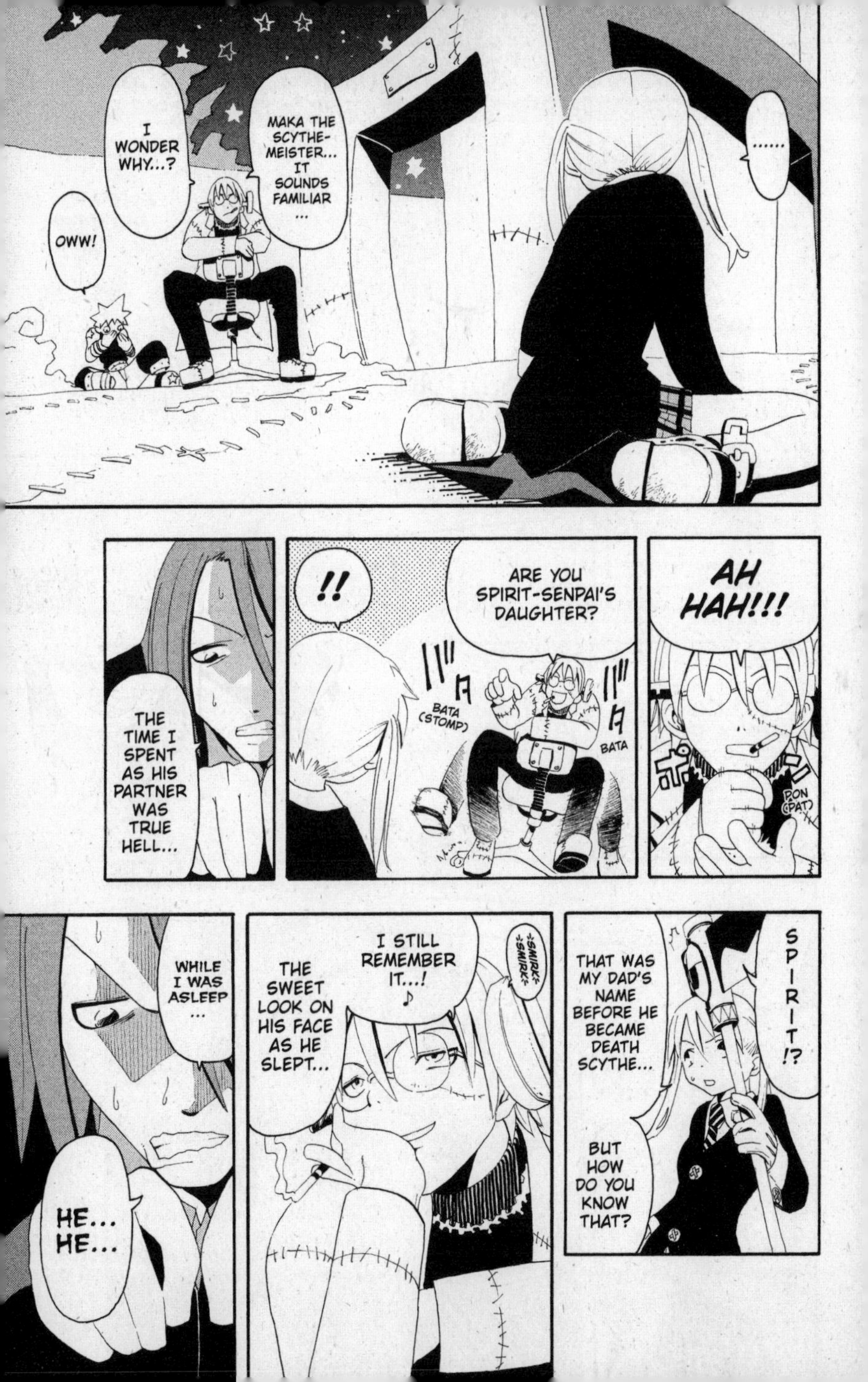
......
MAKA THE SCYTHE-MEISTER... IT SOUNDS FAMILIAR ...
I WONDER WHY...?
OWW!
AH HAH!!!
PON (PAT)
ARE YOU SPIRIT-SENPAI'S DAUGHTER?
!!
BATA (STOMP)
BATA
THE TIME I SPENT AS HIS PARTNER WAS TRUE HELL...
SPIRIT!?
THAT WAS MY DAD'S NAME BEFORE HE BECAME DEATH SCYTHE...
BUT HOW DO YOU KNOW THAT?
SMIRK SMIRK
I STILL REMEMBER IT...! ♪
THE SWEET LOOK ON HIS FACE AS HE SLEPT...
WHILE I WAS ASLEEP ...
HE... HE...

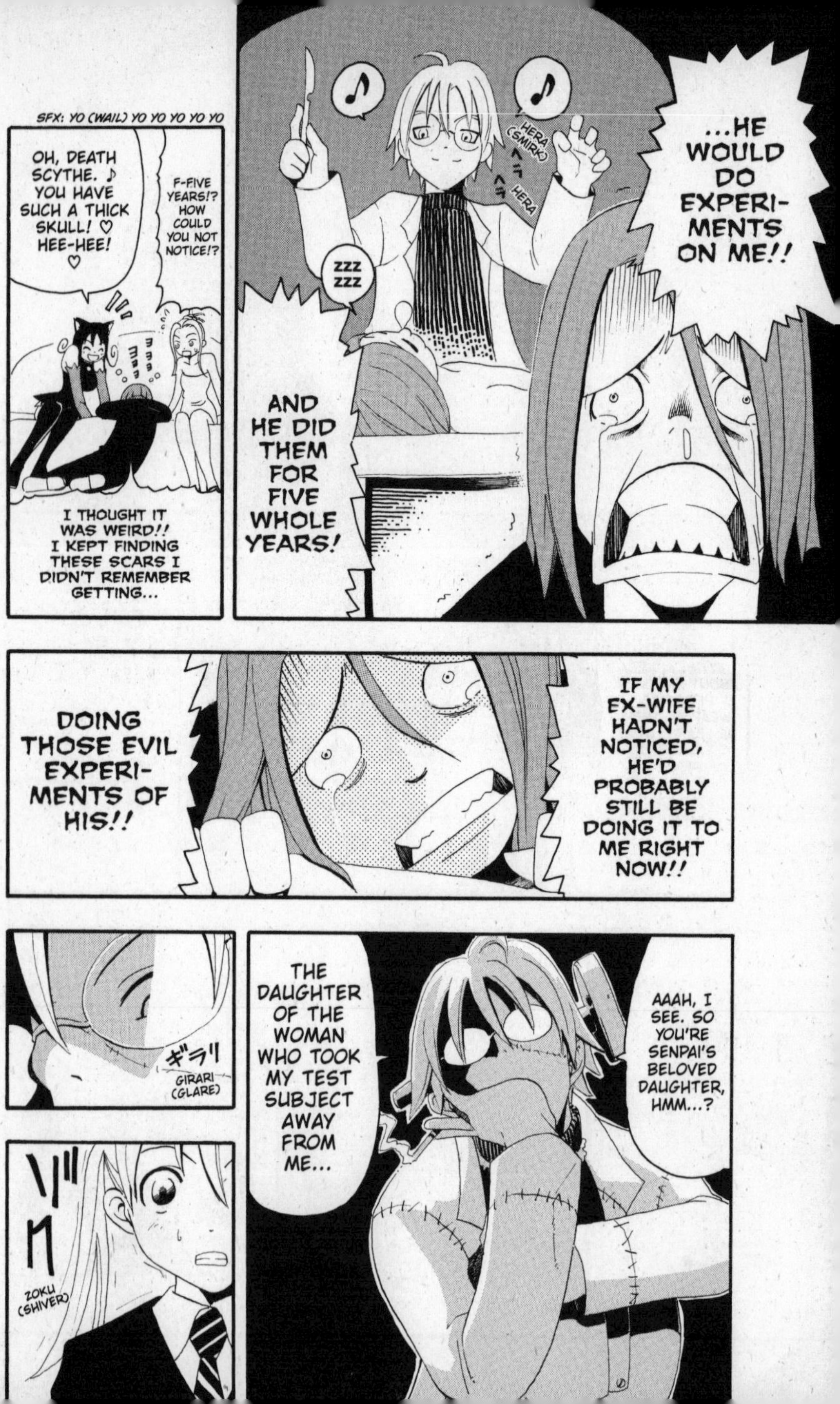

...HE WOULD DO EXPERI-MENTS ON ME!!
HERA (SMIRK) HERA
ZZZ ZZZ
AND HE DID THEM FOR FIVE WHOLE YEARS!
SFX: YO (WAIL) YO YO YO YO YO
F-FIVE YEARS!? HOW COULD YOU NOT NOTICE!?
OH, DEATH SCYTHE. ♪ YOU HAVE SUCH A THICK SKULL! ♡ HEE-HEE! ♡
I THOUGHT IT WAS WEIRD!! I KEPT FINDING THESE SCARS I DIDN'T REMEMBER GETTING...
IF MY EX-WIFE HADN'T NOTICED, HE'D PROBABLY STILL BE DOING IT TO ME RIGHT NOW!!
DOING THOSE EVIL EXPERI-MENTS OF HIS!!
AAAH, I SEE. SO YOU'RE SENPAI'S BELOVED DAUGHTER, HMM...?
THE DAUGHTER OF THE WOMAN WHO TOOK MY TEST SUBJECT AWAY FROM ME...
ギラリ
GIRARI (GLARE)
ゾクッ
ZOKU (SHIVER)

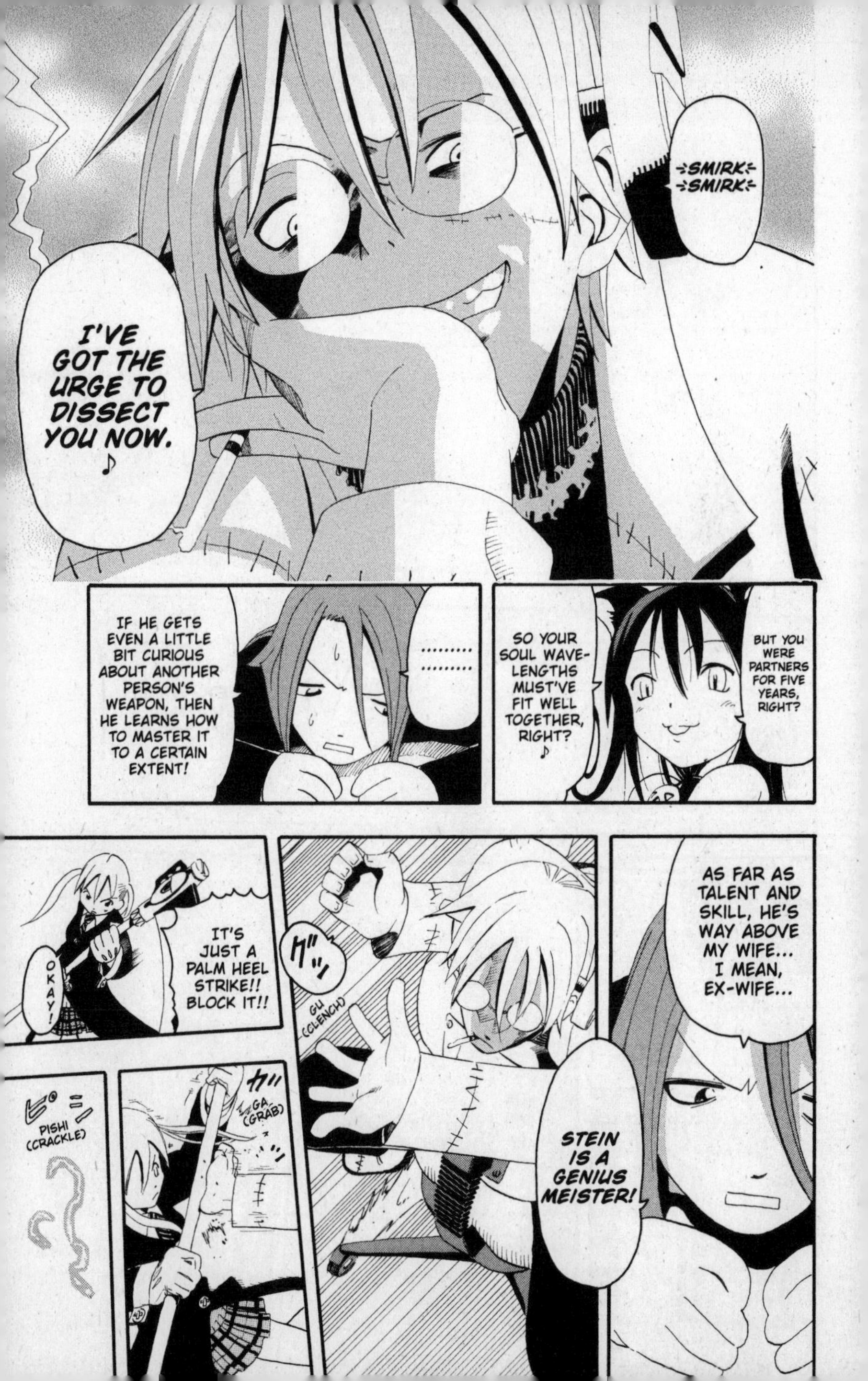

SMIRK SMIRK
I'VE GOT THE URGE TO DISSECT YOU NOW. ♪
BUT YOU WERE PARTNERS FOR FIVE YEARS, RIGHT?
SO YOUR SOUL WAVE-LENGTHS MUST'VE FIT WELL TOGETHER, RIGHT? ♪
....
....
IF HE GETS EVEN A LITTLE BIT CURIOUS ABOUT ANOTHER PERSON'S WEAPON, THEN HE LEARNS HOW TO MASTER IT TO A CERTAIN EXTENT!
AS FAR AS TALENT AND SKILL, HE'S WAY ABOVE MY WIFE... I MEAN, EX-WIFE...
STEIN IS A GENIUS MEISTER!
グッ
GU (CLENCH)
IT'S JUST A PALM HEEL STRIKE!! BLOCK IT!!
OKAY!
GA (GRAB)
PISHI (CRACKLE)

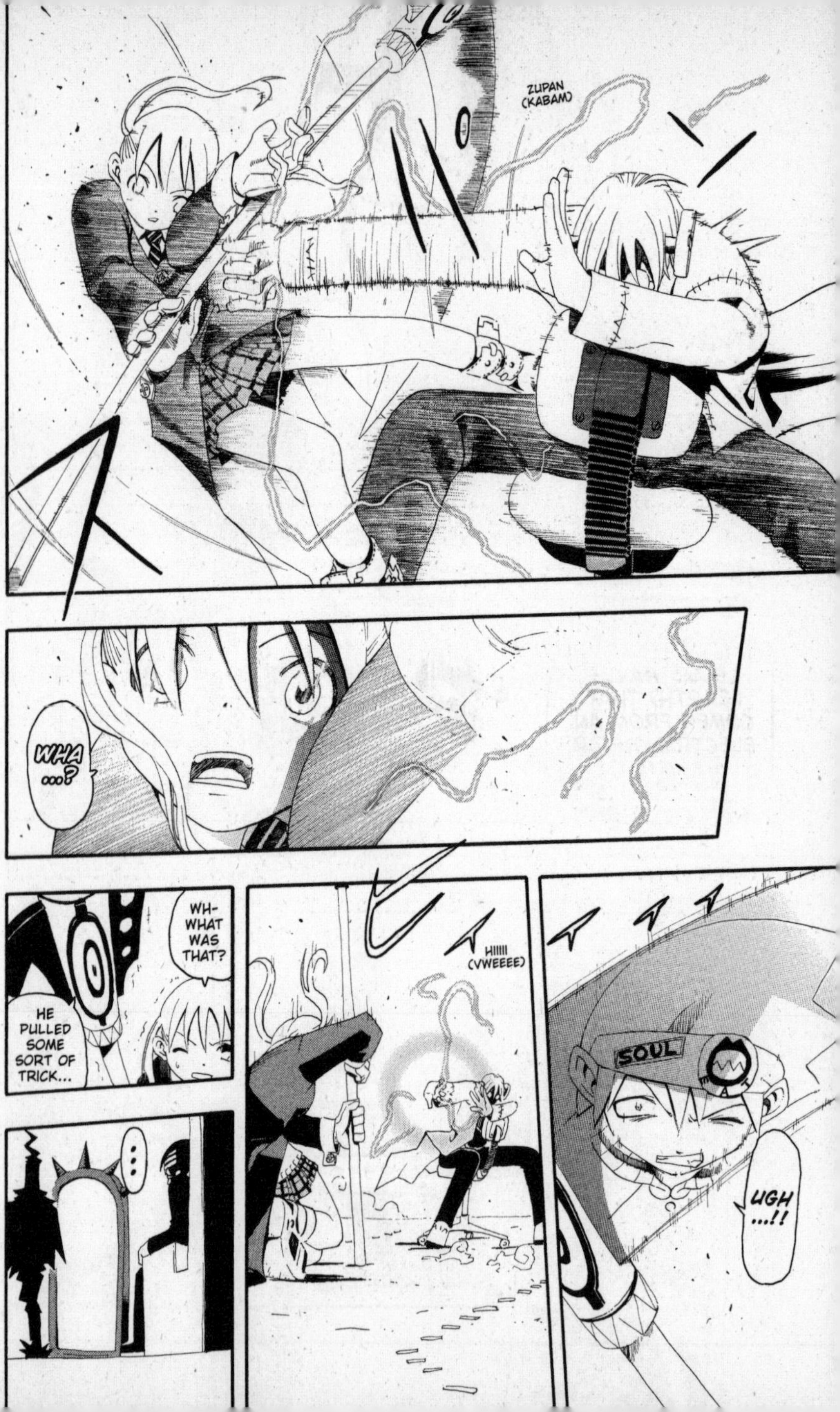
ZUPAN (KABAM)
WHA...?
UGH...!!
HIIII (VWEEEE)
WH-WHAT WAS THAT?
HE PULLED SOME SORT OF TRICK...
...

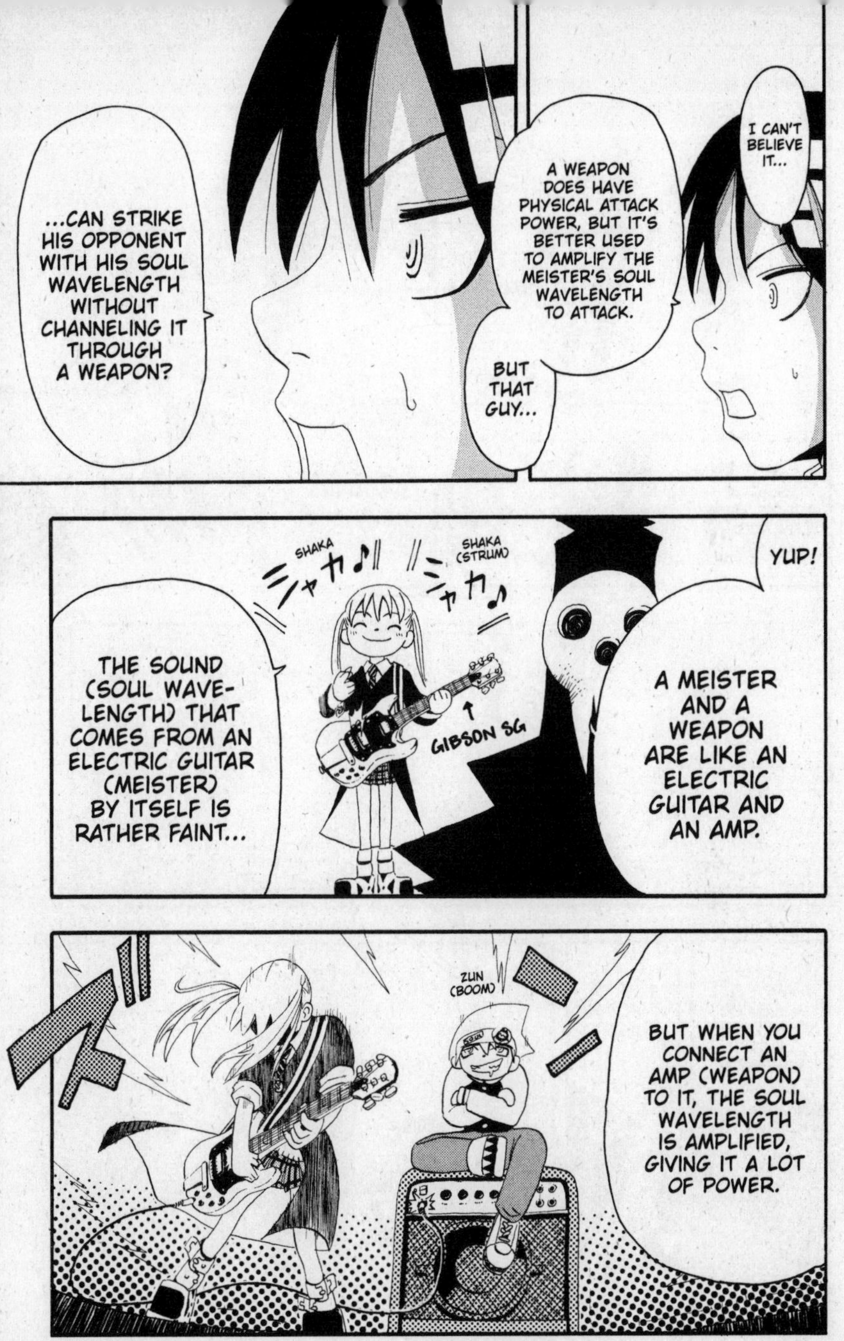

I CAN'T BELIEVE IT...
A WEAPON DOES HAVE PHYSICAL ATTACK POWER, BUT IT'S BETTER USED TO AMPLIFY THE MEISTER'S SOUL WAVELENGTH TO ATTACK.
BUT THAT GUY...
...CAN STRIKE HIS OPPONENT WITH HIS SOUL WAVELENGTH WITHOUT CHANNELING IT THROUGH A WEAPON?
YUP!
A MEISTER AND A WEAPON ARE LIKE AN ELECTRIC GUITAR AND AN AMP.
SHAKA (STRUM)
シャカ♪
SHAKA
シャカ♪
GIBSON SG
THE SOUND (SOUL WAVE-LENGTH) THAT COMES FROM AN ELECTRIC GUITAR (MEISTER) BY ITSELF IS RATHER FAINT...
ZUN (BOOM)
BUT WHEN YOU CONNECT AN AMP (WEAPON) TO IT, THE SOUL WAVELENGTH IS AMPLIFIED, GIVING IT A LOT OF POWER.

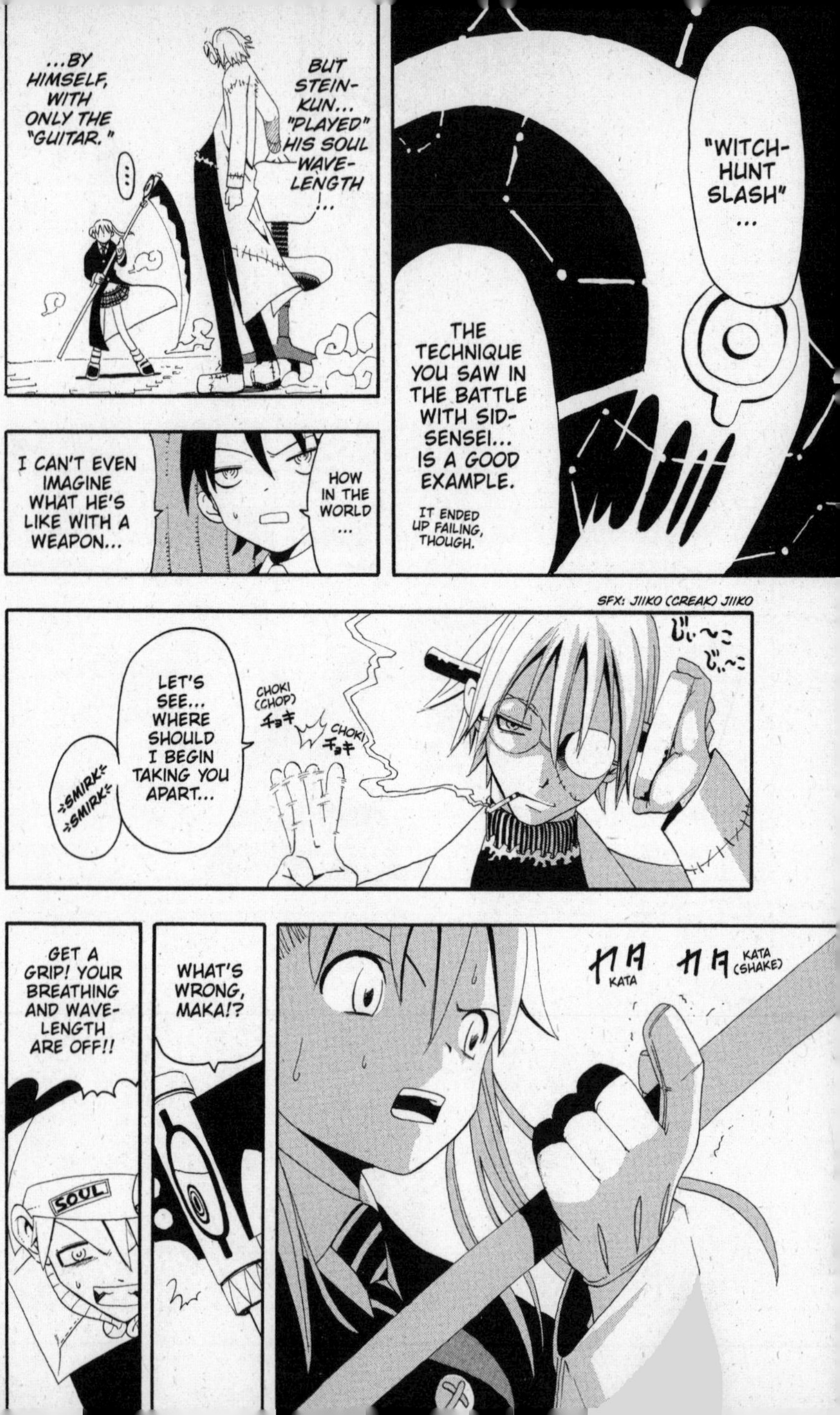
"WITCH-HUNT SLASH"...
THE TECHNIQUE YOU SAW IN THE BATTLE WITH SID-SENSEI... IS A GOOD EXAMPLE.
IT ENDED UP FAILING, THOUGH.
BUT STEIN-KUN... "PLAYED" HIS SOUL WAVE-LENGTH...
...BY HIMSELF, WITH ONLY THE "GUITAR."
...
HOW IN THE WORLD...
I CAN'T EVEN IMAGINE WHAT HE'S LIKE WITH A WEAPON...
SFX: JIIKO (CREAK) JIIKO
じぃ～こ じぃ～こ
CHOKI (CHOP) チョキ
CHOKI チョキ
LET'S SEE... WHERE SHOULD I BEGIN TAKING YOU APART...
SMIRK SMIRK
カタ KATA カタ KATA (SHAKE)
WHAT'S WRONG, MAKA!?
GET A GRIP! YOUR BREATHING AND WAVE-LENGTH ARE OFF!!
SOUL

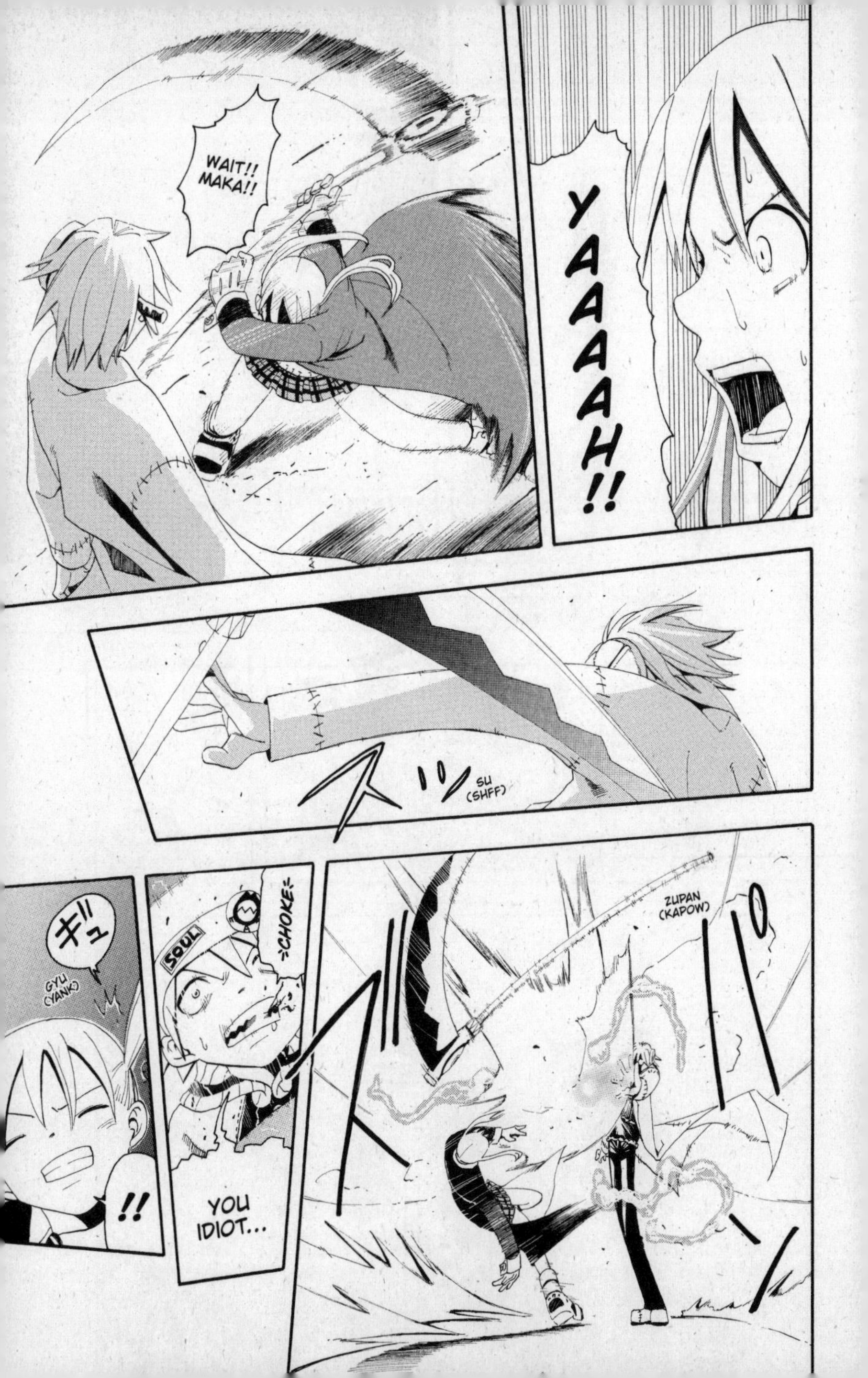
YAAAAAH!!
WAIT!! MAKA!!
スッ
SU (SHFF)
ZUPAN (KAPOW)
CHOKE
YOU IDIOT...
ギュ
GYU (YANK)
!!

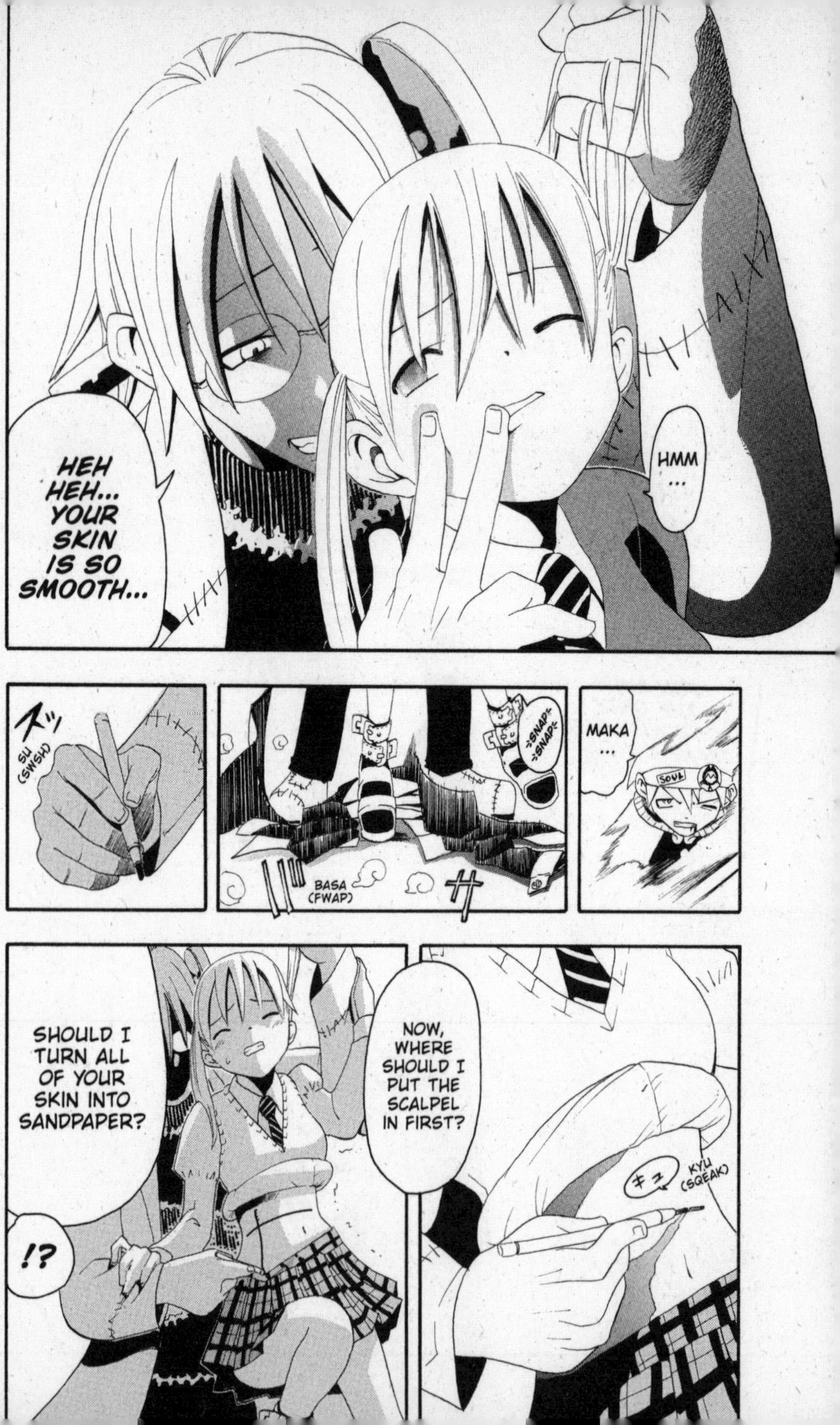
HMM ...
HEH HEH... YOUR SKIN IS SO SMOOTH...
MAKA ...
SNAP SNAP
BASA (FWAP)
ズッ
SU (SWSH)
NOW, WHERE SHOULD I PUT THE SCALPEL IN FIRST?
キュ
KYU (SQEAK)
SHOULD I TURN ALL OF YOUR SKIN INTO SANDPAPER?
!?

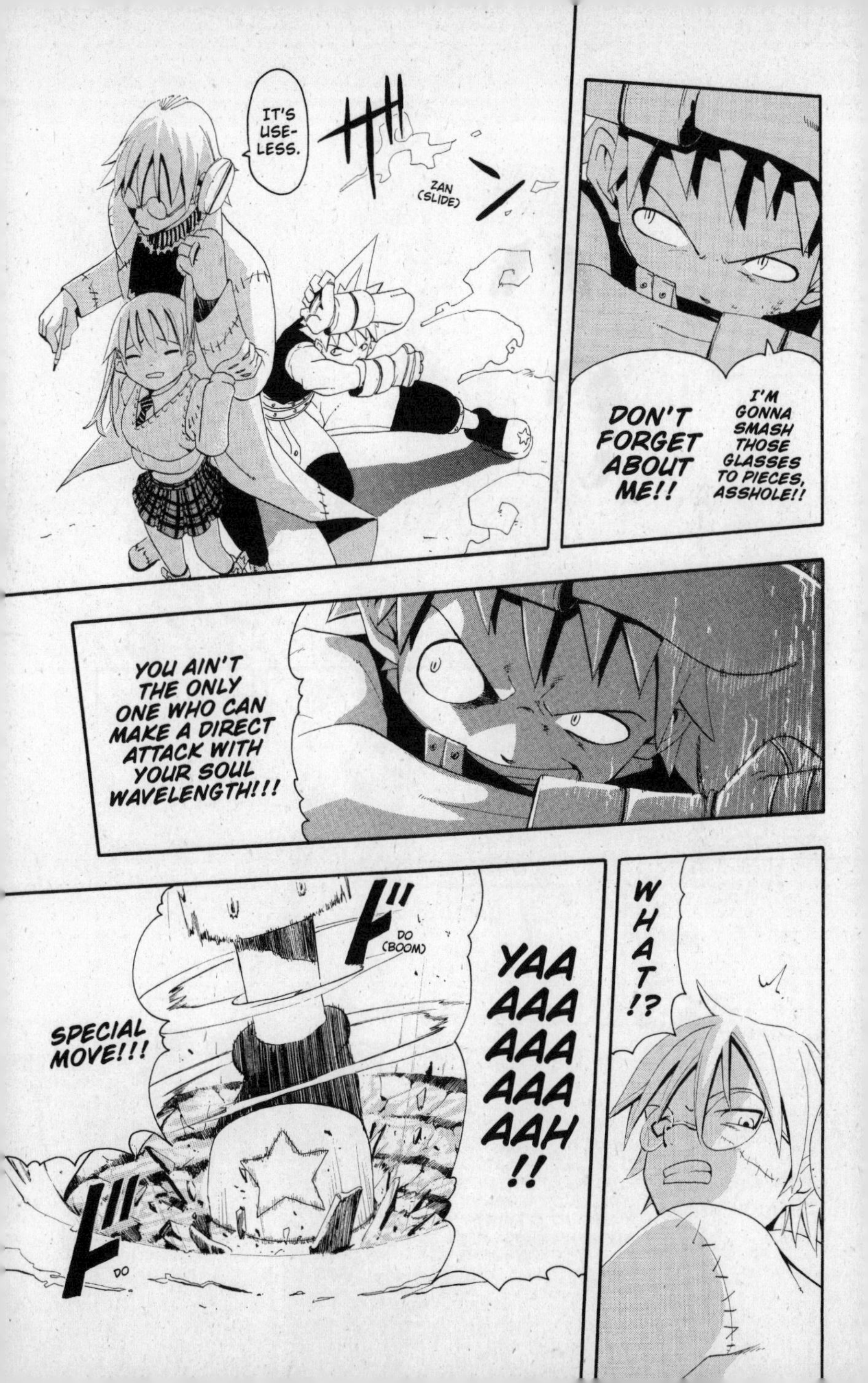
I'M GONNA SMASH THOSE GLASSES TO PIECES, ASSHOLE!!
DON'T FORGET ABOUT ME!!
IT'S USE-LESS.
ZAN (SLIDE)
YOU AIN'T THE ONLY ONE WHO CAN MAKE A DIRECT ATTACK WITH YOUR SOUL WAVELENGTH!!!
WHAT!?
YAAAAAAAAAAAAAAAAH!!
DO (BOOM)
SPECIAL MOVE!!!
DO

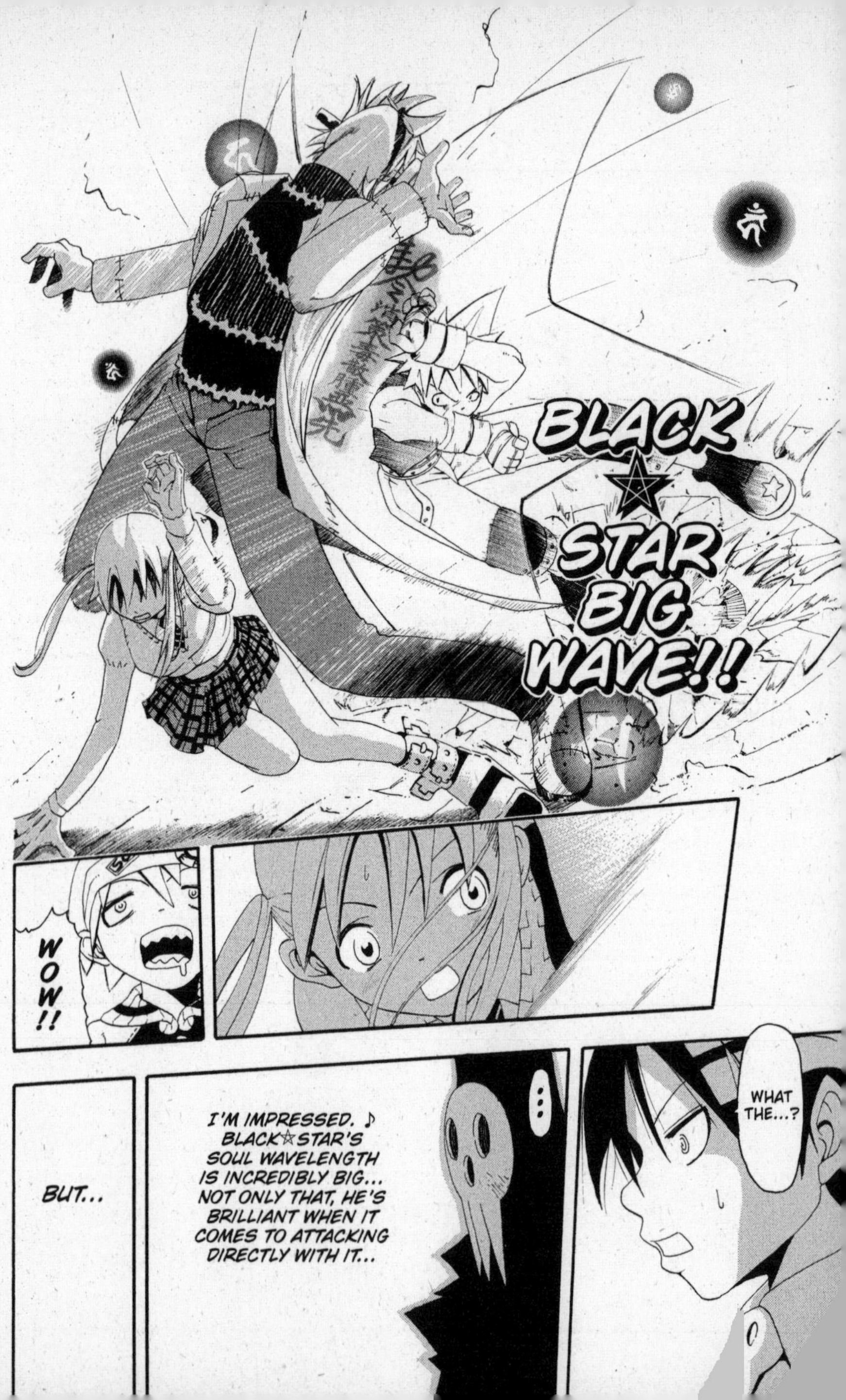
BLACK☆STAR BIG WAVE!!
WOW!!
WHAT THE...?
...
I'M IMPRESSED. ♪ BLACK☆STAR'S SOUL WAVELENGTH IS INCREDIBLY BIG... NOT ONLY THAT, HE'S BRILLIANT WHEN IT COMES TO ATTACKING DIRECTLY WITH IT...
BUT...

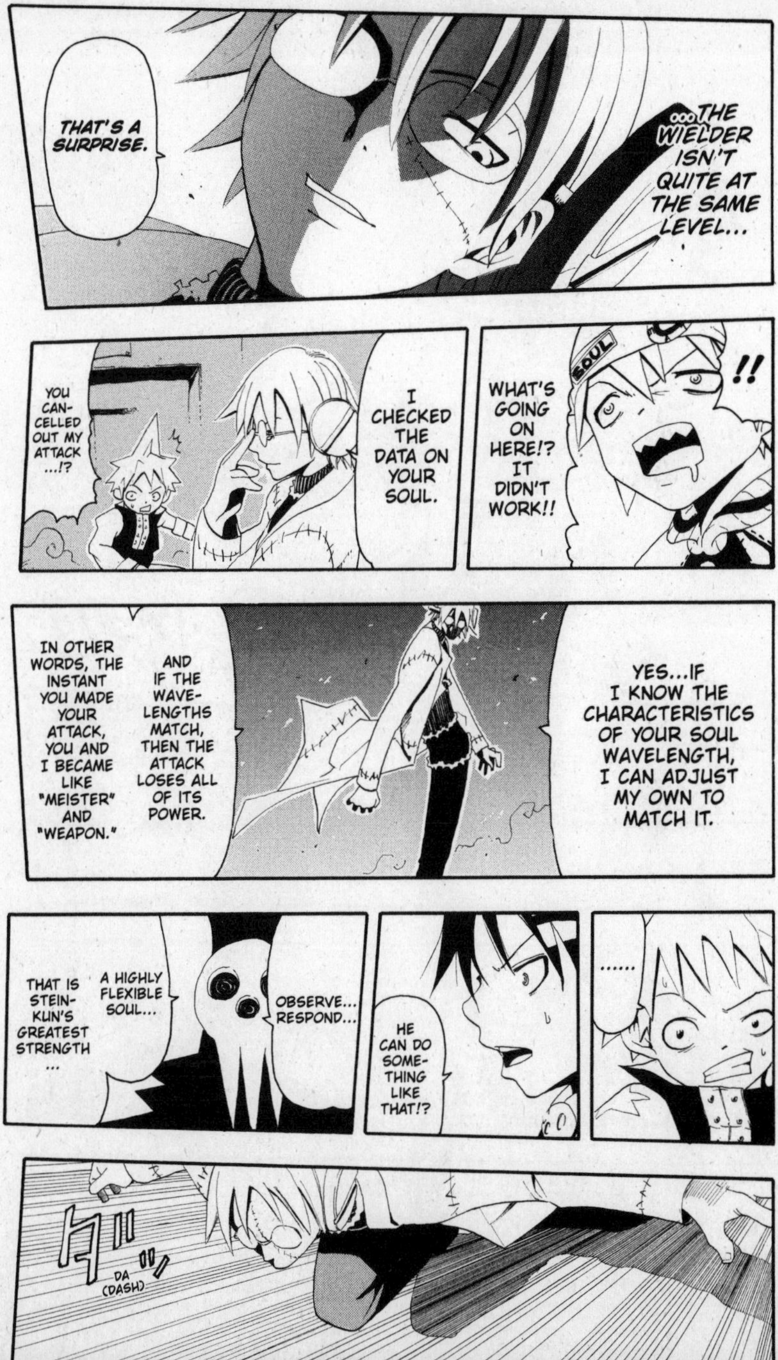
...THE WIELDER ISN'T QUITE AT THE SAME LEVEL...
THAT'S A SURPRISE.
!!
WHAT'S GOING ON HERE!? IT DIDN'T WORK!!
I CHECKED THE DATA ON YOUR SOUL.
YOU CAN-CELLED OUT MY ATTACK ...!?
YES...IF I KNOW THE CHARACTERISTICS OF YOUR SOUL WAVELENGTH, I CAN ADJUST MY OWN TO MATCH IT.
AND IF THE WAVE-LENGTHS MATCH, THEN THE ATTACK LOSES ALL OF ITS POWER.
IN OTHER WORDS, THE INSTANT YOU MADE YOUR ATTACK, YOU AND I BECAME LIKE "MEISTER" AND "WEAPON."
......
HE CAN DO SOME-THING LIKE THAT!?
OBSERVE... RESPOND...
A HIGHLY FLEXIBLE SOUL...
THAT IS STEIN-KUN'S GREATEST STRENGTH ...
DA (DASH)

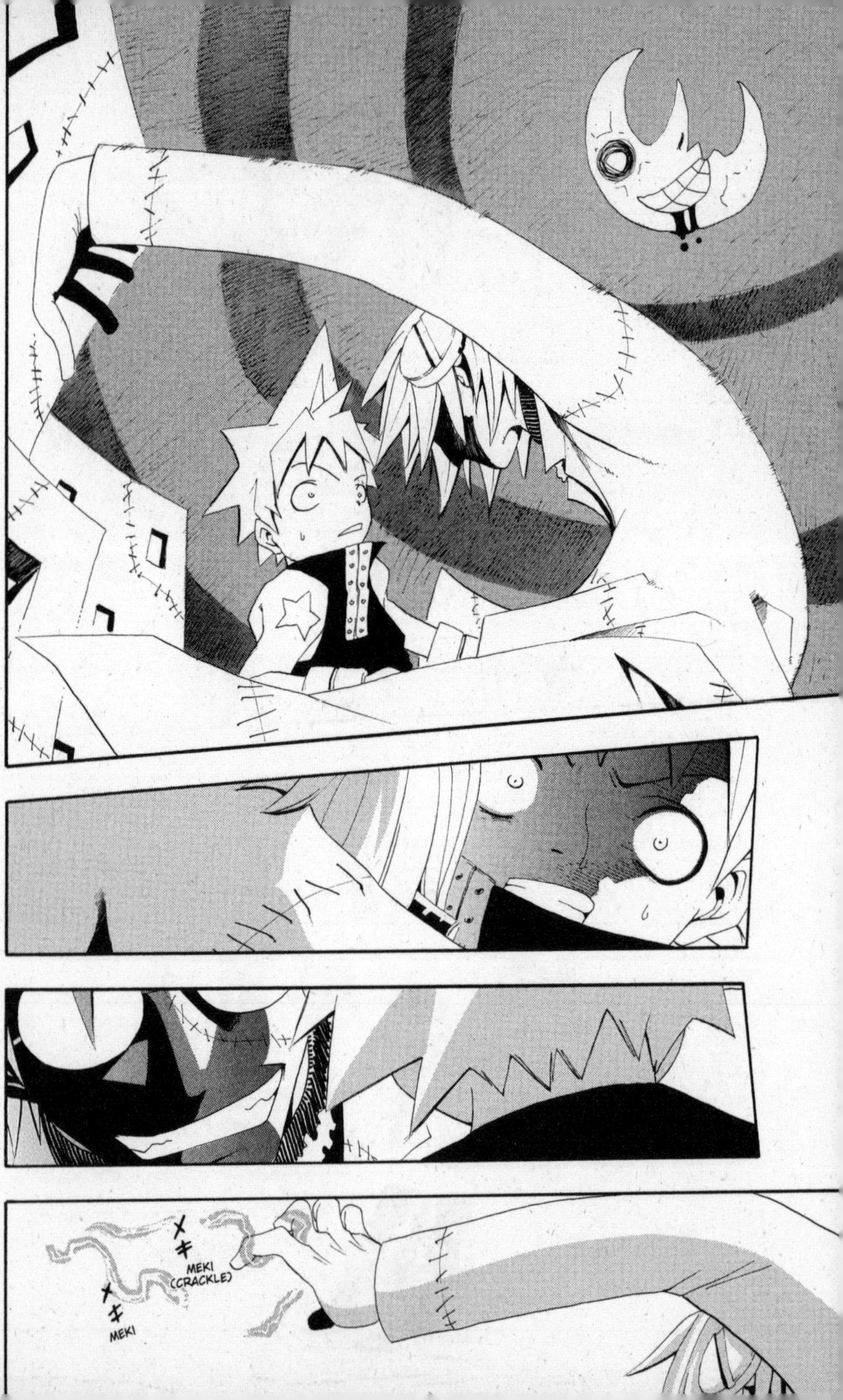
メキ
MEKI
(CRACKLE)
メキ
MEKI

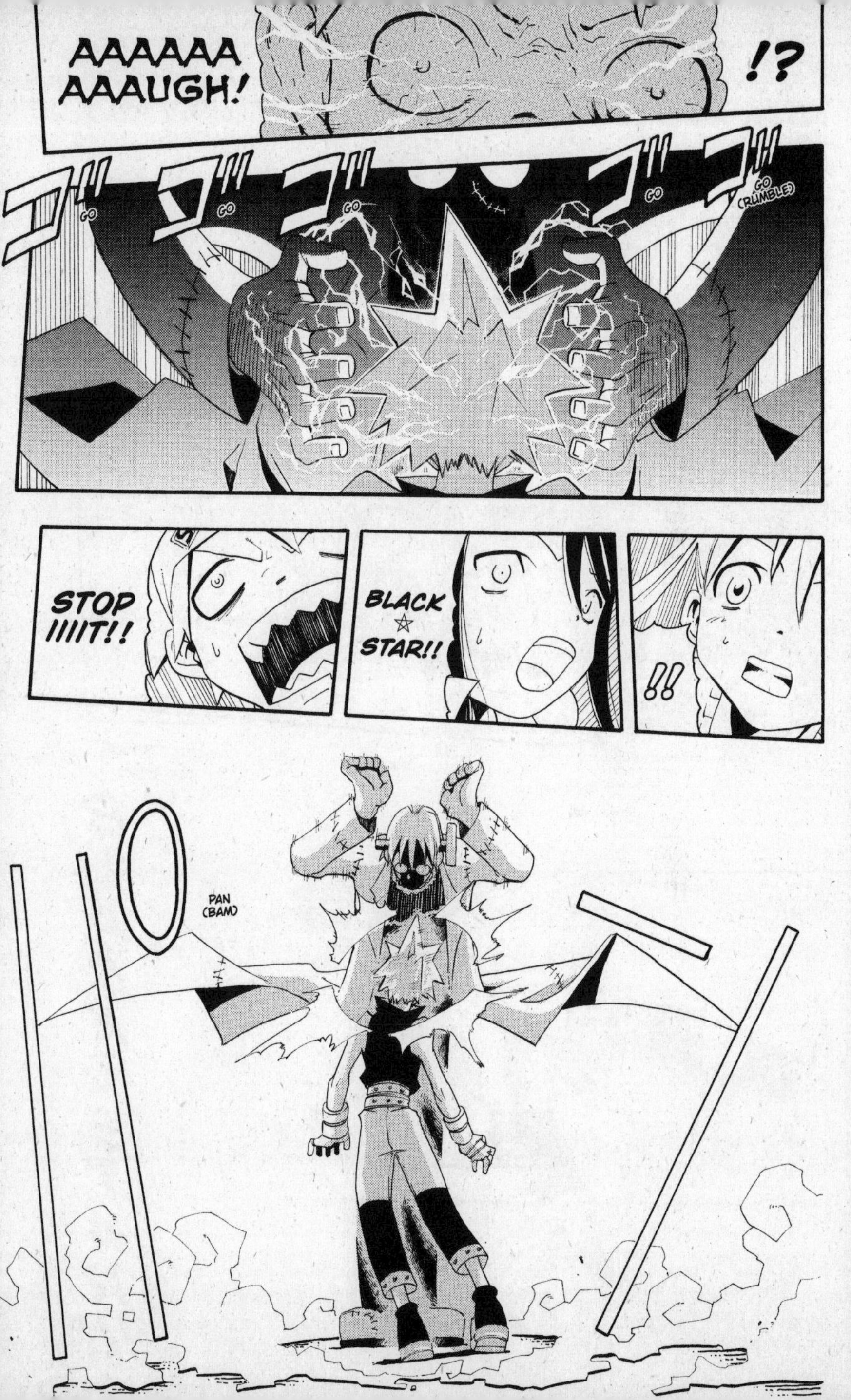
!?
AAAAAA
AAAUGH!
ゴゴゴゴゴ
GO GO GO GO GO (RUMBLE)
!!
BLACK ☆ STAR!!
STOP IIIIT!!
PAN
(BAM)

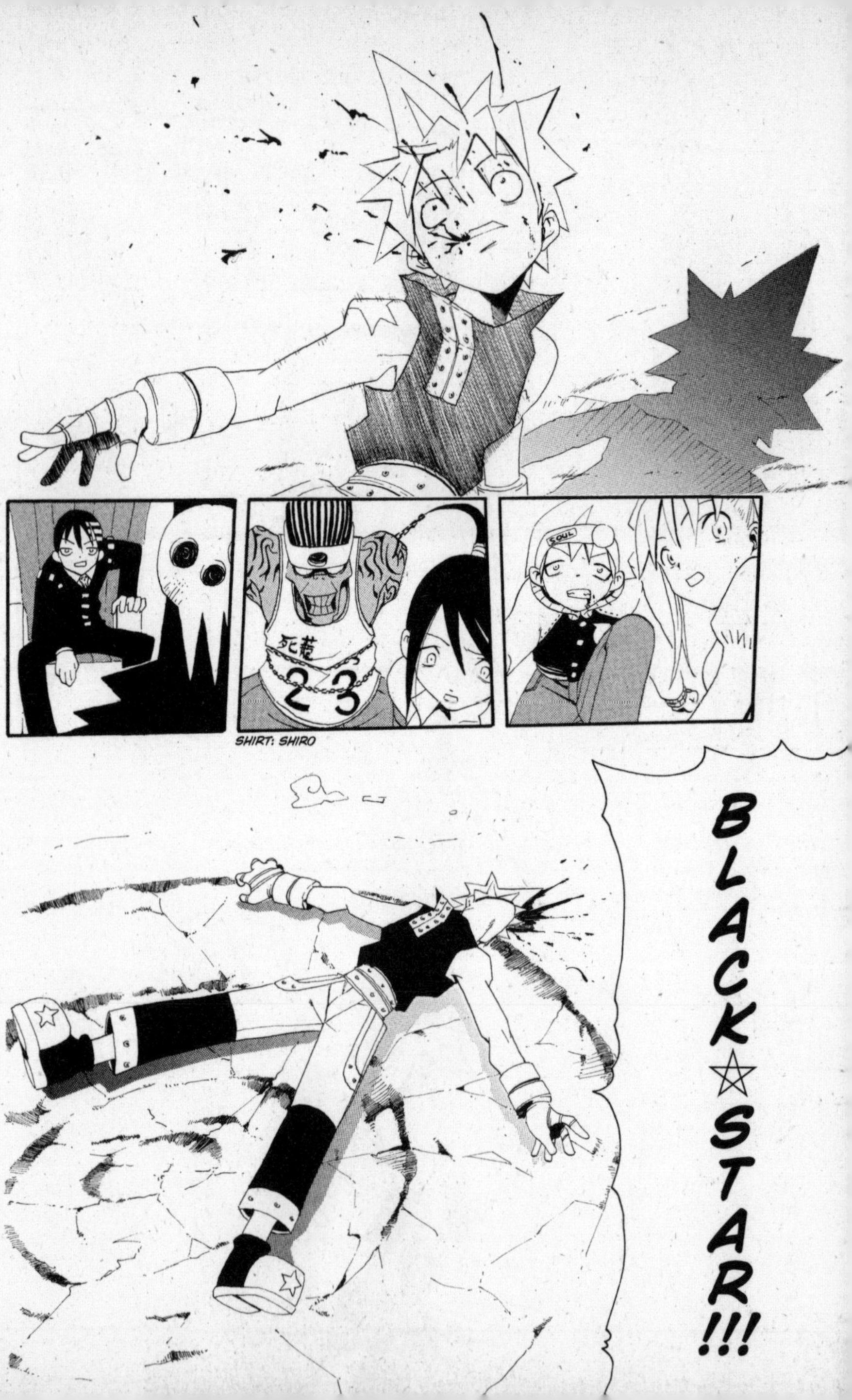
死舞
23
SOUL
SHIRT: SHIRO
BLACK☆STAR!!!

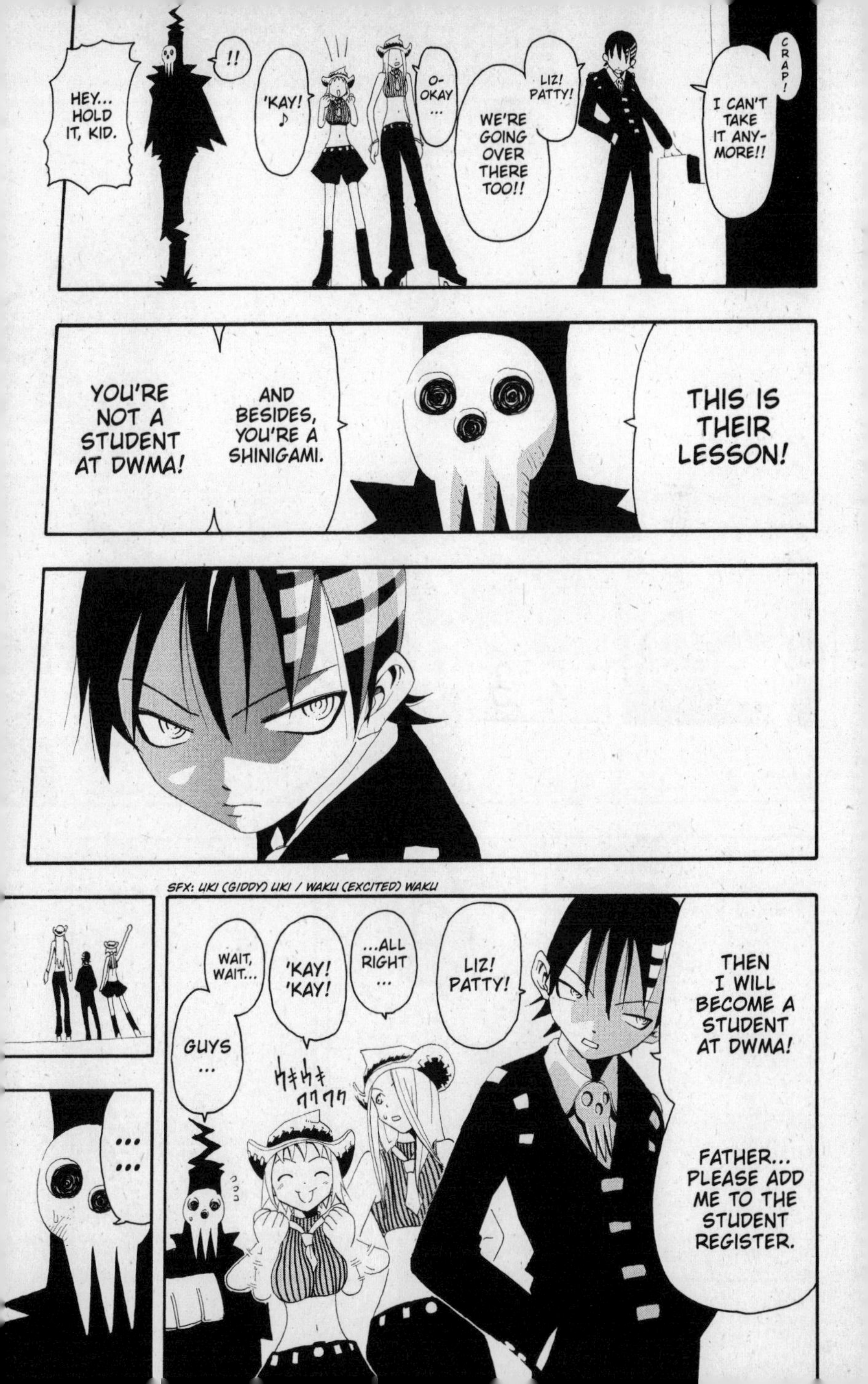
CRAP!
I CAN'T TAKE IT ANY-MORE!!
LIZ! PATTY!
WE'RE GOING OVER THERE TOO!!
O-OKAY...
'KAY! ♪
!!
HEY... HOLD IT, KID.
THIS IS THEIR LESSON!
AND BESIDES, YOU'RE A SHINIGAMI.
YOU'RE NOT A STUDENT AT DWMA!
SFX: UKI (GIDDY) UKI / WAKU (EXCITED) WAKU
THEN I WILL BECOME A STUDENT AT DWMA!
FATHER... PLEASE ADD ME TO THE STUDENT REGISTER.
LIZ! PATTY!
...ALL RIGHT...
'KAY! 'KAY!
ウキウキ ワクワク
WAIT, WAIT... GUYS...
......

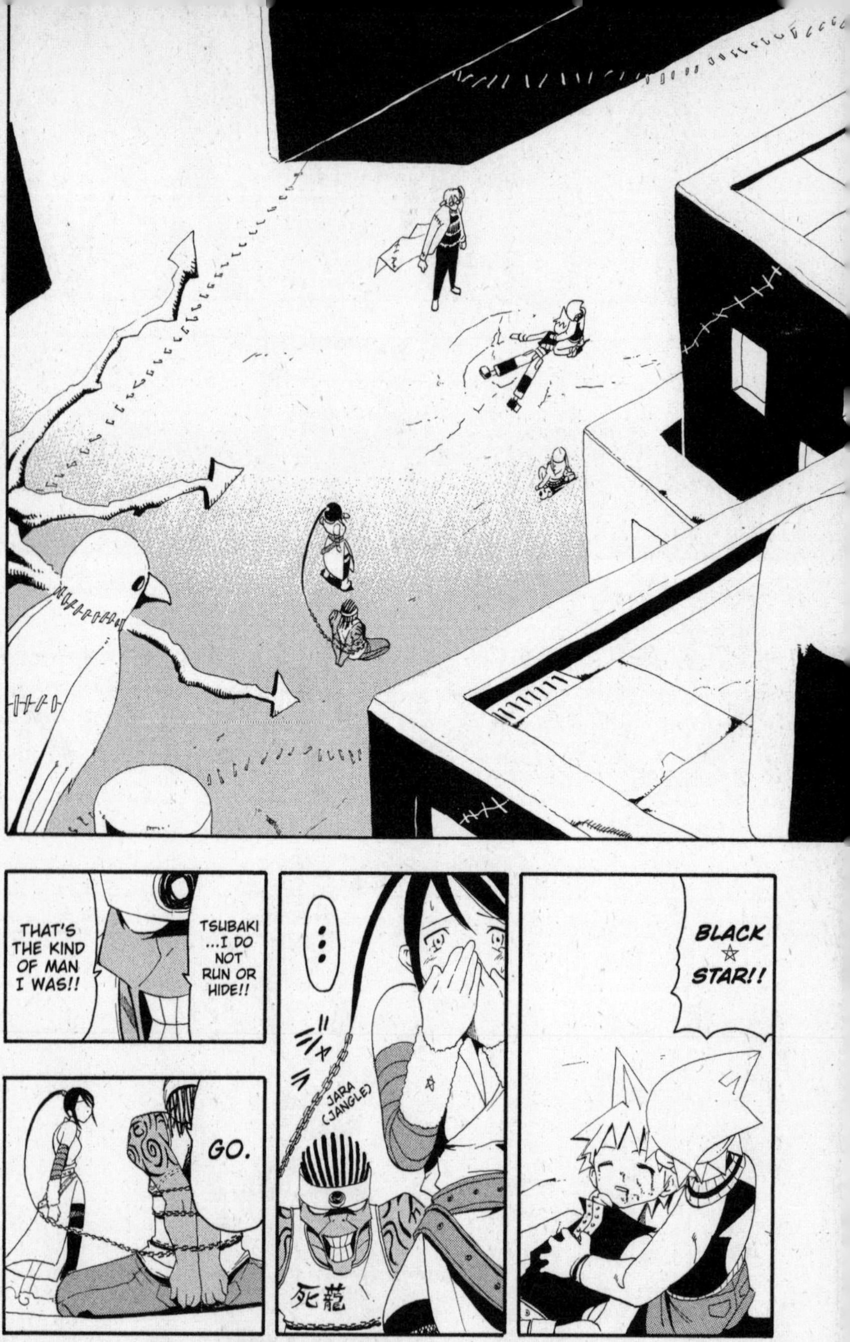
BLACK
☆
STAR!!
...
ジャラ
JARA (JANGLE)
死龍
TSUBAKI ...I DO NOT RUN OR HIDE!!
THAT'S THE KIND OF MAN I WAS!!
GO.

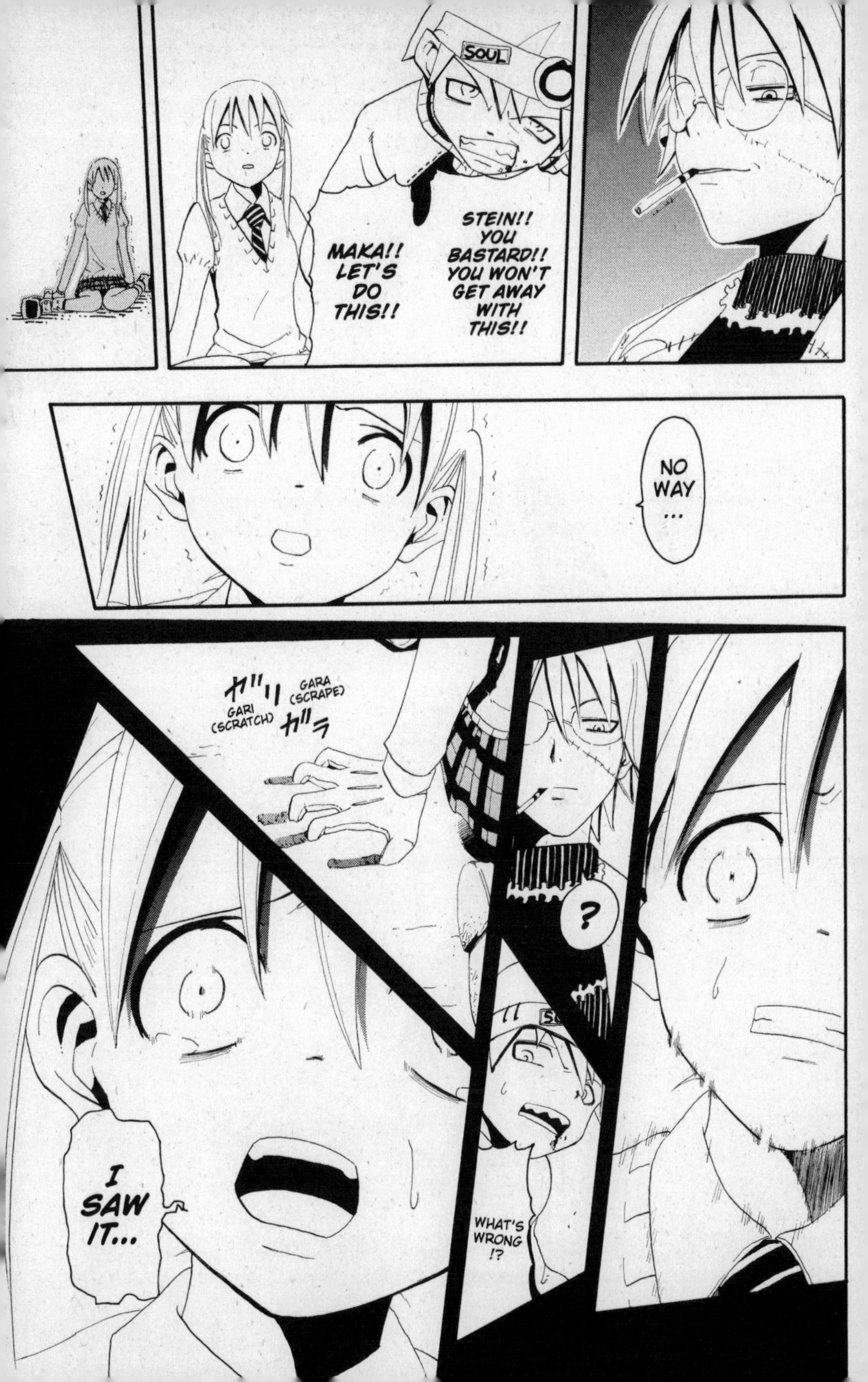
SOUL
STEIN!! YOU BASTARD!! YOU WON'T GET AWAY WITH THIS!!
MAKA!! LET'S DO THIS!!
NO WAY...
?
SOUL
WHAT'S WRONG !?
ガラ GARA (SCRAPE)
ガリ GARI (SCRATCH)
I SAW IT...

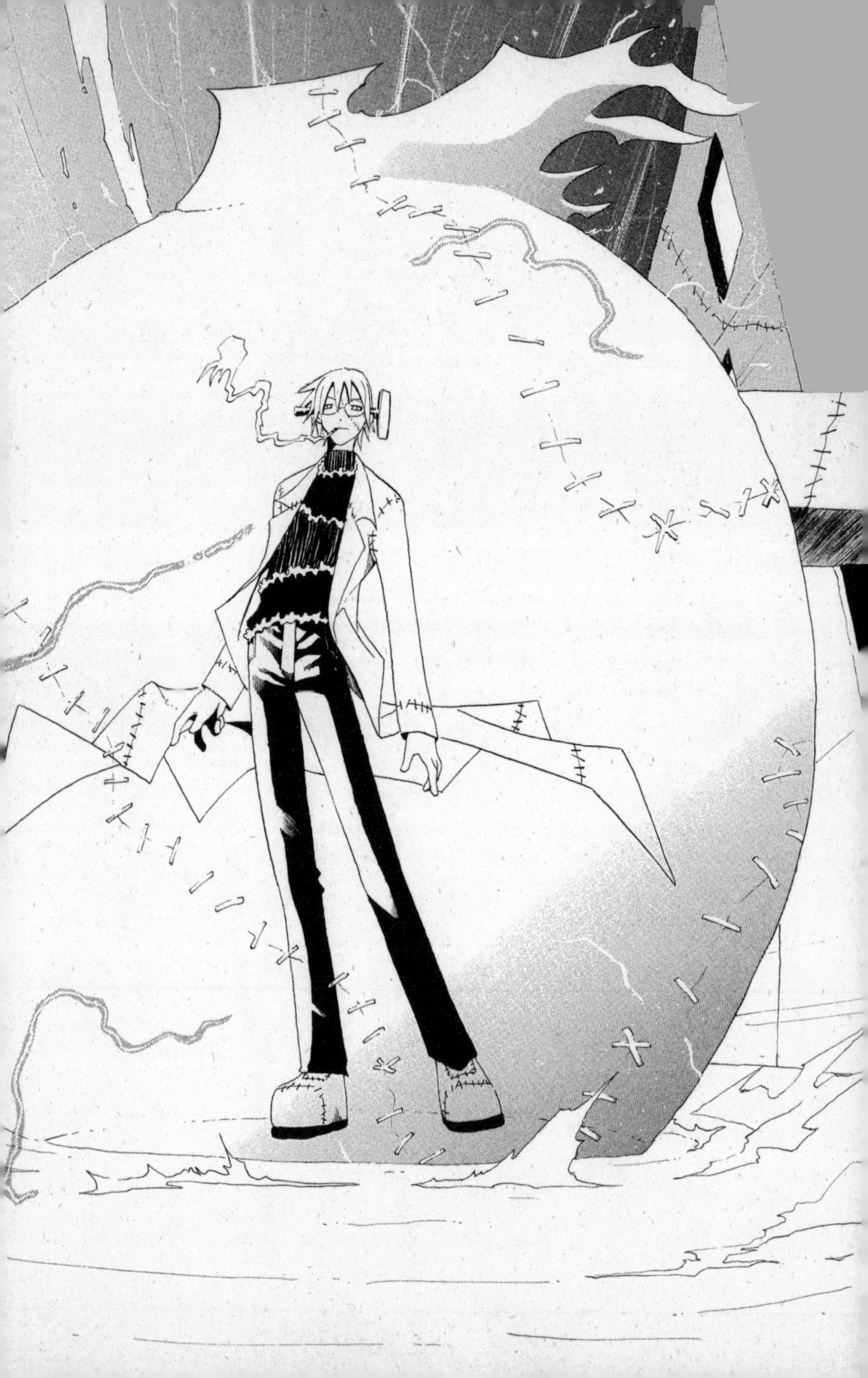

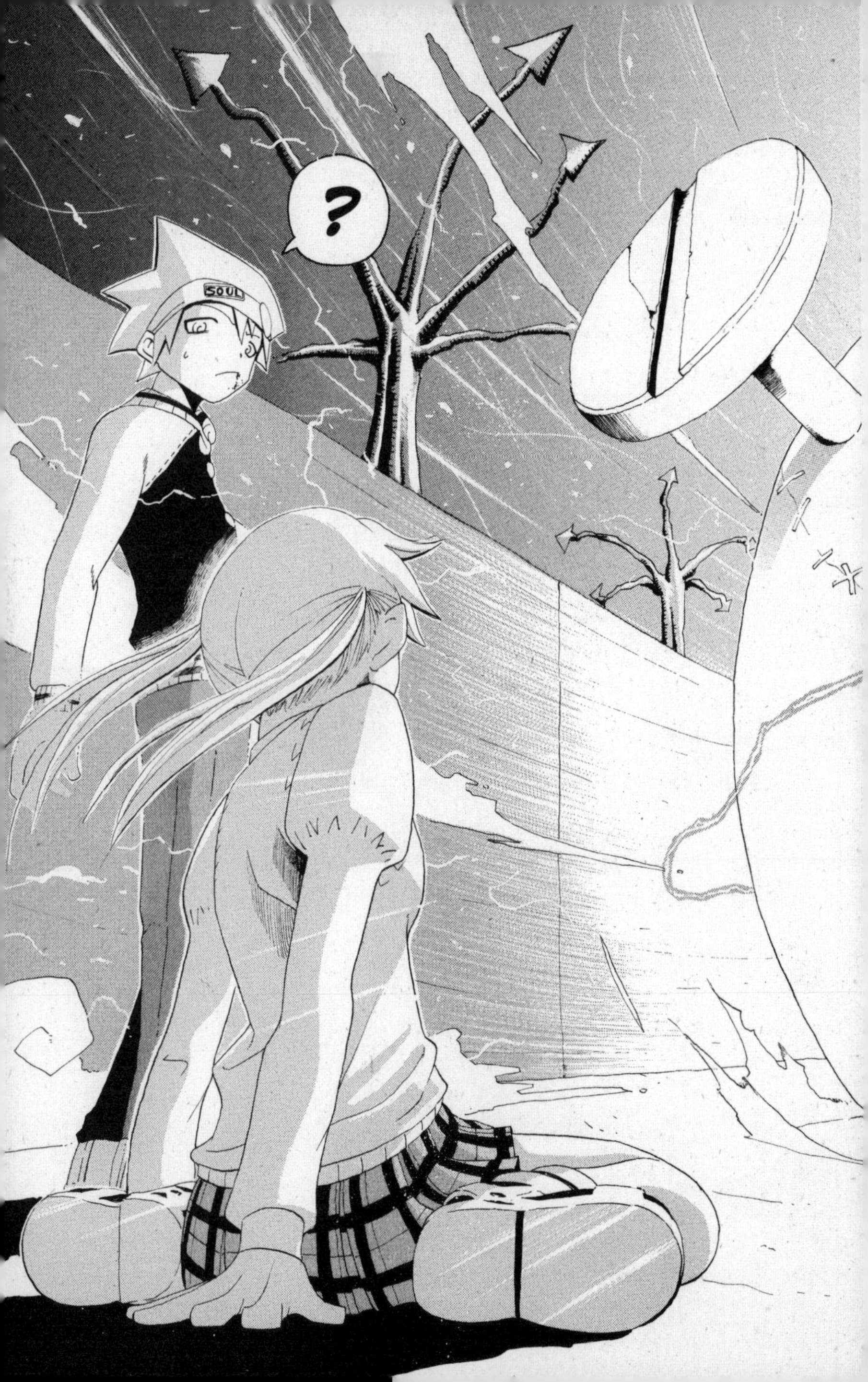
?
SOUL

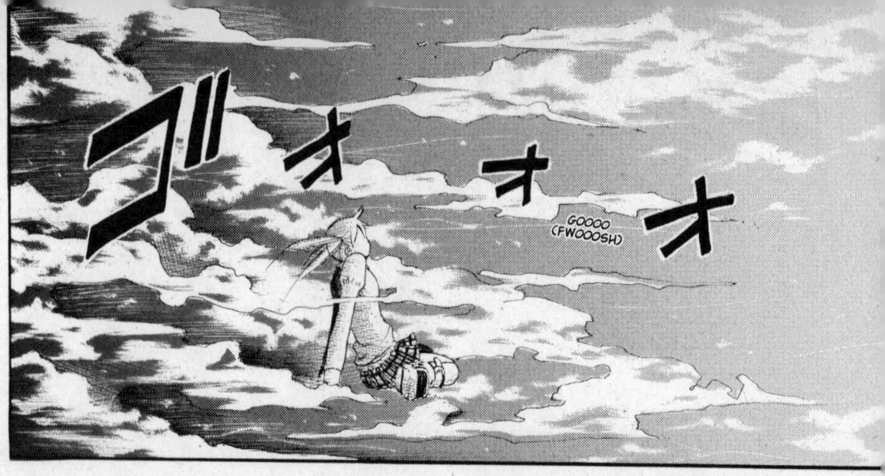
ゴォォォ
GOOOO (FWOOOSH)
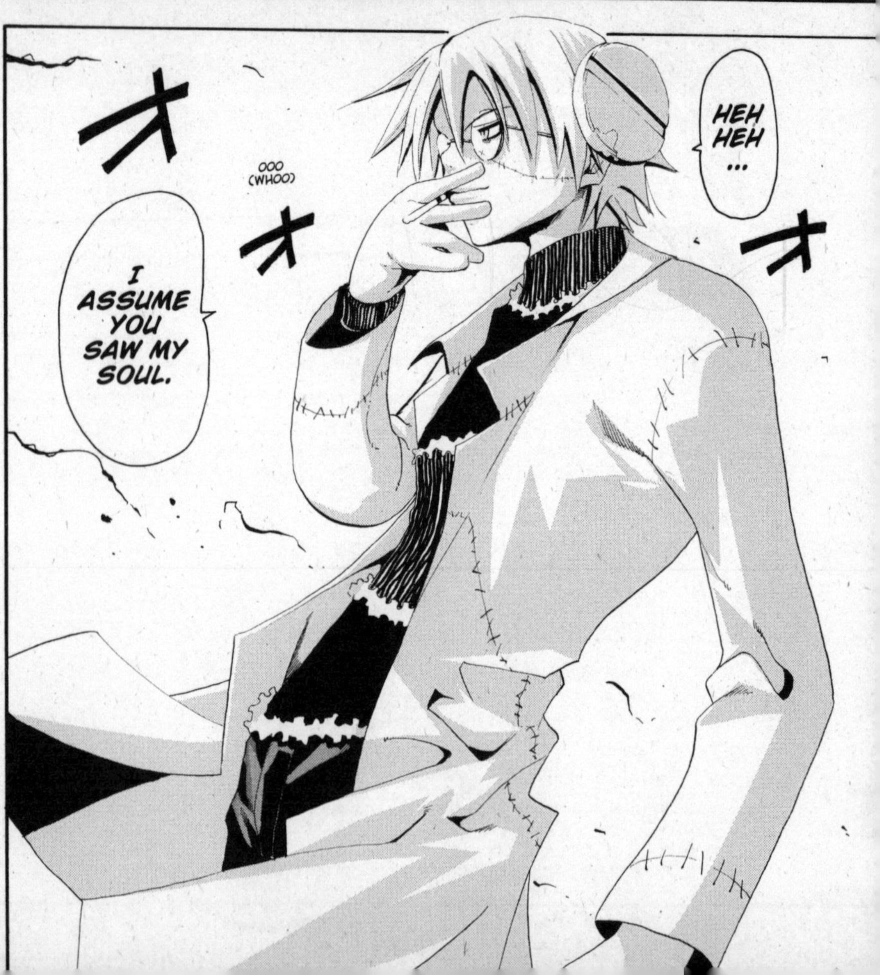
HEH HEH ...
オ
オ
OOO (WHOO)
I ASSUME YOU SAW MY SOUL.
オ

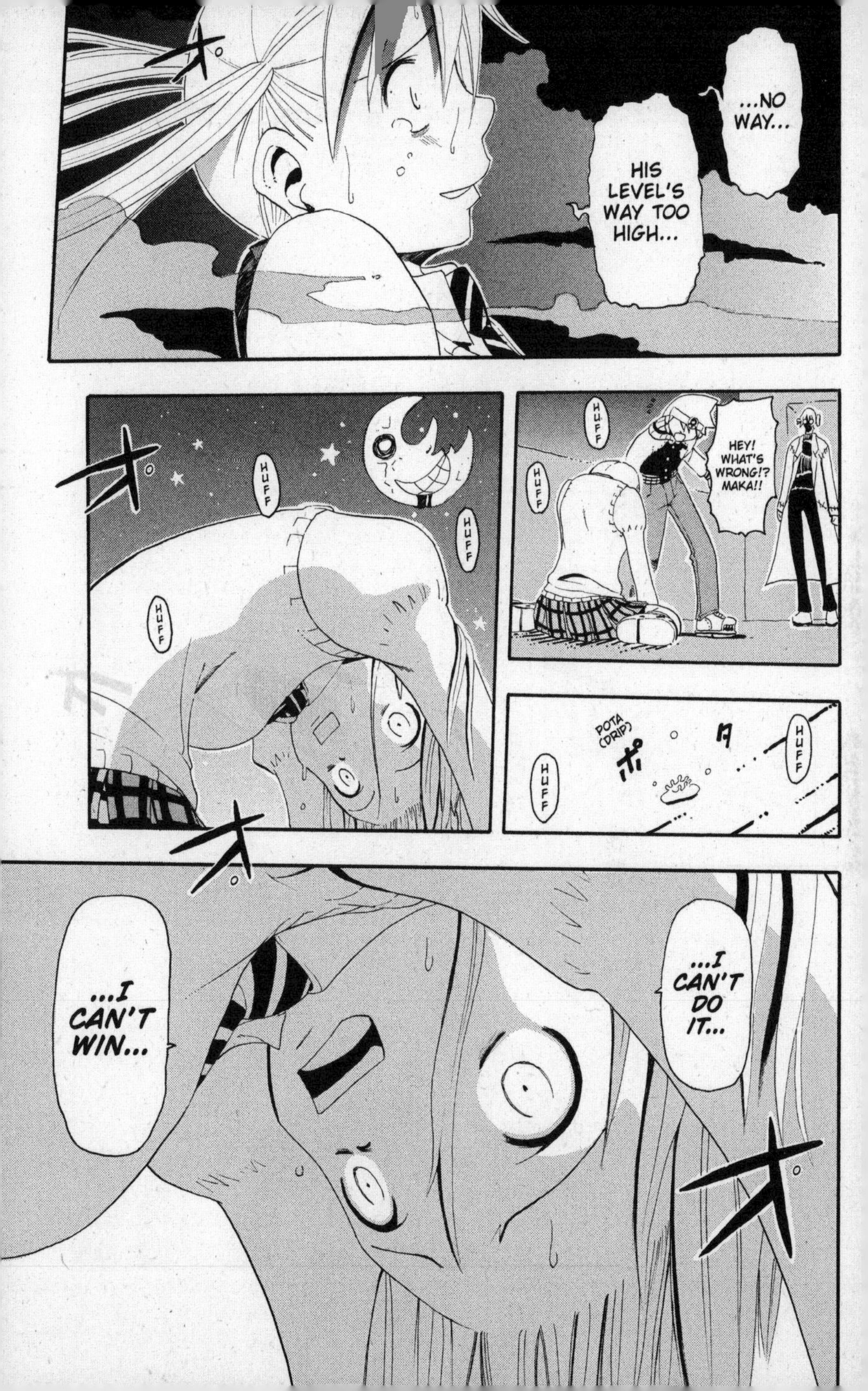
...NO WAY...
HIS LEVEL'S WAY TOO HIGH...
HUFF
HUFF
HEY! WHAT'S WRONG!? MAKA!!
HUFF
POTA (DRIP)
HUFF
HUFF
HUFF
HUFF
...I CAN'T DO IT...
...I CAN'T WIN...

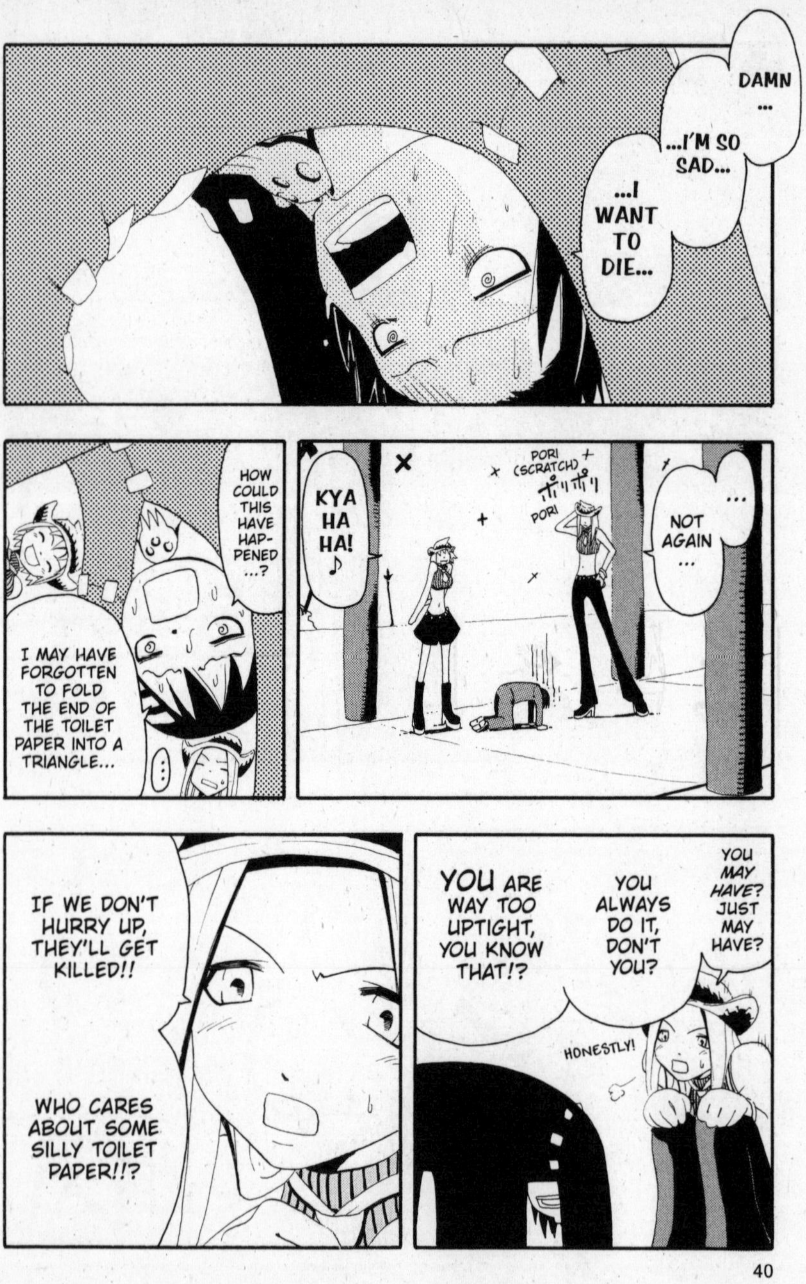
DAMN ...
...I'M SO SAD...
...I WANT TO DIE...
... NOT AGAIN ...
PORI (SCRATCH)
ポリポリ
PORI
KYA HA HA! ♪
HOW COULD THIS HAVE HAP-PENED ...?
I MAY HAVE FORGOTTEN TO FOLD THE END OF THE TOILET PAPER INTO A TRIANGLE...
...
YOU MAY HAVE? JUST MAY HAVE?
YOU ALWAYS DO IT, DON'T YOU?
YOU ARE WAY TOO UPTIGHT, YOU KNOW THAT!?
HONESTLY!
IF WE DON'T HURRY UP, THEY'LL GET KILLED!!
WHO CARES ABOUT SOME SILLY TOILET PAPER!!?

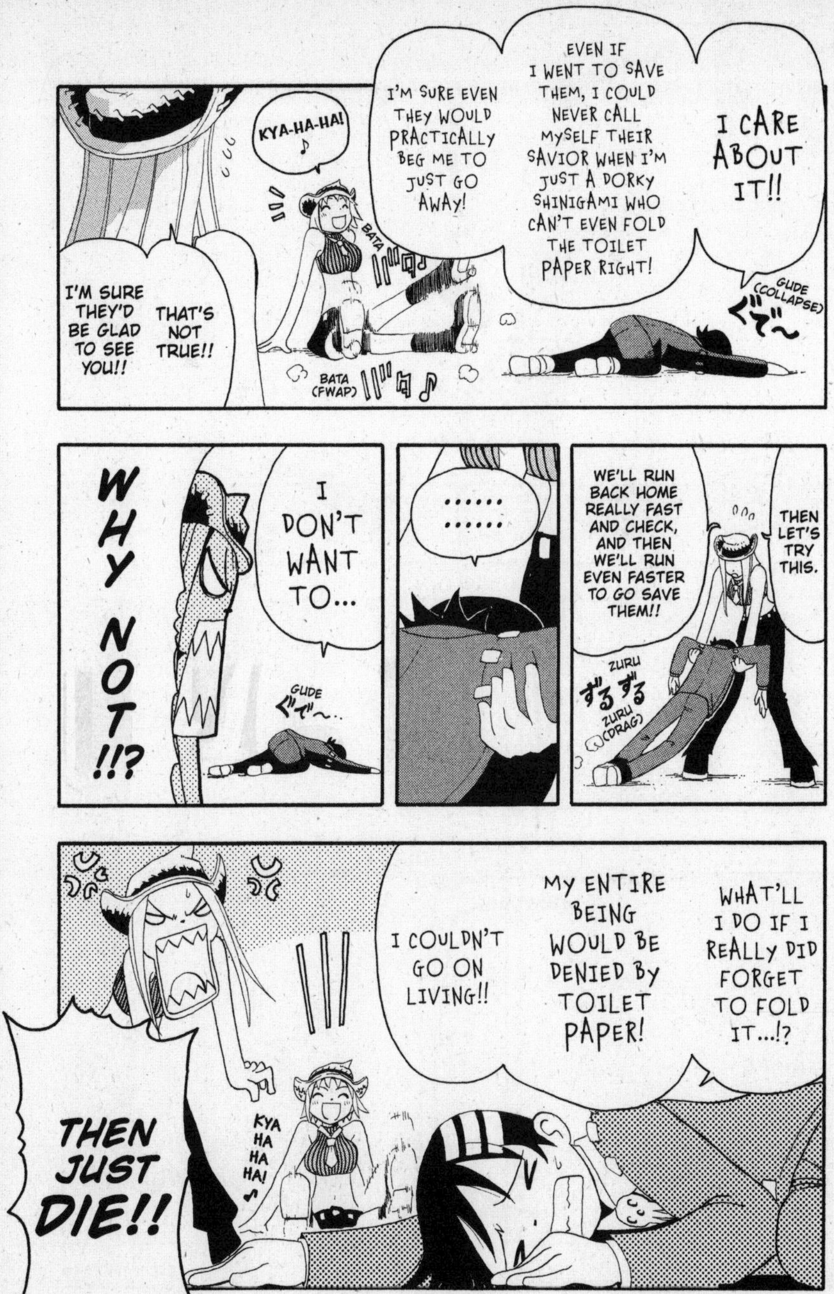
I CARE ABOUT IT!!
EVEN IF I WENT TO SAVE THEM, I COULD NEVER CALL MYSELF THEIR SAVIOR WHEN I'M JUST A DORKY SHINIGAMI WHO CAN'T EVEN FOLD THE TOILET PAPER RIGHT!
I'M SURE EVEN THEY WOULD PRACTICALLY BEG ME TO JUST GO AWAY!
KYA-HA-HA! ♪
BATA
GUDE (COLLAPSE)
ぐで〜
THAT'S NOT TRUE!!
I'M SURE THEY'D BE GLAD TO SEE YOU!!
BATA (FWAP)
THEN LET'S TRY THIS.
WE'LL RUN BACK HOME REALLY FAST AND CHECK, AND THEN WE'LL RUN EVEN FASTER TO GO SAVE THEM!!
ZURU ZURU (DRAG)
ずるずる
....
I DON'T WANT TO...
GUDE
ぐで〜
WHY NOT!!?
WHAT'LL I DO IF I REALLY DID FORGET TO FOLD IT...!?
MY ENTIRE BEING WOULD BE DENIED BY TOILET PAPER!
I COULDN'T GO ON LIVING!!
KYA HA HA HA! ♪
THEN JUST DIE!!

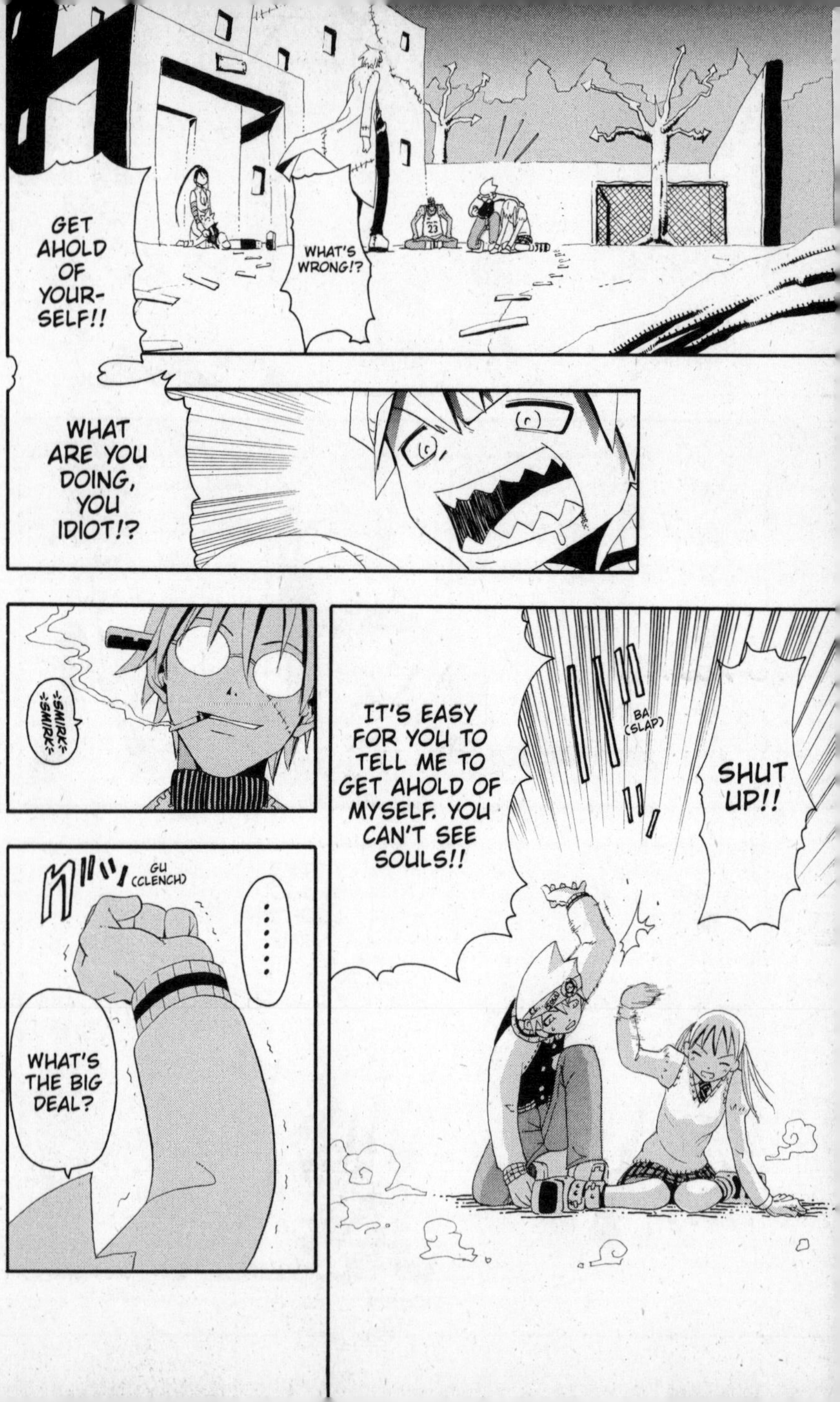
WHAT'S WRONG!?
GET AHOLD OF YOURSELF!!
WHAT ARE YOU DOING, YOU IDIOT!?
SHUT UP!!
BA (SLAP)
IT'S EASY FOR YOU TO TELL ME TO GET AHOLD OF MYSELF. YOU CAN'T SEE SOULS!!
SMIRK SMIRK
GU (CLENCH)
......
WHAT'S THE BIG DEAL?

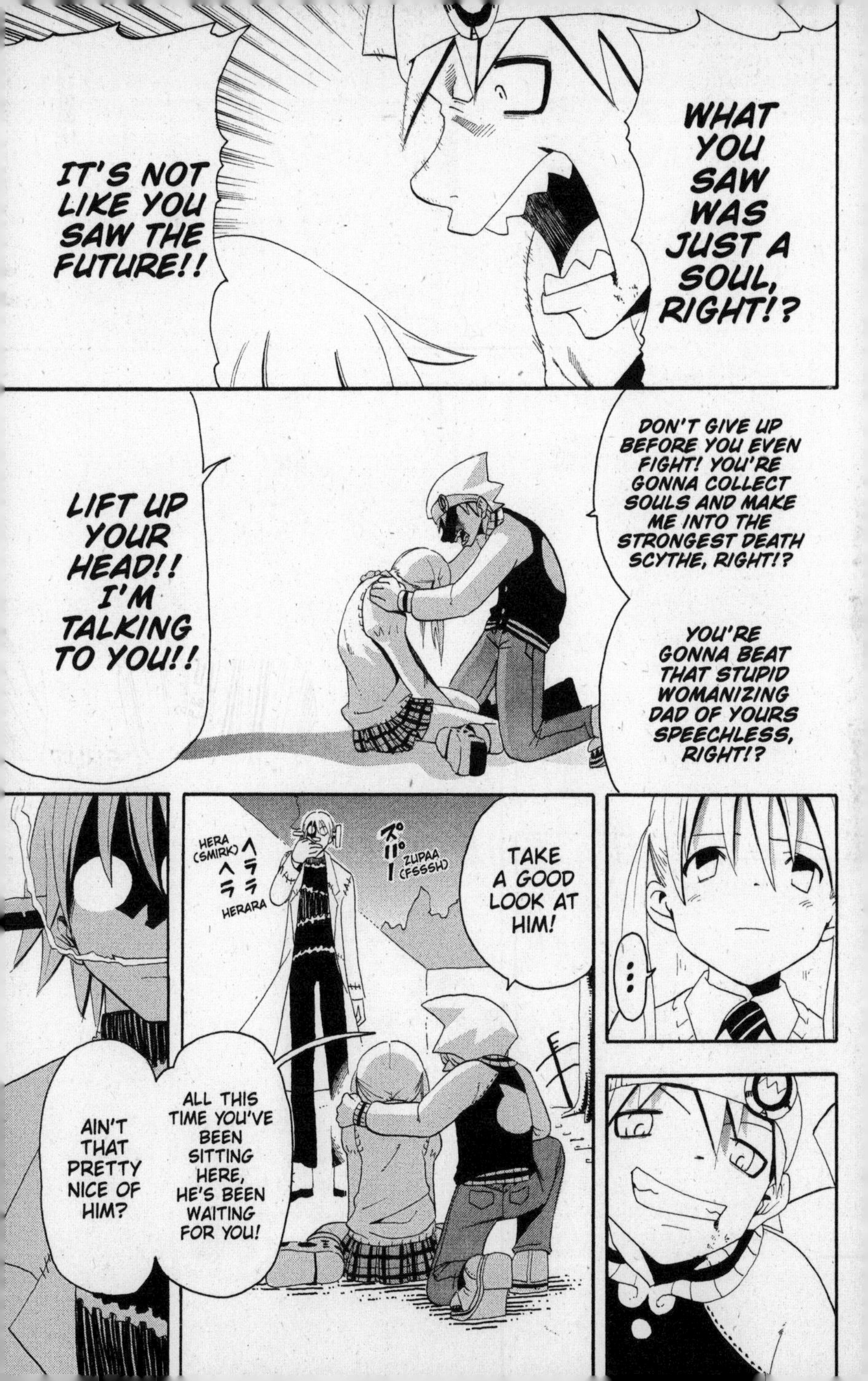
WHAT YOU SAW WAS JUST A SOUL, RIGHT!?
IT'S NOT LIKE YOU SAW THE FUTURE!!
DON'T GIVE UP BEFORE YOU EVEN FIGHT! YOU'RE GONNA COLLECT SOULS AND MAKE ME INTO THE STRONGEST DEATH SCYTHE, RIGHT!?
YOU'RE GONNA BEAT THAT STUPID WOMANIZING DAD OF YOURS SPEECHLESS, RIGHT!?
LIFT UP YOUR HEAD!! I'M TALKING TO YOU!!
...
TAKE A GOOD LOOK AT HIM!
ZUPAA (FSSSH)
HERA (SMIRK)
HERARA
ALL THIS TIME YOU'VE BEEN SITTING HERE, HE'S BEEN WAITING FOR YOU!
AIN'T THAT PRETTY NICE OF HIM?

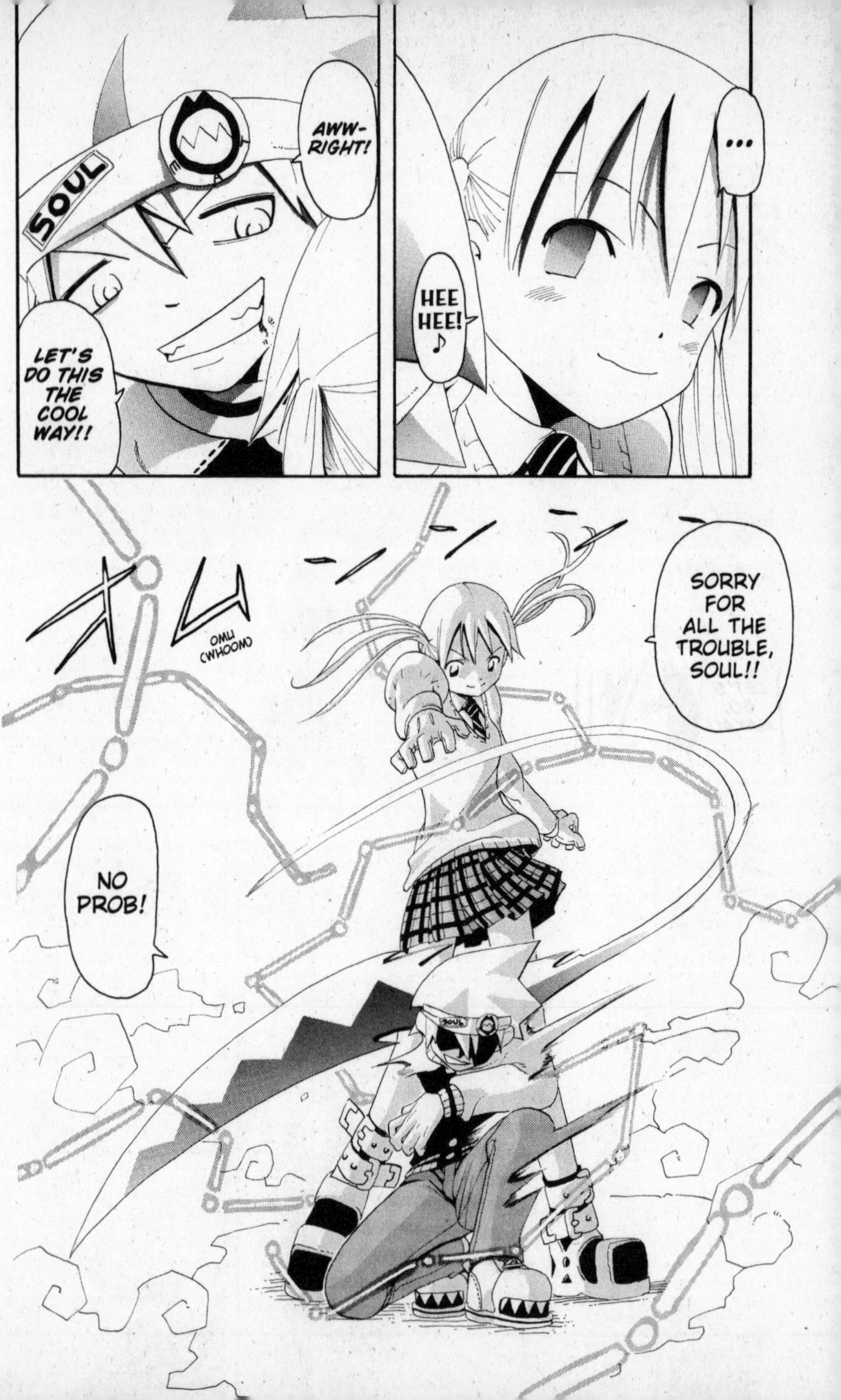
...
HEE HEE! ♪
AWW-RIGHT!
LET'S DO THIS THE COOL WAY!!
SORRY FOR ALL THE TROUBLE, SOUL!!
オム
OMU (WHOOM)
NO PROB!

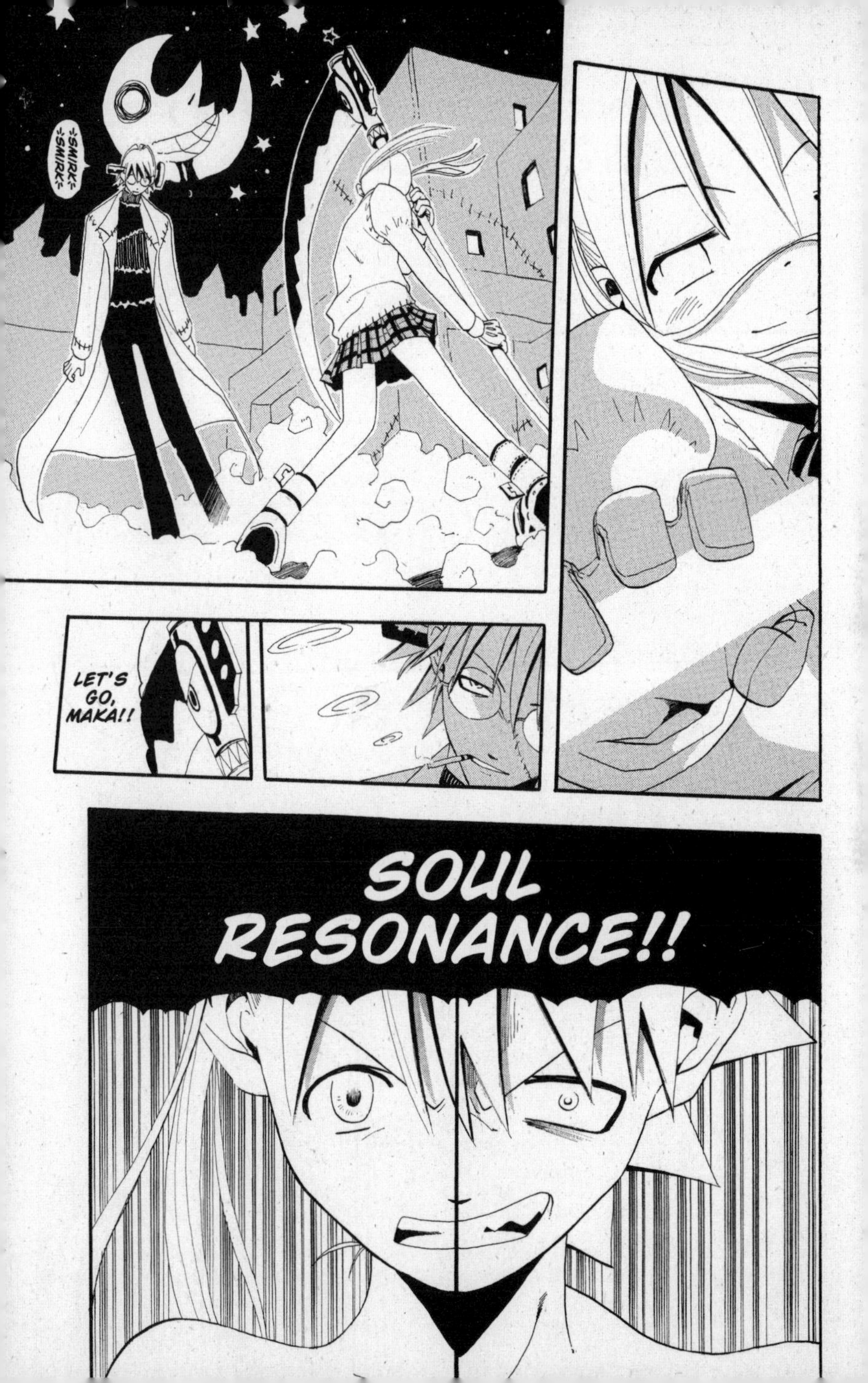

SMIRK SMIRK
LET'S GO, MAKA!!
SOUL RESONANCE!!

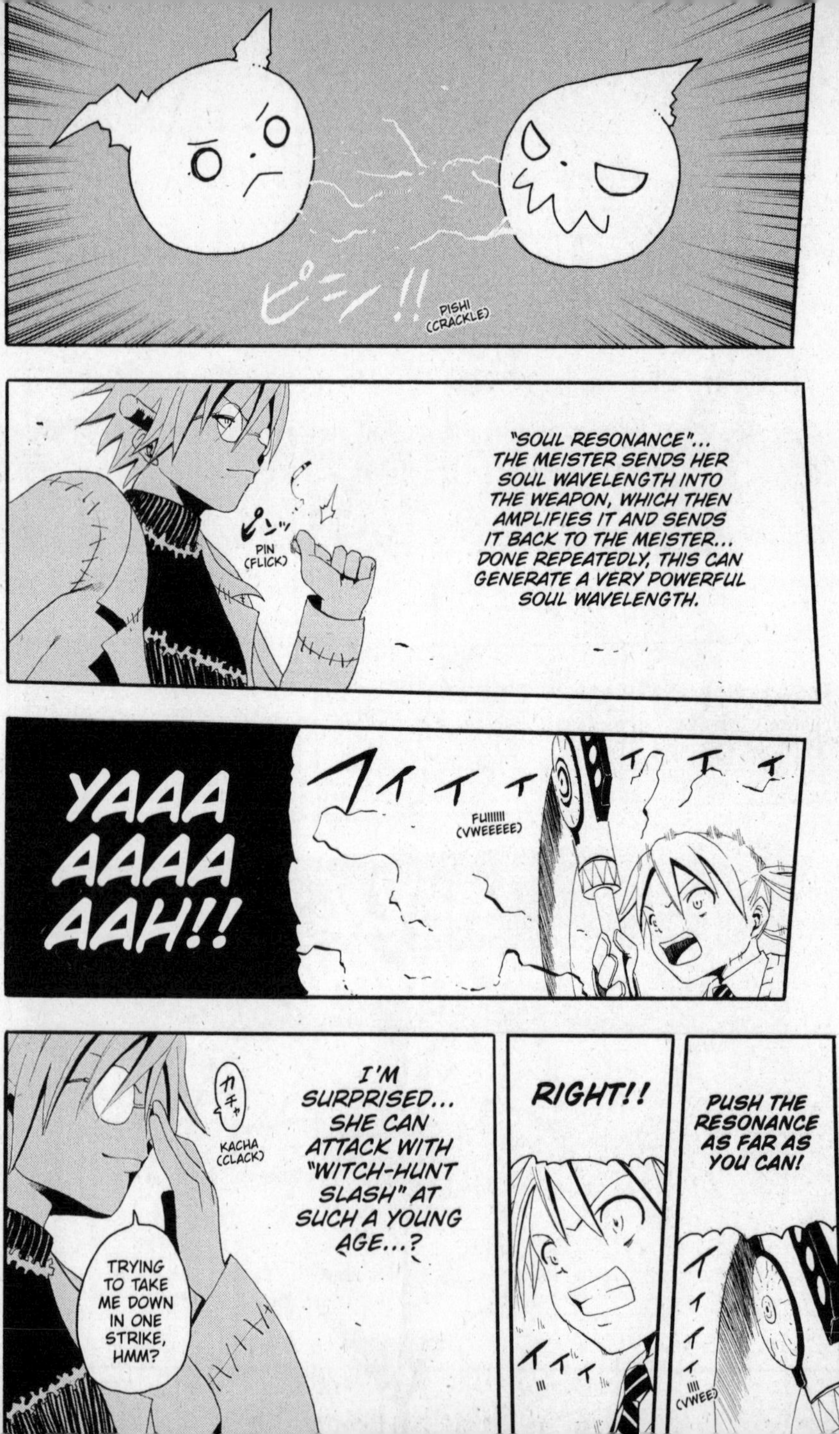
ピーン!!
PISHI (CRACKLE)
"SOUL RESONANCE"... THE MEISTER SENDS HER SOUL WAVELENGTH INTO THE WEAPON, WHICH THEN AMPLIFIES IT AND SENDS IT BACK TO THE MEISTER... DONE REPEATEDLY, THIS CAN GENERATE A VERY POWERFUL SOUL WAVELENGTH.
ピンッ
PIN (FLICK)
FUIIIIII (VWEEEEE)
YAAA AAAA AAH!!
PUSH THE RESONANCE AS FAR AS YOU CAN!
IIII (VWEE)
RIGHT!!
I'M SURPRISED... SHE CAN ATTACK WITH "WITCH-HUNT SLASH" AT SUCH A YOUNG AGE...?
カチャ
KACHA (CLACK)
TRYING TO TAKE ME DOWN IN ONE STRIKE, HMM?

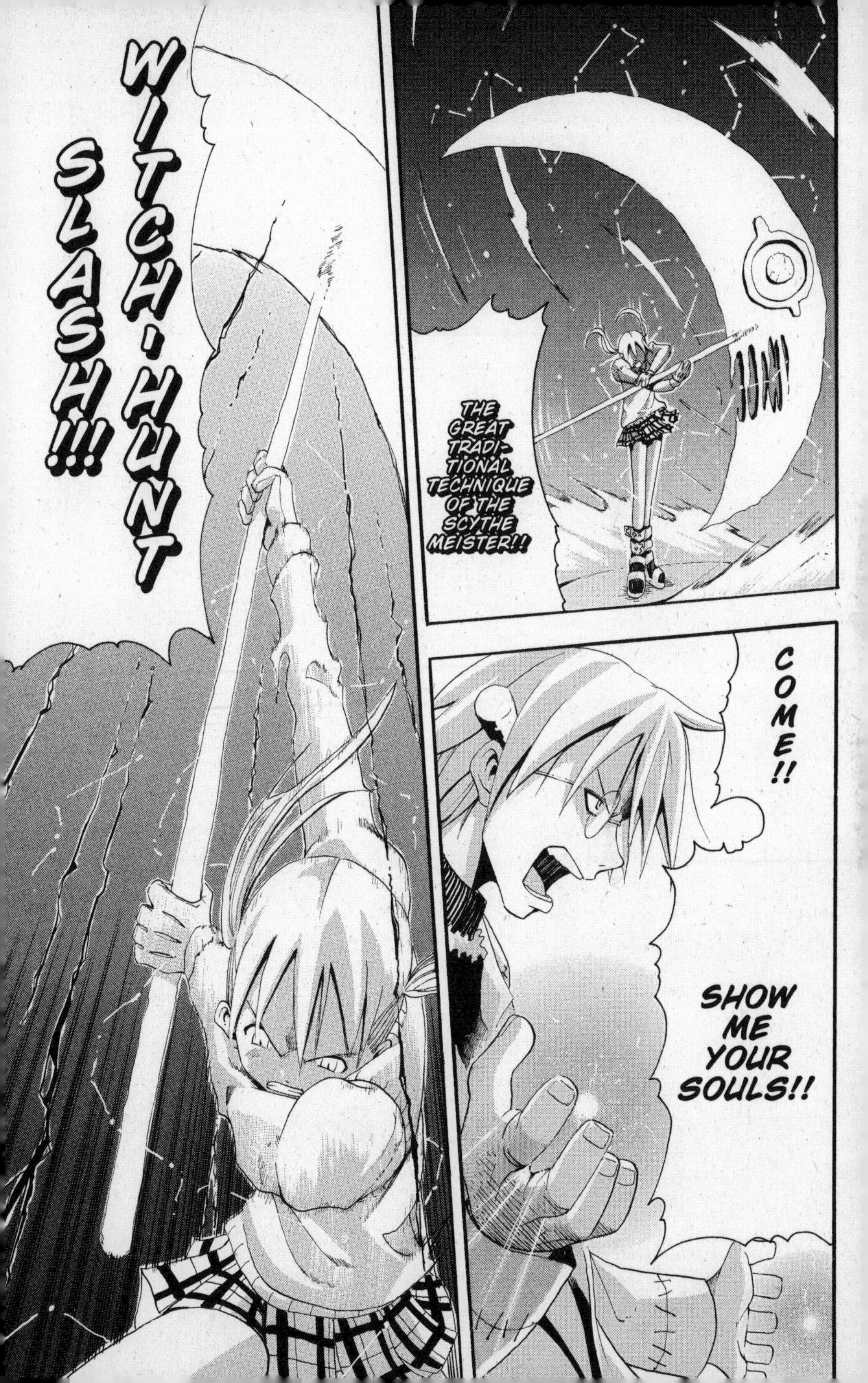
THE GREAT TRADI-TIONAL TECHNIQUE OF THE SCYTHE MEISTER!!
COME!!
SHOW ME YOUR SOULS!!
WITCH-HUNT SLASH!!!

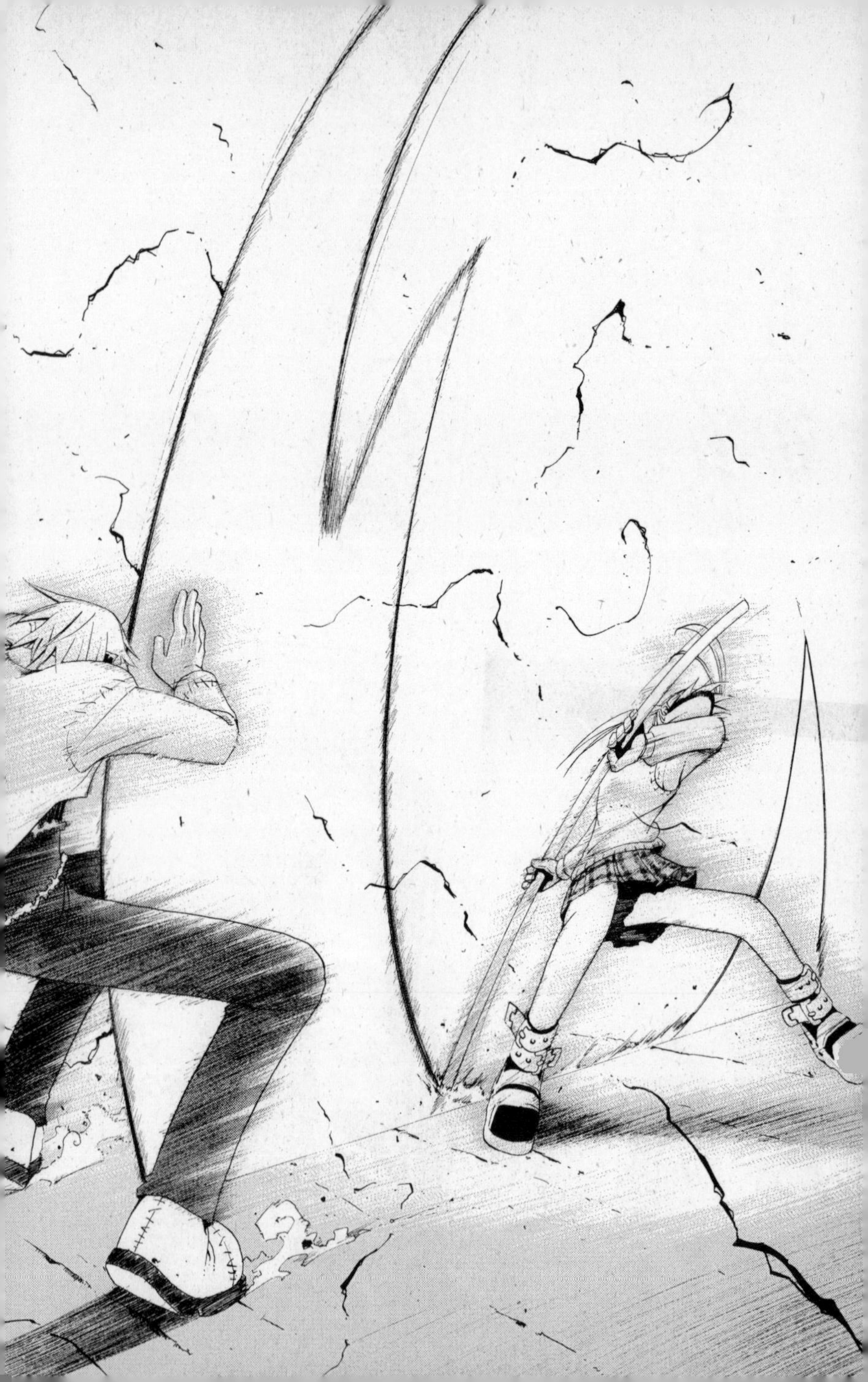

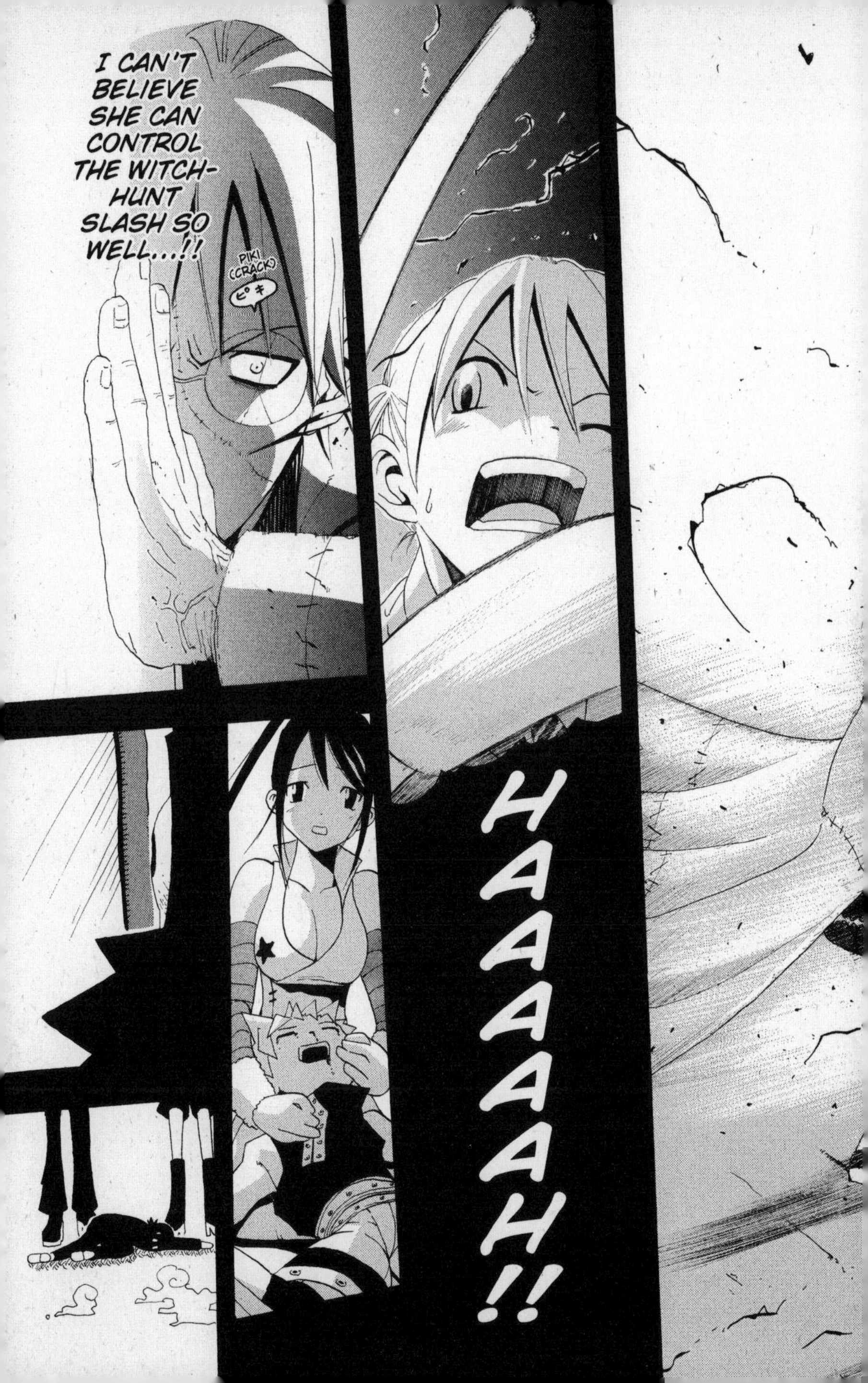
HAAAAAH!!
I CAN'T BELIEVE SHE CAN CONTROL THE WITCH-HUNT SLASH SO WELL...!!
PIKI (CRACK)
ピキ

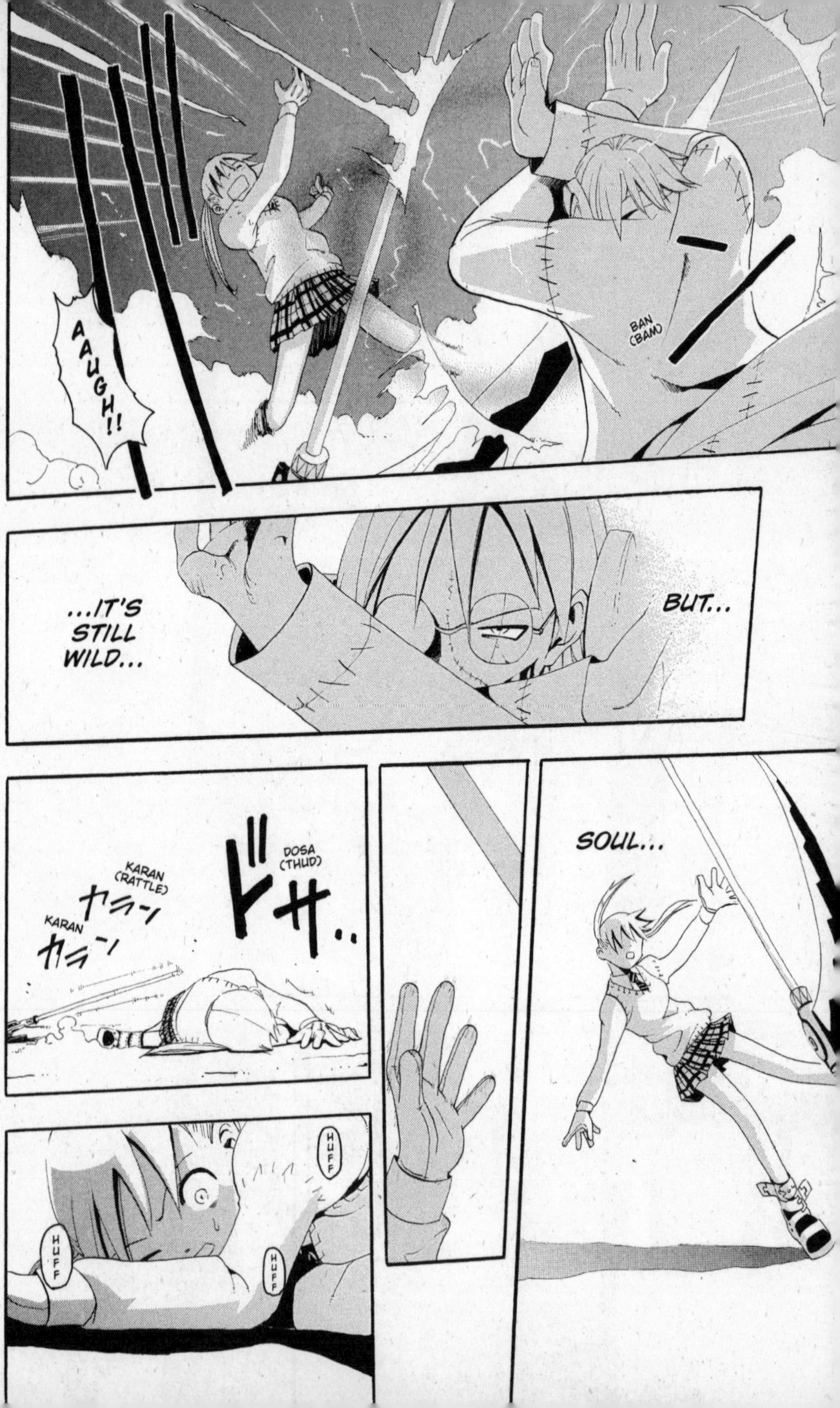

BAN (BAM)
AAUGH!!
BUT...
...IT'S STILL WILD...
SOUL...
DOSA (THUD)
ドサ..
KARAN (RATTLE)
KARAN
HUFF
HUFF
HUFF

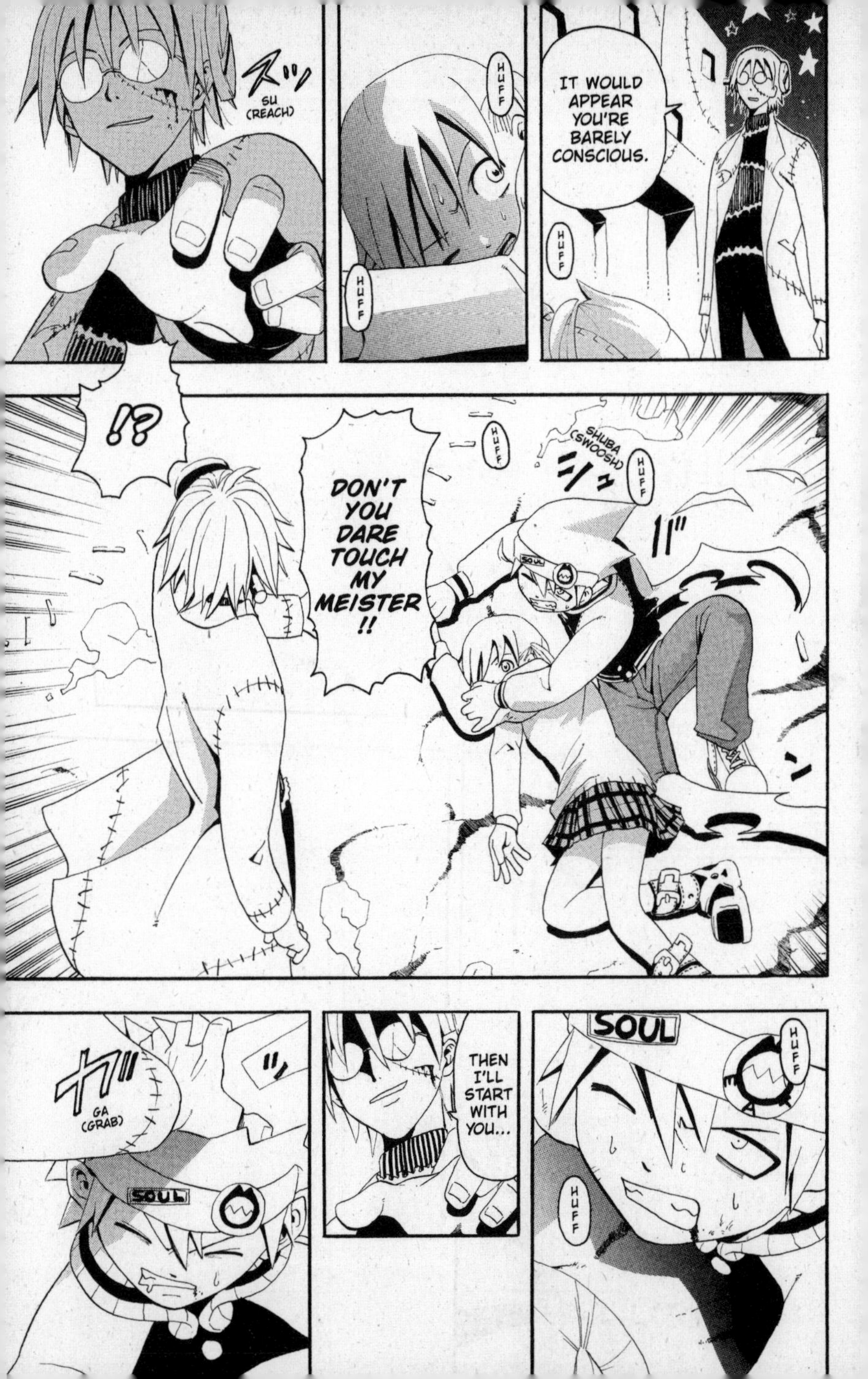

IT WOULD APPEAR YOU'RE BARELY CONSCIOUS.
HUFF
HUFF
HUFF
HUFF
SU (REACH)
HUFF
SHUBA (SWOOSH)
HUFF
DON'T YOU DARE TOUCH MY MEISTER!!
!?
SOUL
HUFF
HUFF
THEN I'LL START WITH YOU...
GA (GRAB)
SOUL

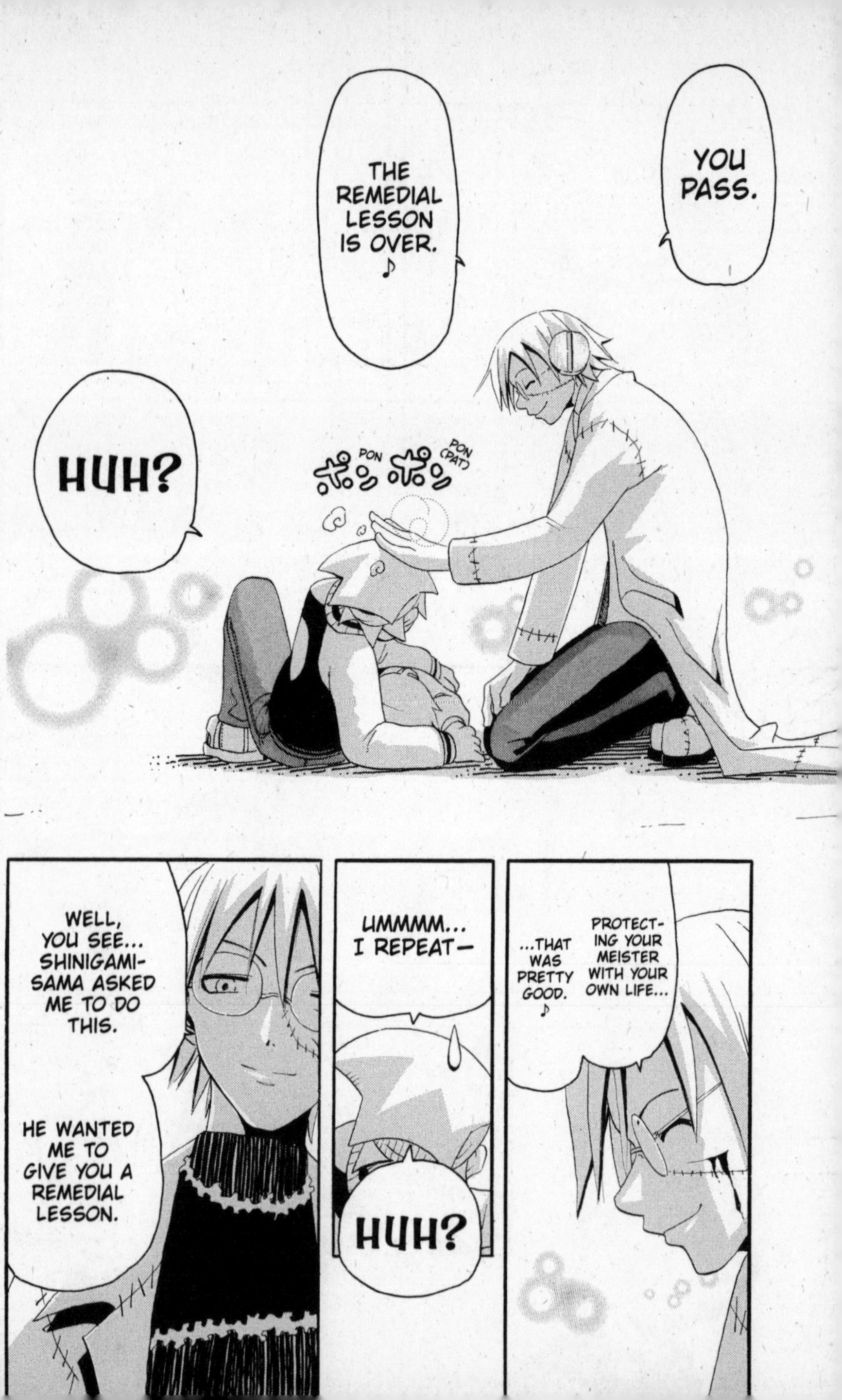

YOU PASS.
THE REMEDIAL LESSON IS OVER. ♪
PON (PAT)
PON
HUH?
PROTECT-ING YOUR MEISTER WITH YOUR OWN LIFE...
...THAT WAS PRETTY GOOD. ♪
UMMMM... I REPEAT—
HUH?
WELL, YOU SEE... SHINIGAMI-SAMA ASKED ME TO DO THIS.
HE WANTED ME TO GIVE YOU A REMEDIAL LESSON.

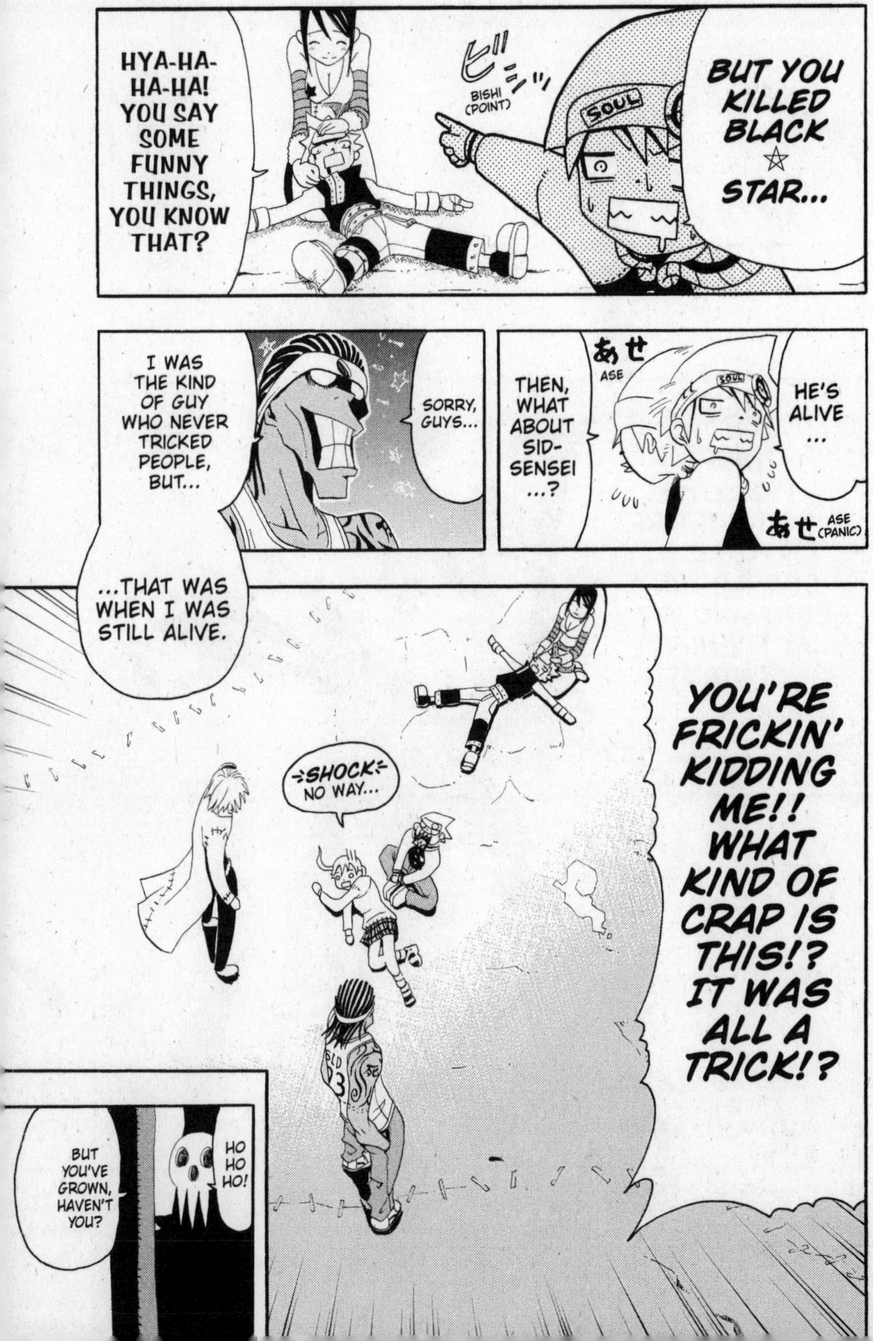
BUT YOU KILLED BLACK☆STAR...
ビッ
BISHI (POINT)
HYA-HA-HA-HA! YOU SAY SOME FUNNY THINGS, YOU KNOW THAT?
HE'S ALIVE ...
あせ
ASE (PANIC)
あせ
ASE
THEN, WHAT ABOUT SID-SENSEI ...?
SORRY, GUYS...
I WAS THE KIND OF GUY WHO NEVER TRICKED PEOPLE, BUT...
...THAT WAS WHEN I WAS STILL ALIVE.
YOU'RE FRICKIN' KIDDING ME!! WHAT KIND OF CRAP IS THIS!? IT WAS ALL A TRICK!?
SHOCK
NO WAY...
HO HO HO!
BUT YOU'VE GROWN, HAVEN'T YOU?

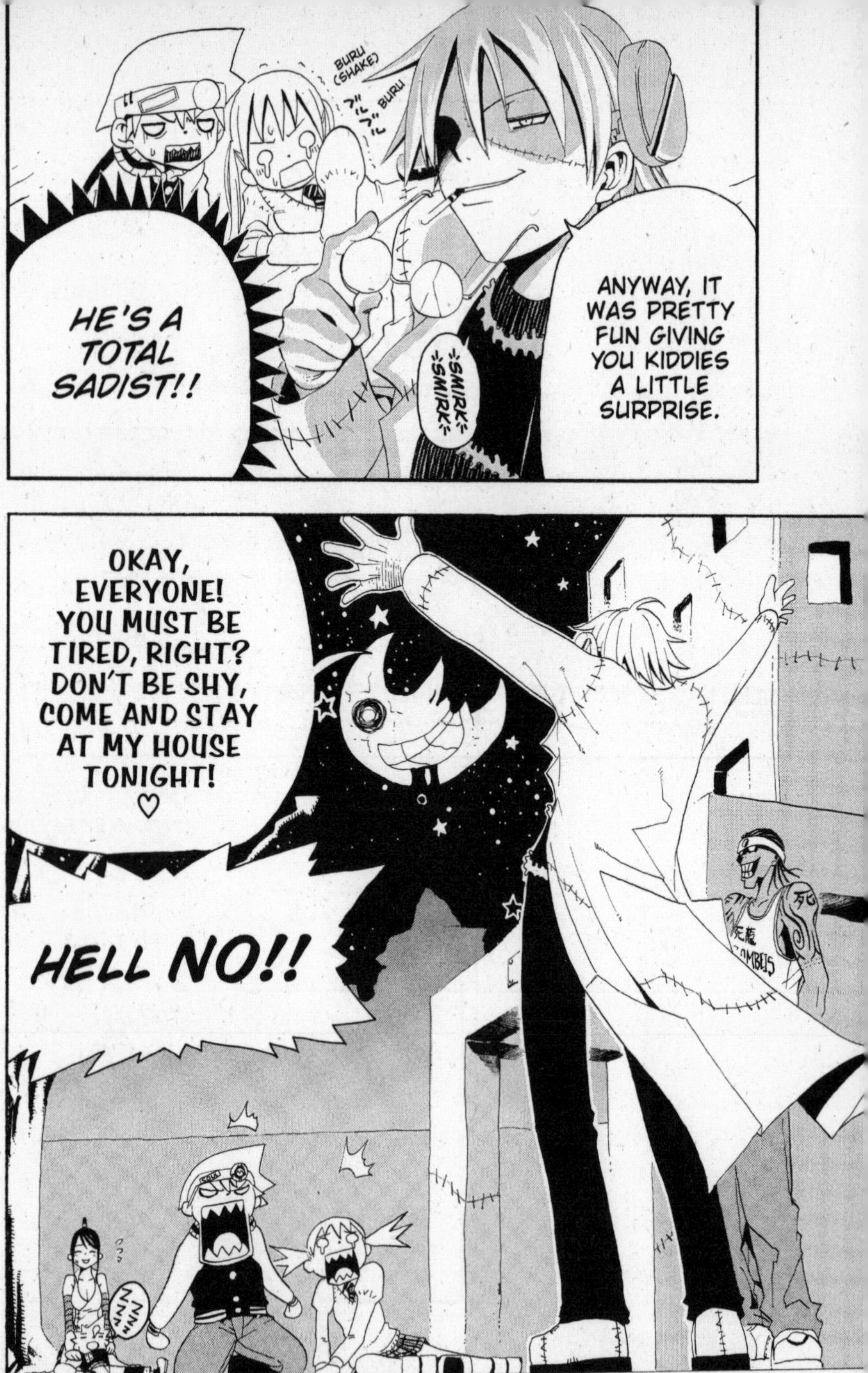
BURU (SHAKE)
BURU
ANYWAY, IT WAS PRETTY FUN GIVING YOU KIDDIES A LITTLE SURPRISE.
SMIRK SMIRK
HE'S A TOTAL SADIST!!
OKAY, EVERYONE! YOU MUST BE TIRED, RIGHT? DON'T BE SHY, COME AND STAY AT MY HOUSE TONIGHT! ♡
HELL NO!!
ZZZ

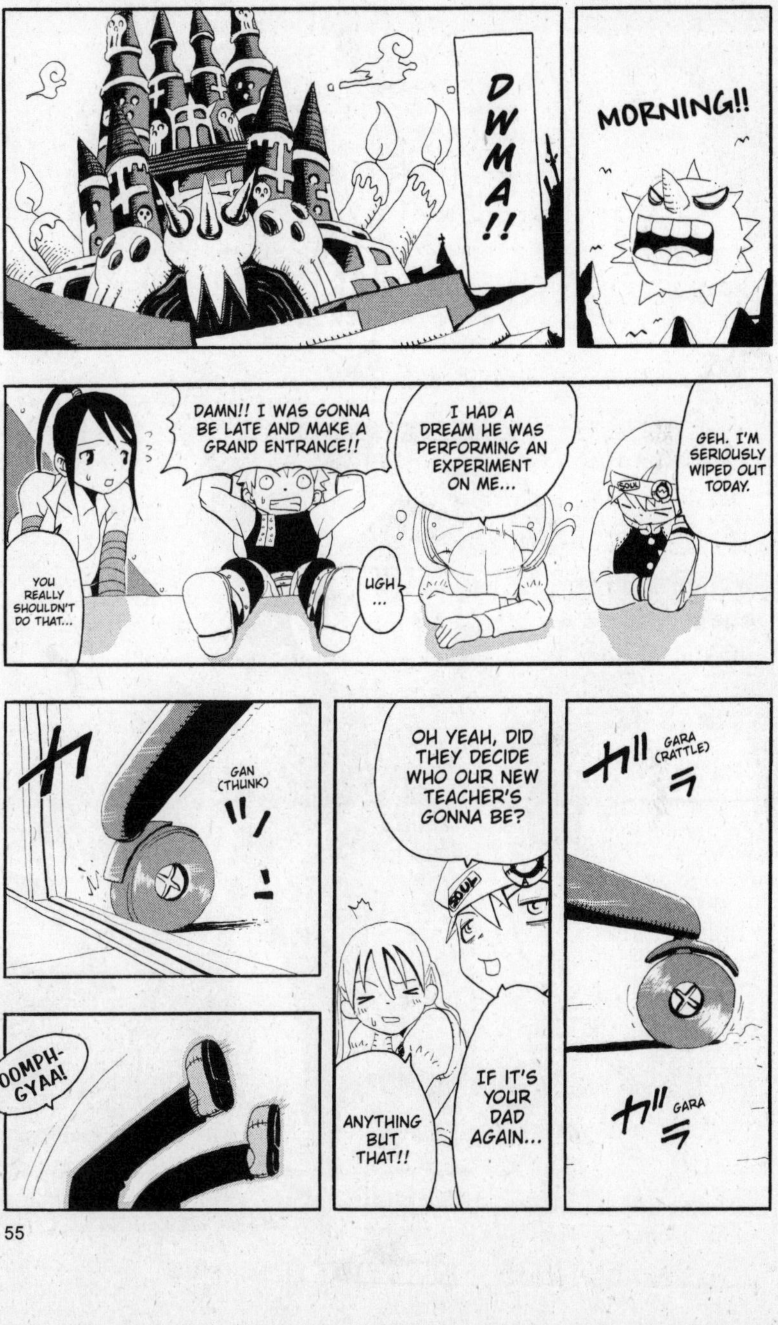

MORNING!!
DWMA!!
GEH. I'M SERIOUSLY WIPED OUT TODAY.
I HAD A DREAM HE WAS PERFORMING AN EXPERIMENT ON ME...
UGH...
DAMN!! I WAS GONNA BE LATE AND MAKE A GRAND ENTRANCE!!
YOU REALLY SHOULDN'T DO THAT...
GARA (RATTLE)
GARA
OH YEAH, DID THEY DECIDE WHO OUR NEW TEACHER'S GONNA BE?
IF IT'S YOUR DAD AGAIN...
ANYTHING BUT THAT!!
GAN (THUNK)
OOMPH-GYAA!

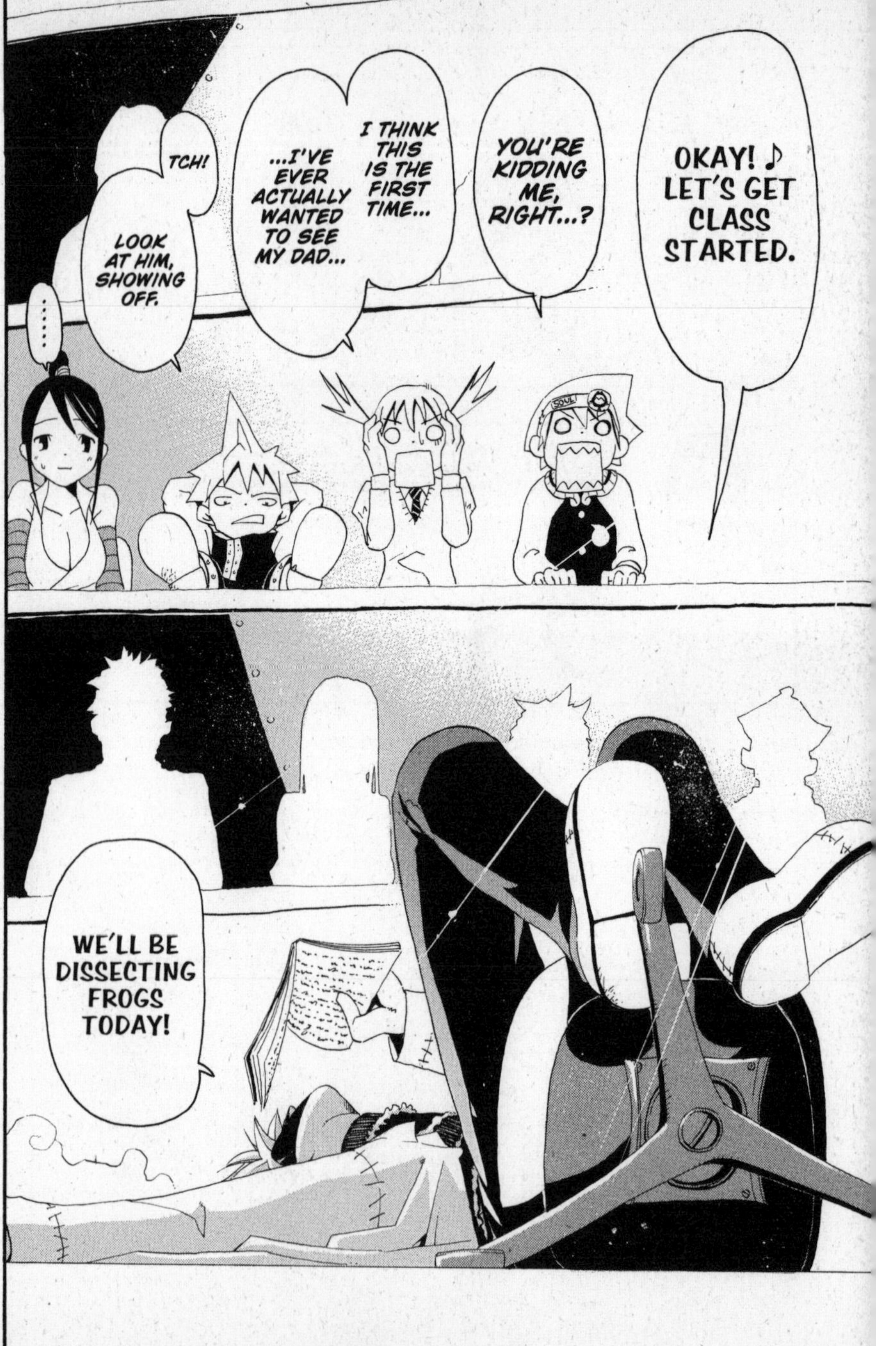
OKAY! ♪ LET'S GET CLASS STARTED.
YOU'RE KIDDING ME, RIGHT...?
I THINK THIS IS THE FIRST TIME...
...I'VE EVER ACTUALLY WANTED TO SEE MY DAD...
TCH!
LOOK AT HIM, SHOWING OFF.
......
WE'LL BE DISSECTING FROGS TODAY!

SOUL EATER

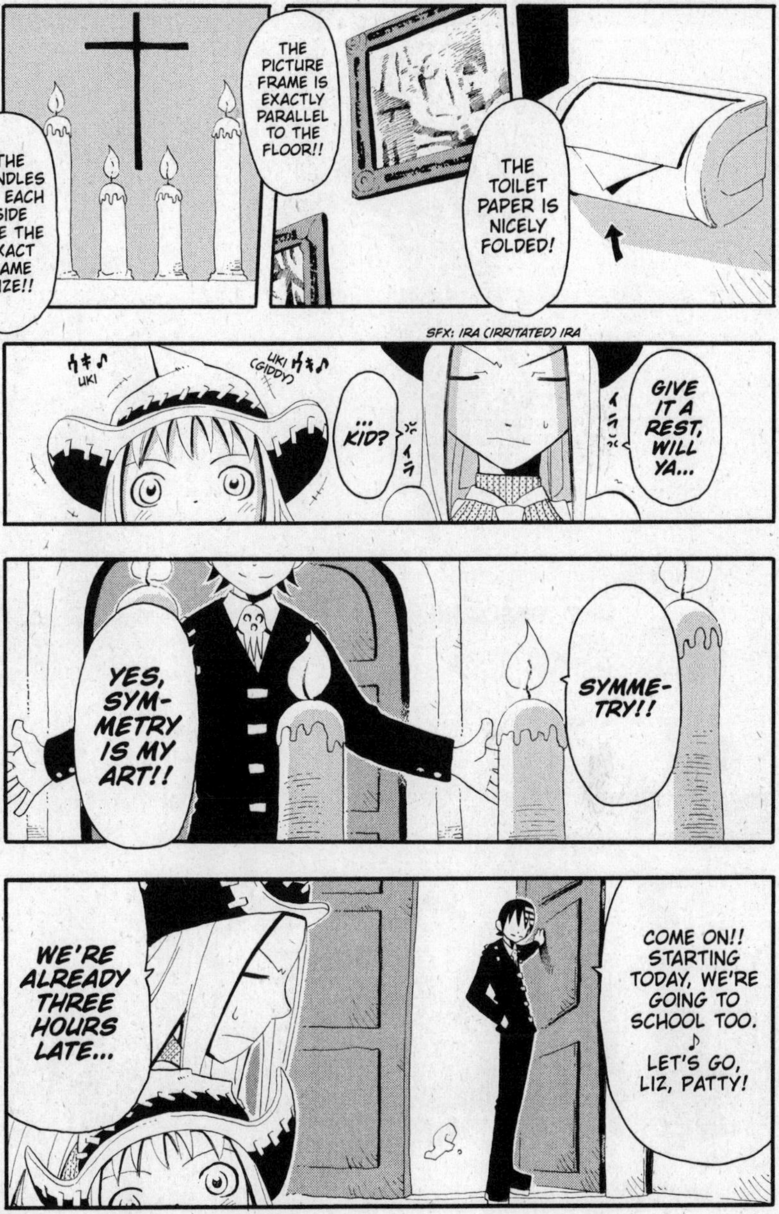
THE TOILET PAPER IS NICELY FOLDED!
THE PICTURE FRAME IS EXACTLY PARALLEL TO THE FLOOR!!
THE CANDLES ON EACH SIDE ARE THE EXACT SAME SIZE!!
SFX: IRA (IRRITATED) IRA
GIVE IT A REST, WILL YA...
...KID?
UKI (GIDDY)
UKI
SYMME-TRY!!
YES, SYMMETRY IS MY ART!!
COME ON!! STARTING TODAY, WE'RE GOING TO SCHOOL TOO. ♪ LET'S GO, LIZ, PATTY!
WE'RE ALREADY THREE HOURS LATE...

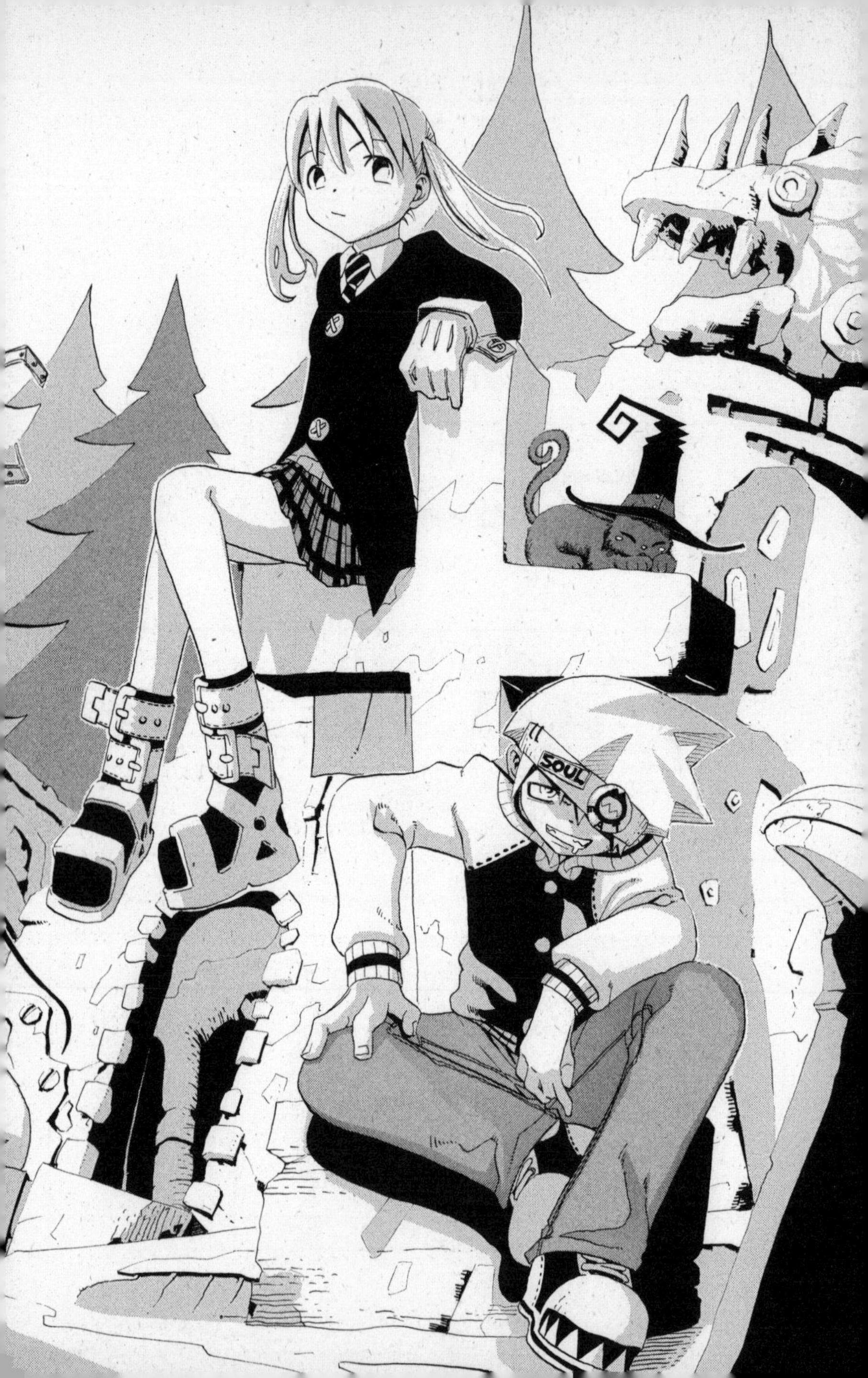
SOUL

CHAPTER 3: THE "NEW STUDENT" AND "SOUL OBSERVATION"

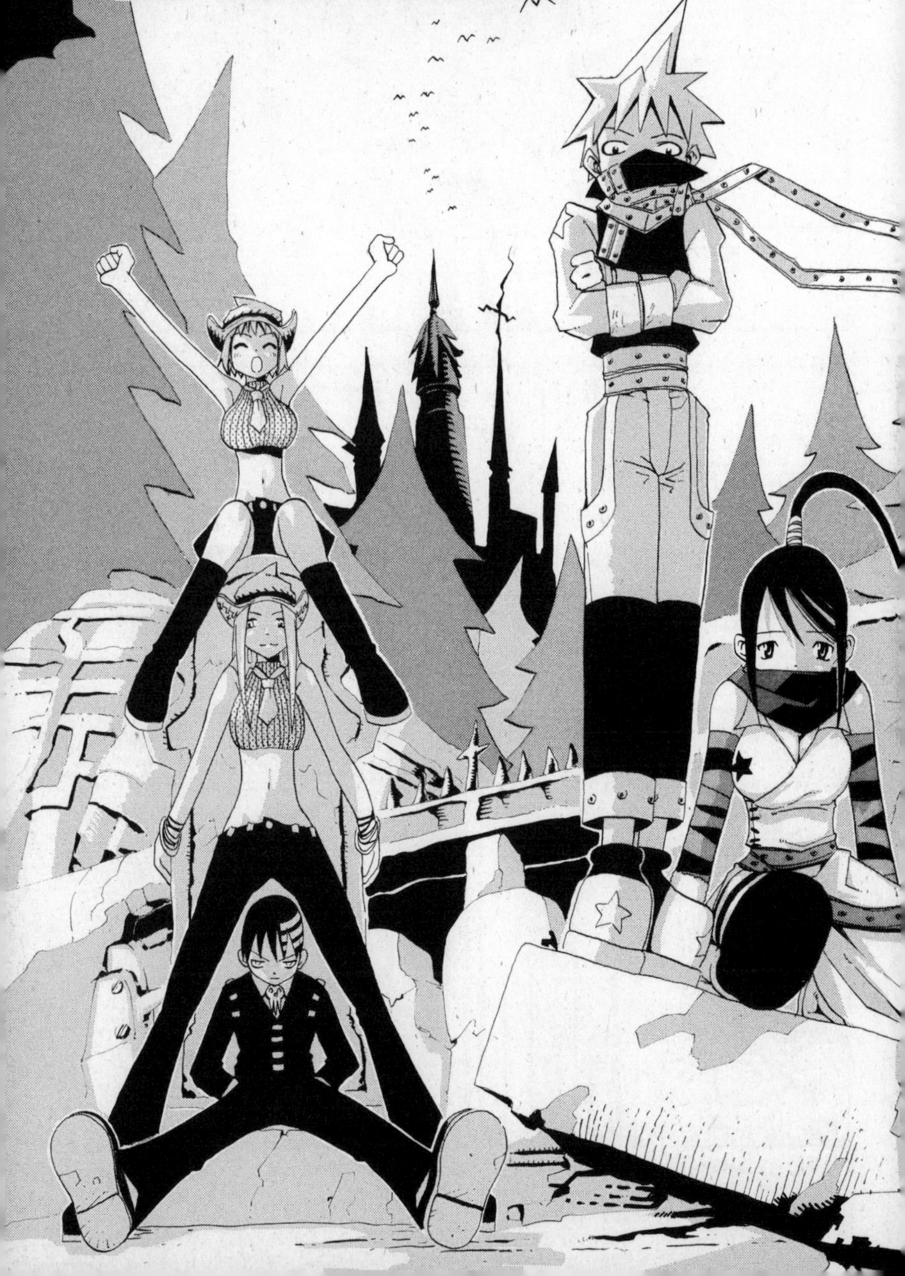

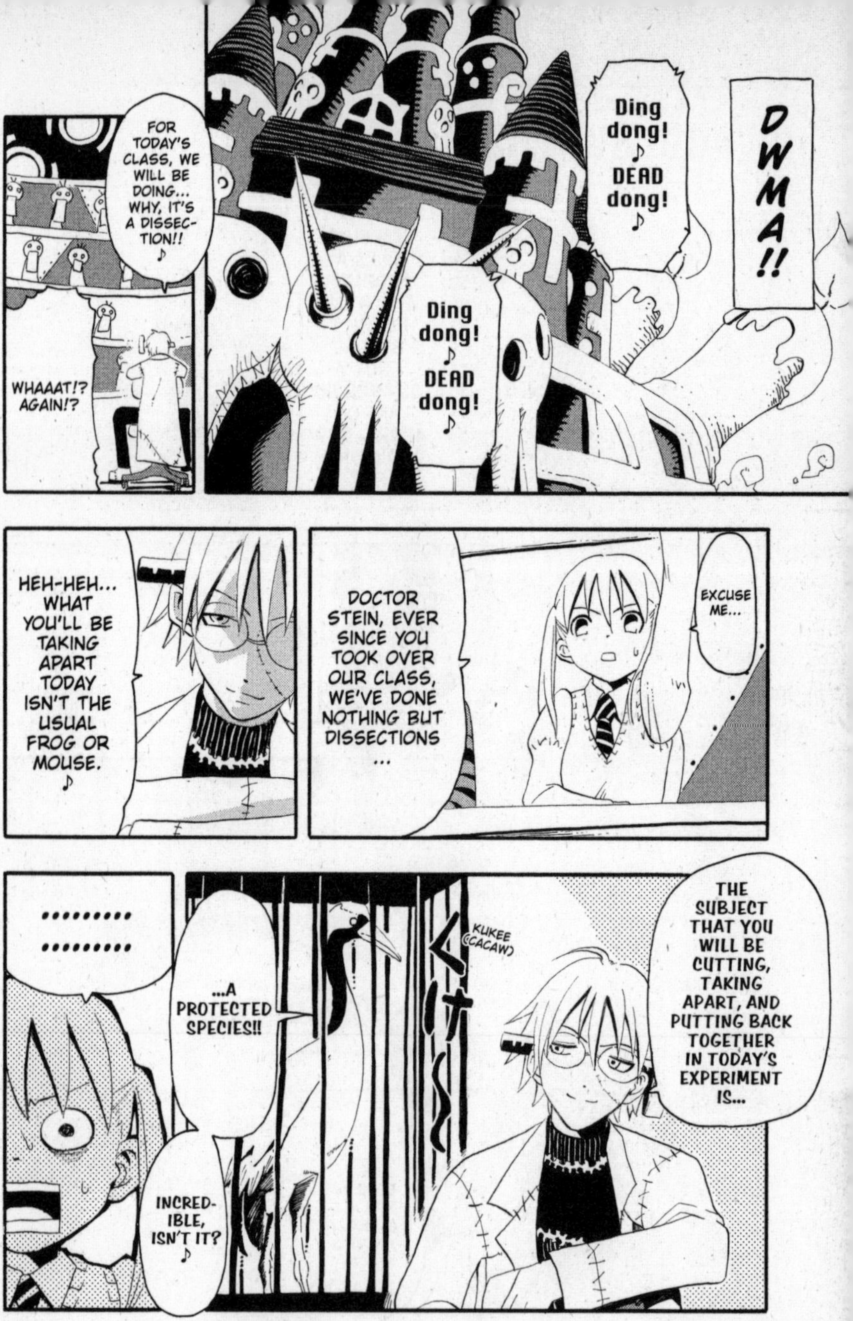
DWMA!!
Ding dong! ♪ DEAD dong! ♪
Ding dong! ♪ DEAD dong! ♪
FOR TODAY'S CLASS, WE WILL BE DOING... WHY, IT'S A DISSECTION!! ♪
WHAAAT!? AGAIN!?
EXCUSE ME...
DOCTOR STEIN, EVER SINCE YOU TOOK OVER OUR CLASS, WE'VE DONE NOTHING BUT DISSECTIONS ...
HEH-HEH... WHAT YOU'LL BE TAKING APART TODAY ISN'T THE USUAL FROG OR MOUSE. ♪
THE SUBJECT THAT YOU WILL BE CUTTING, TAKING APART, AND PUTTING BACK TOGETHER IN TODAY'S EXPERIMENT IS...
KUKEE (CACAW)
...A PROTECTED SPECIES!!
INCRED-IBLE, ISN'T IT? ♪
....
....

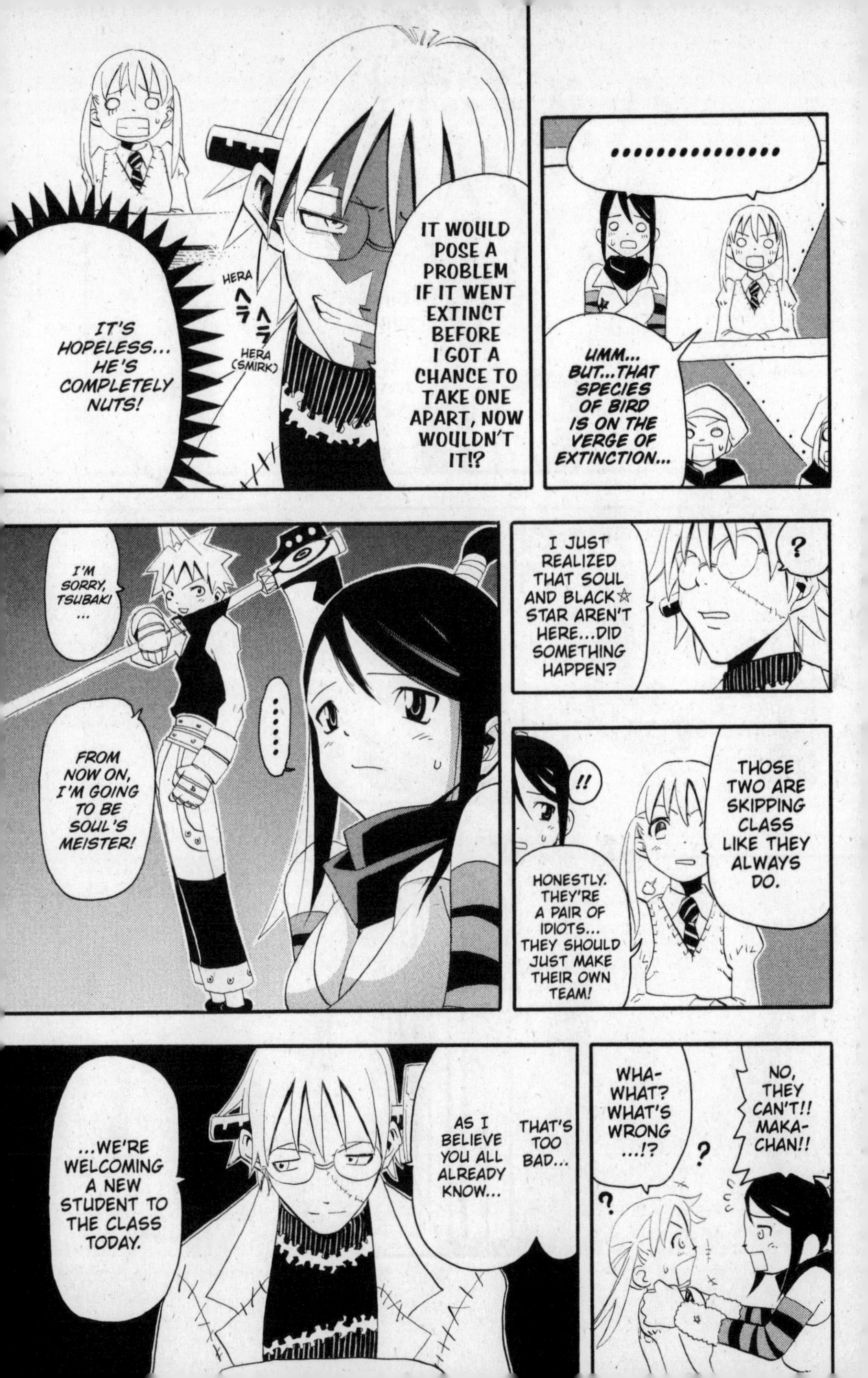
....
UMM... BUT...THAT SPECIES OF BIRD IS ON THE VERGE OF EXTINCTION...
IT WOULD POSE A PROBLEM IF IT WENT EXTINCT BEFORE I GOT A CHANCE TO TAKE ONE APART, NOW WOULDN'T IT!?
HERA
HERA (SMIRK)
IT'S HOPELESS... HE'S COMPLETELY NUTS!
I JUST REALIZED THAT SOUL AND BLACK☆STAR AREN'T HERE...DID SOMETHING HAPPEN?
?
THOSE TWO ARE SKIPPING CLASS LIKE THEY ALWAYS DO.
!!
HONESTLY. THEY'RE A PAIR OF IDIOTS... THEY SHOULD JUST MAKE THEIR OWN TEAM!
I'M SORRY, TSUBAKI...
......
FROM NOW ON, I'M GOING TO BE SOUL'S MEISTER!
NO, THEY CAN'T!! MAKA-CHAN!!
WHA-WHAT? WHAT'S WRONG...!?
?
?
THAT'S TOO BAD...
AS I BELIEVE YOU ALL ALREADY KNOW...
...WE'RE WELCOMING A NEW STUDENT TO THE CLASS TODAY.

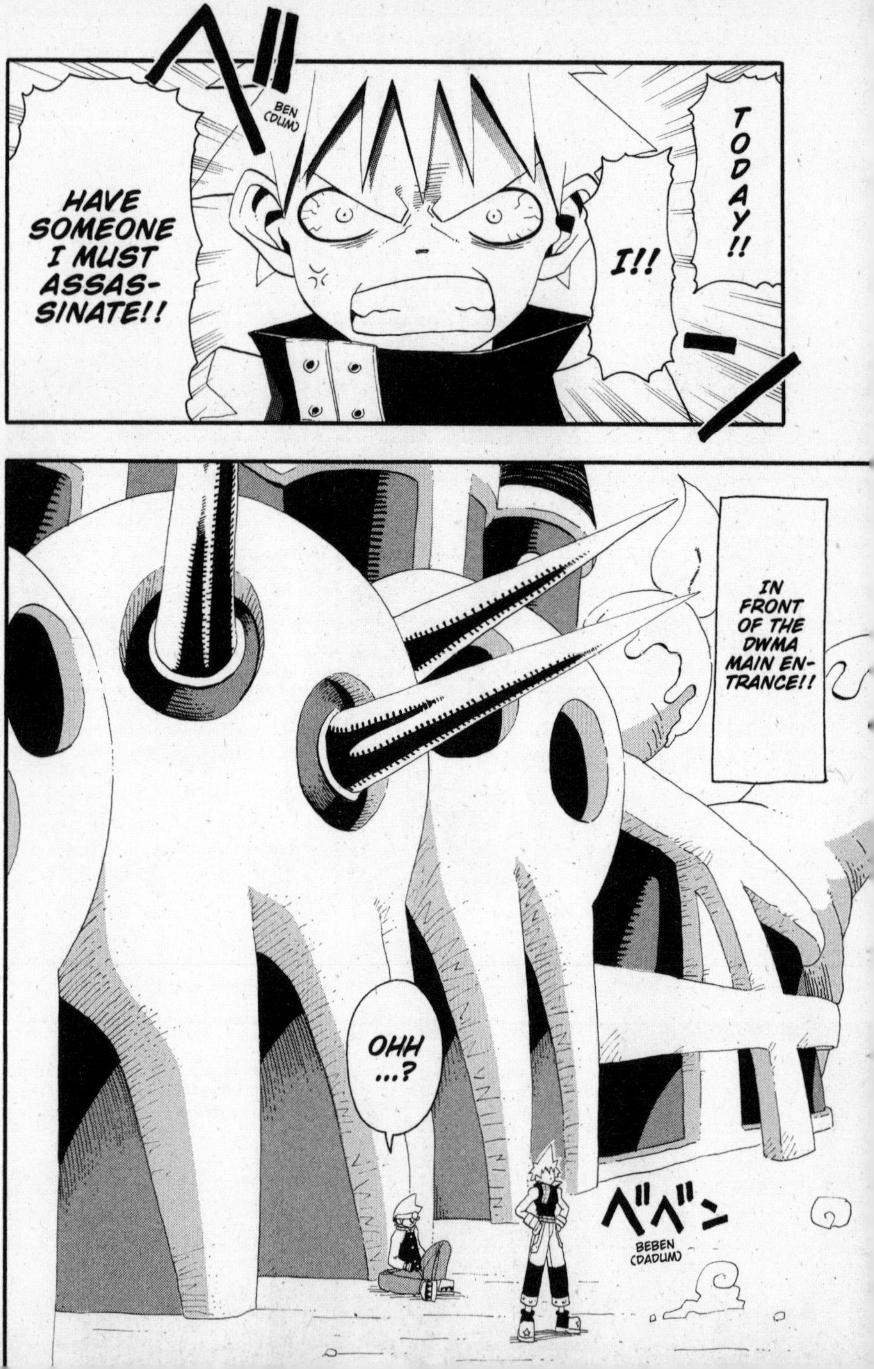
TODAY!!
I!!
HAVE SOMEONE I MUST ASSAS-SINATE!!
BEN (DUM)
IN FRONT OF THE DWMA MAIN EN-TRANCE!!
OHH ...?
べべン
BEBEN (DADUM)

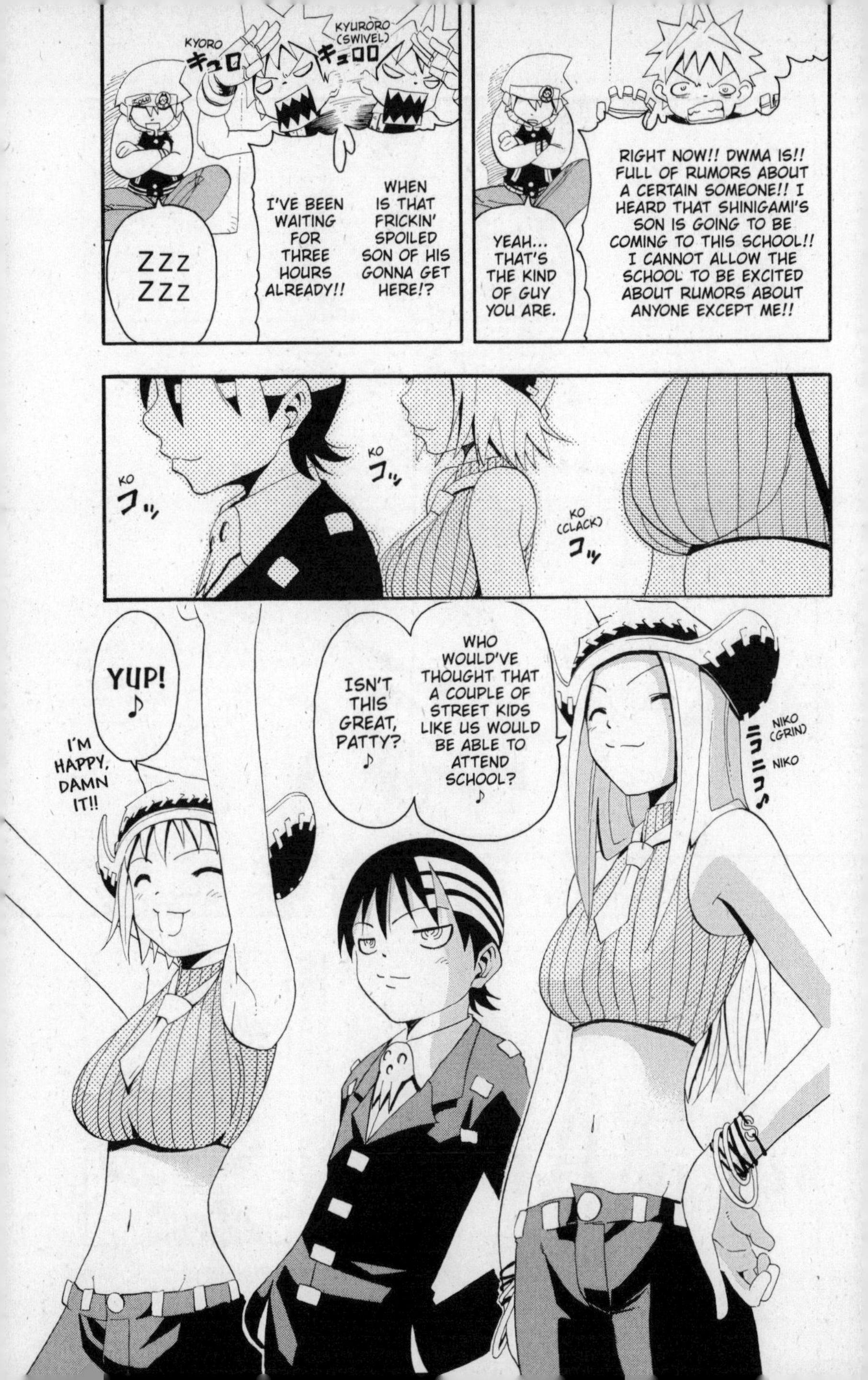
RIGHT NOW!! DWMA IS!! FULL OF RUMORS ABOUT A CERTAIN SOMEONE!! I HEARD THAT SHINIGAMI'S SON IS GOING TO BE COMING TO THIS SCHOOL!! I CANNOT ALLOW THE SCHOOL TO BE EXCITED ABOUT RUMORS ABOUT ANYONE EXCEPT ME!!
YEAH... THAT'S THE KIND OF GUY YOU ARE.
KYURORO (SWIVEL)
キュロロ
KYORO
キョロ
WHEN IS THAT FRICKIN' SPOILED SON OF HIS GONNA GET HERE!?
I'VE BEEN WAITING FOR THREE HOURS ALREADY!!
ZZZ ZZZ
KO (CLACK)
コッ
KO
コッ
KO
コッ
NIKO (GRIN) NIKO
ニコニコ
WHO WOULD'VE THOUGHT THAT A COUPLE OF STREET KIDS LIKE US WOULD BE ABLE TO ATTEND SCHOOL? ♪
ISN'T THIS GREAT, PATTY? ♪
YUP! ♪
I'M HAPPY, DAMN IT!!

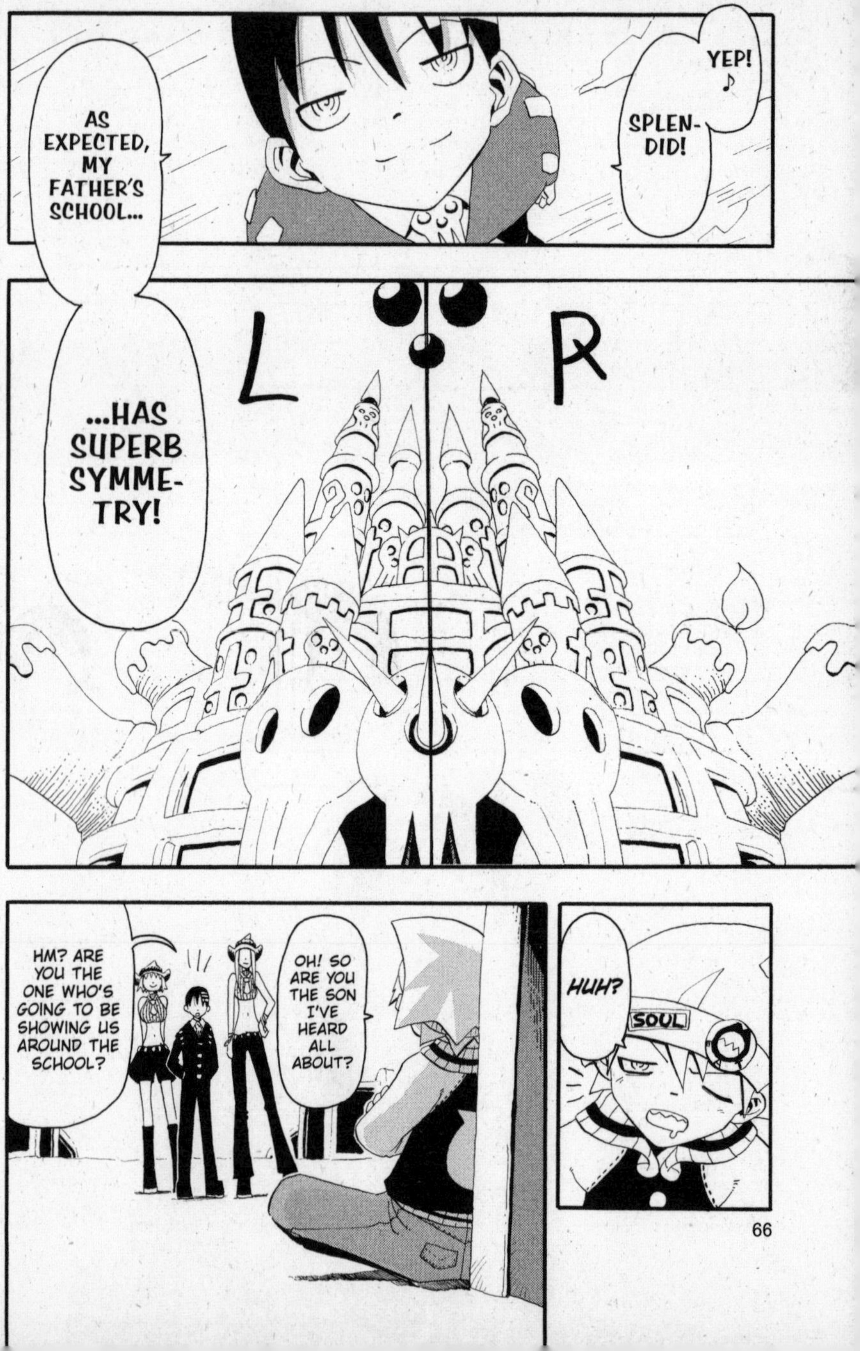
YEP! ♪
SPLEN-DID!
AS EXPECTED, MY FATHER'S SCHOOL...
...HAS SUPERB SYMME-TRY!
L
R
HUH?
SOUL
OH! SO ARE YOU THE SON I'VE HEARD ALL ABOUT?
HM? ARE YOU THE ONE WHO'S GOING TO BE SHOWING US AROUND THE SCHOOL?

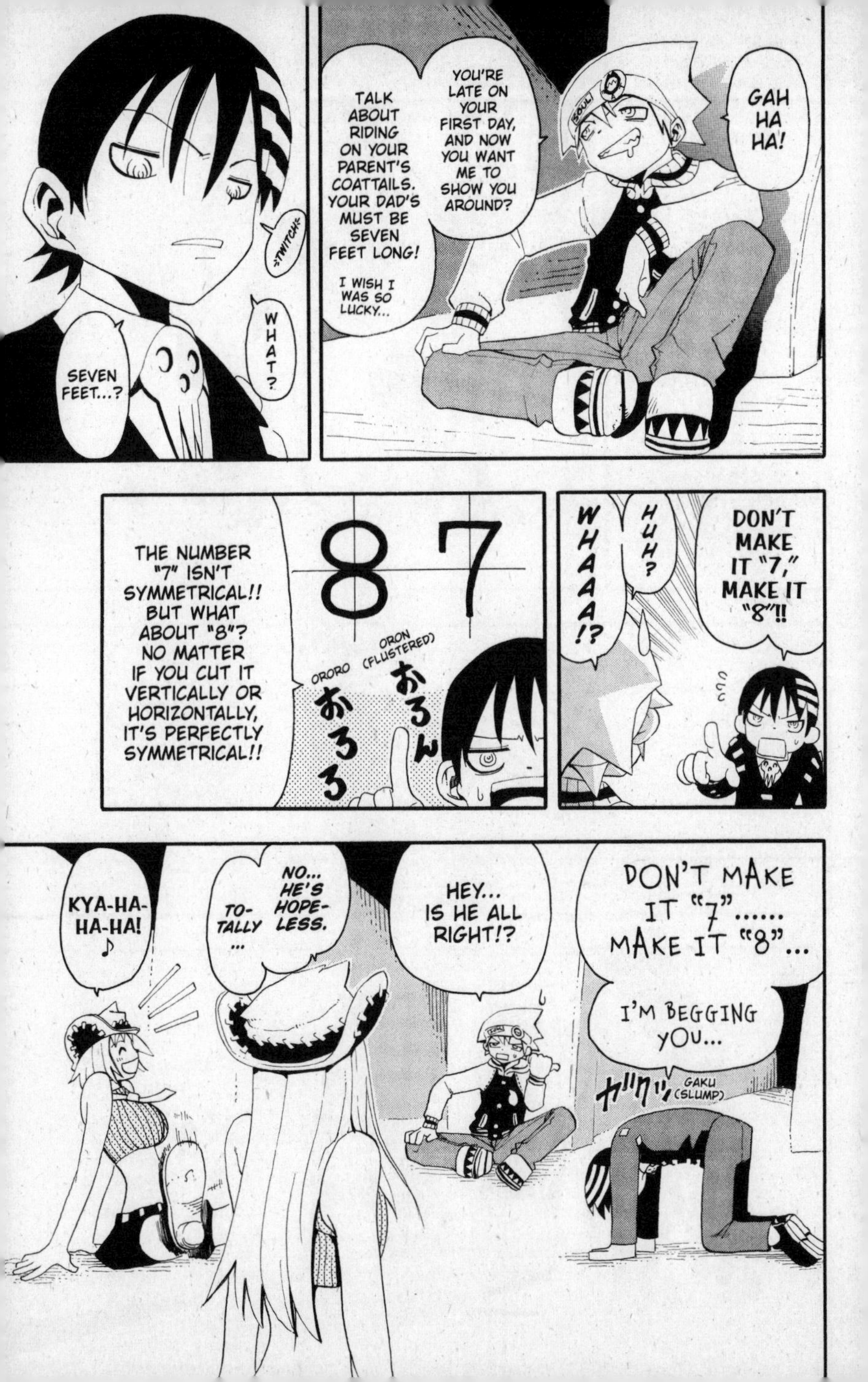
GAH HA HA!
YOU'RE LATE ON YOUR FIRST DAY, AND NOW YOU WANT ME TO SHOW YOU AROUND?
TALK ABOUT RIDING ON YOUR PARENT'S COATTAILS. YOUR DAD'S MUST BE SEVEN FEET LONG!
I WISH I WAS SO LUCKY...
TWITCH
WHAT?
SEVEN FEET...?
DON'T MAKE IT "7," MAKE IT "8"!!
HUH?
WHAAAA!?
8 7
THE NUMBER "7" ISN'T SYMMETRICAL!! BUT WHAT ABOUT "8"? NO MATTER IF YOU CUT IT VERTICALLY OR HORIZONTALLY, IT'S PERFECTLY SYMMETRICAL!!
おろん
ORON (FLUSTERED)
おろろ
ORORO
DON'T MAKE IT "7"...... MAKE IT "8"...
I'M BEGGING YOU...
ガクッ
GAKU (SLUMP)
HEY... IS HE ALL RIGHT!?
NO... HE'S HOPELESS.
TO-TALLY...
KYA-HA-HA-HA! ♪

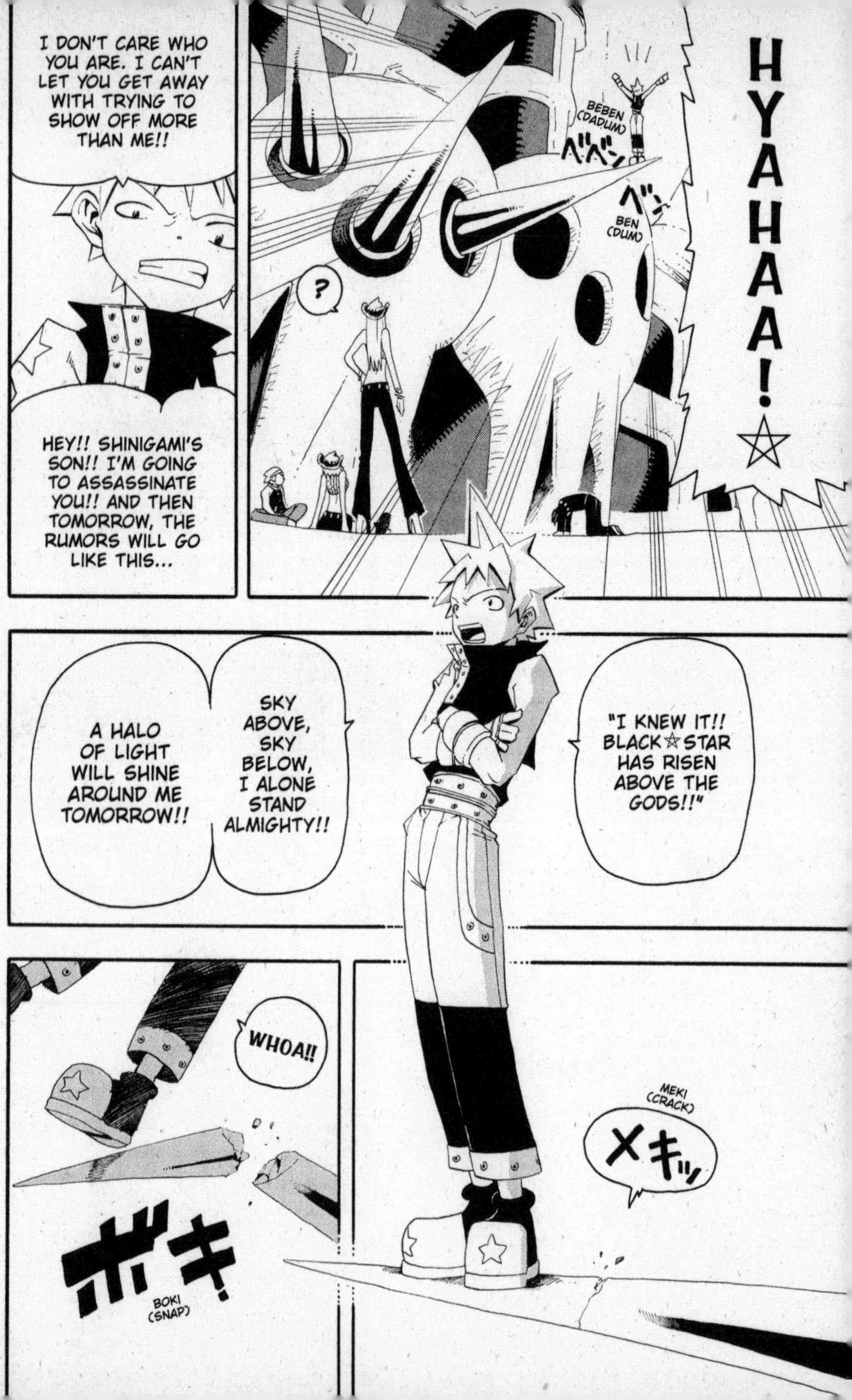
HYAHAHA!☆
BEBEN (DADUM)
ベベン
ベン
BEN (DUM)
?
I DON'T CARE WHO YOU ARE. I CAN'T LET YOU GET AWAY WITH TRYING TO SHOW OFF MORE THAN ME!!
HEY!! SHINIGAMI'S SON!! I'M GOING TO ASSASSINATE YOU!! AND THEN TOMORROW, THE RUMORS WILL GO LIKE THIS...
"I KNEW IT!! BLACK☆STAR HAS RISEN ABOVE THE GODS!!"
SKY ABOVE, SKY BELOW, I ALONE STAND ALMIGHTY!!
A HALO OF LIGHT WILL SHINE AROUND ME TOMORROW!!
MEKI (CRACK)
メキッ
WHOA!!
ボキ
BOKI (SNAP)

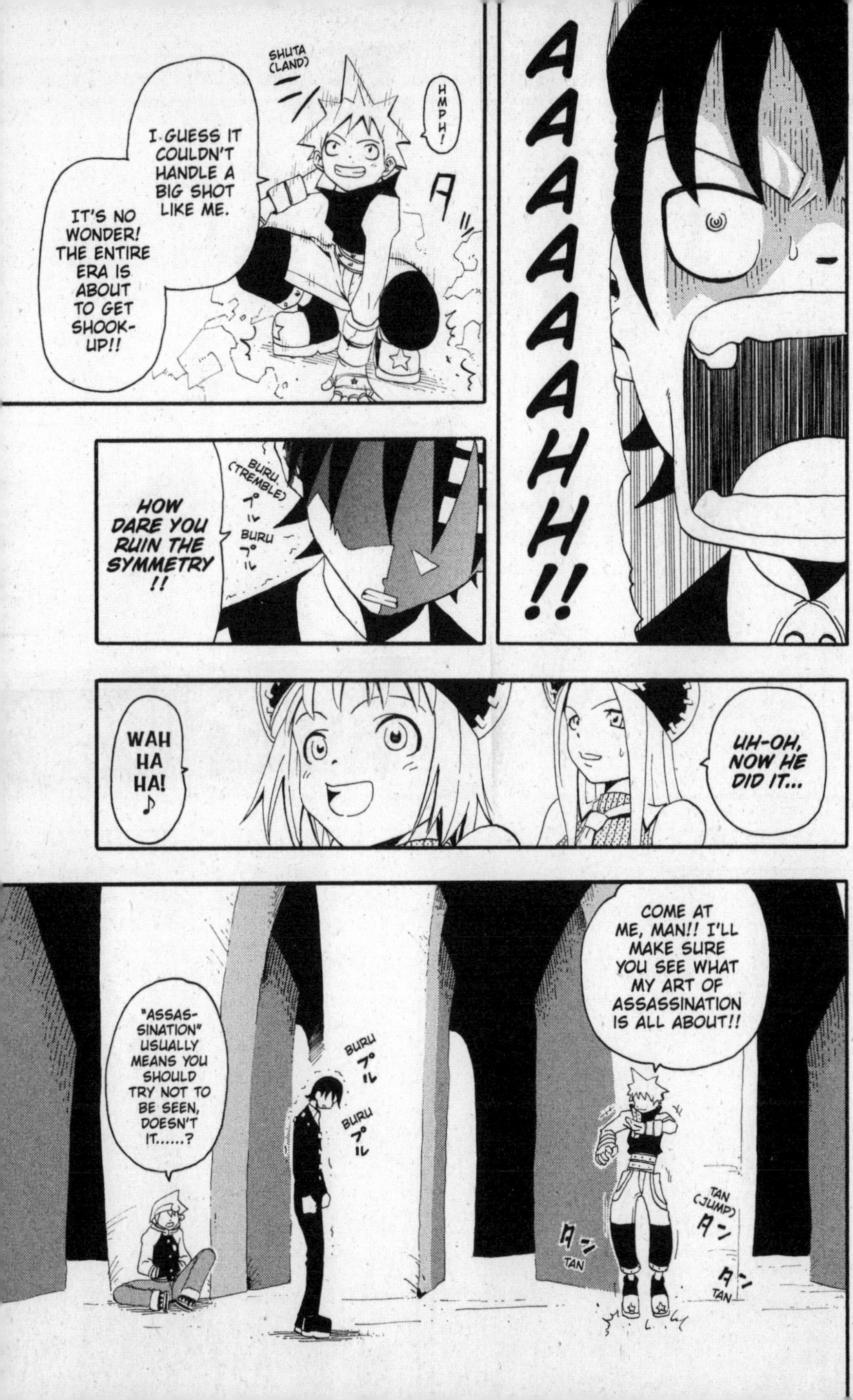
AAAAAAAHH!!
SHUTA (LAND)
HMPH!
I GUESS IT COULDN'T HANDLE A BIG SHOT LIKE ME.
IT'S NO WONDER! THE ENTIRE ERA IS ABOUT TO GET SHOOK-UP!!
BURU (TREMBLE)
BURU
HOW DARE YOU RUIN THE SYMMETRY!!
UH-OH, NOW HE DID IT...
WAH HA HA! ♪
COME AT ME, MAN!! I'LL MAKE SURE YOU SEE WHAT MY ART OF ASSASSINATION IS ALL ABOUT!!
BURU
BURU
"ASSAS-SINATION" USUALLY MEANS YOU SHOULD TRY NOT TO BE SEEN, DOESN'T IT......?
TAN (JUMP)
TAN
TAN

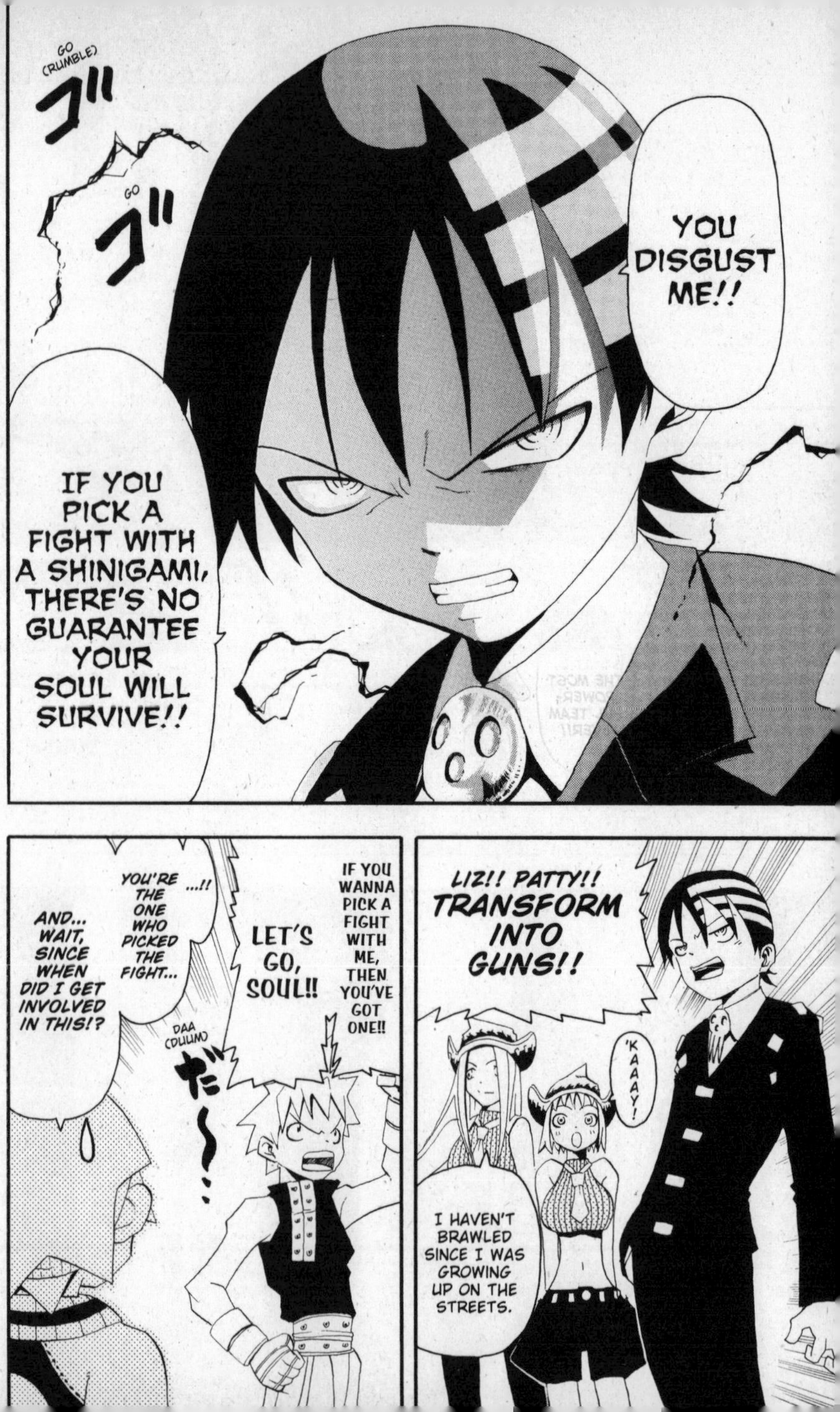
YOU DISGUST ME!!
GO (RUMBLE)
ゴ
GO
ゴ
IF YOU PICK A FIGHT WITH A SHINIGAMI, THERE'S NO GUARANTEE YOUR SOUL WILL SURVIVE!!
LIZ!! PATTY!! TRANSFORM INTO GUNS!!
'KAAAAY!
I HAVEN'T BRAWLED SINCE I WAS GROWING UP ON THE STREETS.
IF YOU WANNA PICK A FIGHT WITH ME, THEN YOU'VE GOT ONE!!
LET'S GO, SOUL!!
...!!
YOU'RE THE ONE WHO PICKED THE FIGHT...
AND... WAIT, SINCE WHEN DID I GET INVOLVED IN THIS!?
DAA (DUUM)
だ～っ

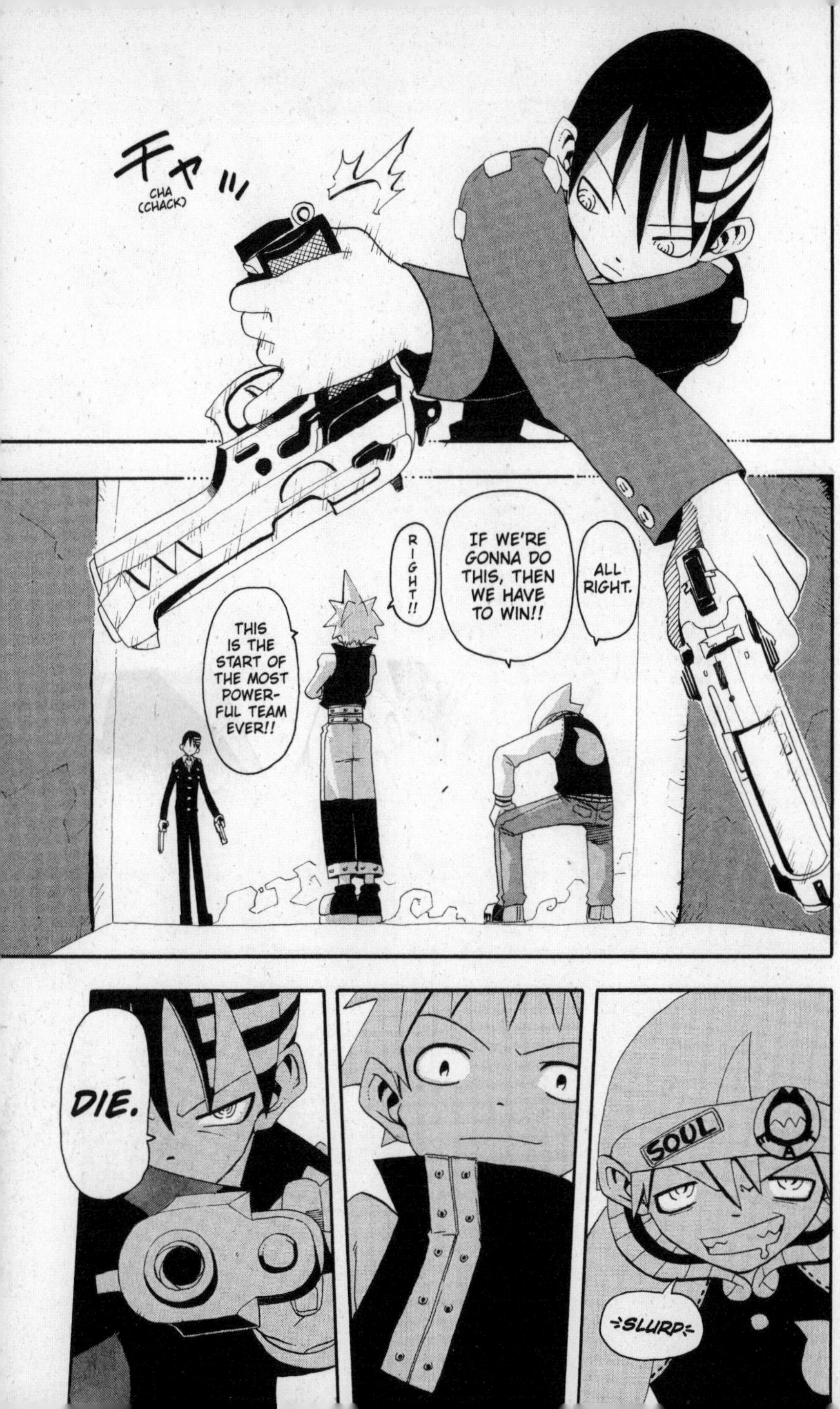
チャッ
CHA (CHACK)
ALL RIGHT.
IF WE'RE GONNA DO THIS, THEN WE HAVE TO WIN!!
RIGHT!!
THIS IS THE START OF THE MOST POWER-FUL TEAM EVER!!
SLURP
DIE.

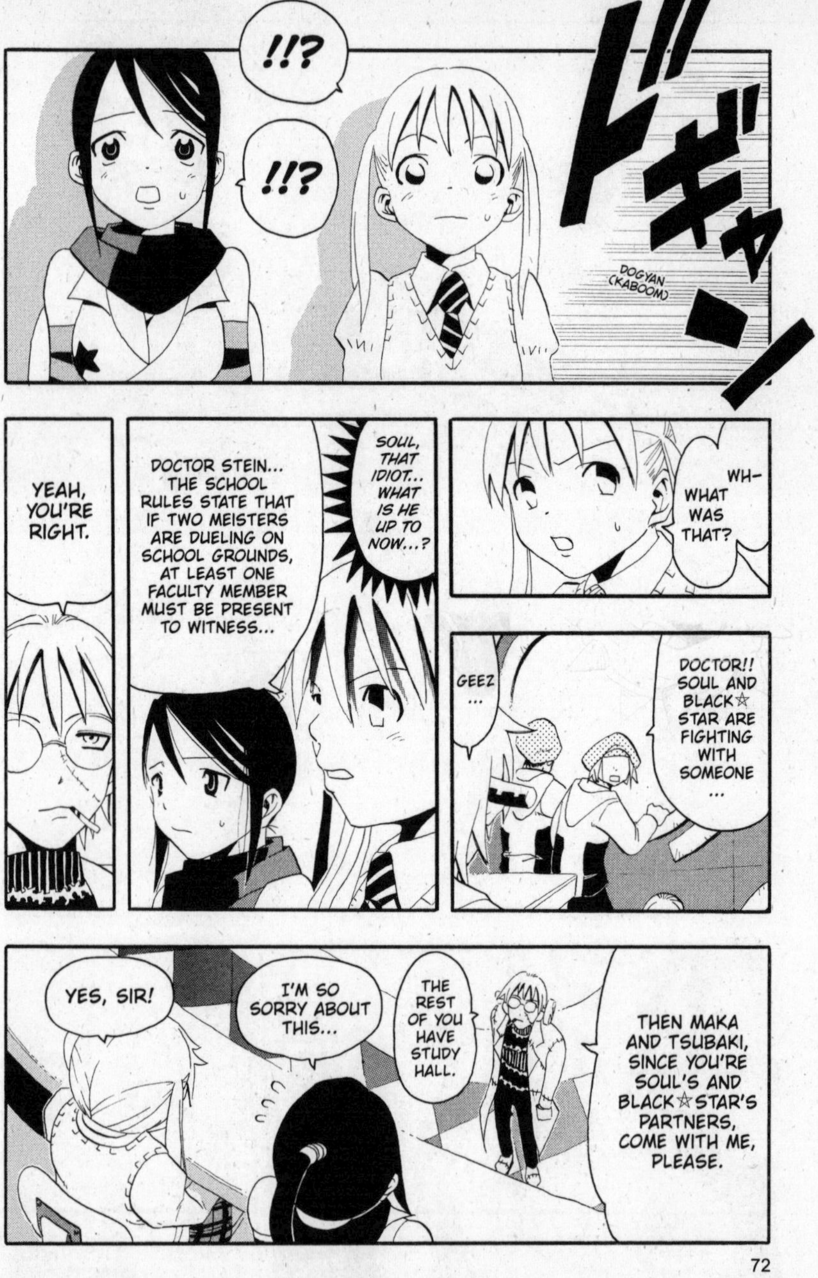
DOGYAN (KABOOM)
!!?
!!?
WH- WHAT WAS THAT?
DOCTOR!! SOUL AND BLACK☆STAR ARE FIGHTING WITH SOMEONE...
GEEZ...
SOUL, THAT IDIOT... WHAT IS HE UP TO NOW...?
DOCTOR STEIN... THE SCHOOL RULES STATE THAT IF TWO MEISTERS ARE DUELING ON SCHOOL GROUNDS, AT LEAST ONE FACULTY MEMBER MUST BE PRESENT TO WITNESS...
YEAH, YOU'RE RIGHT.
THEN MAKA AND TSUBAKI, SINCE YOU'RE SOUL'S AND BLACK☆STAR'S PARTNERS, COME WITH ME, PLEASE.
THE REST OF YOU HAVE STUDY HALL.
I'M SO SORRY ABOUT THIS...
YES, SIR!

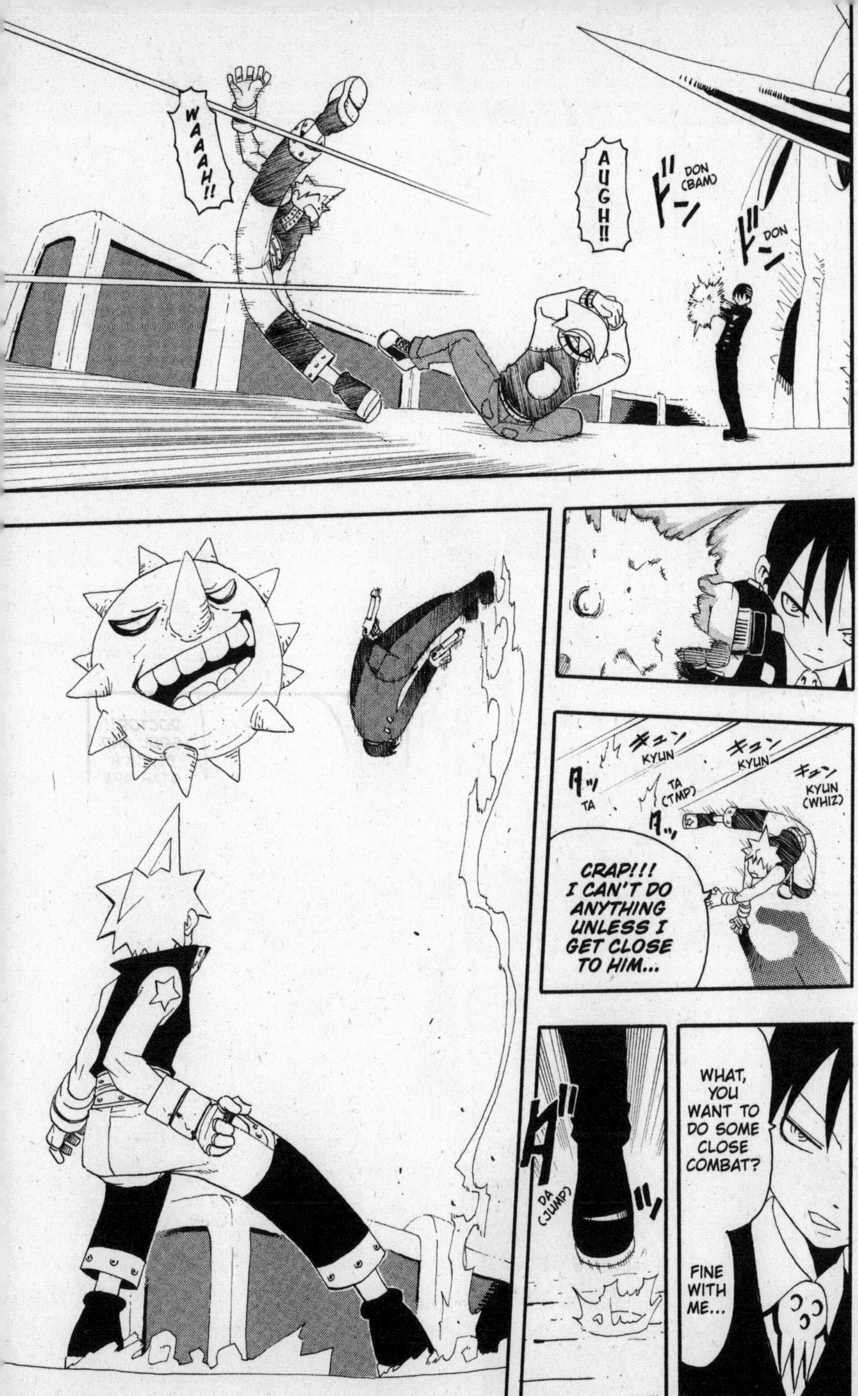
ドン
DON (BAM)
ドン
DON
AUGH!!
WAAAH!!
キュン
KYUN (WHIZ)
キュン
KYUN
キュン
KYUN
タッ
TA (TMP)
タッ
TA
CRAP!!! I CAN'T DO ANYTHING UNLESS I GET CLOSE TO HIM...
WHAT, YOU WANT TO DO SOME CLOSE COMBAT?
FINE WITH ME...
ダッ
DA (JUMP)

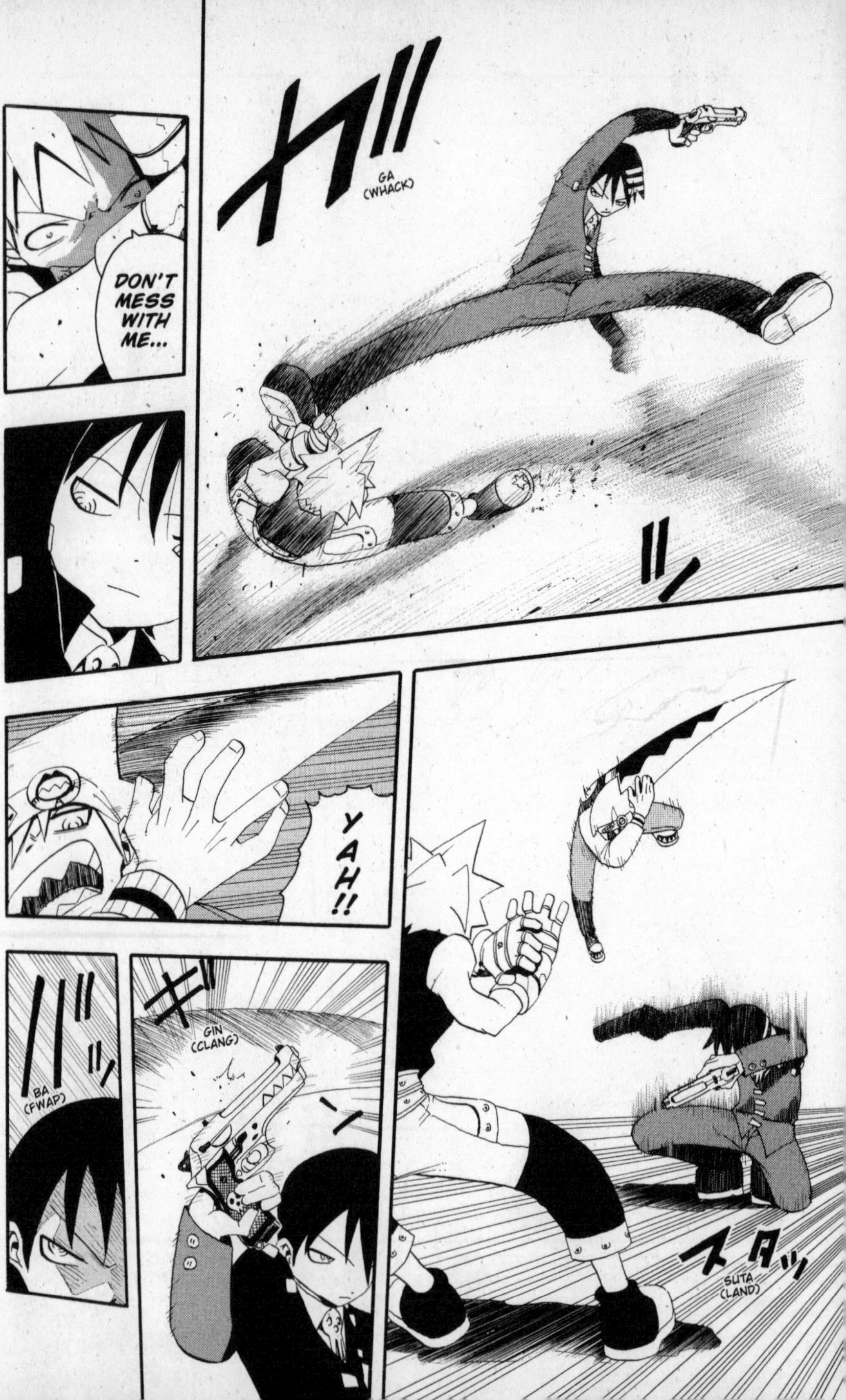
GA (WHACK)
DON'T MESS WITH ME...
SUTA (LAND)
YAH!!
GIN (CLANG)
BA (FWAP)

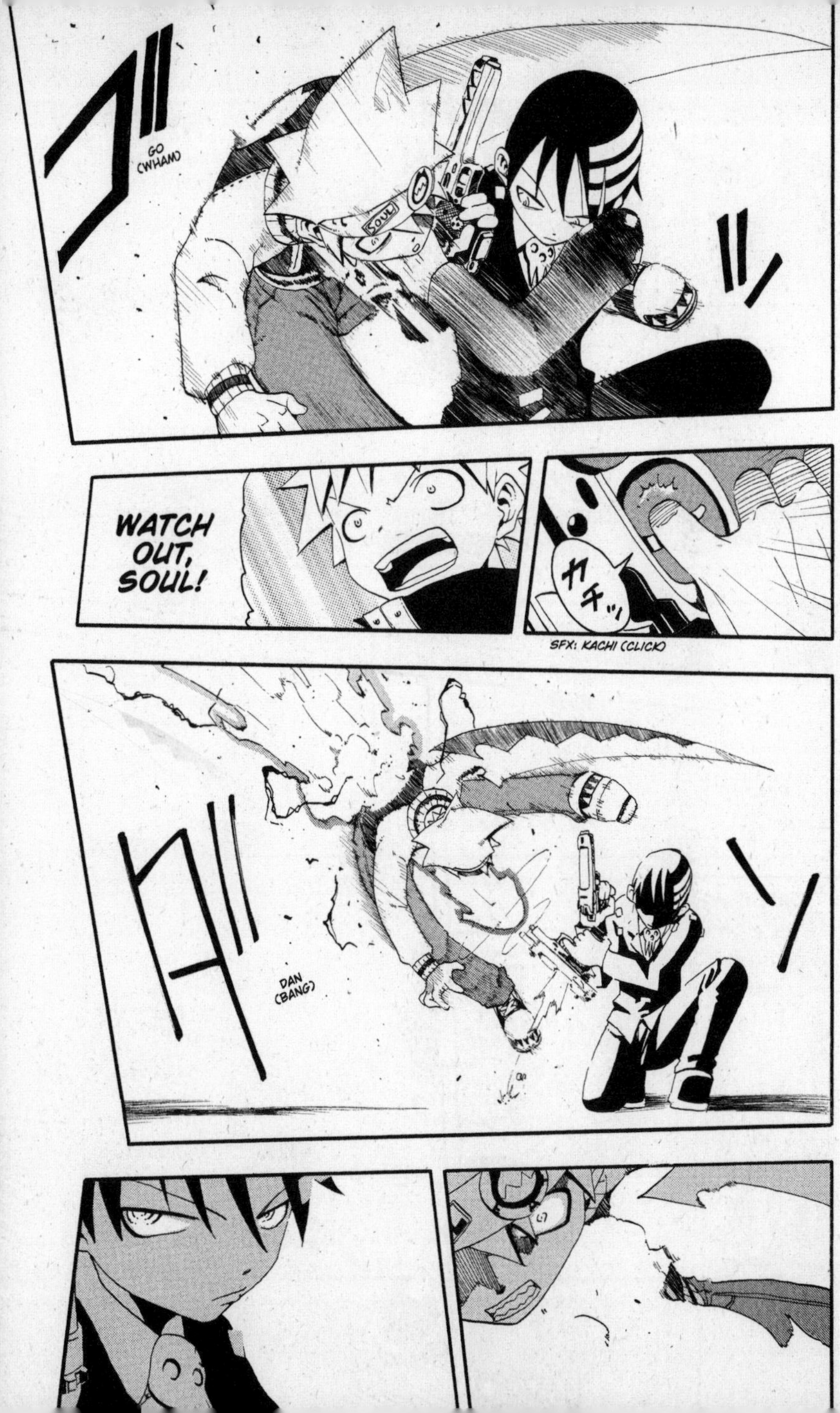
GO
(WHAM)
カチッ
SFX: KACHI (CLICK)
WATCH OUT, SOUL!
DAN
(BANG)

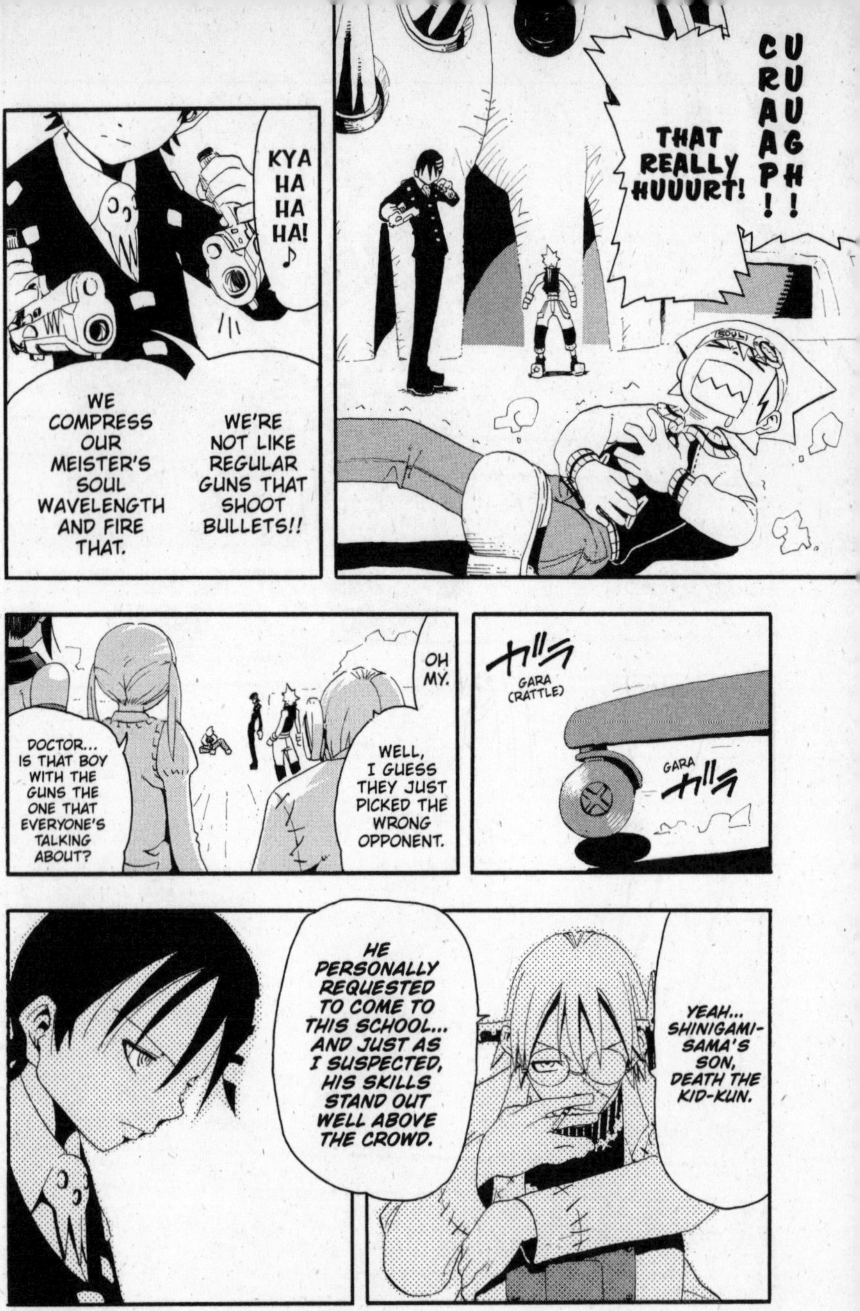
UUUUGH!
CRAAAP!
THAT REALLY HUUURT!
KYA HA HA HA! ♪
WE'RE NOT LIKE REGULAR GUNS THAT SHOOT BULLETS!!
WE COMPRESS OUR MEISTER'S SOUL WAVELENGTH AND FIRE THAT.
ガラ
GARA (RATTLE)
GARA
ガラ
OH MY.
WELL, I GUESS THEY JUST PICKED THE WRONG OPPONENT.
DOCTOR... IS THAT BOY WITH THE GUNS THE ONE THAT EVERYONE'S TALKING ABOUT?
YEAH... SHINIGAMI-SAMA'S SON, DEATH THE KID-KUN.
HE PERSONALLY REQUESTED TO COME TO THIS SCHOOL... AND JUST AS I SUSPECTED, HIS SKILLS STAND OUT WELL ABOVE THE CROWD.

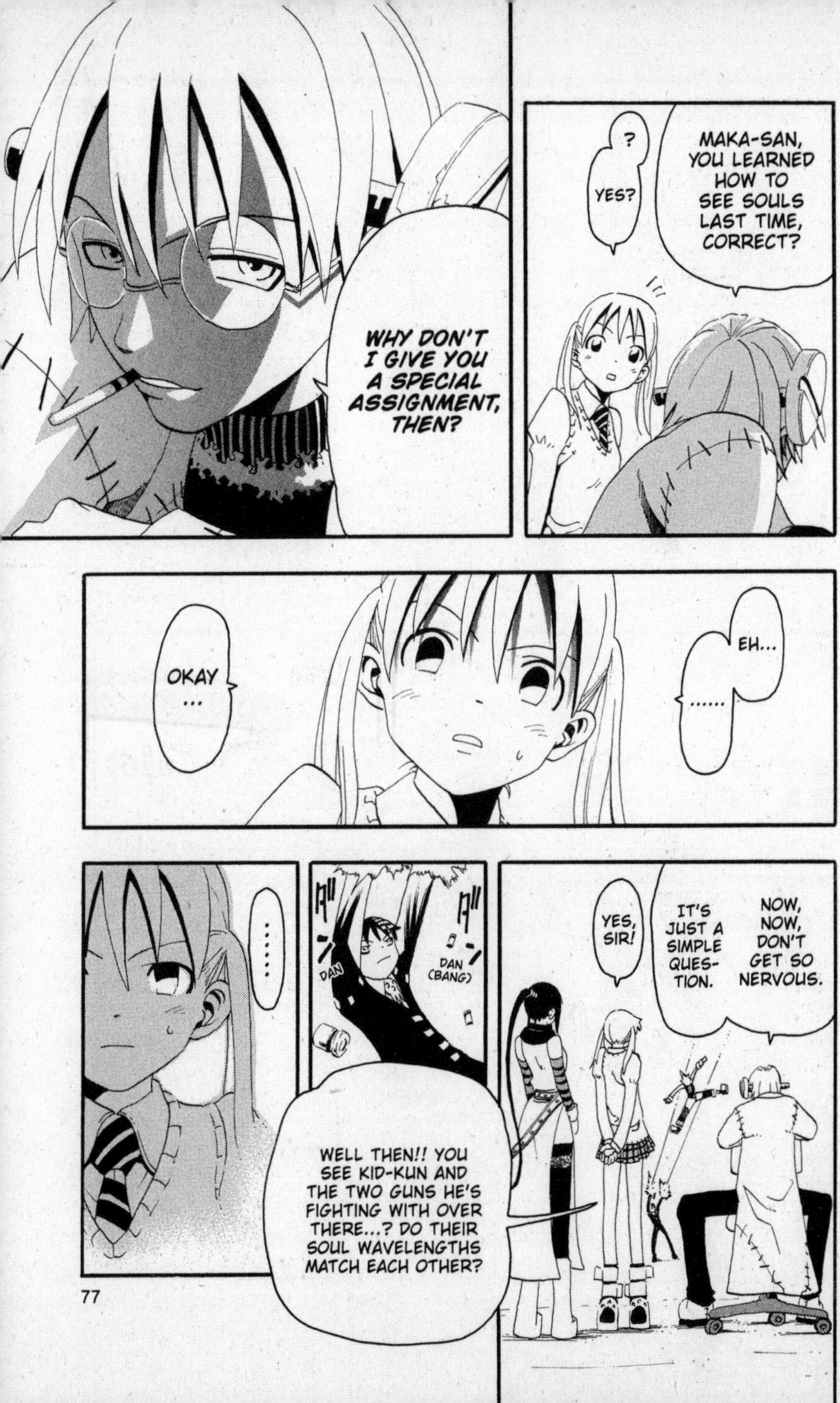
MAKA-SAN, YOU LEARNED HOW TO SEE SOULS LAST TIME, CORRECT?
? YES?
WHY DON'T I GIVE YOU A SPECIAL ASSIGNMENT, THEN?
EH... ......
OKAY ...
NOW, NOW, DON'T GET SO NERVOUS.
IT'S JUST A SIMPLE QUES-TION.
YES, SIR!
WELL THEN!! YOU SEE KID-KUN AND THE TWO GUNS HE'S FIGHTING WITH OVER THERE...? DO THEIR SOUL WAVELENGTHS MATCH EACH OTHER?
DAN (BANG)
DAN
......

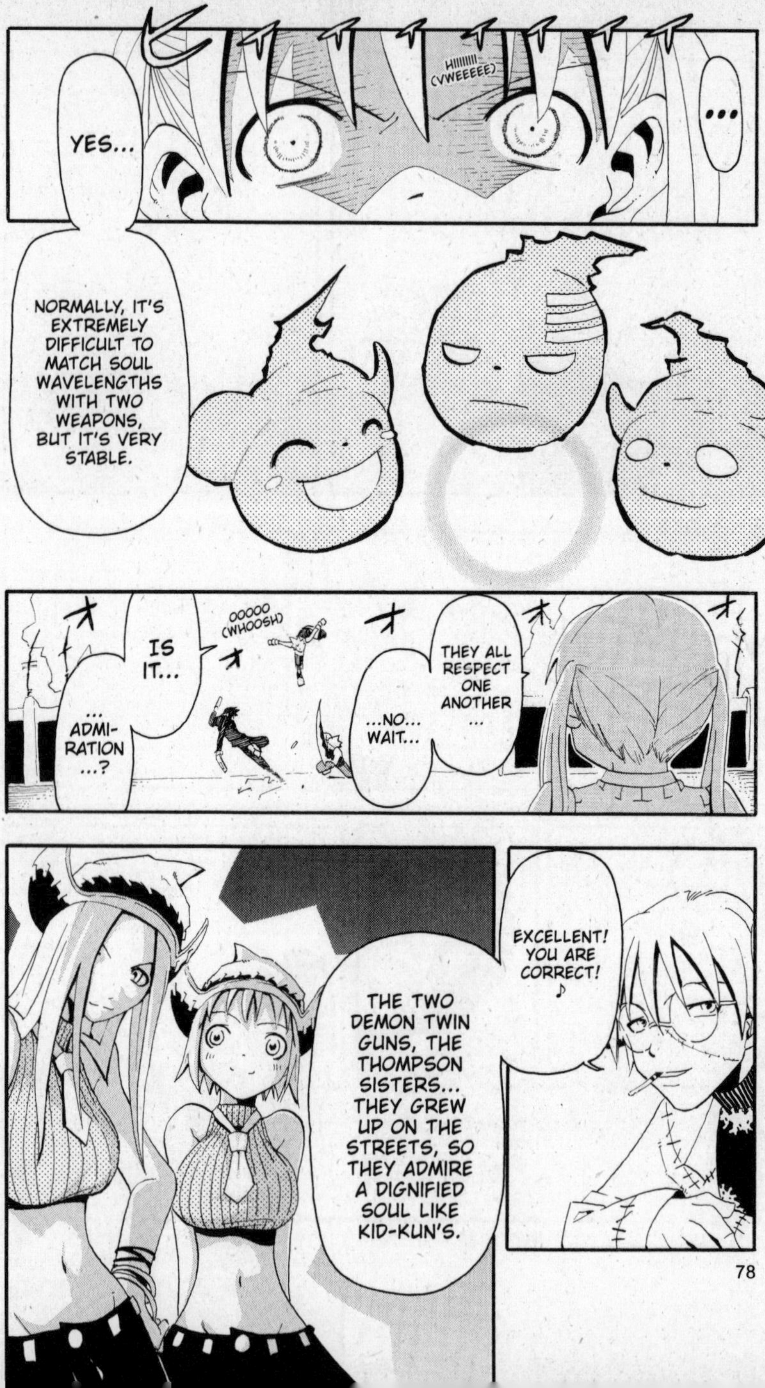
...
HIIIIIII- (VWEEEEE)
YES...
NORMALLY, IT'S EXTREMELY DIFFICULT TO MATCH SOUL WAVELENGTHS WITH TWO WEAPONS, BUT IT'S VERY STABLE.
THEY ALL RESPECT ONE ANOTHER ...
...NO... WAIT...
OOOOO (WHOOSH)
IS IT...
...ADMIRATION ...?
EXCELLENT! YOU ARE CORRECT! ♪
THE TWO DEMON TWIN GUNS, THE THOMPSON SISTERS... THEY GREW UP ON THE STREETS, SO THEY ADMIRE A DIGNIFIED SOUL LIKE KID-KUN'S.

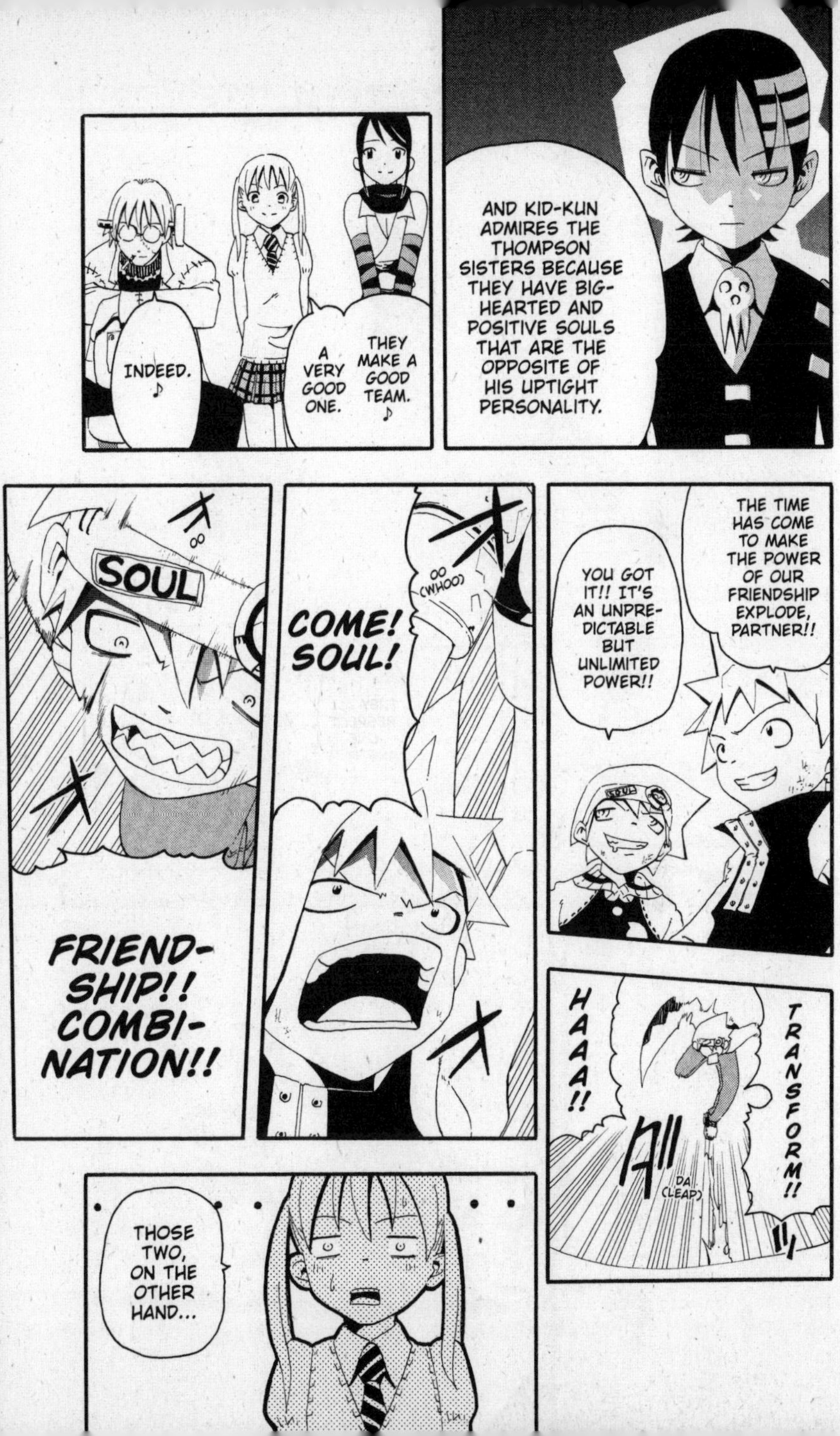
AND KID-KUN ADMIRES THE THOMPSON SISTERS BECAUSE THEY HAVE BIG-HEARTED AND POSITIVE SOULS THAT ARE THE OPPOSITE OF HIS UPTIGHT PERSONALITY.
THEY MAKE A GOOD TEAM. ♪
A VERY GOOD ONE.
INDEED. ♪
THE TIME HAS COME TO MAKE THE POWER OF OUR FRIENDSHIP EXPLODE, PARTNER!!
YOU GOT IT!! IT'S AN UNPREDICTABLE BUT UNLIMITED POWER!!
TRANSFORM!!
HAAAA!!
DA (LEAP)
OO (WHOO)
COME! SOUL!
SOUL
FRIENDSHIP!! COMBINATION!!
THOSE TWO, ON THE OTHER HAND...

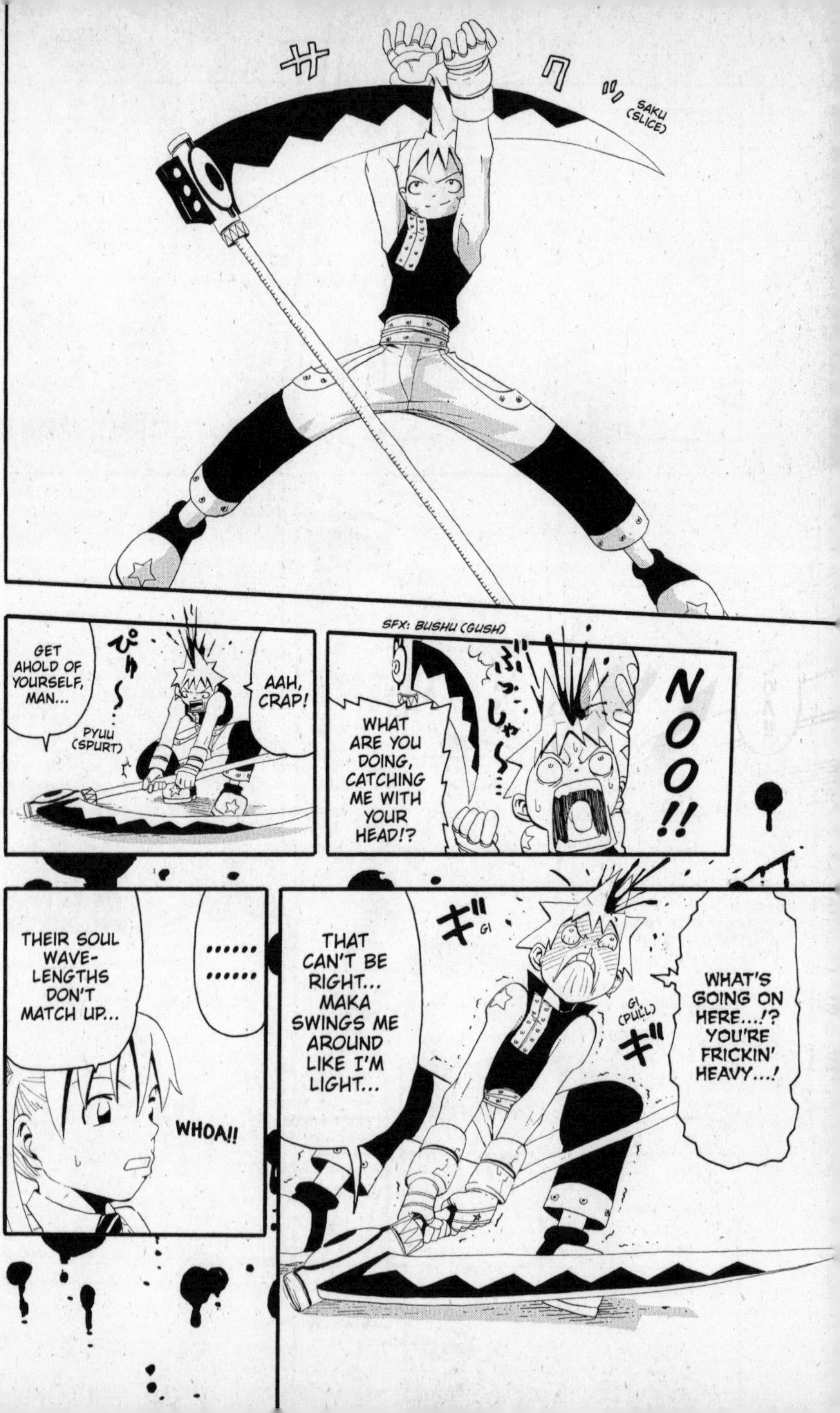
サク
SAKU (SLICE)
SFX: BUSHU (GUSH)
ぶっしゃ~
NOO!!
WHAT ARE YOU DOING, CATCHING ME WITH YOUR HEAD!?
AAH, CRAP!
ぴゅ~
PYUU (SPURT)
GET AHOLD OF YOURSELF, MAN...
WHAT'S GOING ON HERE...!? YOU'RE FRICKIN' HEAVY....!
ギ
GI
THAT CAN'T BE RIGHT... MAKA SWINGS ME AROUND LIKE I'M LIGHT...
GI (PULL)
ギ
......
......
THEIR SOUL WAVE-LENGTHS DON'T MATCH UP...
WHOA!!

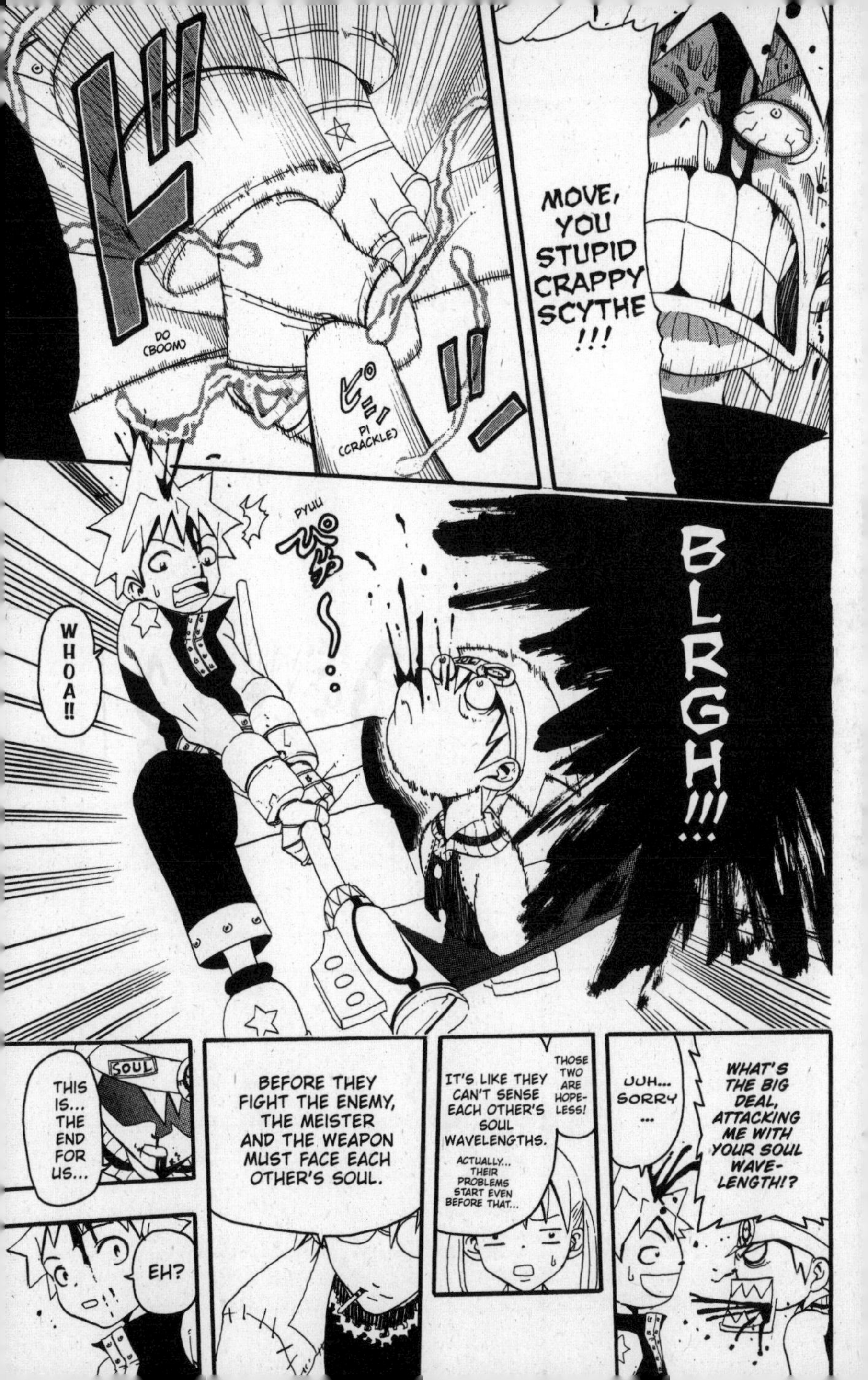
MOVE, YOU STUPID CRAPPY SCYTHE!!!
DO (BOOM)
PI (CRACKLE)
BLRGH!!!
PYUU
WHOA!!
WHAT'S THE BIG DEAL, ATTACKING ME WITH YOUR SOUL WAVE-LENGTH!?
UUH... SORRY...
THOSE TWO ARE HOPE-LESS!
IT'S LIKE THEY CAN'T SENSE EACH OTHER'S SOUL WAVELENGTHS.
ACTUALLY... THEIR PROBLEMS START EVEN BEFORE THAT...
BEFORE THEY FIGHT THE ENEMY, THE MEISTER AND THE WEAPON MUST FACE EACH OTHER'S SOUL.
SOUL
THIS IS... THE END FOR US...
EH?

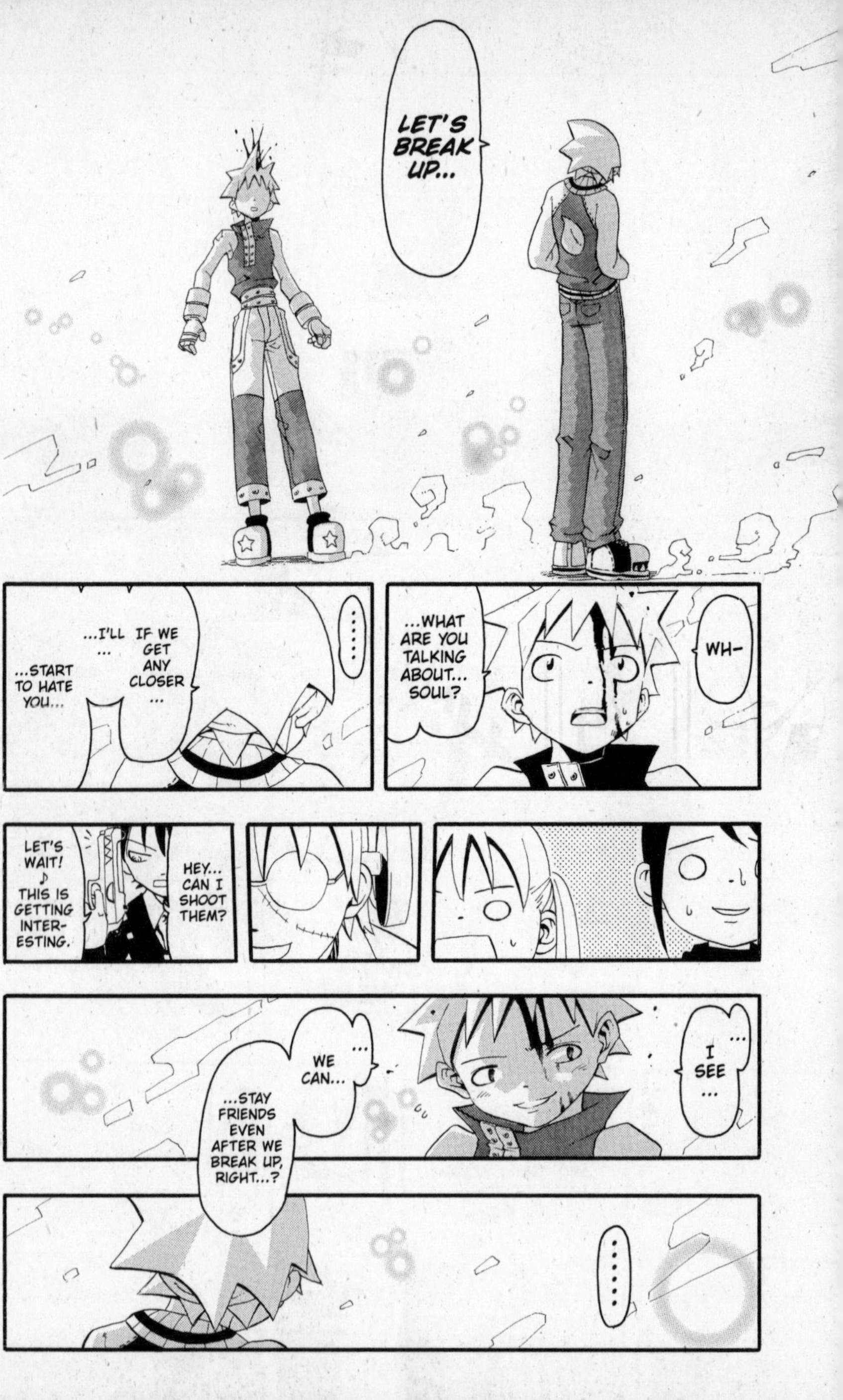
LET'S BREAK UP...
WH-
...WHAT ARE YOU TALKING ABOUT... SOUL?
......
IF WE GET ANY CLOSER ...
...I'LL ...
...START TO HATE YOU...
HEY... CAN I SHOOT THEM?
LET'S WAIT! ♪ THIS IS GETTING INTER-ESTING.
... I SEE ...
... WE CAN...
...STAY FRIENDS EVEN AFTER WE BREAK UP, RIGHT...?
......

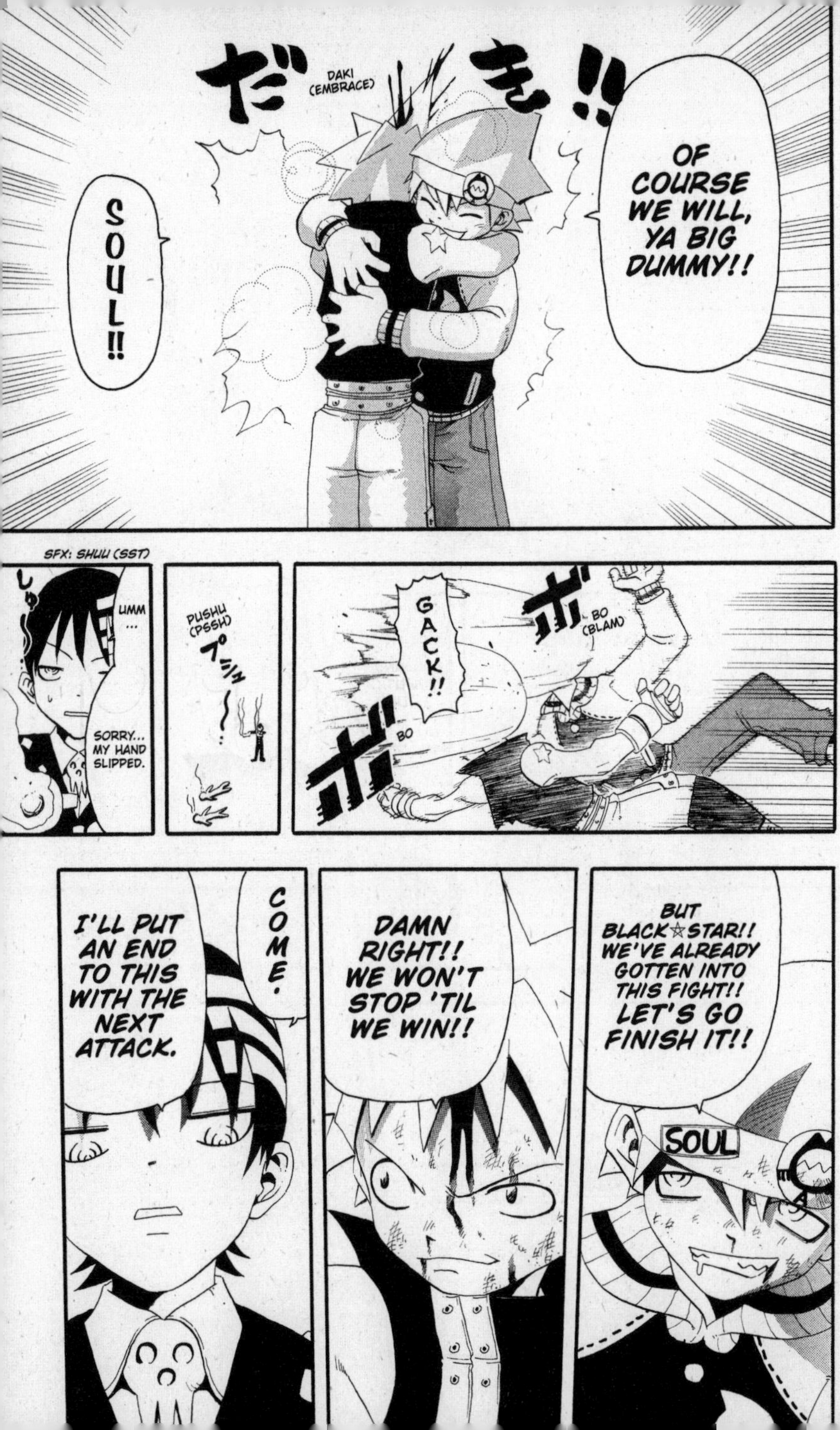
だき!!
DAKI (EMBRACE)
OF COURSE WE WILL, YA BIG DUMMY!!
SOUL!!
ボ
BO (BLAM)
GACK!!
ボ
BO
PUSHU (PSSH)
プシュ~
SFX: SHUU (SST)
しゅ
UMM ...
SORRY... MY HAND SLIPPED.
BUT BLACK☆STAR!! WE'VE ALREADY GOTTEN INTO THIS FIGHT!! LET'S GO FINISH IT!!
SOUL
DAMN RIGHT!! WE WON'T STOP 'TIL WE WIN!!
COME.
I'LL PUT AN END TO THIS WITH THE NEXT ATTACK.

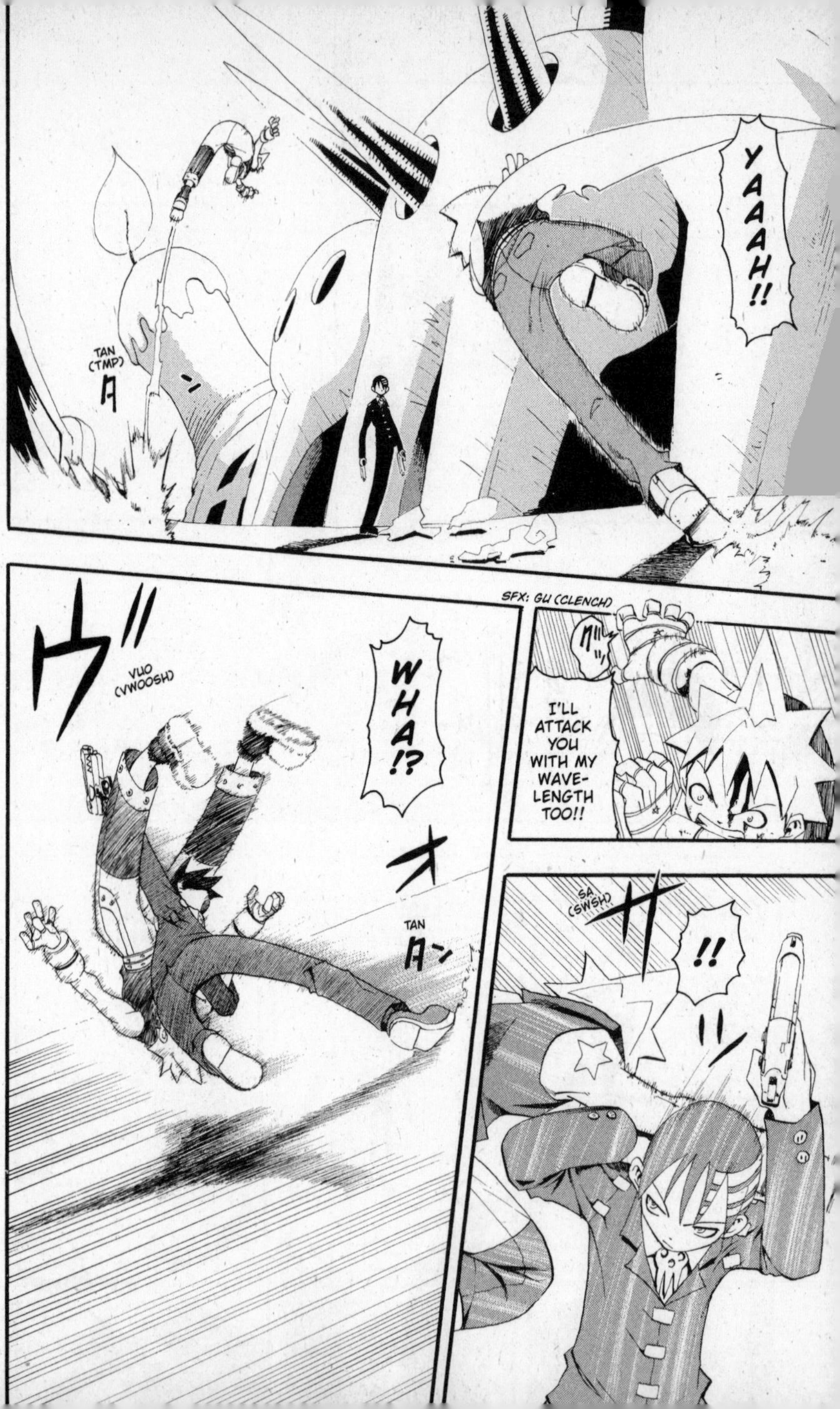
YAAAAH!!
TAN (TMP)
SFX: GU (CLENCH)
I'LL ATTACK YOU WITH MY WAVE-LENGTH TOO!!
SA (SWSH)
!!
WHA!?
VUO (VWOOSH)
TAN

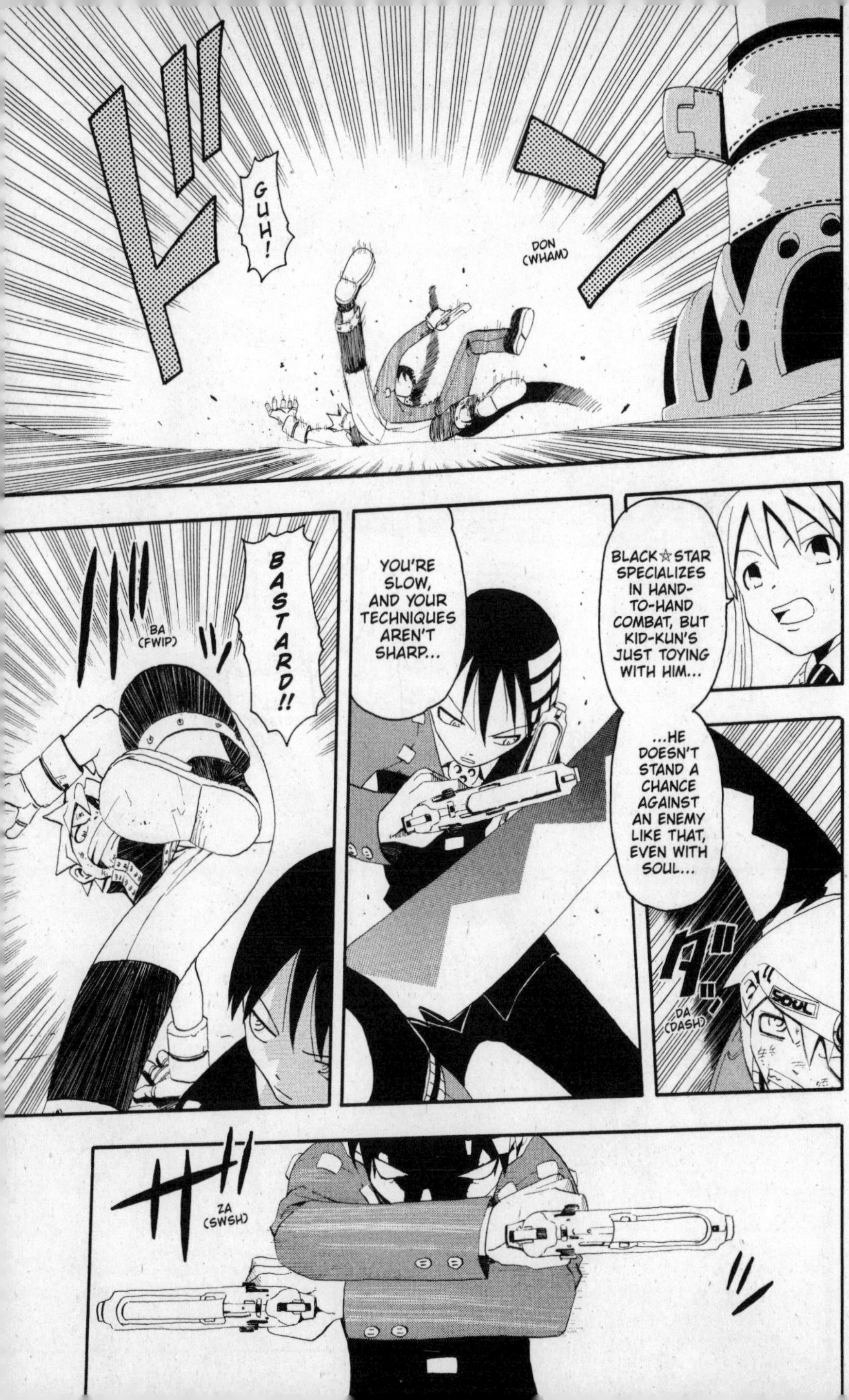
GUH!
DON (WHAM)
BLACK☆STAR SPECIALIZES IN HAND-TO-HAND COMBAT, BUT KID-KUN'S JUST TOYING WITH HIM...
...HE DOESN'T STAND A CHANCE AGAINST AN ENEMY LIKE THAT, EVEN WITH SOUL...
DA (DASH)
SOUL
YOU'RE SLOW, AND YOUR TECHNIQUES AREN'T SHARP...
BASTARD!!
BA (FWIP)
ZA (SWSH)

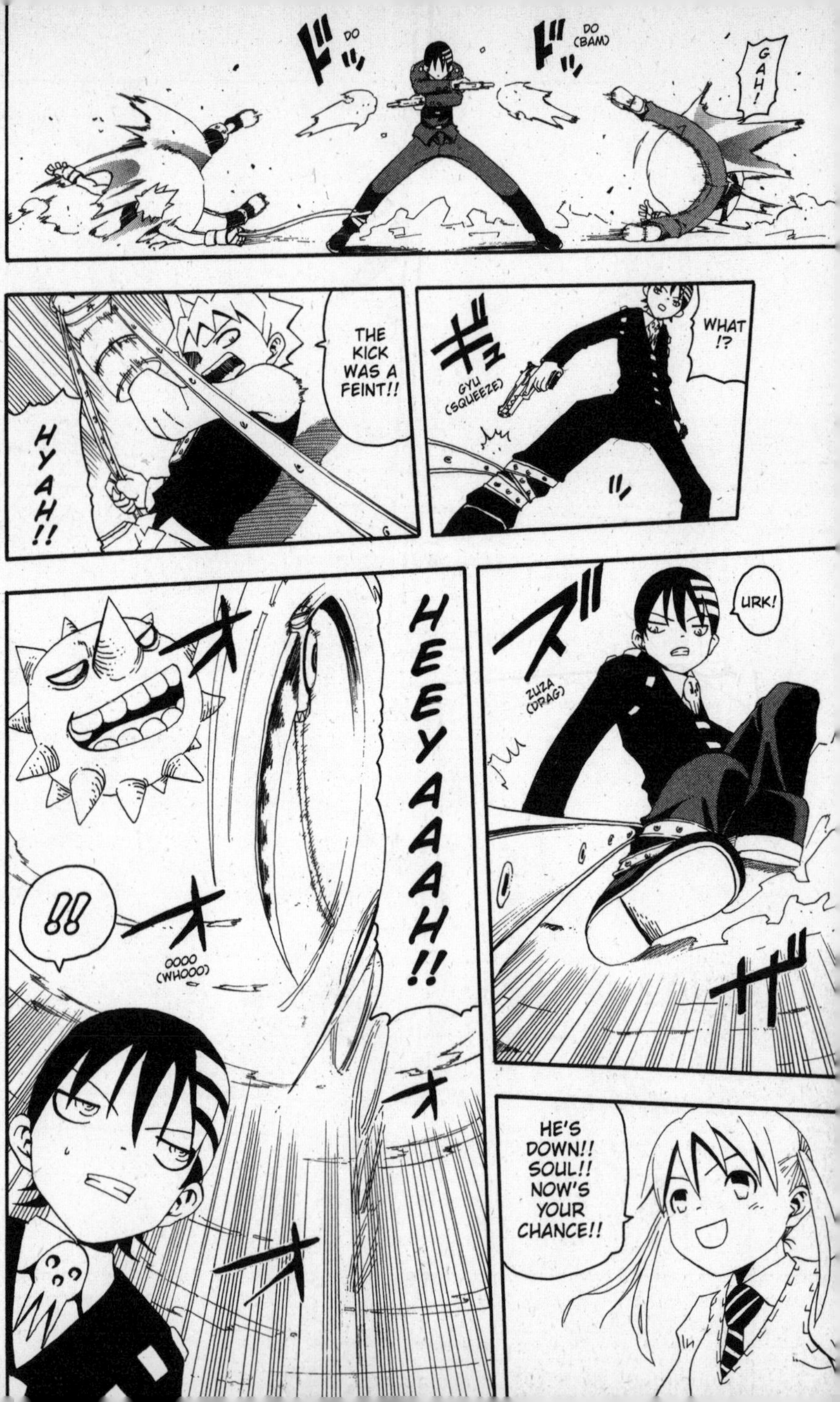
GAH!
DO (BAM)
DO
WHAT!?
GYU (SQUEEZE)
THE KICK WAS A FEINT!!
HYAH!!
URK!
ZUZA (DRAG)
HE'S DOWN!! SOUL!! NOW'S YOUR CHANCE!!
HEEYAAAAH!!
!!
OOOO (WHOOO)

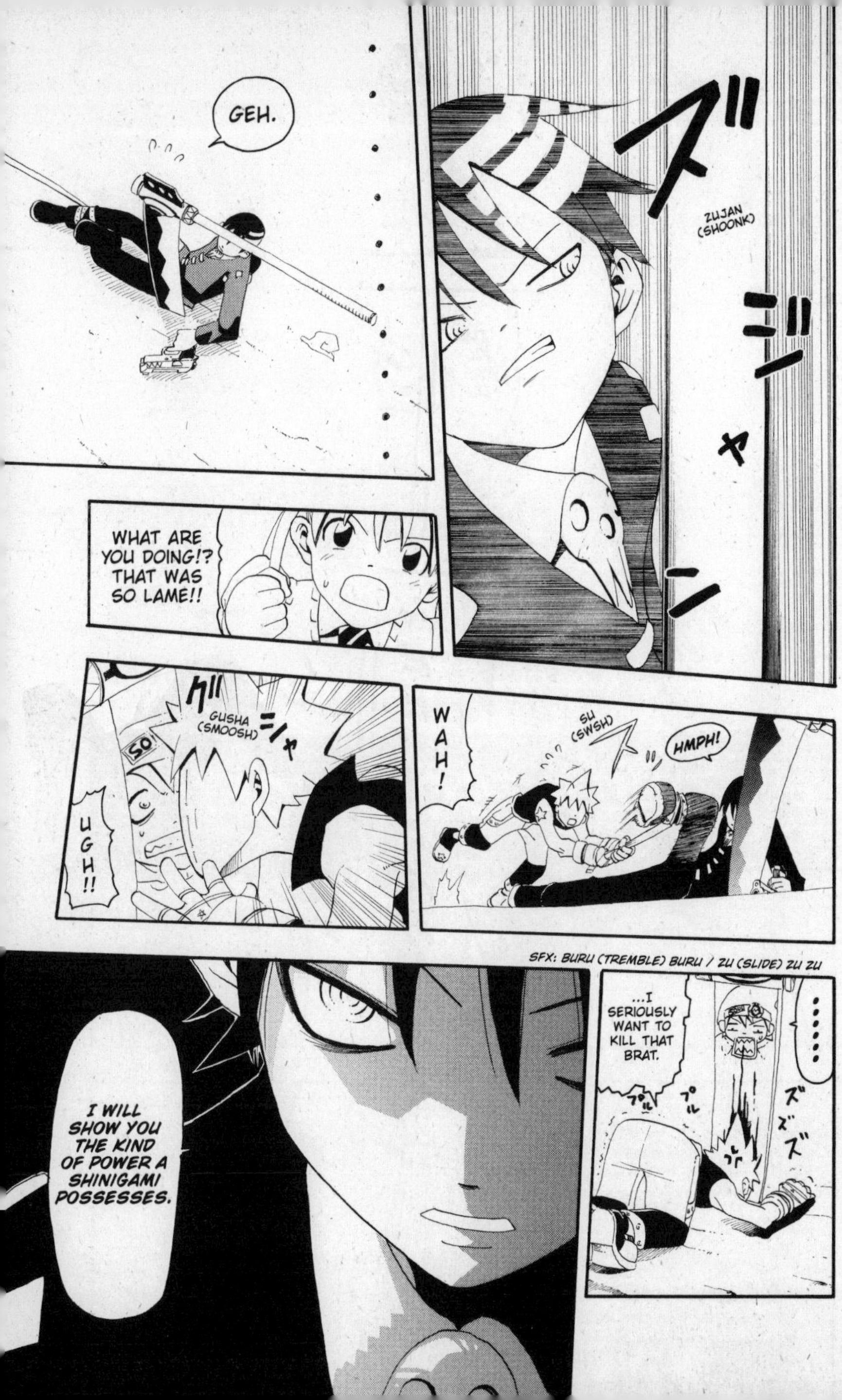
ZUJAN (SHOONK)
GEH.
WHAT ARE YOU DOING!? THAT WAS SO LAME!!
WAH!
SU (SWSH)
HMPH!
GUSHA (SMOOSH)
SO
UGH!!
SFX: BURU (TREMBLE) BURU / ZU (SLIDE) ZU ZU
...I SERIOUSLY WANT TO KILL THAT BRAT.
......
I WILL SHOW YOU THE KIND OF POWER A SHINIGAMI POSSESSES.

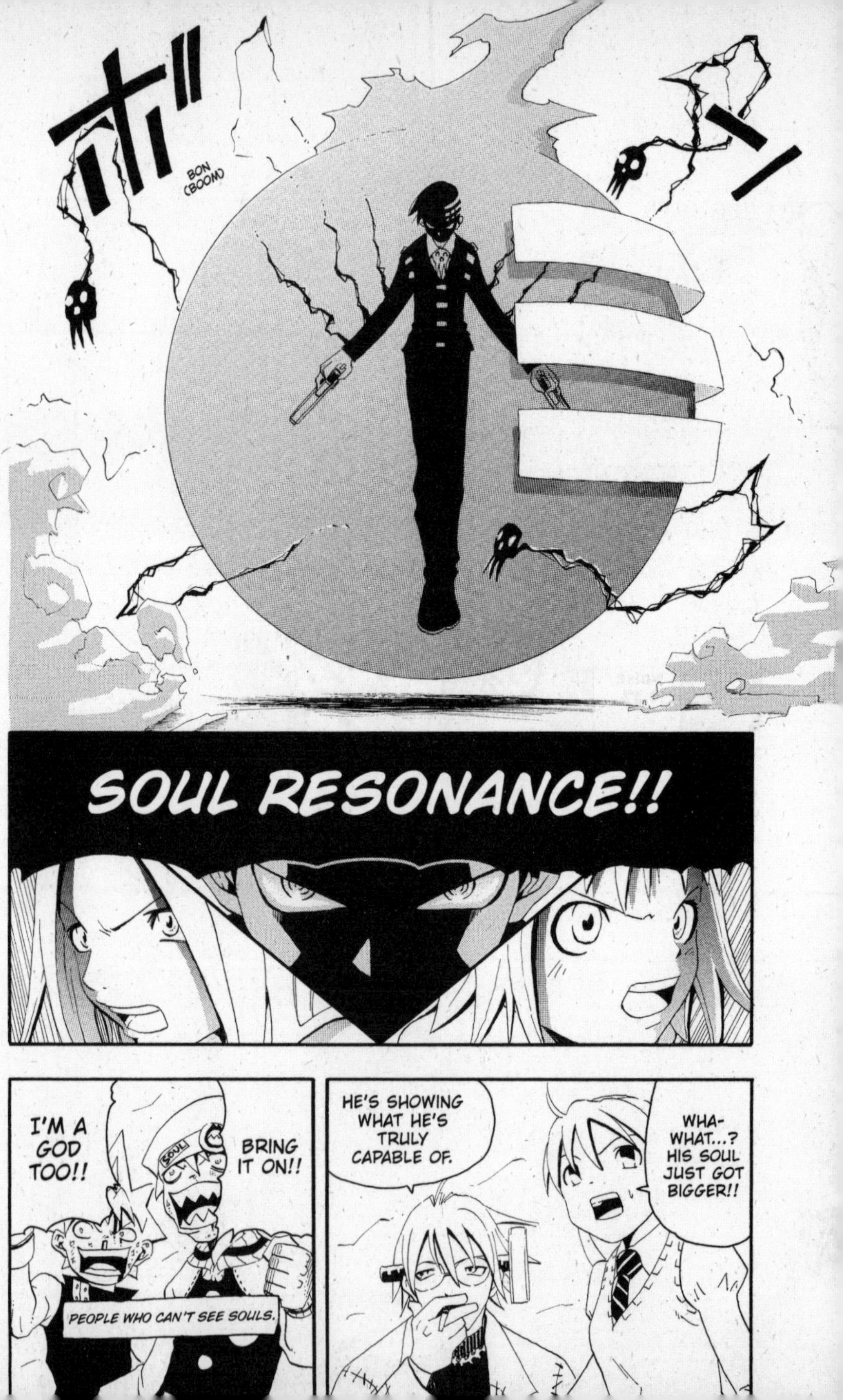
BON (BOOM)
SOUL RESONANCE!!
WHA-WHAT...? HIS SOUL JUST GOT BIGGER!!
HE'S SHOWING WHAT HE'S TRULY CAPABLE OF.
BRING IT ON!!
I'M A GOD TOO!!
PEOPLE WHO CAN'T SEE SOULS.

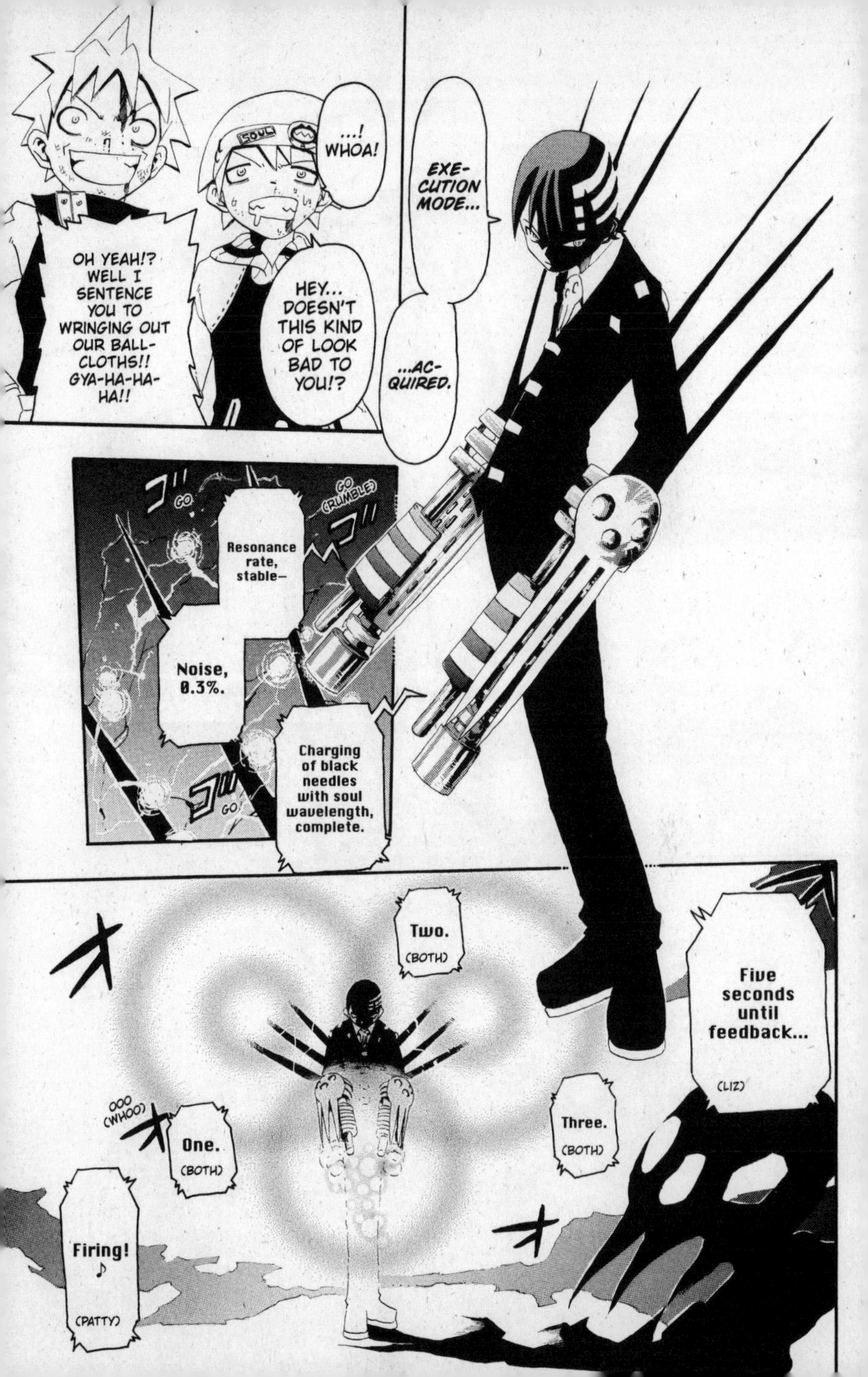
EXE-CUTION MODE...
...AC-QUIRED.
...! WHOA!
HEY... DOESN'T THIS KIND OF LOOK BAD TO YOU!?
OH YEAH!? WELL I SENTENCE YOU TO WRINGING OUT OUR BALL-CLOTHS!! GYA-HA-HA-HA!!
GO (RUMBLE)
GO
Resonance rate, stable—
Noise, 0.3%.
Charging of black needles with soul wavelength, complete.
GO
Five seconds until feedback...
(LIZ)
Three.
(BOTH)
Two.
(BOTH)
OOO (WHOO)
One.
(BOTH)
Firing! ♪
(PATTY)

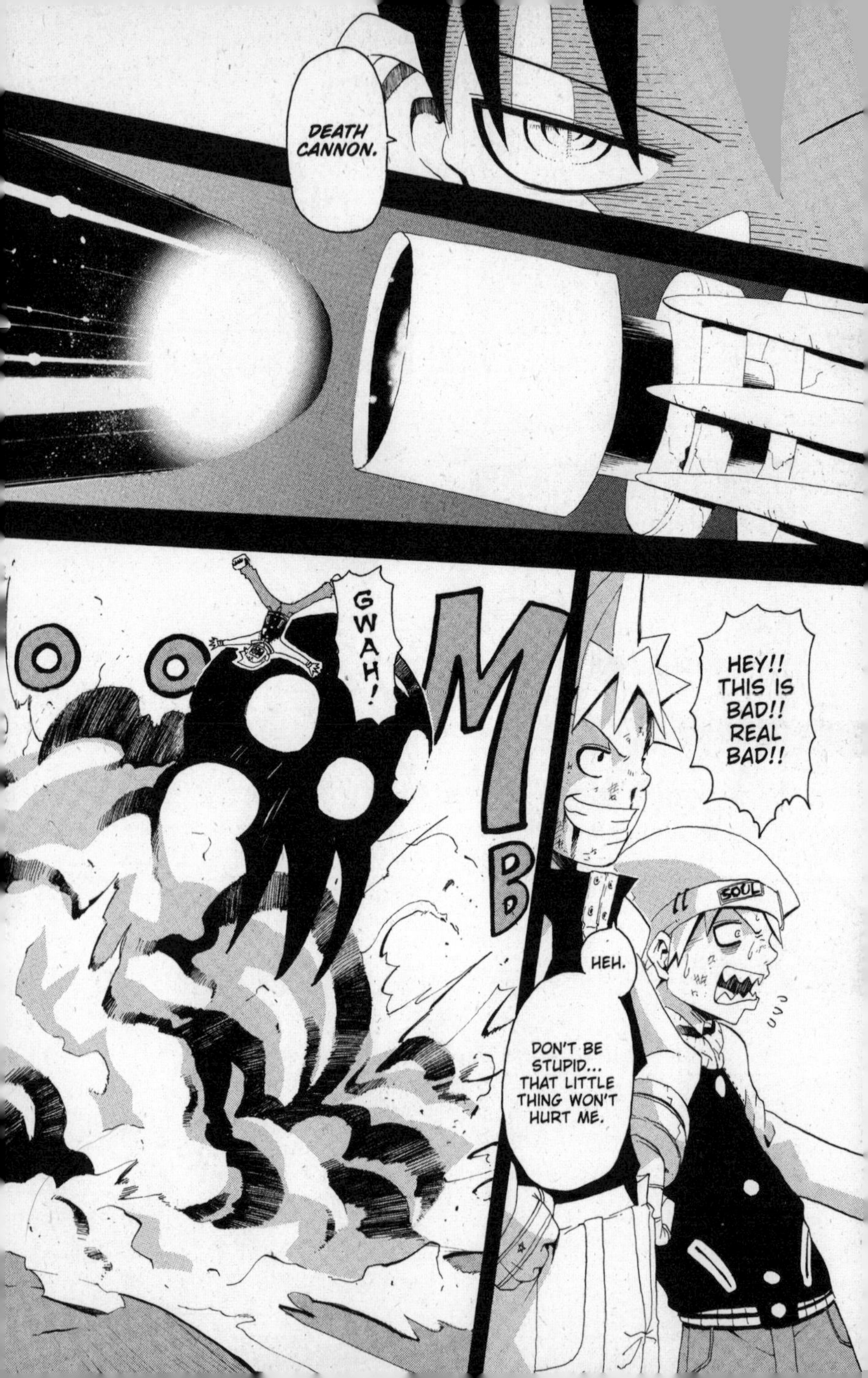
DEATH CANNON.
HEY!! THIS IS BAD!! REAL BAD!!
HEH.
DON'T BE STUPID... THAT LITTLE THING WON'T HURT ME.
GWAH!

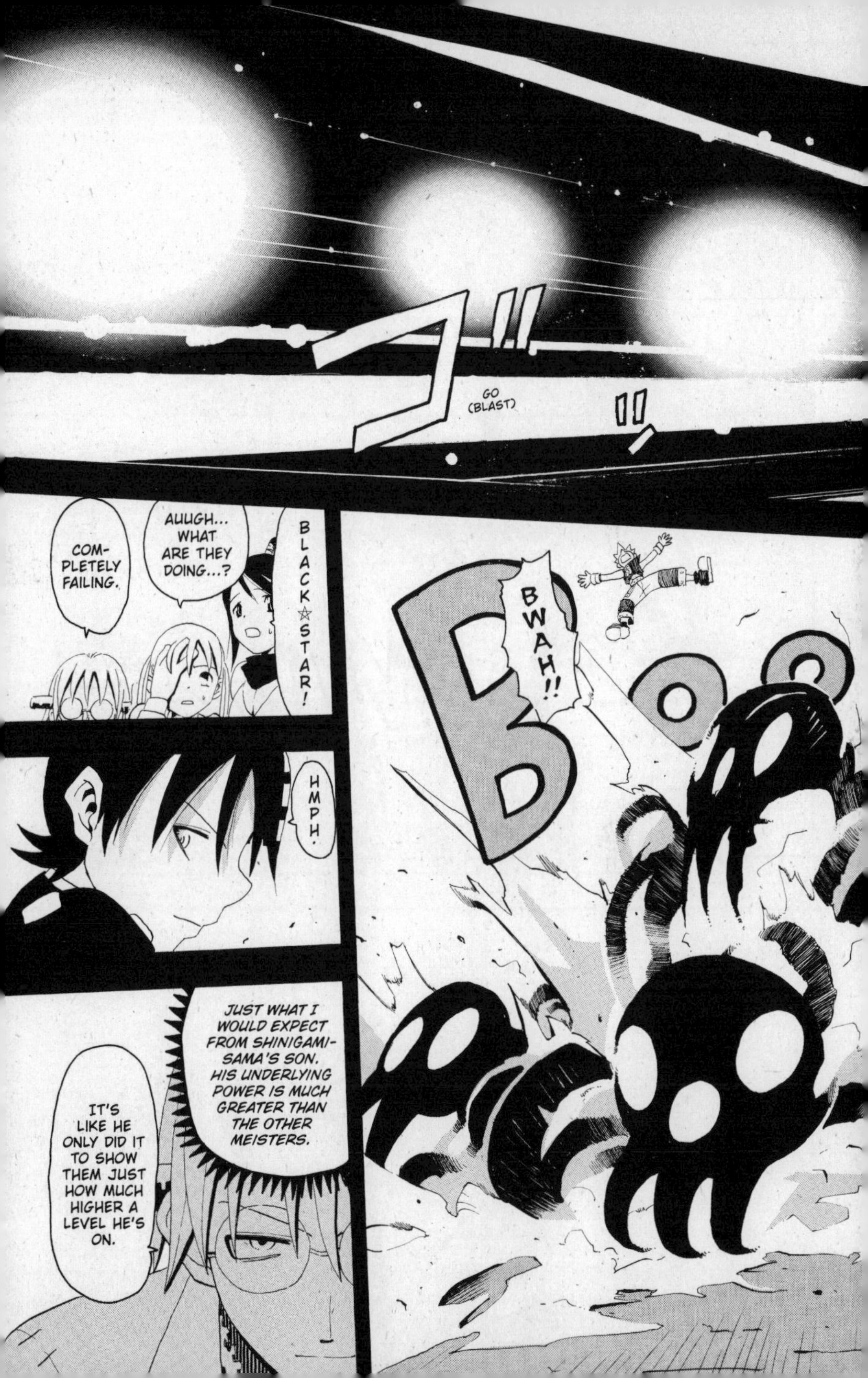

GO (BLAST)
BWAH!!
BLACK☆STAR!
AUUGH... WHAT ARE THEY DOING...?
COMPLETELY FAILING.
HMPH.
JUST WHAT I WOULD EXPECT FROM SHINIGAMI-SAMA'S SON. HIS UNDERLYING POWER IS MUCH GREATER THAN THE OTHER MEISTERS.
IT'S LIKE HE ONLY DID IT TO SHOW THEM JUST HOW MUCH HIGHER A LEVEL HE'S ON.

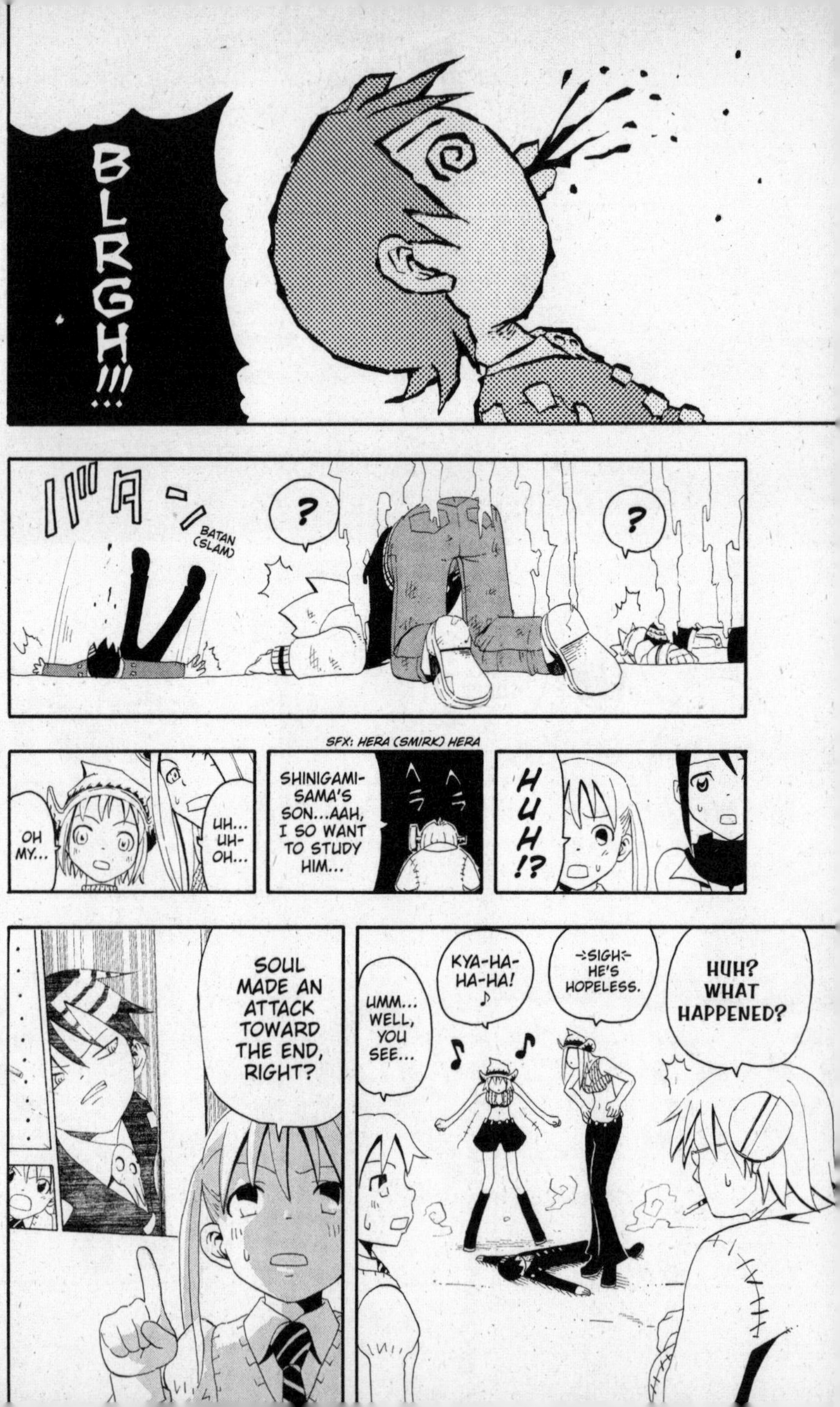
BLRGH!!!...
?
?
バターン
BATAN (SLAM)
SFX: HERA (SMIRK) HERA
HUH!?
SHINIGAMI-SAMA'S SON...AAH, I SO WANT TO STUDY HIM...
UH... UH-OH...
OH MY...
HUH? WHAT HAPPENED?
-SIGH- HE'S HOPELESS.
KYA-HA-HA-HA! ♪
UMM... WELL, YOU SEE...
SOUL MADE AN ATTACK TOWARD THE END, RIGHT?

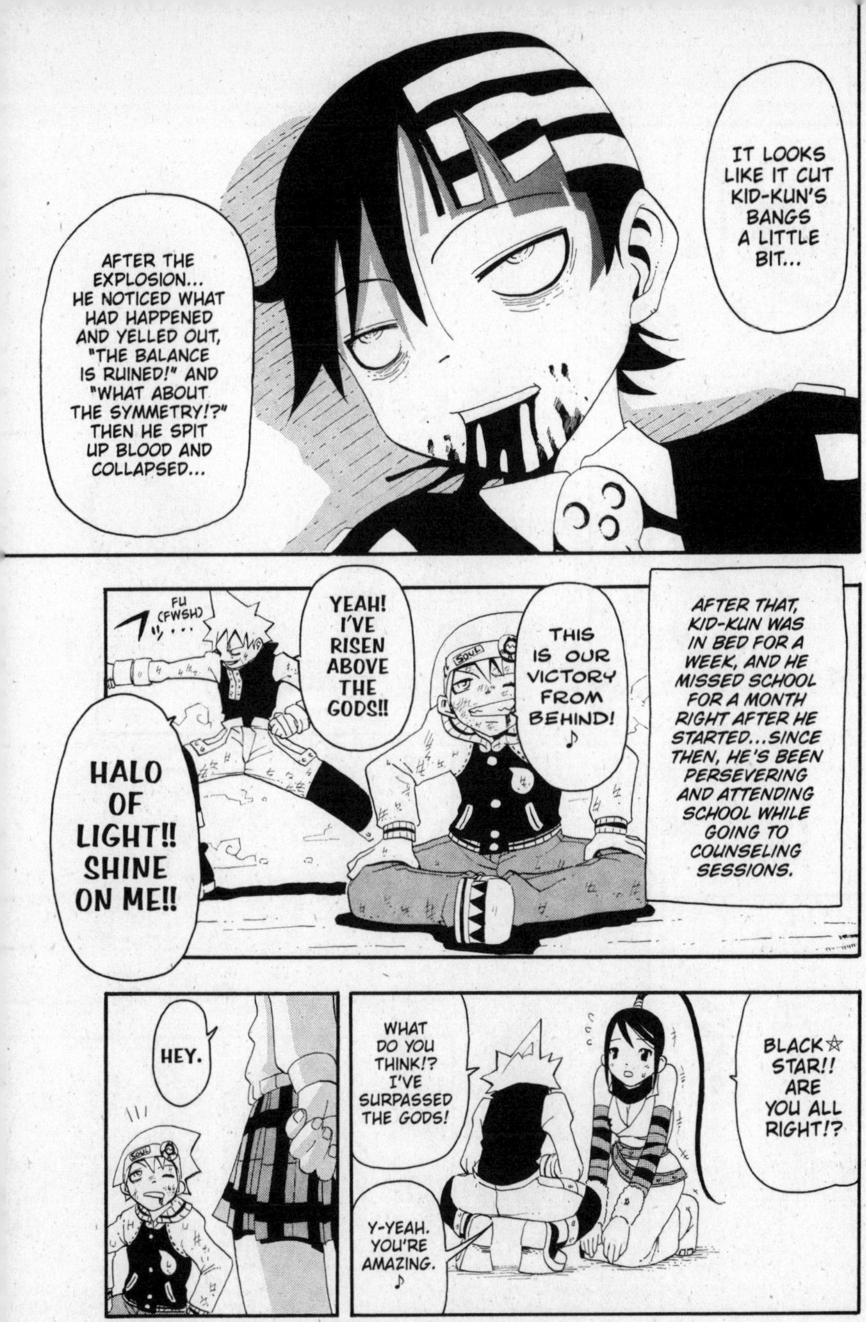
IT LOOKS LIKE IT CUT KID-KUN'S BANGS A LITTLE BIT...
AFTER THE EXPLOSION... HE NOTICED WHAT HAD HAPPENED AND YELLED OUT, "THE BALANCE IS RUINED!" AND "WHAT ABOUT THE SYMMETRY!?" THEN HE SPIT UP BLOOD AND COLLAPSED...
AFTER THAT, KID-KUN WAS IN BED FOR A WEEK, AND HE MISSED SCHOOL FOR A MONTH RIGHT AFTER HE STARTED...SINCE THEN, HE'S BEEN PERSEVERING AND ATTENDING SCHOOL WHILE GOING TO COUNSELING SESSIONS.
THIS IS OUR VICTORY FROM BEHIND! ♪
YEAH! I'VE RISEN ABOVE THE GODS!!
FU (FWSH)
HALO OF LIGHT!! SHINE ON ME!!
BLACK☆STAR!! ARE YOU ALL RIGHT!?
WHAT DO YOU THINK!? I'VE SURPASSED THE GODS!
Y-YEAH. YOU'RE AMAZING. ♪
HEY.

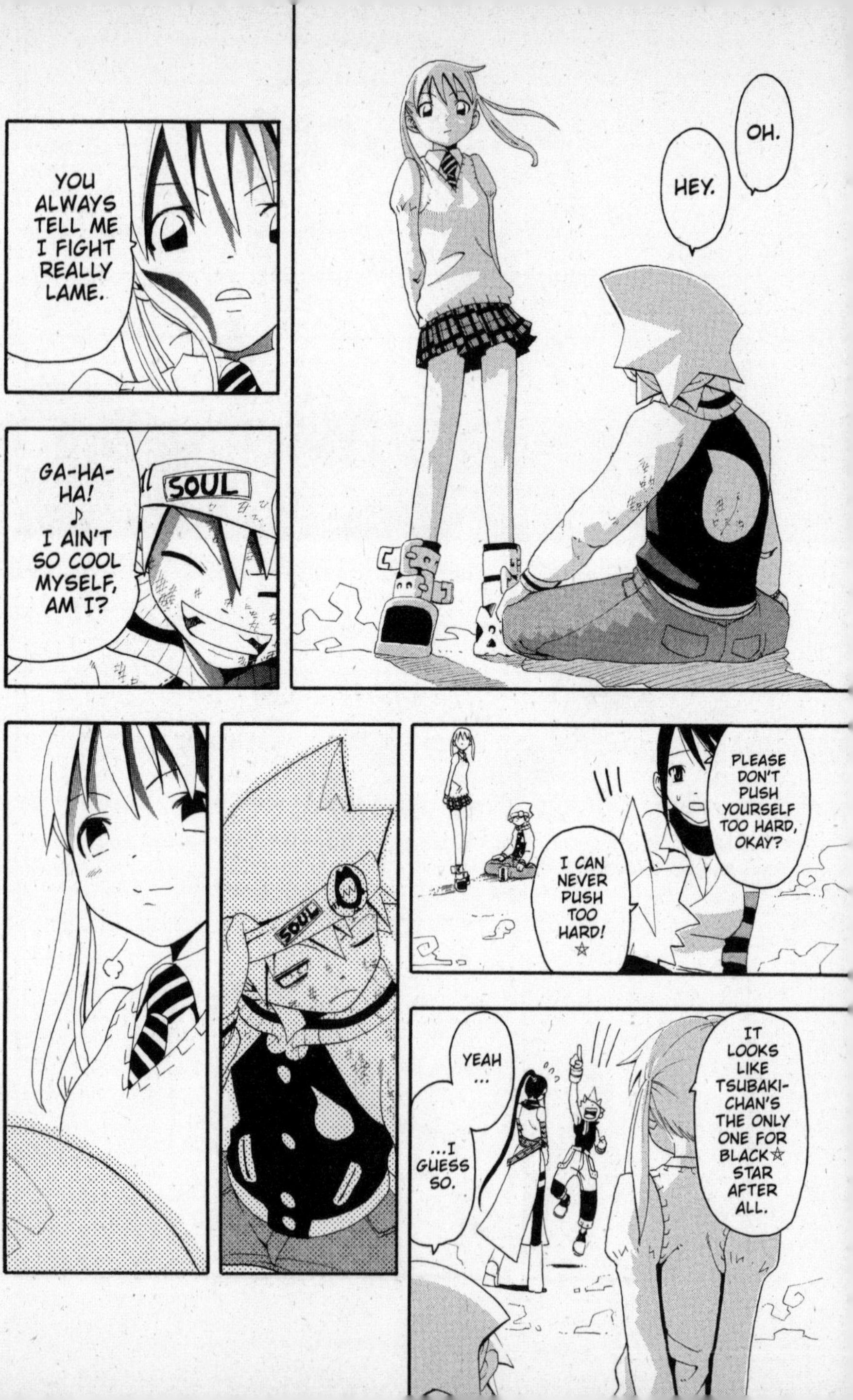
OH.
HEY.
YOU ALWAYS TELL ME I FIGHT REALLY LAME.
GA-HA-HA! ♪ I AIN'T SO COOL MYSELF, AM I?
PLEASE DON'T PUSH YOURSELF TOO HARD, OKAY?
I CAN NEVER PUSH TOO HARD! ☆
IT LOOKS LIKE TSUBAKI-CHAN'S THE ONLY ONE FOR BLACK☆STAR AFTER ALL.
YEAH...
...I GUESS SO.
SOUL
SOUL

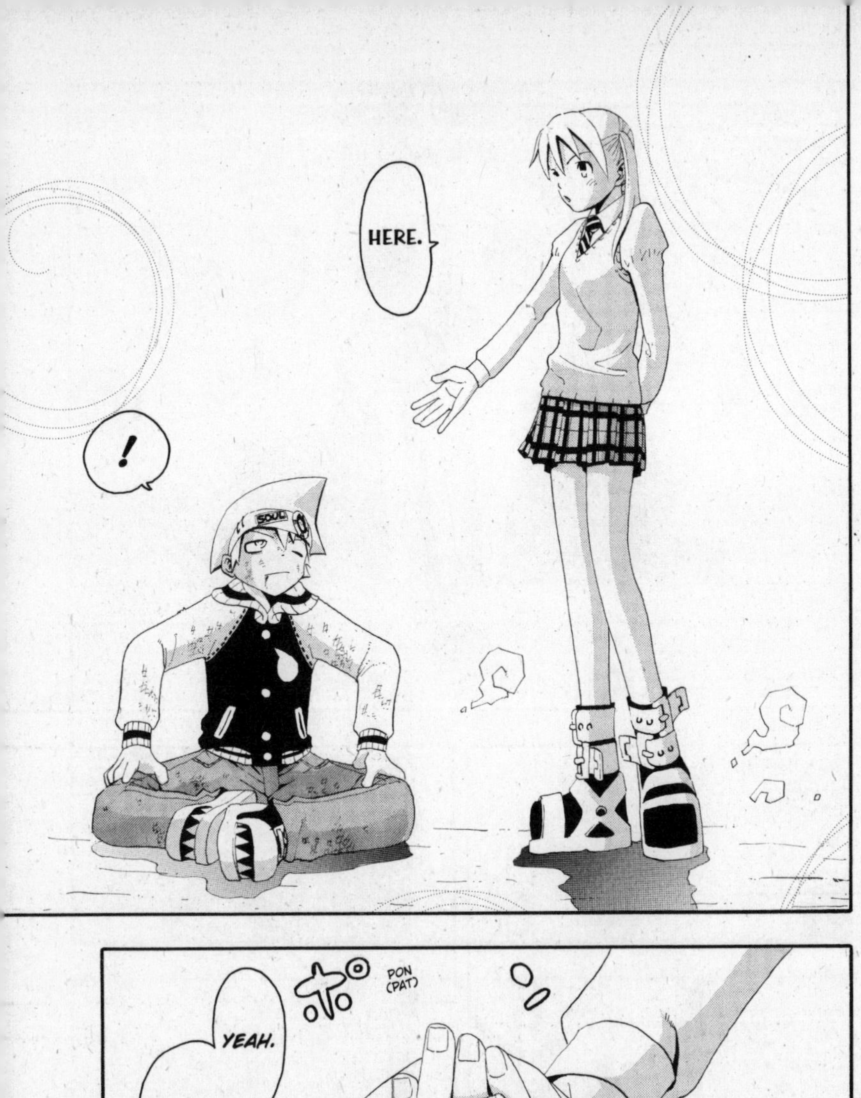
HERE.
!

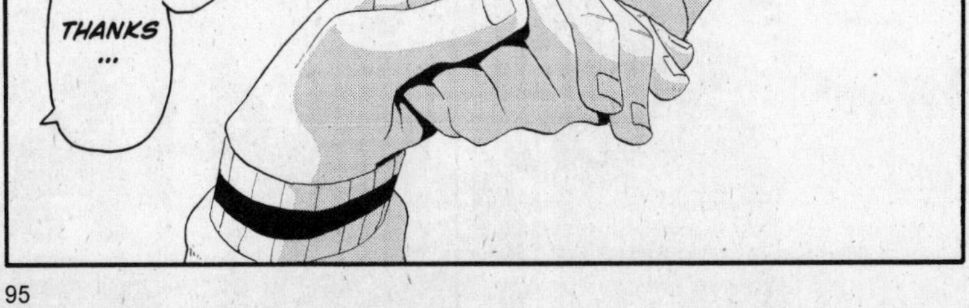
PON
(PAT)
YEAH.
THANKS
...

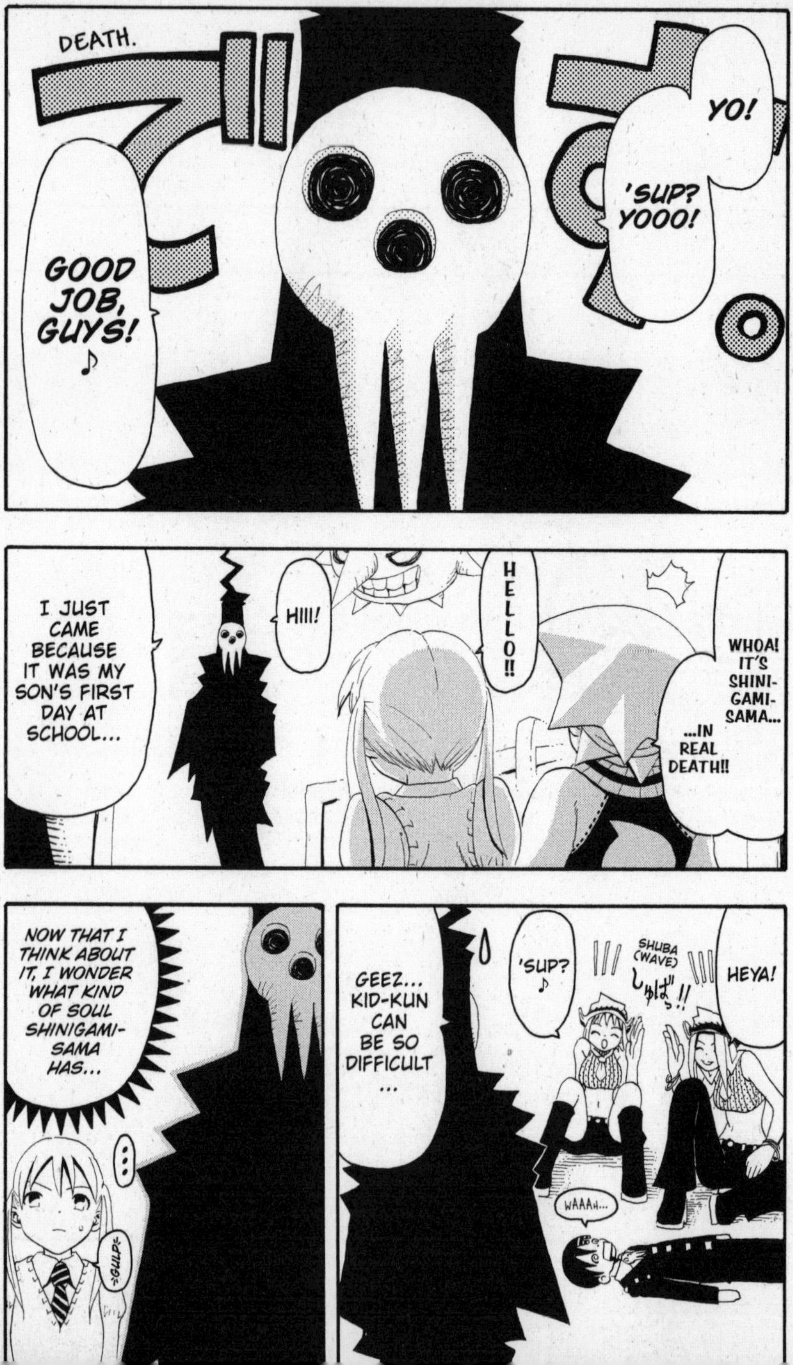
YO!
'SUP? YOOO!
DEATH.
GOOD JOB, GUYS! ♪
WHOA! IT'S SHINIGAMI-SAMA...
...IN REAL DEATH!!
HELLO!!
HIII!
I JUST CAME BECAUSE IT WAS MY SON'S FIRST DAY AT SCHOOL...
HEYA!
SHUBA (WAVE)
しゅばっ!!
'SUP? ♪
GEEZ... KID-KUN CAN BE SO DIFFICULT...
WAAAH...
NOW THAT I THINK ABOUT IT, I WONDER WHAT KIND OF SOUL SHINIGAMI-SAMA HAS...
...
GULP

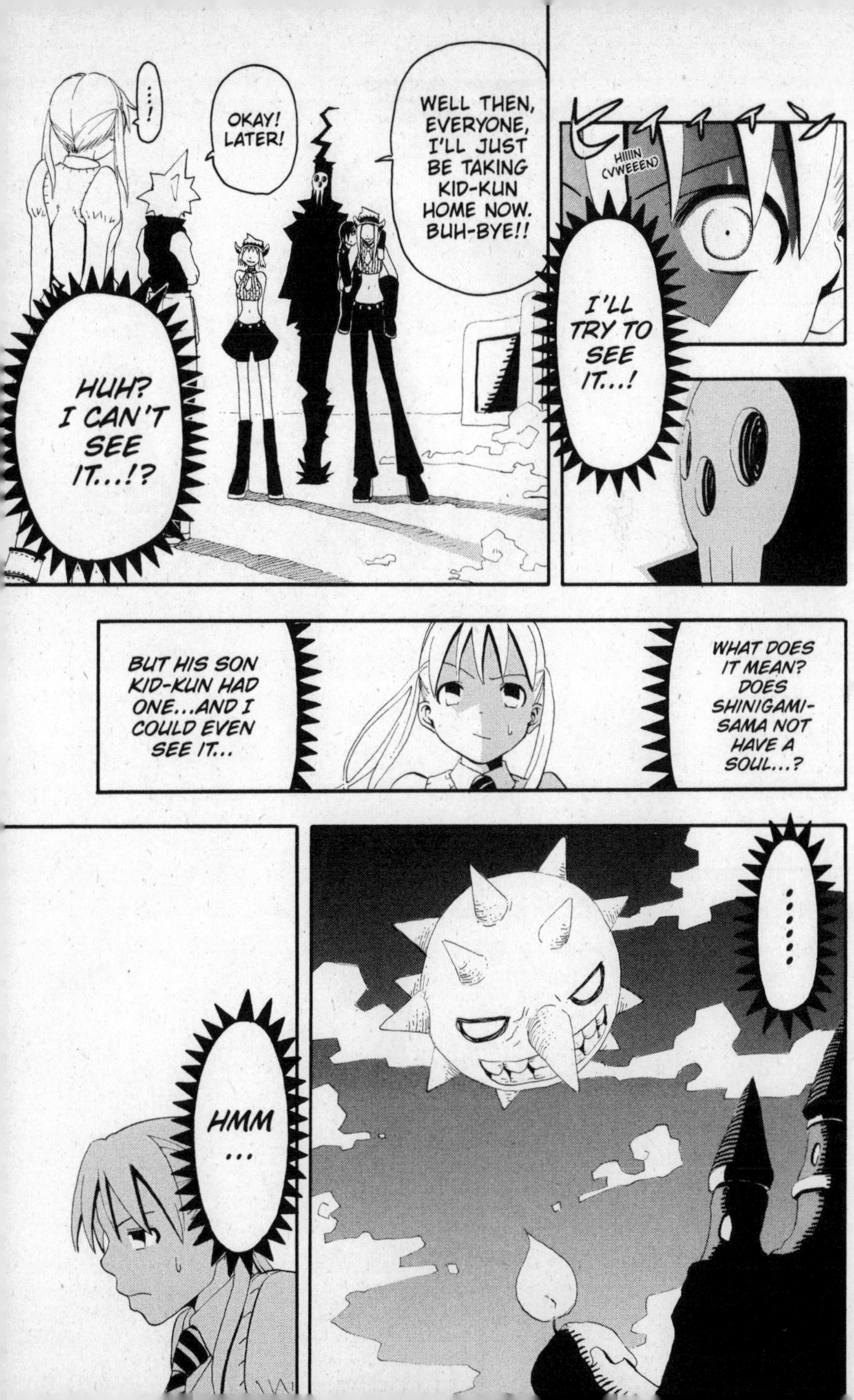
HIIIIN (VWEEEN)
I'LL TRY TO SEE IT...!
WELL THEN, EVERYONE, I'LL JUST BE TAKING KID-KUN HOME NOW. BUH-BYE!!
OKAY! LATER!
...!
HUH? I CAN'T SEE IT...!?
WHAT DOES IT MEAN? DOES SHINIGAMI-SAMA NOT HAVE A SOUL...?
BUT HIS SON KID-KUN HAD ONE...AND I COULD EVEN SEE IT...
......
HMM ...

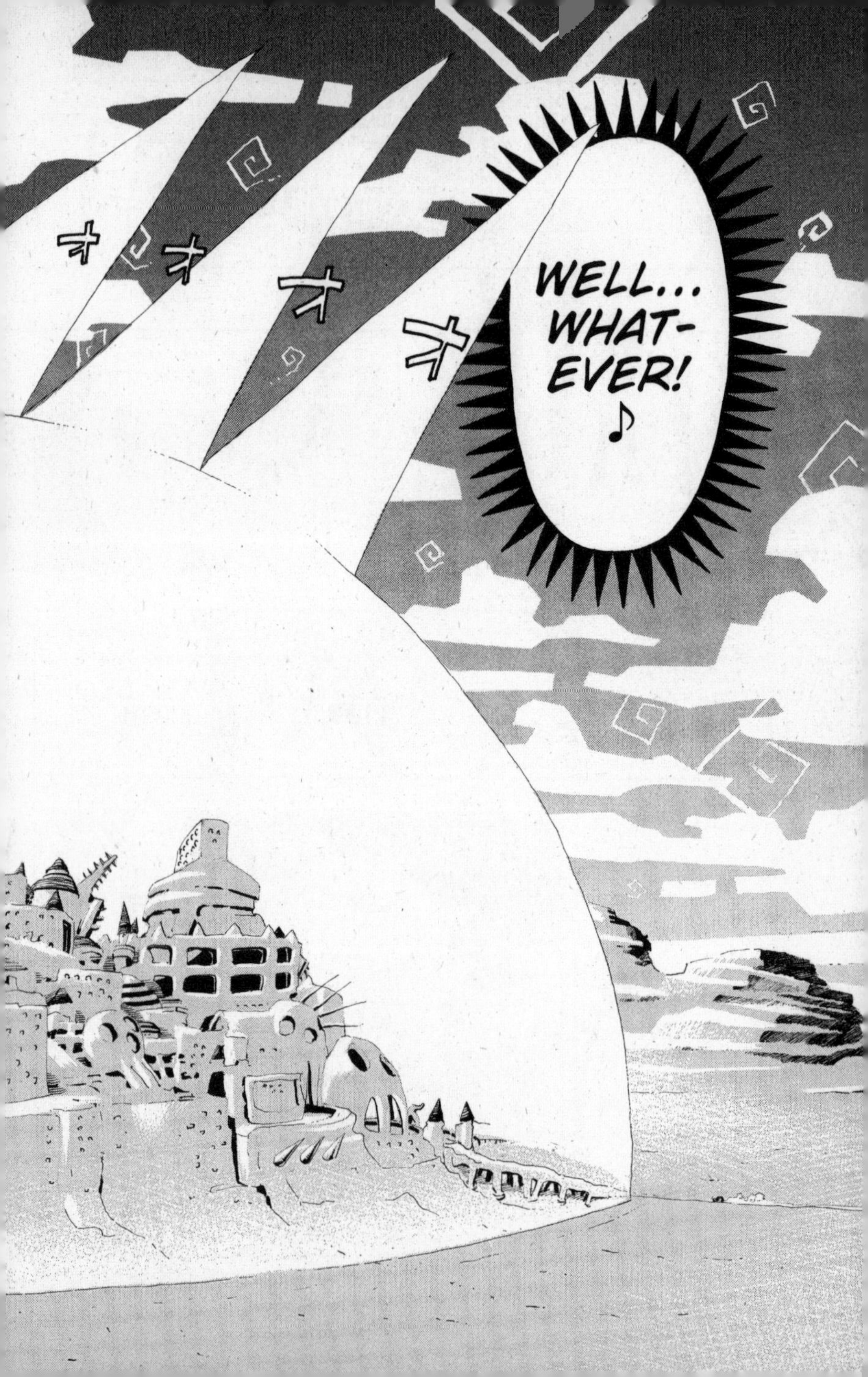
WELL... WHAT-EVER! ♪
オオオオ

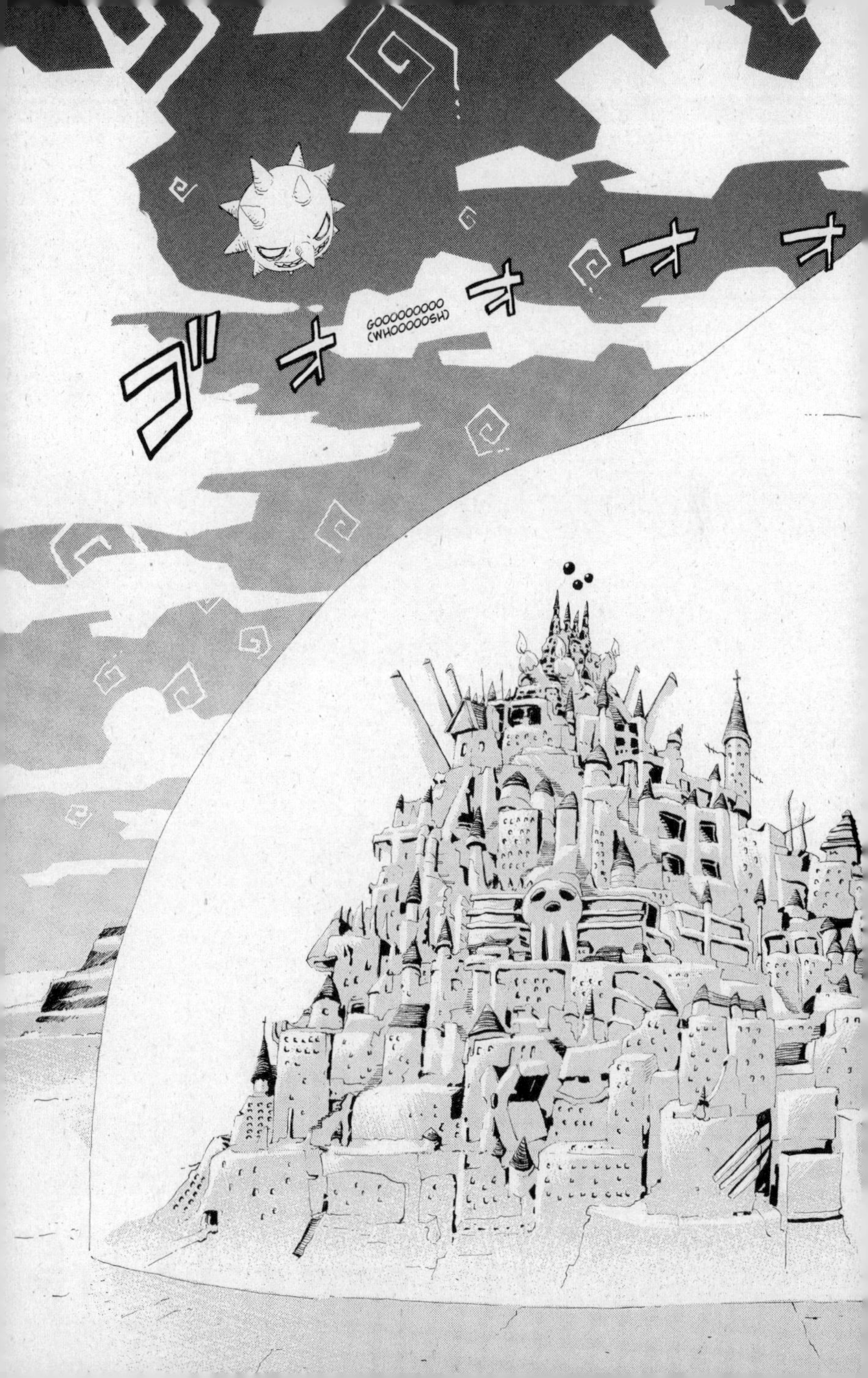
ゴオオオオ
GOOOOOOOOO
(WHOOOOOOSH)

SOUL EATER

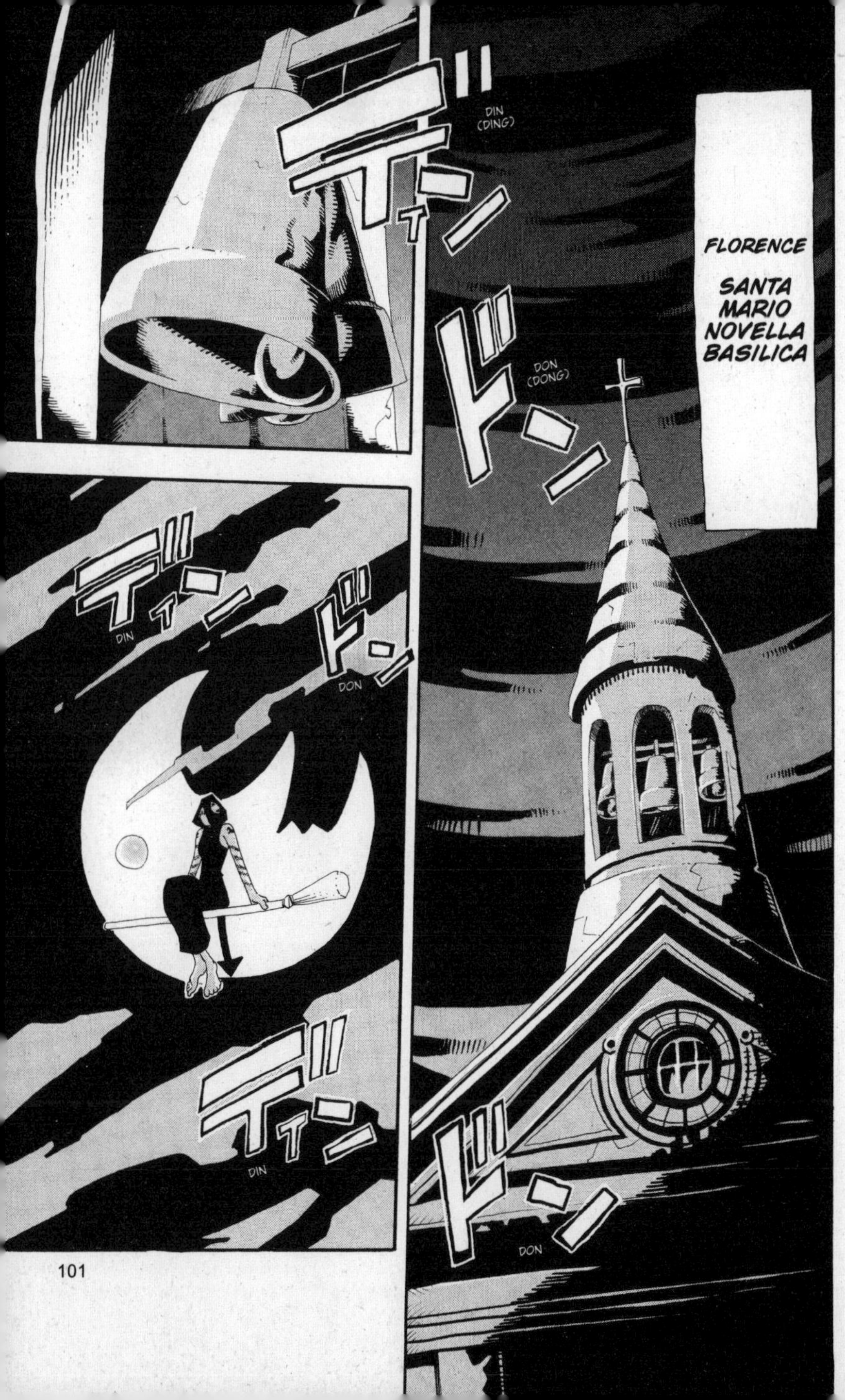
FLORENCE
SANTA MARIO NOVELLA BASILICA
DIN (DING)
DON (DONG)
DON
DIN
DON
DIN

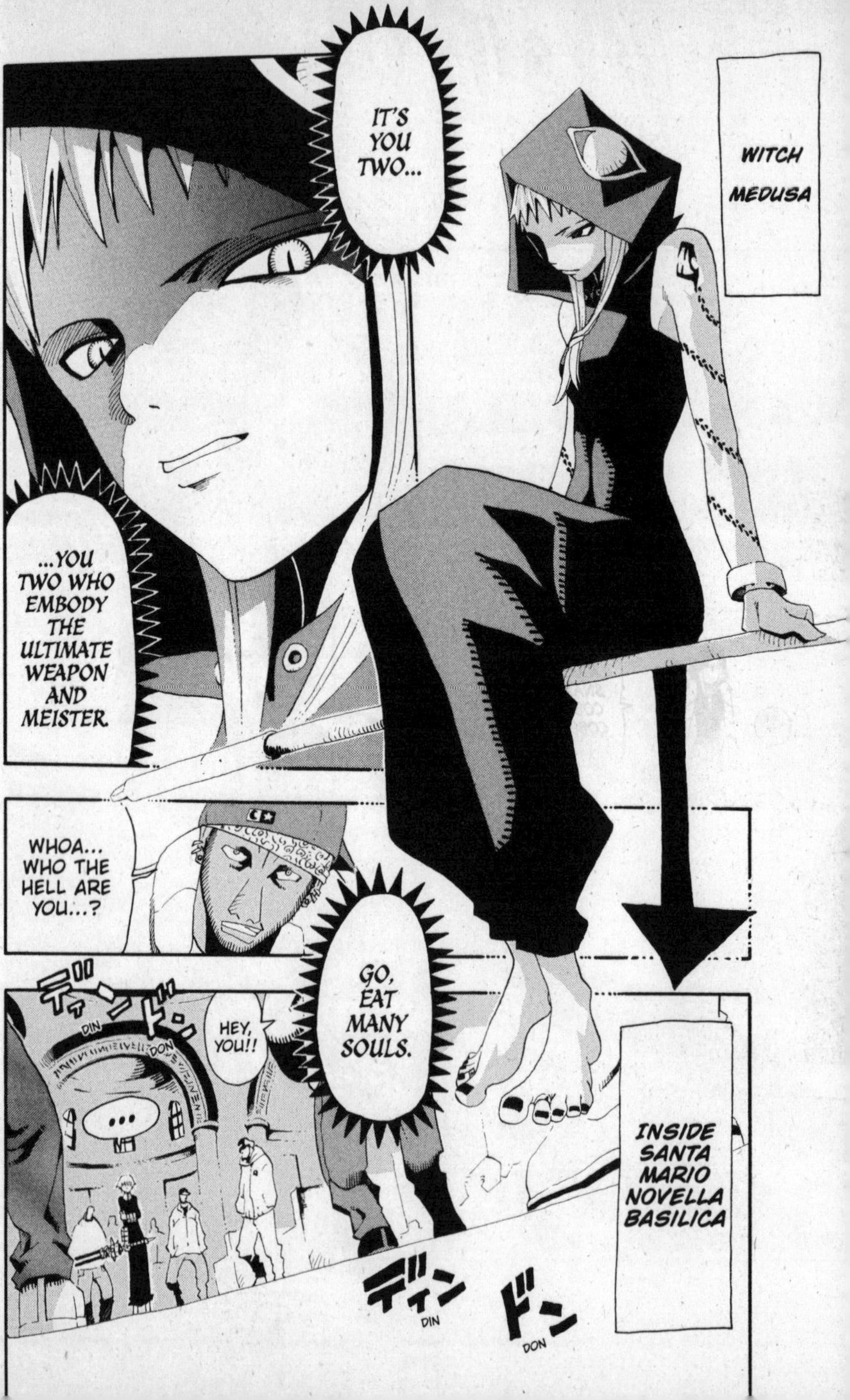

WITCH MEDUSA
IT'S YOU TWO...
...YOU TWO WHO EMBODY THE ULTIMATE WEAPON AND MEISTER.
WHOA... WHO THE HELL ARE YOU...?
GO, EAT MANY SOULS.
INSIDE SANTA MARIO NOVELLA BASILICA
HEY, YOU!!
...
DIN DON
ディン ドン
DIN DON

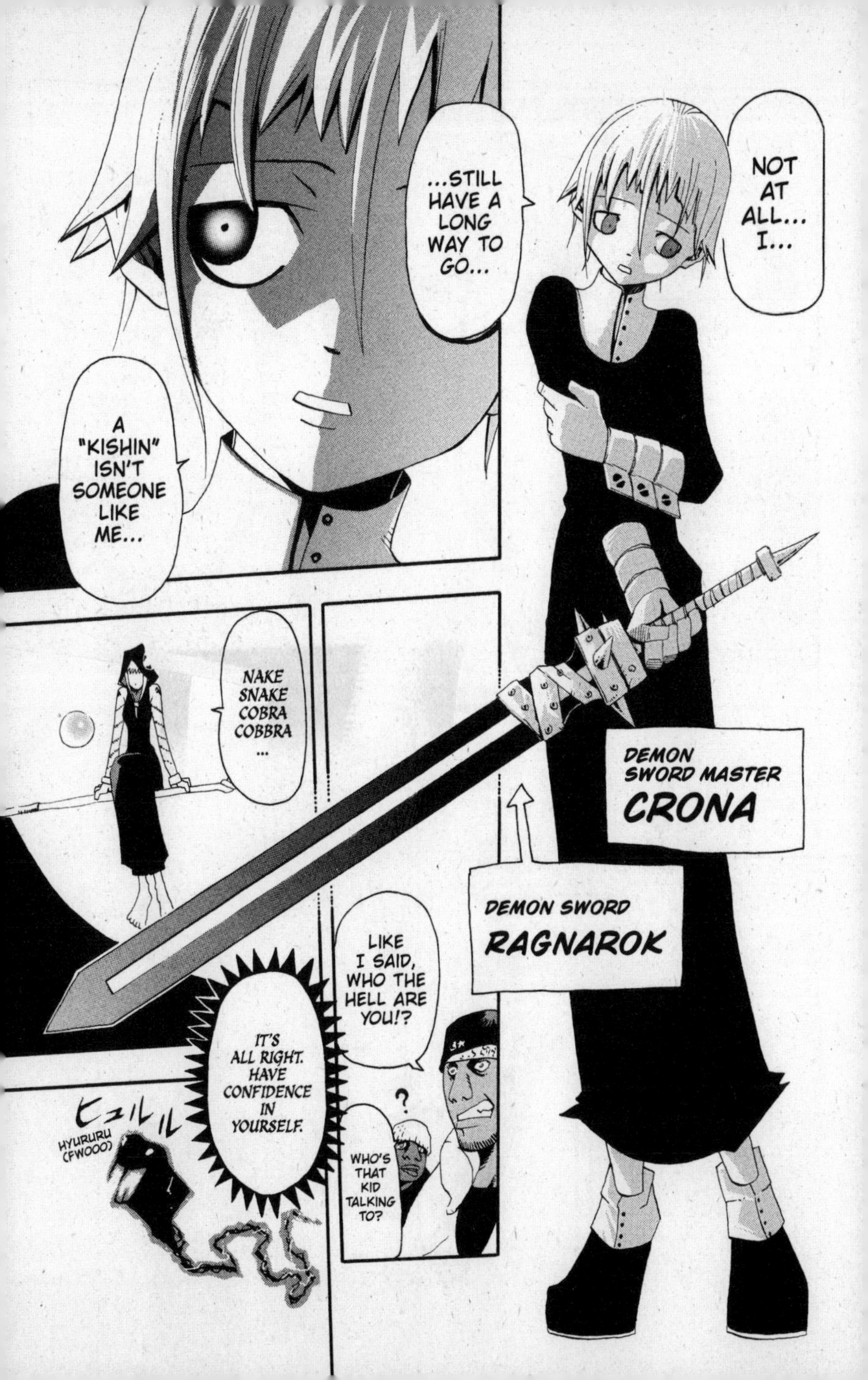
NOT AT ALL... I...
DEMON SWORD MASTER CRONA
DEMON SWORD RAGNAROK
...STILL HAVE A LONG WAY TO GO...
A "KISHIN" ISN'T SOMEONE LIKE ME...
LIKE I SAID, WHO THE HELL ARE YOU!?
?
WHO'S THAT KID TALKING TO?
NAKE SNAKE COBRA COBBRA ...
IT'S ALL RIGHT. HAVE CONFIDENCE IN YOURSELF.
ヒュルルル
HYURURU (FWOOO)

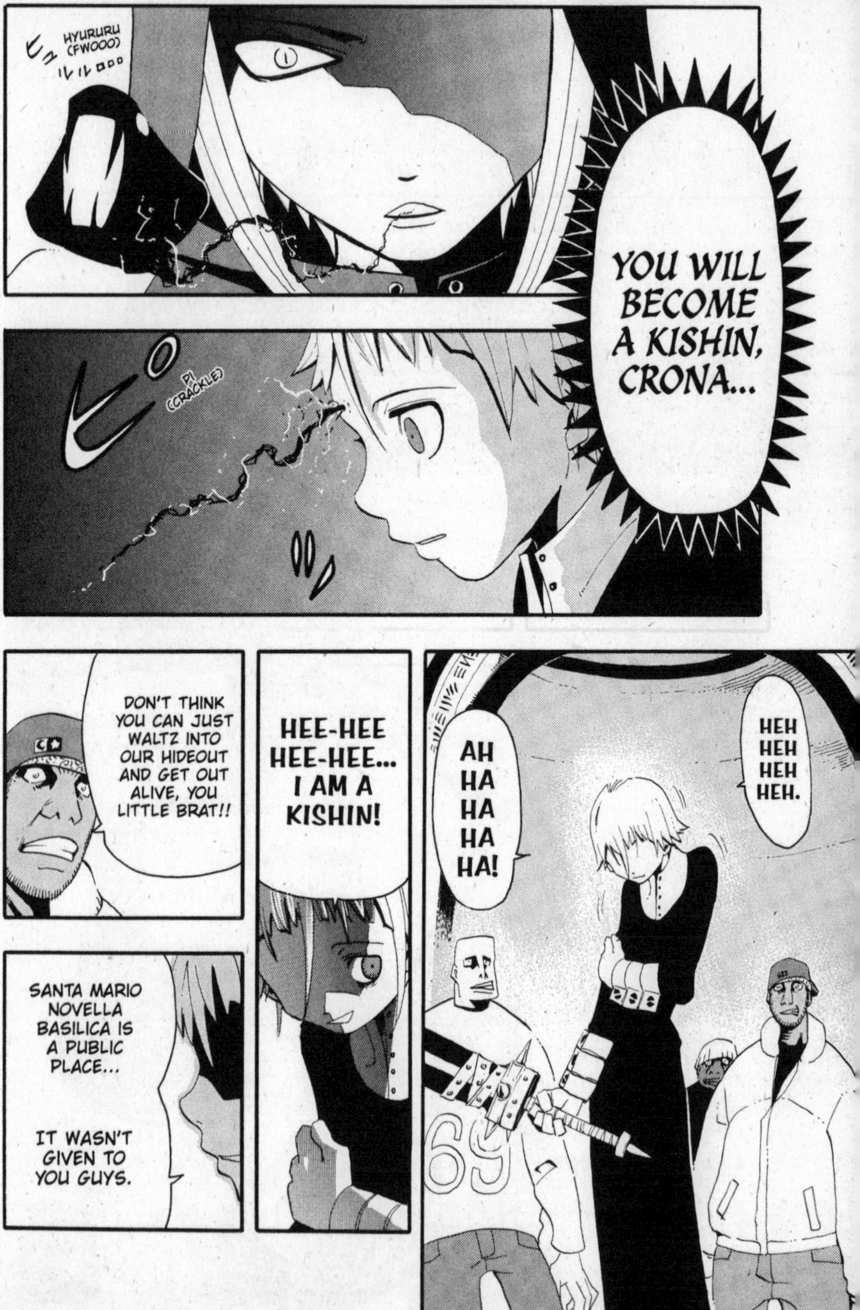
YOU WILL BECOME A KISHIN, CRONA...
HYURURU (FWOOO)
PI (CRACKLE)
HEH HEH HEH HEH.
AH HA HA HA HA HA!
HEE-HEE HEE-HEE... I AM A KISHIN!
DON'T THINK YOU CAN JUST WALTZ INTO OUR HIDEOUT AND GET OUT ALIVE, YOU LITTLE BRAT!!
SANTA MARIO NOVELLA BASILICA IS A PUBLIC PLACE...
IT WASN'T GIVEN TO YOU GUYS.

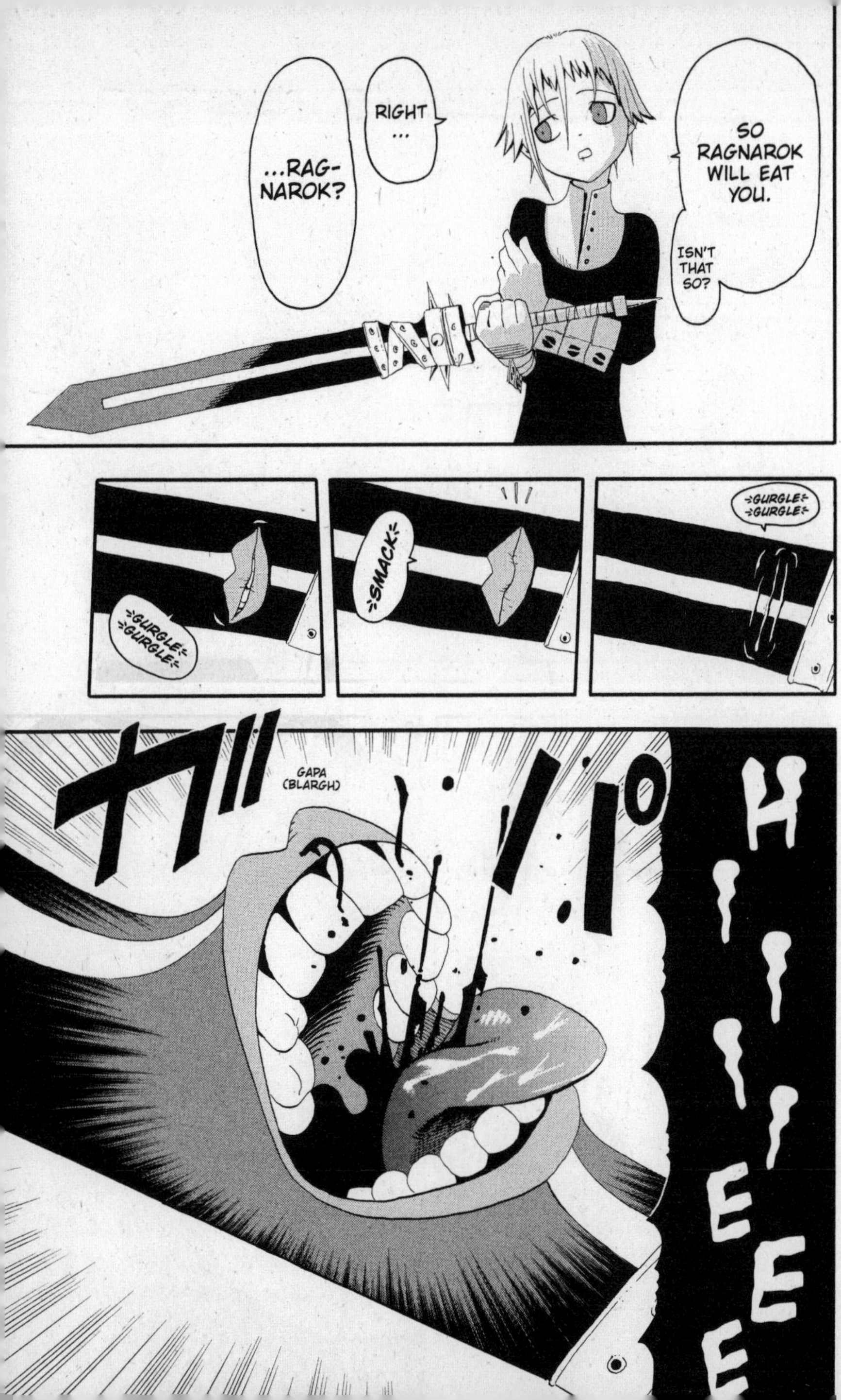
SO RAGNAROK WILL EAT YOU.
ISN'T THAT SO?
RIGHT...
...RAG-NAROK?
GURGLE GURGLE
SMACK
GURGLE GURGLE
GAPA (BLARGH)

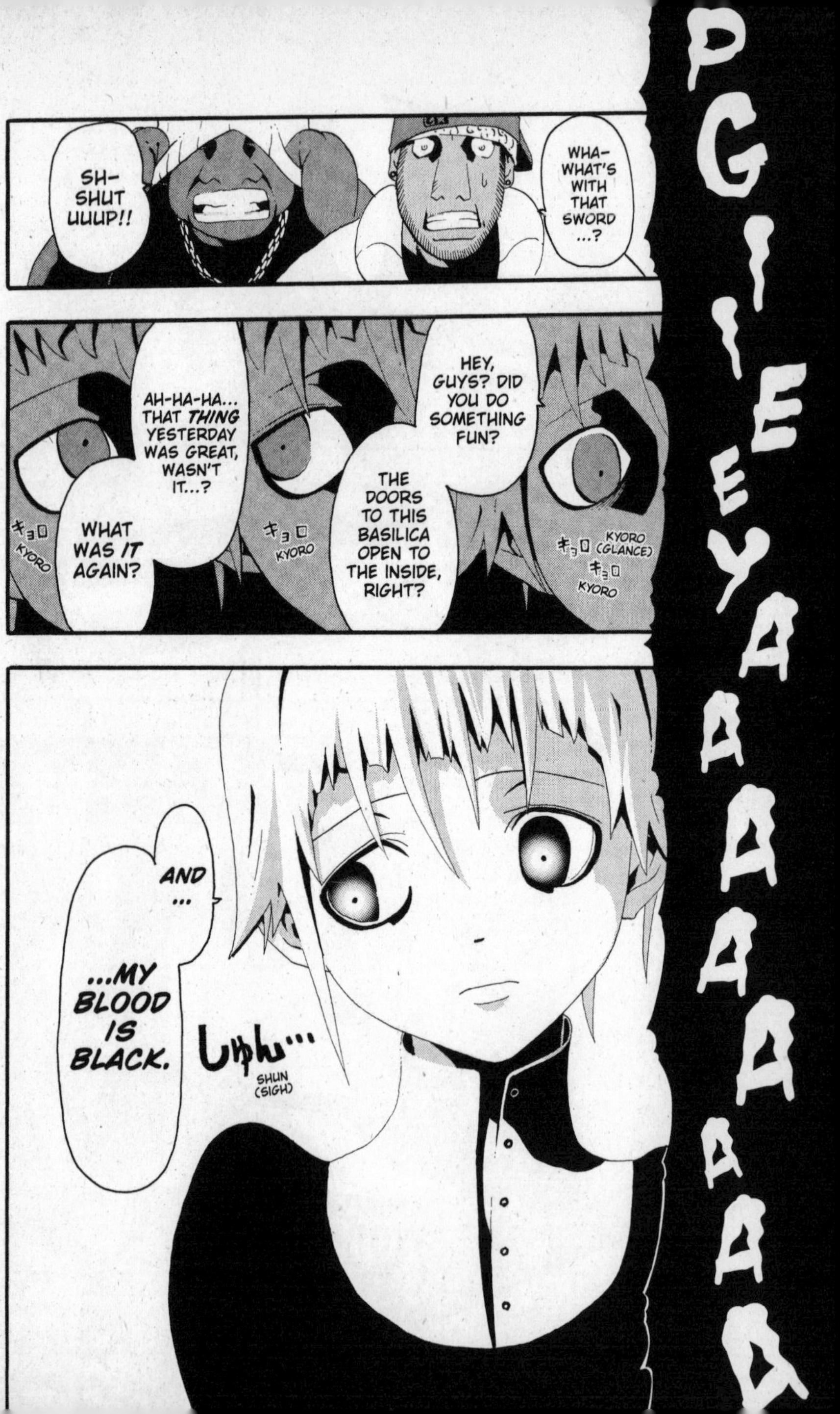
PGIIEEYAAAAAAAAAA
WHA- WHAT'S WITH THAT SWORD ...?
SH- SHUT UUUP!!
HEY, GUYS? DID YOU DO SOMETHING FUN?
キョロ KYORO (GLANCE)
キョロ KYORO
THE DOORS TO THIS BASILICA OPEN TO THE INSIDE, RIGHT?
キョロ KYORO
AH-HA-HA... THAT *THING* YESTERDAY WAS GREAT, WASN'T IT...?
WHAT WAS *IT* AGAIN?
キョロ KYORO
AND ...
...MY BLOOD IS BLACK.
しゅん… SHUN (SIGH)

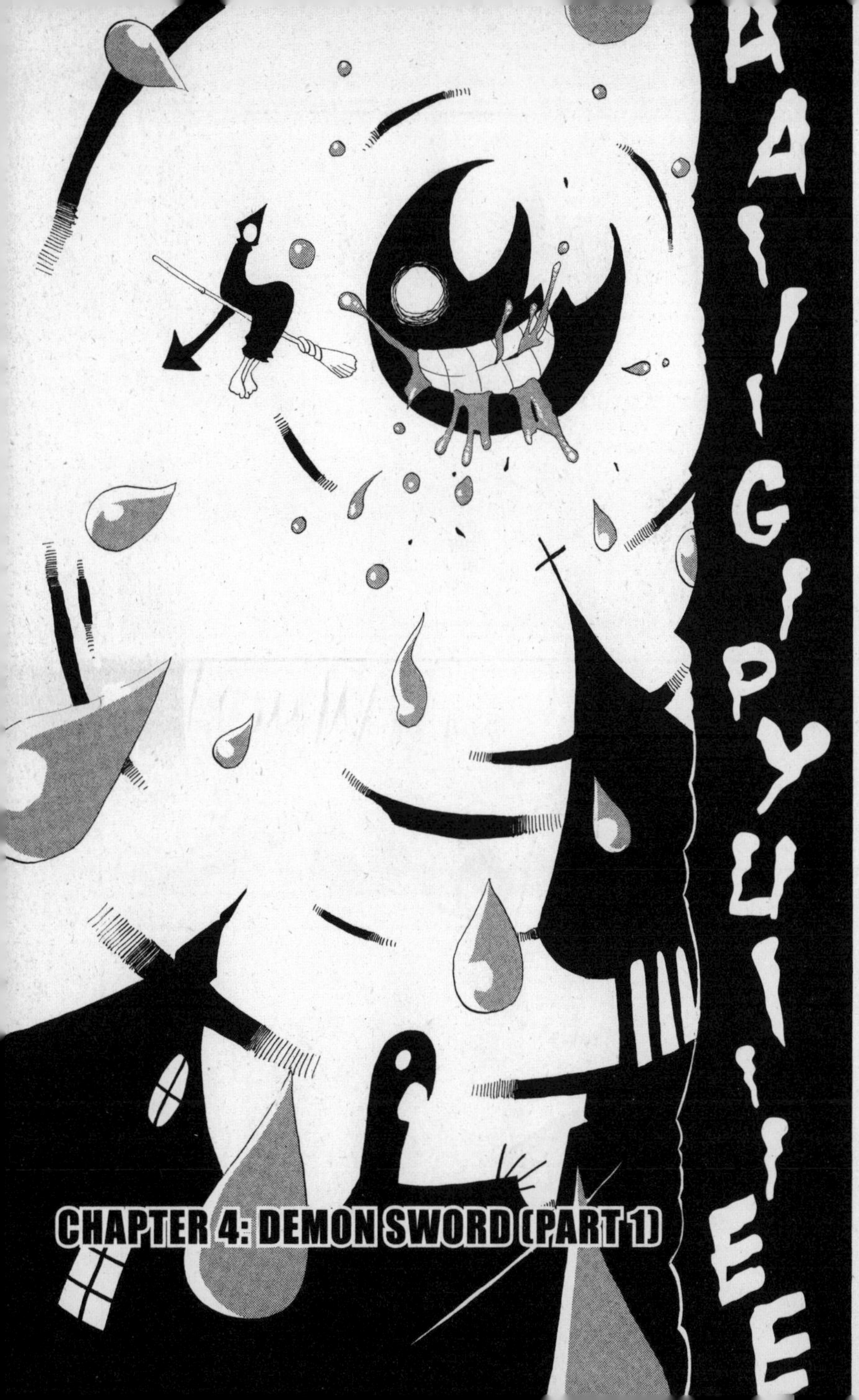

CHAPTER 4: DEMON SWORD (PART 1)

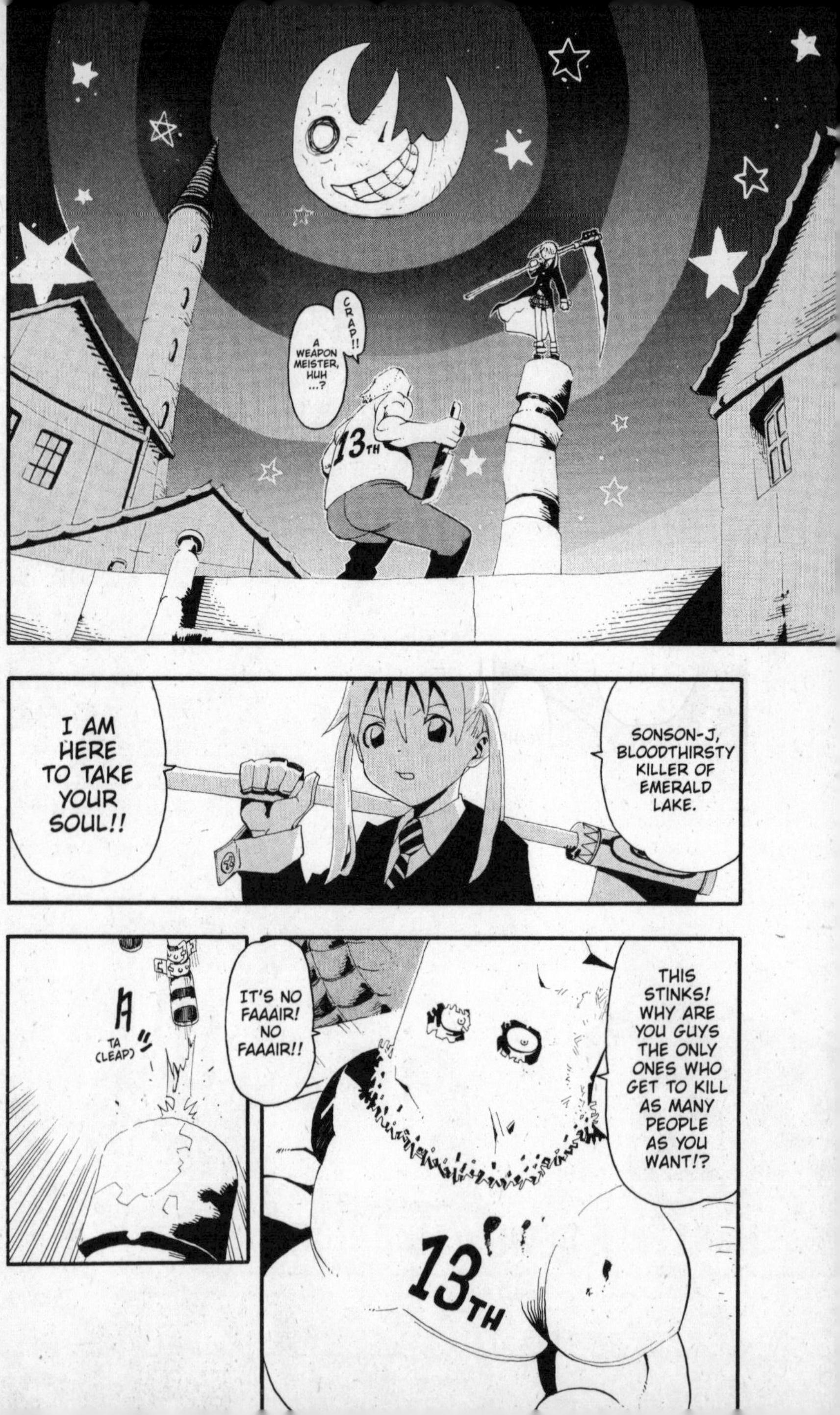
CRAP!!
A WEAPON MEISTER, HUH ...?
SONSON-J, BLOODTHIRSTY KILLER OF EMERALD LAKE.
I AM HERE TO TAKE YOUR SOUL!!
THIS STINKS! WHY ARE YOU GUYS THE ONLY ONES WHO GET TO KILL AS MANY PEOPLE AS YOU WANT!?
IT'S NO FAAAIR! NO FAAAIR!!
TA (LEAP)

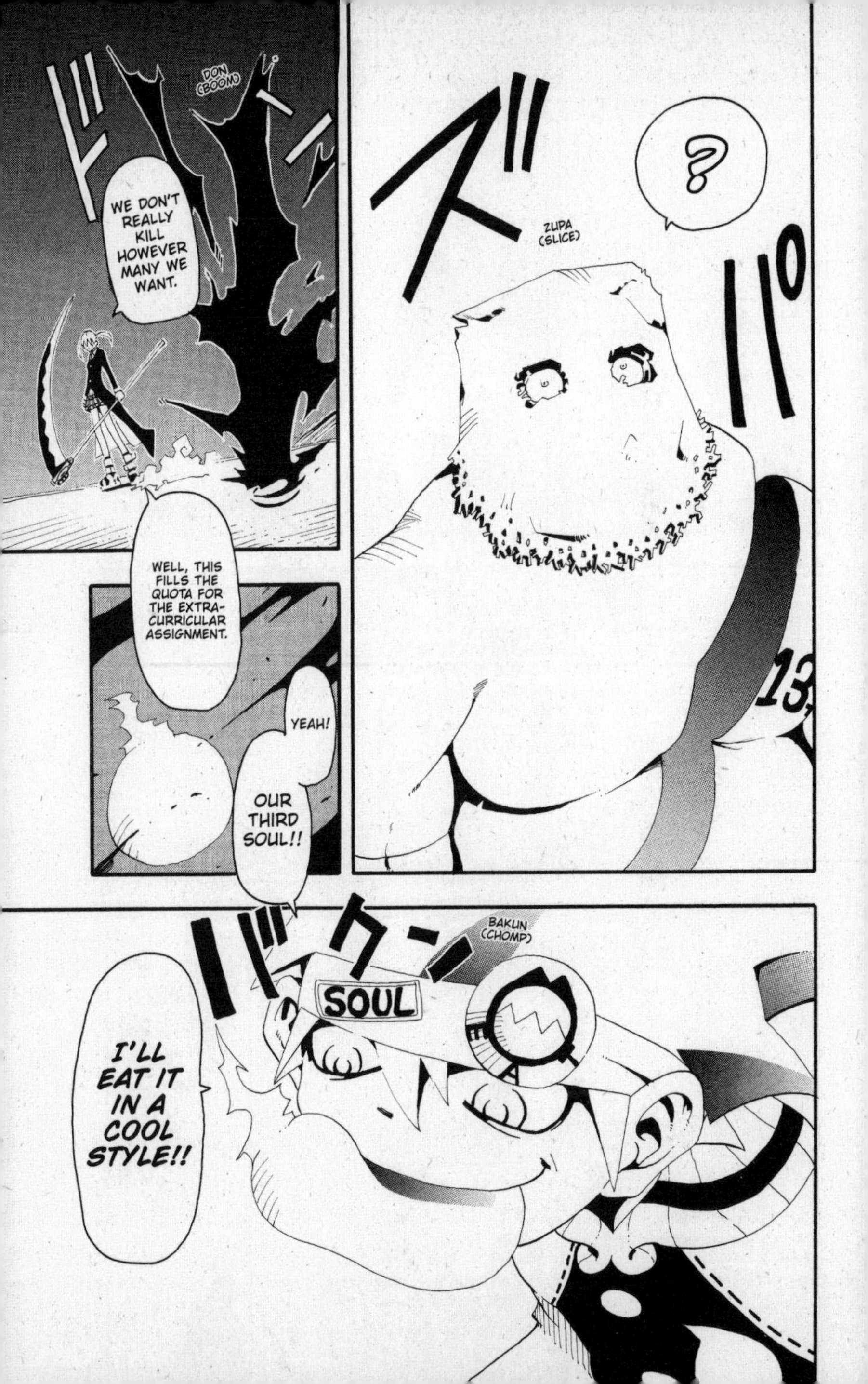
?
ZUPA (SLICE)
DON (BOOM)
WE DON'T REALLY KILL HOWEVER MANY WE WANT.
WELL, THIS FILLS THE QUOTA FOR THE EXTRA-CURRICULAR ASSIGNMENT.
YEAH!
OUR THIRD SOUL!!
BAKUN (CHOMP)
SOUL
I'LL EAT IT IN A COOL STYLE!!

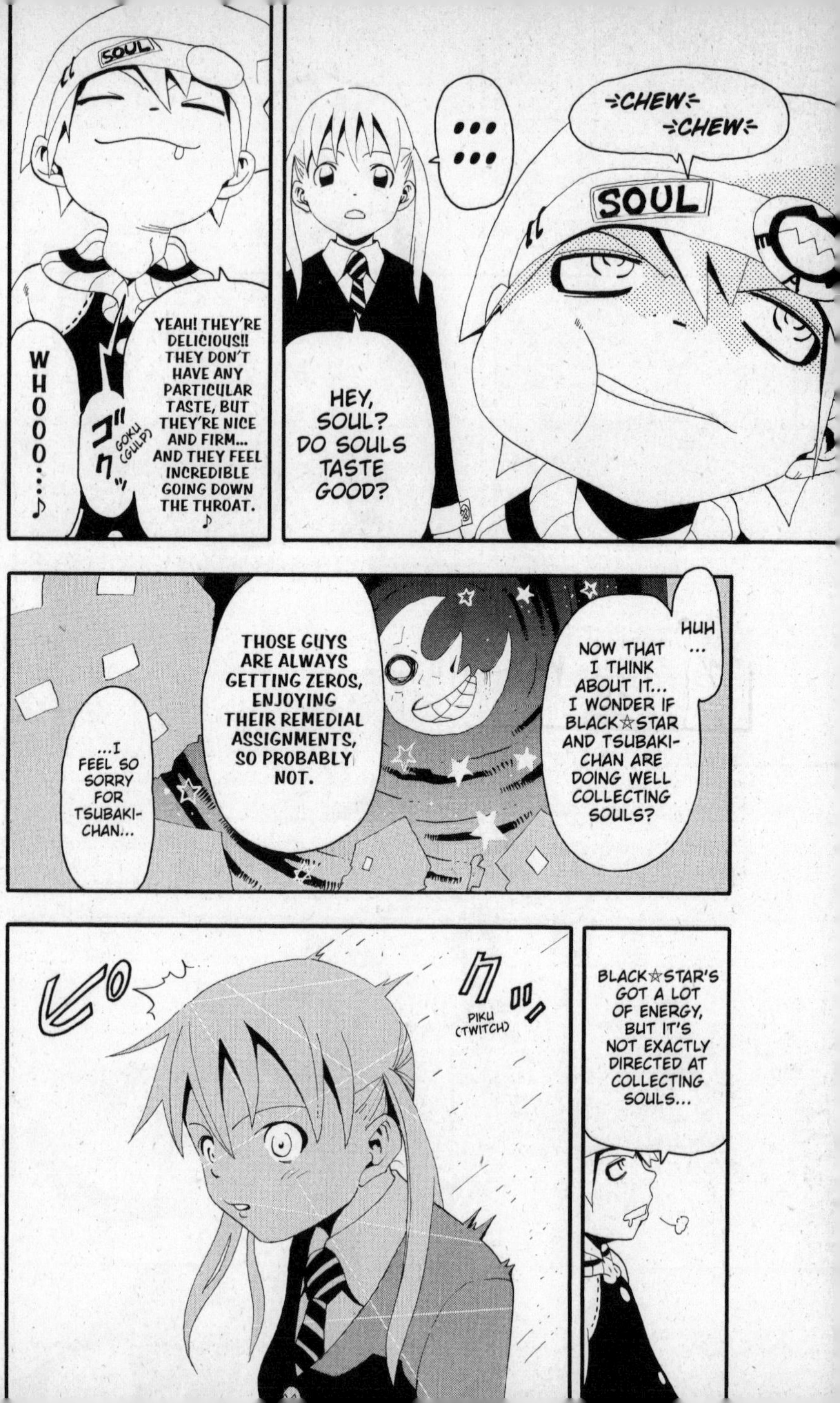

-CHEW- -CHEW-
......
HEY, SOUL? DO SOULS TASTE GOOD?
YEAH! THEY'RE DELICIOUS!! THEY DON'T HAVE ANY PARTICULAR TASTE, BUT THEY'RE NICE AND FIRM... AND THEY FEEL INCREDIBLE GOING DOWN THE THROAT. ♪
GOKU (GULP)
WHOOOO...♪
HUH...
NOW THAT I THINK ABOUT IT... I WONDER IF BLACK☆STAR AND TSUBAKI-CHAN ARE DOING WELL COLLECTING SOULS?
THOSE GUYS ARE ALWAYS GETTING ZEROS, ENJOYING THEIR REMEDIAL ASSIGNMENTS, SO PROBABLY NOT.
...I FEEL SO SORRY FOR TSUBAKI-CHAN...
BLACK☆STAR'S GOT A LOT OF ENERGY, BUT IT'S NOT EXACTLY DIRECTED AT COLLECTING SOULS...
PIKU (TWITCH)

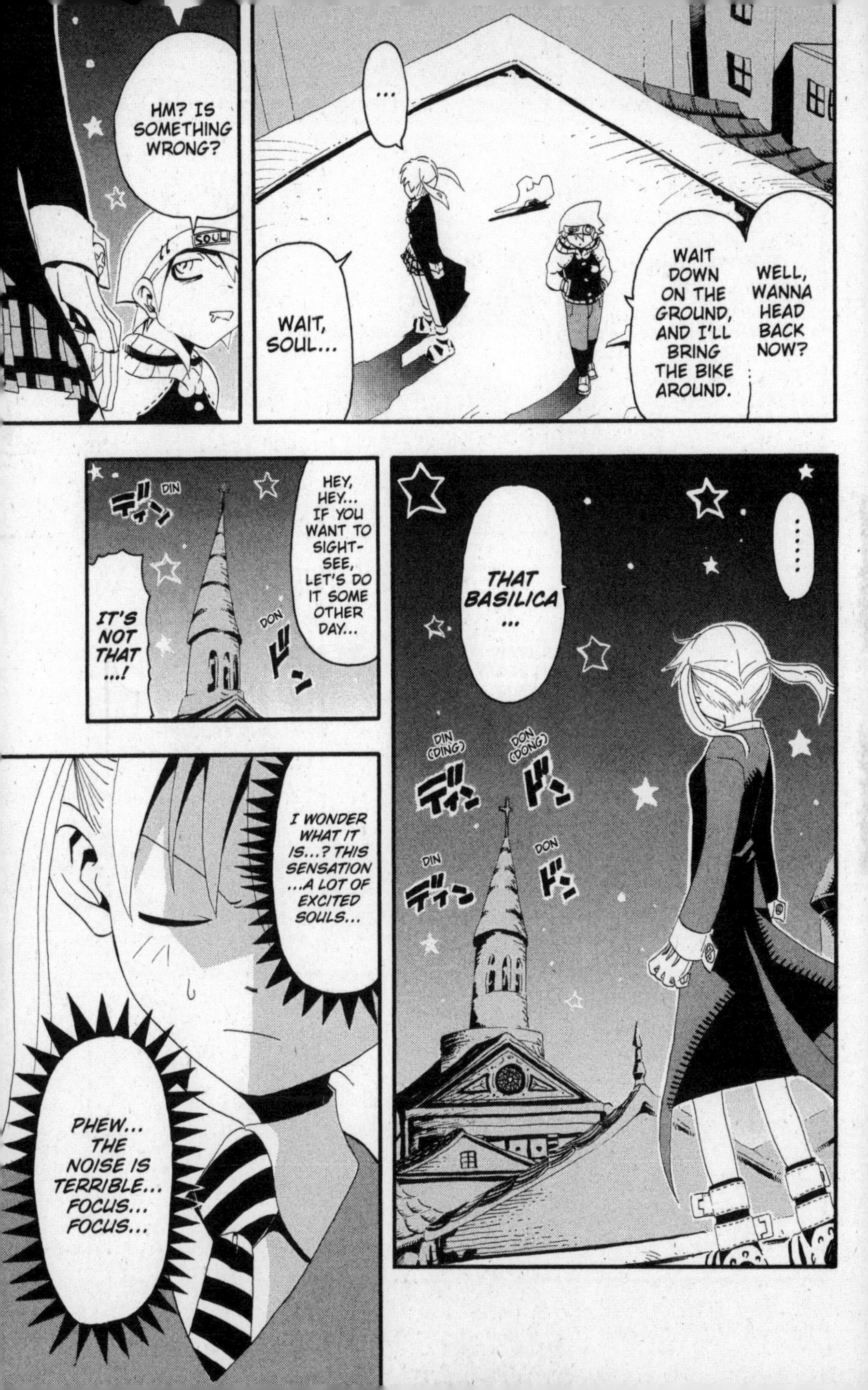
WELL, WANNA HEAD BACK NOW?
WAIT DOWN ON THE GROUND, AND I'LL BRING THE BIKE AROUND.
...
WAIT, SOUL...
HM? IS SOMETHING WRONG?
SOUL
......
THAT BASILICA ...
DIN (DING)
ディン
DON (DONG)
ドン
DIN
ディン
DON
ドン
HEY, HEY... IF YOU WANT TO SIGHT-SEE, LET'S DO IT SOME OTHER DAY...
DIN
ディン
DON
ドン
IT'S NOT THAT ...!
I WONDER WHAT IT IS...? THIS SENSATION ...A LOT OF EXCITED SOULS...
PHEW... THE NOISE IS TERRIBLE... FOCUS... FOCUS...

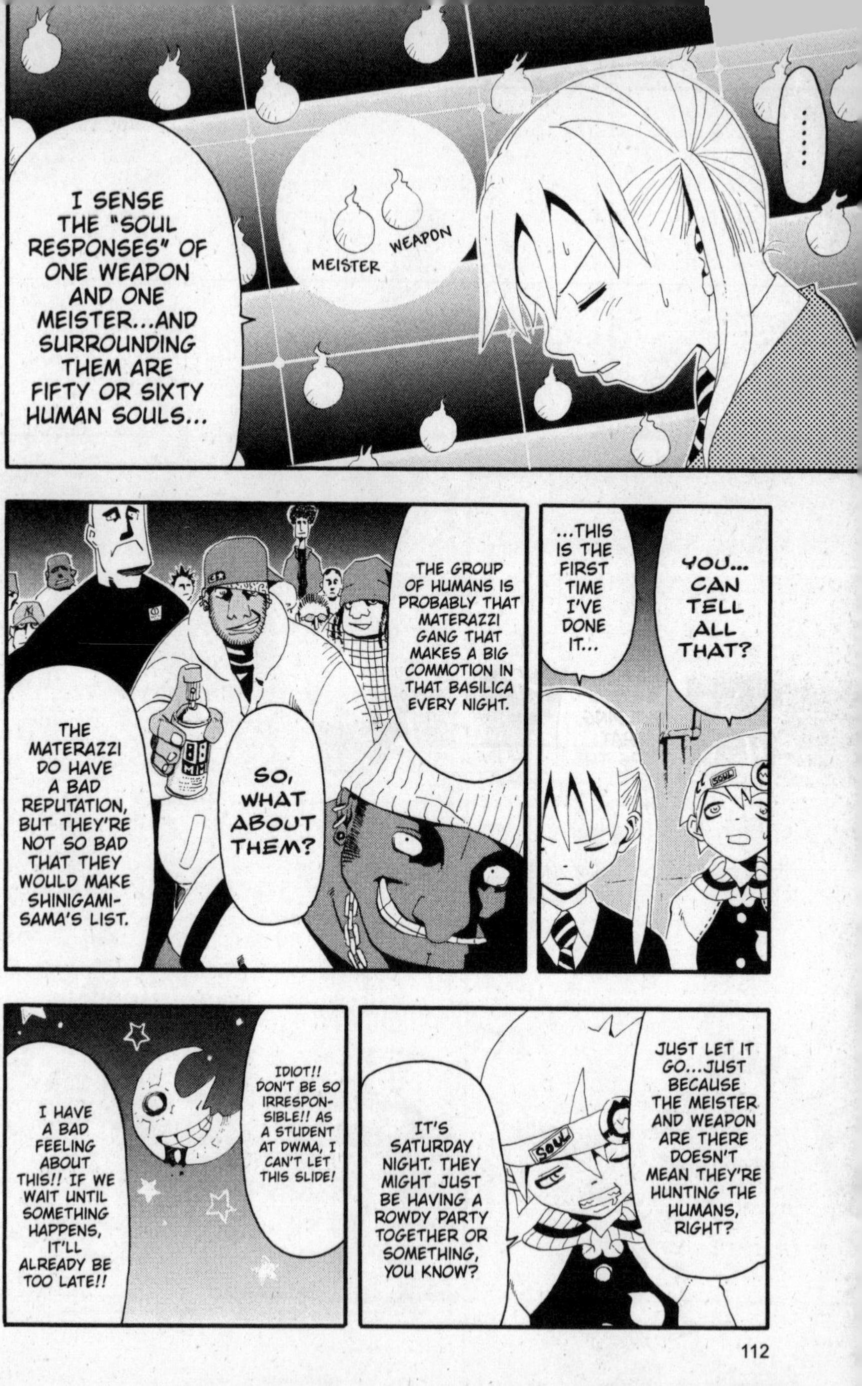
......
WEAPON
MEISTER
I SENSE THE "SOUL RESPONSES" OF ONE WEAPON AND ONE MEISTER...AND SURROUNDING THEM ARE FIFTY OR SIXTY HUMAN SOULS...
YOU... CAN TELL ALL THAT?
...THIS IS THE FIRST TIME I'VE DONE IT...
THE GROUP OF HUMANS IS PROBABLY THAT MATERAZZI GANG THAT MAKES A BIG COMMOTION IN THAT BASILICA EVERY NIGHT.
SO, WHAT ABOUT THEM?
THE MATERAZZI DO HAVE A BAD REPUTATION, BUT THEY'RE NOT SO BAD THAT THEY WOULD MAKE SHINIGAMI-SAMA'S LIST.
JUST LET IT GO...JUST BECAUSE THE MEISTER AND WEAPON ARE THERE DOESN'T MEAN THEY'RE HUNTING THE HUMANS, RIGHT?
IT'S SATURDAY NIGHT. THEY MIGHT JUST BE HAVING A ROWDY PARTY TOGETHER OR SOMETHING, YOU KNOW?
IDIOT!! DON'T BE SO IRRESPONSIBLE!! AS A STUDENT AT DWMA, I CAN'T LET THIS SLIDE!
I HAVE A BAD FEELING ABOUT THIS!! IF WE WAIT UNTIL SOMETHING HAPPENS, IT'LL ALREADY BE TOO LATE!!

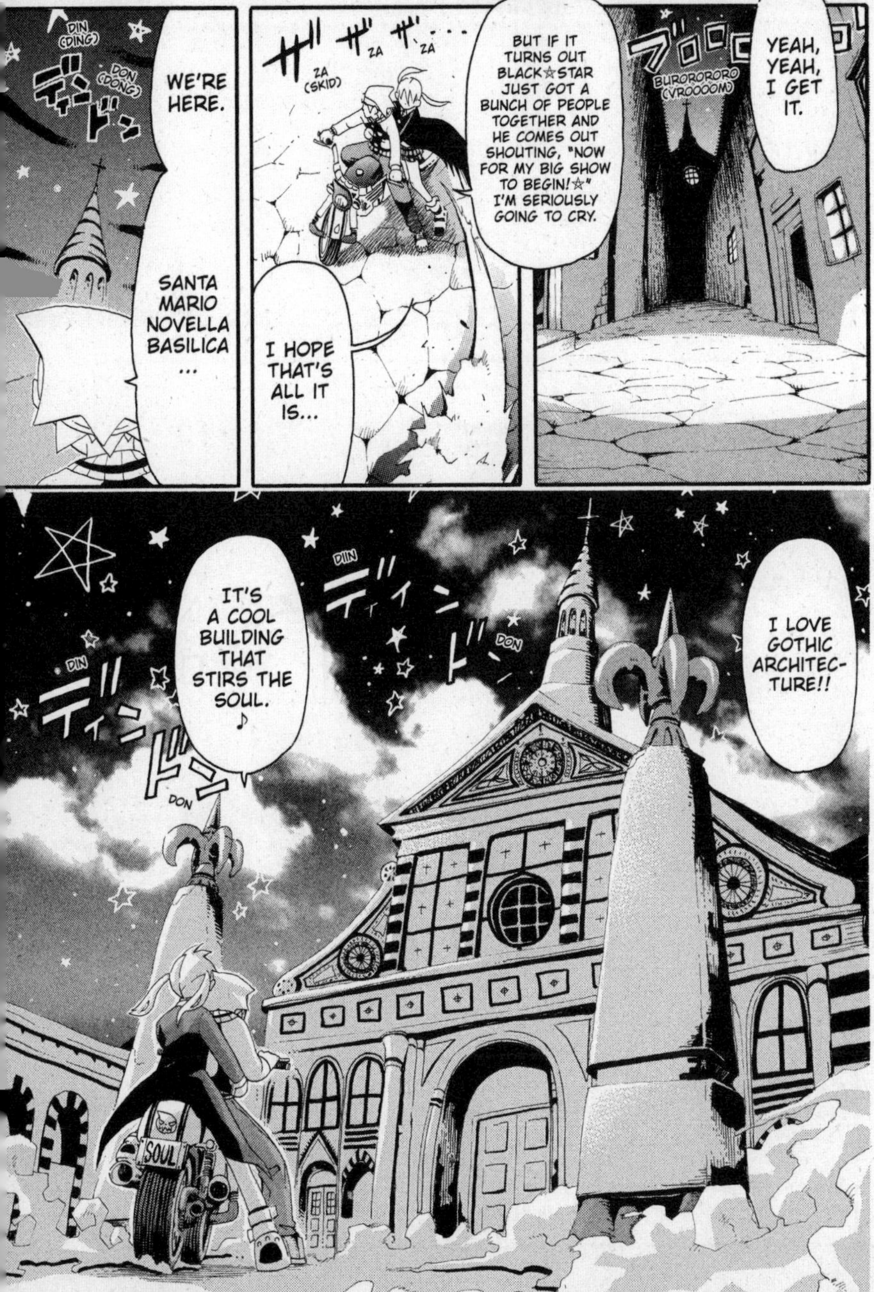
BURORORORO (VROOOOM)
YEAH, YEAH, I GET IT.
ZA (SKID) ZA ZA
BUT IF IT TURNS OUT BLACK☆STAR JUST GOT A BUNCH OF PEOPLE TOGETHER AND HE COMES OUT SHOUTING, "NOW FOR MY BIG SHOW TO BEGIN!☆" I'M SERIOUSLY GOING TO CRY.
I HOPE THAT'S ALL IT IS...
DIN (DING) DON (DONG)
WE'RE HERE.
SANTA MARIO NOVELLA BASILICA ...
I LOVE GOTHIC ARCHITECTURE!!
DIIN DON
IT'S A COOL BUILDING THAT STIRS THE SOUL. ♪
DIIN DON
SOUL

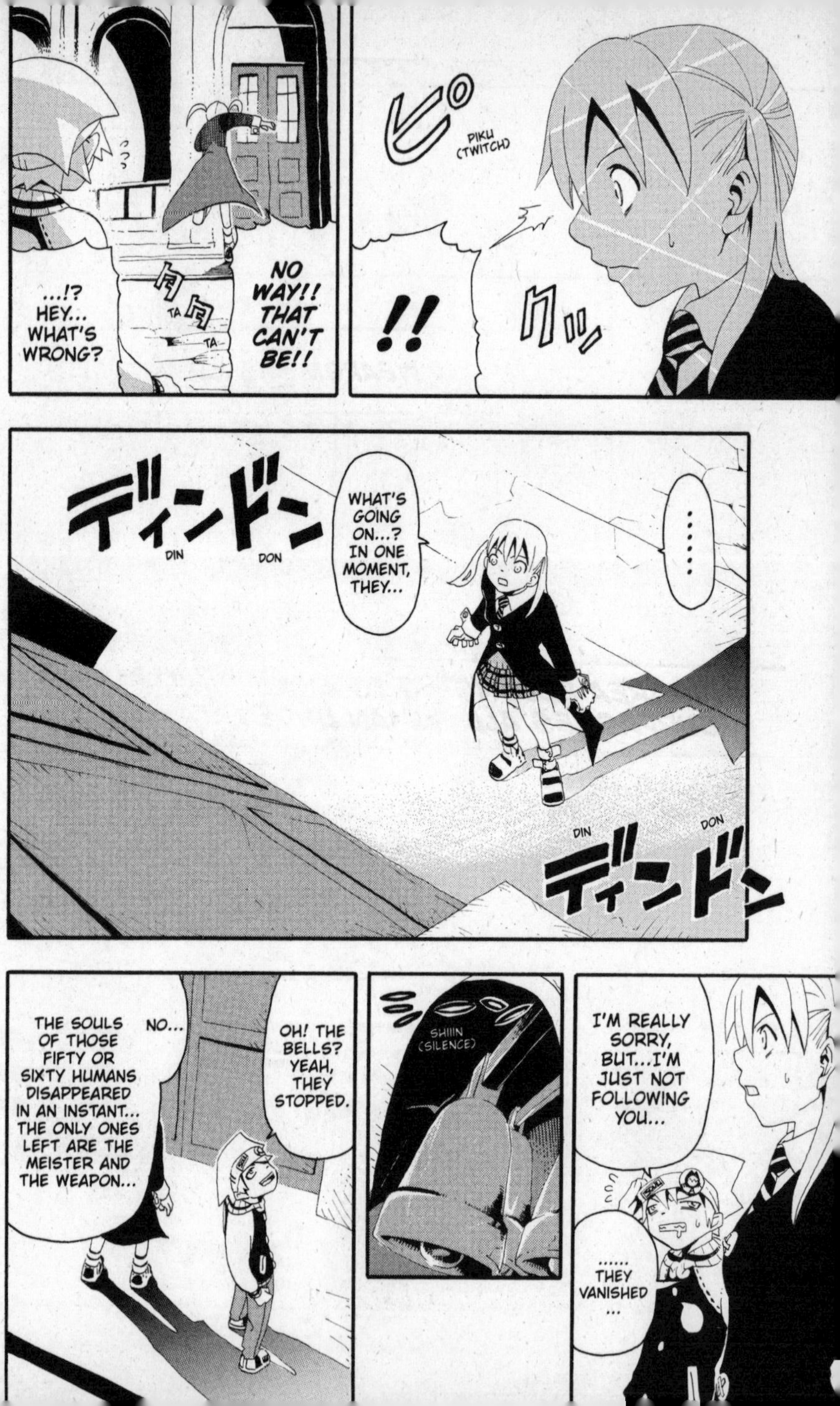
ピ
PIKU (TWITCH)
!!
NO WAY!! THAT CAN'T BE!!
...!? HEY... WHAT'S WRONG?
TA TA
......
WHAT'S GOING ON...? IN ONE MOMENT, THEY...
ディンドン
DIN DON
DIN DON
ディンドン
I'M REALLY SORRY, BUT...I'M JUST NOT FOLLOWING YOU...
...... THEY VANISHED ...
SHIIN (SILENCE)
OH! THE BELLS? YEAH, THEY STOPPED.
NO...
THE SOULS OF THOSE FIFTY OR SIXTY HUMANS DISAPPEARED IN AN INSTANT... THE ONLY ONES LEFT ARE THE MEISTER AND THE WEAPON...

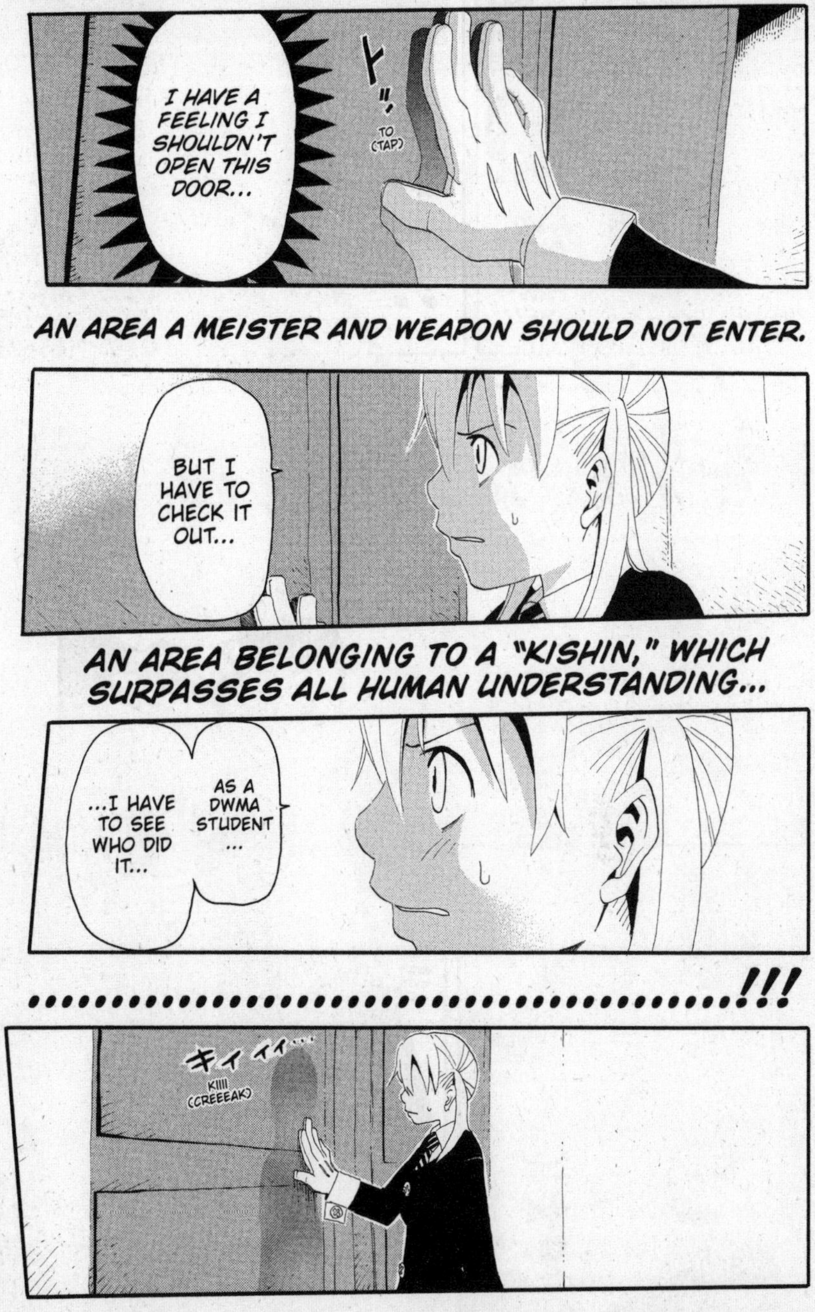
ト"
TO (TAP)
I HAVE A FEELING I SHOULDN'T OPEN THIS DOOR...
AN AREA A MEISTER AND WEAPON SHOULD NOT ENTER.
BUT I HAVE TO CHECK IT OUT...
AN AREA BELONGING TO A "KISHIN," WHICH SURPASSES ALL HUMAN UNDERSTANDING...
AS A DWMA STUDENT ...
...I HAVE TO SEE WHO DID IT...
......................................!!!
キイイイ...
KIIII (CREEEAK)

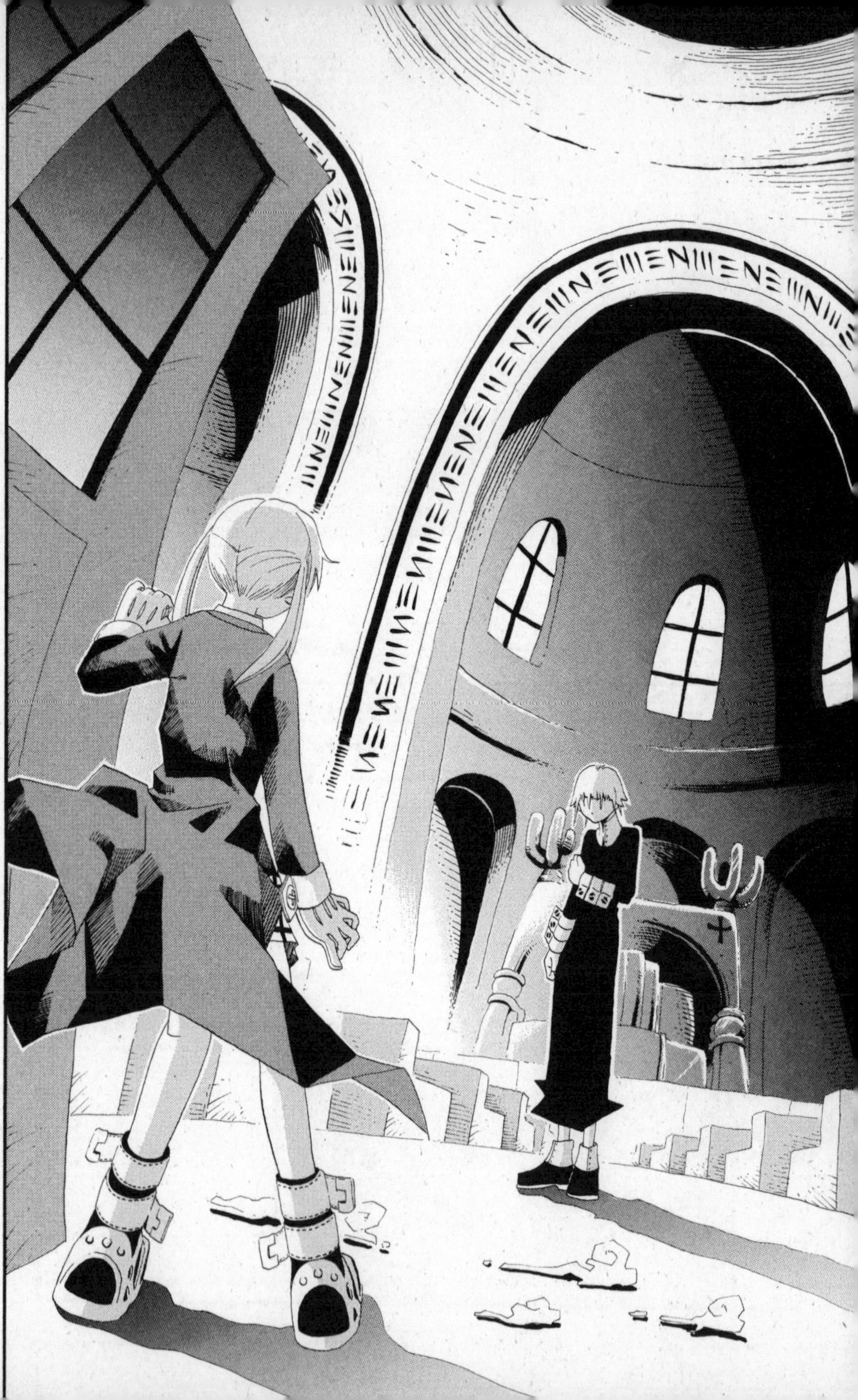

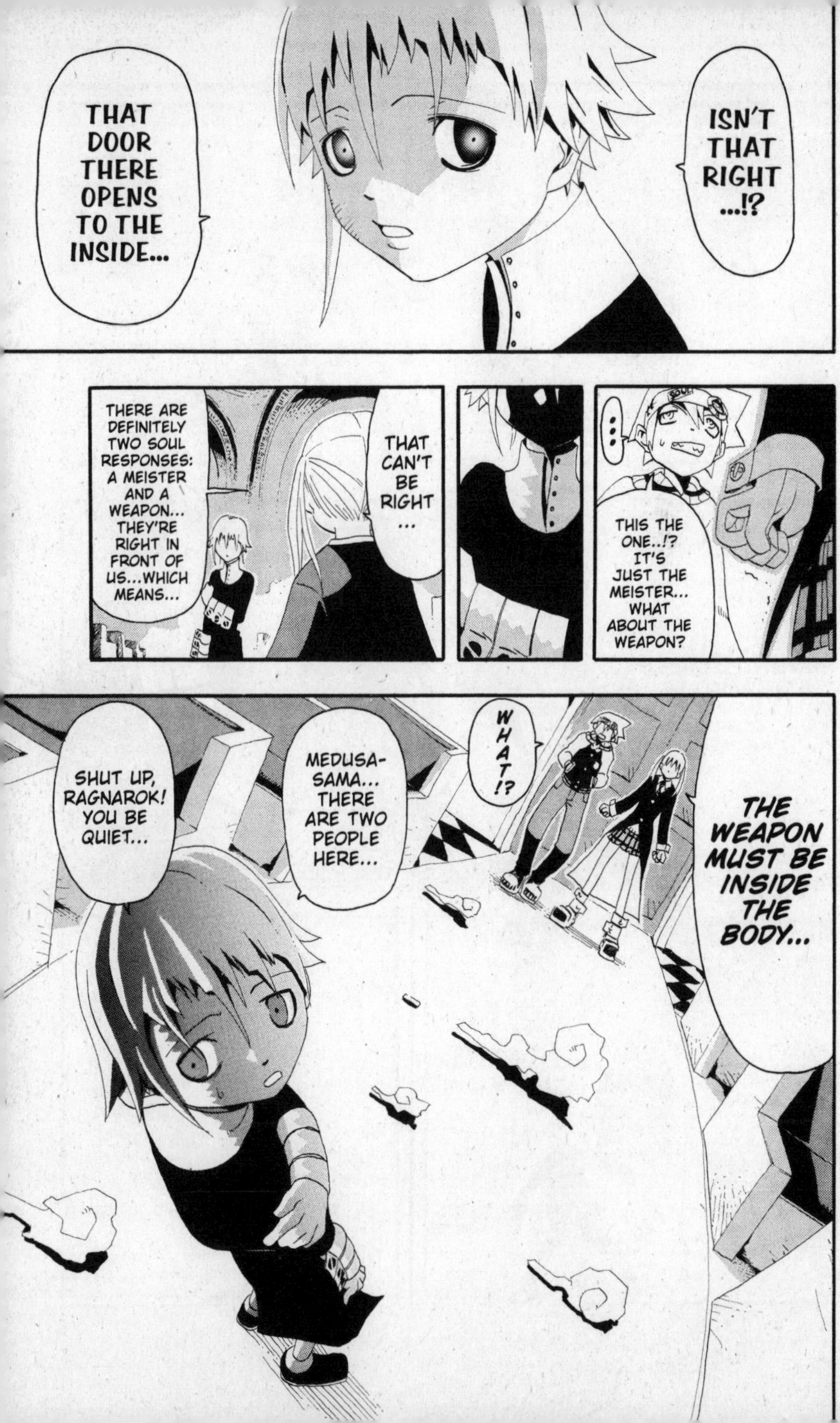
ISN'T THAT RIGHT ...!?
THAT DOOR THERE OPENS TO THE INSIDE...
...
THIS THE ONE..!? IT'S JUST THE MEISTER... WHAT ABOUT THE WEAPON?
THAT CAN'T BE RIGHT ...
THERE ARE DEFINITELY TWO SOUL RESPONSES: A MEISTER AND A WEAPON... THEY'RE RIGHT IN FRONT OF US...WHICH MEANS...
THE WEAPON MUST BE INSIDE THE BODY...
WHAT!?
MEDUSA-SAMA... THERE ARE TWO PEOPLE HERE...
SHUT UP, RAGNAROK! YOU BE QUIET...

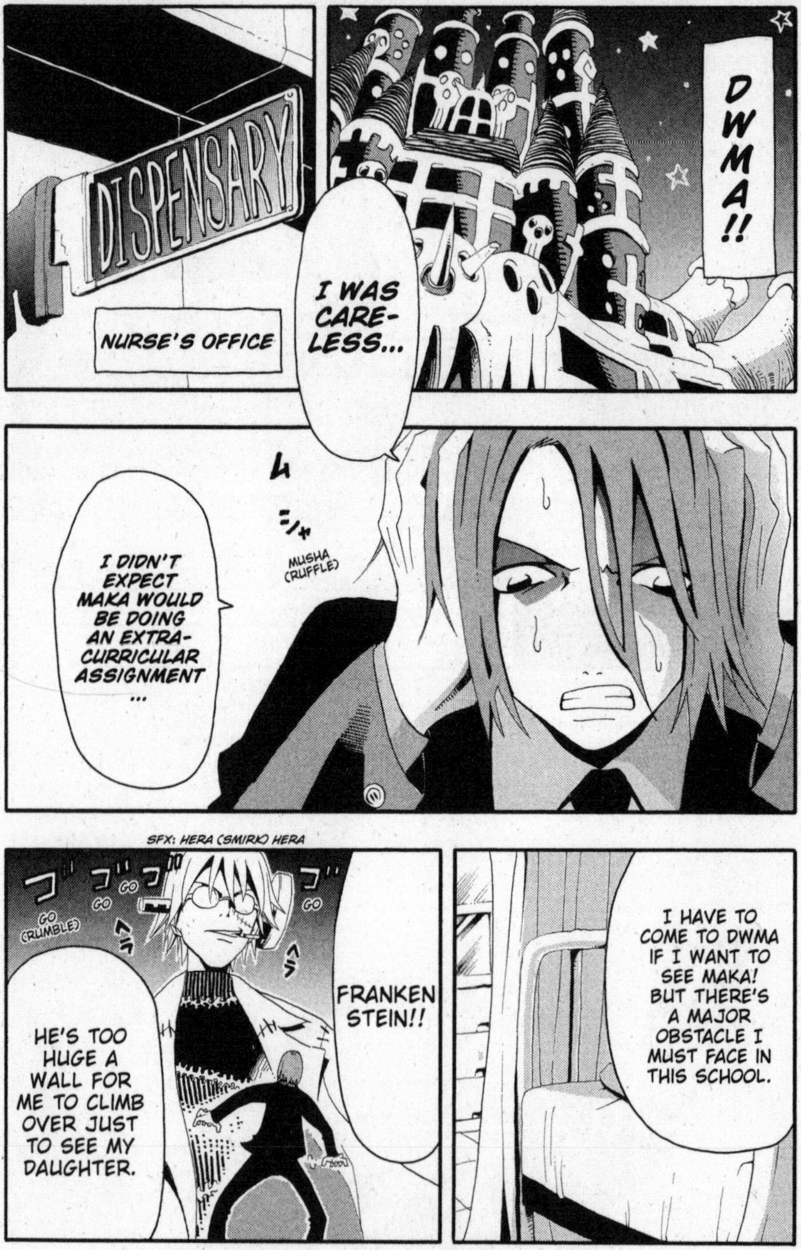
DWMA!!
DISPENSARY
NURSE'S OFFICE
I WAS CARE-LESS...
MUSHA (RUFFLE)
I DIDN'T EXPECT MAKA WOULD BE DOING AN EXTRA-CURRICULAR ASSIGNMENT ...
I HAVE TO COME TO DWMA IF I WANT TO SEE MAKA! BUT THERE'S A MAJOR OBSTACLE I MUST FACE IN THIS SCHOOL.
SFX: HERA (SMIRK) HERA
FRANKEN STEIN!!
GO GO GO GO (RUMBLE)
HE'S TOO HUGE A WALL FOR ME TO CLIMB OVER JUST TO SEE MY DAUGHTER.

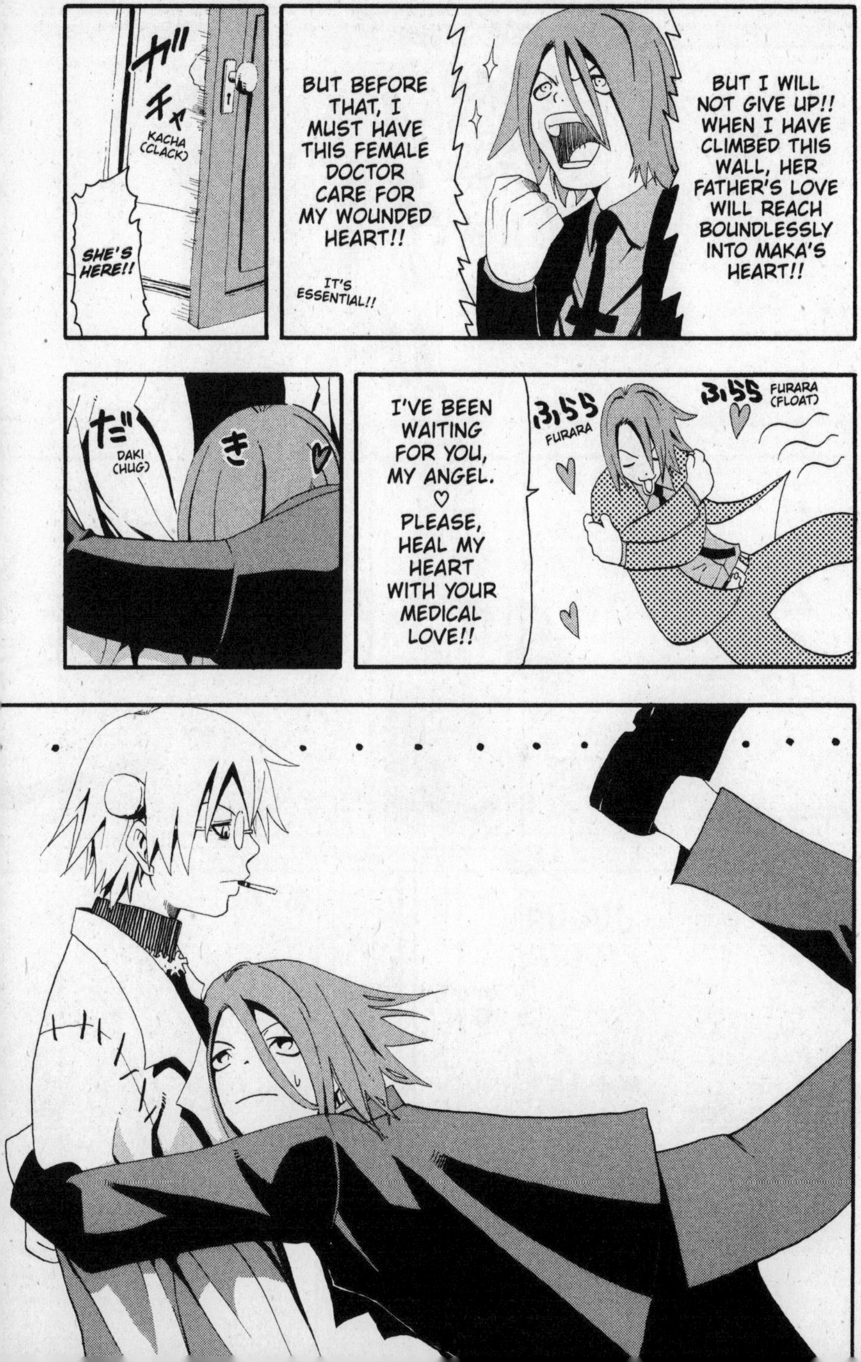
BUT I WILL NOT GIVE UP!! WHEN I HAVE CLIMBED THIS WALL, HER FATHER'S LOVE WILL REACH BOUNDLESSLY INTO MAKA'S HEART!!
BUT BEFORE THAT, I MUST HAVE THIS FEMALE DOCTOR CARE FOR MY WOUNDED HEART!!
IT'S ESSENTIAL!!
ガチャ
KACHA (CLACK)
SHE'S HERE!!
ふらら
FURARA (FLOAT)
ふらら
FURARA
I'VE BEEN WAITING FOR YOU, MY ANGEL. ♡ PLEASE, HEAL MY HEART WITH YOUR MEDICAL LOVE!!
だき
DAKI (HUG)
• • • • • • • • • • • • •

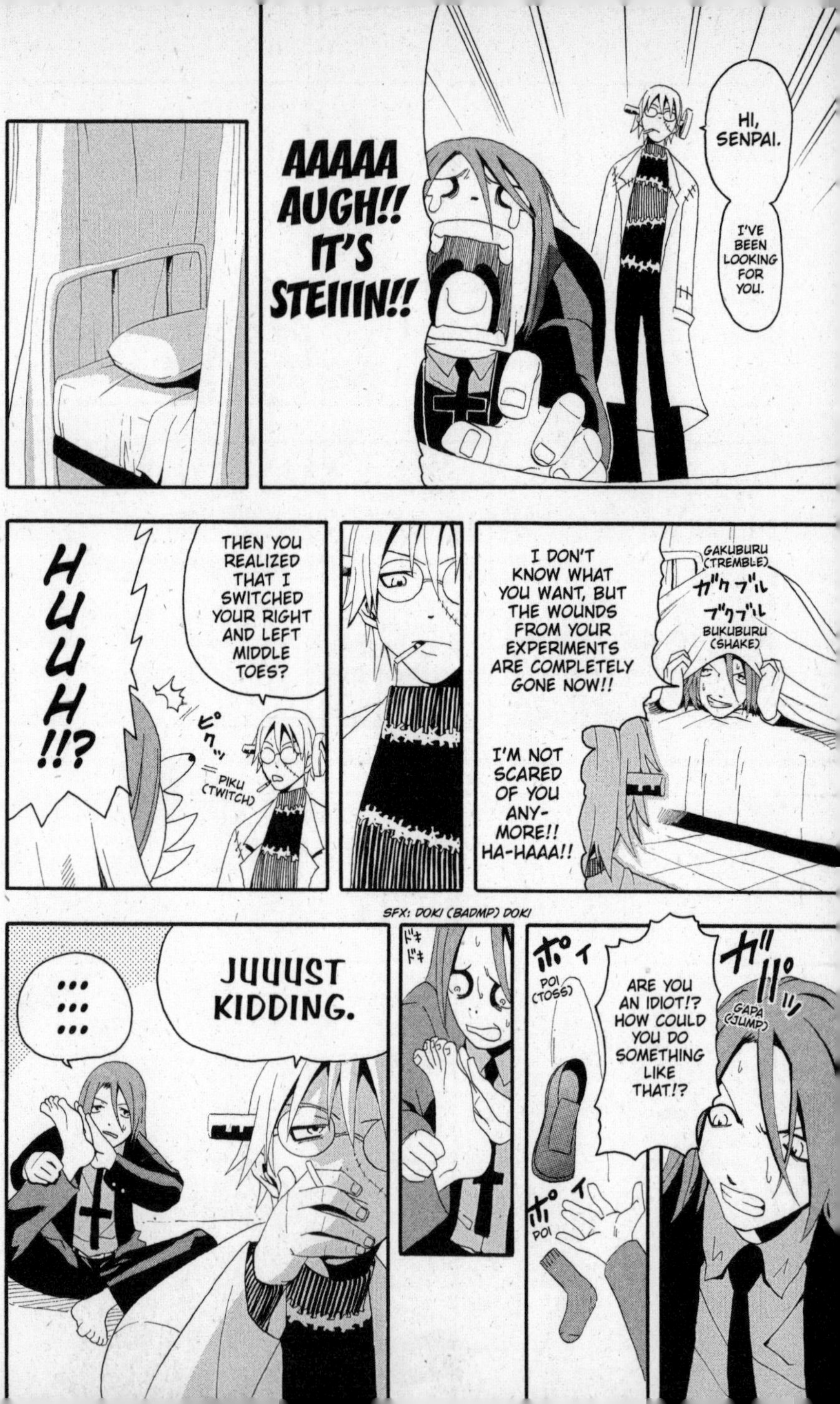
HI, SENPAI.
I'VE BEEN LOOKING FOR YOU.
AAAAA AUGH!! IT'S STEIIIN!!
GAKUBURU (TREMBLE)
ガクブル
ブクブル
BUKUBURU (SHAKE)
I DON'T KNOW WHAT YOU WANT, BUT THE WOUNDS FROM YOUR EXPERIMENTS ARE COMPLETELY GONE NOW!!
I'M NOT SCARED OF YOU ANY-MORE!! HA-HAAA!!
THEN YOU REALIZED THAT I SWITCHED YOUR RIGHT AND LEFT MIDDLE TOES?
ピクッ
PIKU (TWITCH)
HUUUH!!?
SFX: DOKI (BADMP) DOKI
ガバッ
GAPA (JUMP)
ARE YOU AN IDIOT!? HOW COULD YOU DO SOMETHING LIKE THAT!?
ポイ
POI (TOSS)
ポイ
POI
ドキドキ
JUUUST KIDDING.
....

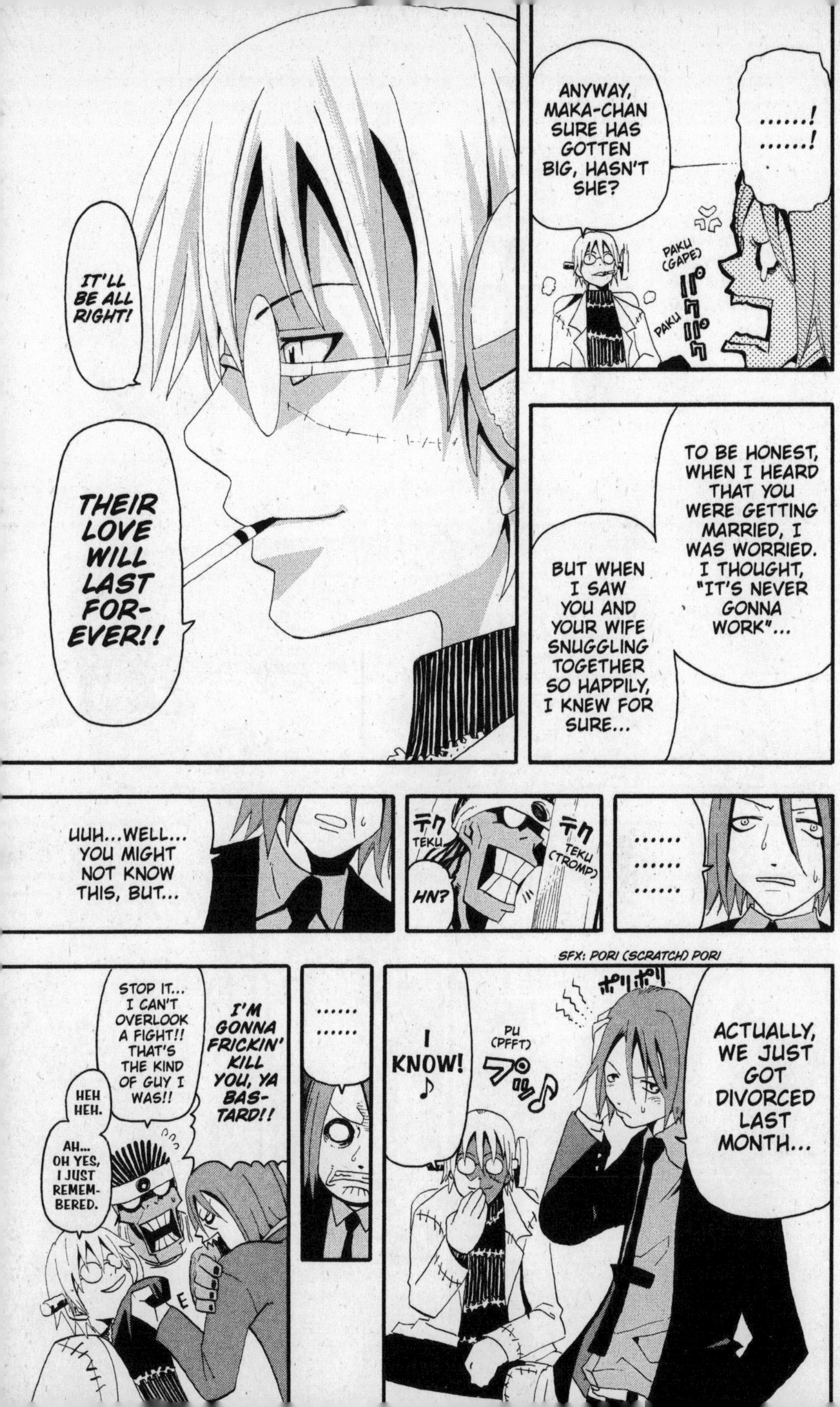
......!
......!
ANYWAY, MAKA-CHAN SURE HAS GOTTEN BIG, HASN'T SHE?
PAKU (GAPE)
PAKU
TO BE HONEST, WHEN I HEARD THAT YOU WERE GETTING MARRIED, I WAS WORRIED. I THOUGHT, "IT'S NEVER GONNA WORK"...
BUT WHEN I SAW YOU AND YOUR WIFE SNUGGLING TOGETHER SO HAPPILY, I KNEW FOR SURE...
IT'LL BE ALL RIGHT!
THEIR LOVE WILL LAST FOR-EVER!!
......
......
......
TEKU (TROMP)
TEKU
HN?
UUH...WELL... YOU MIGHT NOT KNOW THIS, BUT...
SFX: PORI (SCRATCH) PORI
ACTUALLY, WE JUST GOT DIVORCED LAST MONTH...
PU (PFFT)
I KNOW! ♪
......
......
I'M GONNA FRICKIN' KILL YOU, YA BAS-TARD!!
STOP IT... I CAN'T OVERLOOK A FIGHT!! THAT'S THE KIND OF GUY I WAS!!
HEH HEH.
AH... OH YES, I JUST REMEM-BERED.

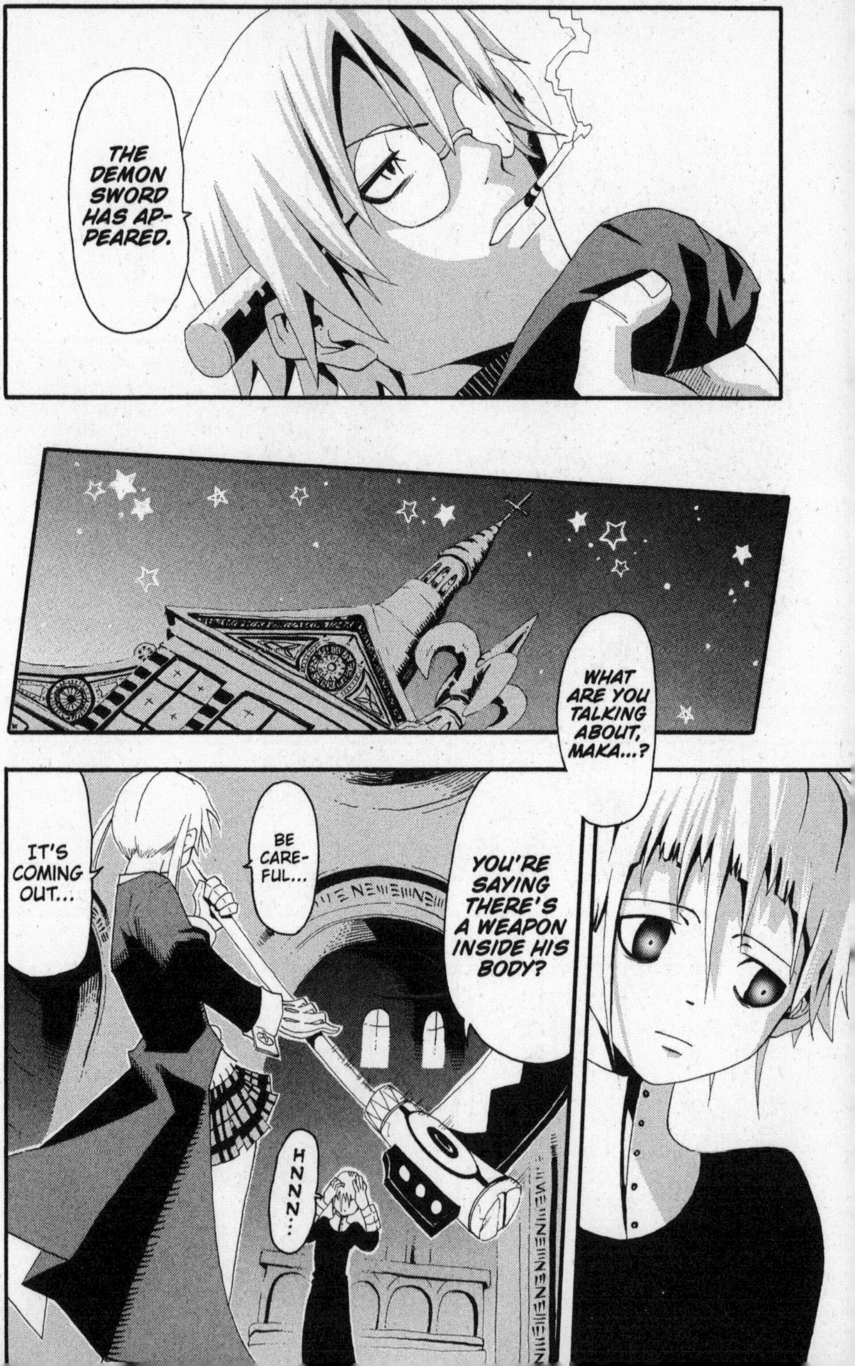
THE DEMON SWORD HAS APPEARED.
WHAT ARE YOU TALKING ABOUT, MAKA...?
YOU'RE SAYING THERE'S A WEAPON INSIDE HIS BODY?
BE CAREFUL...
IT'S COMING OUT...
HNNN...

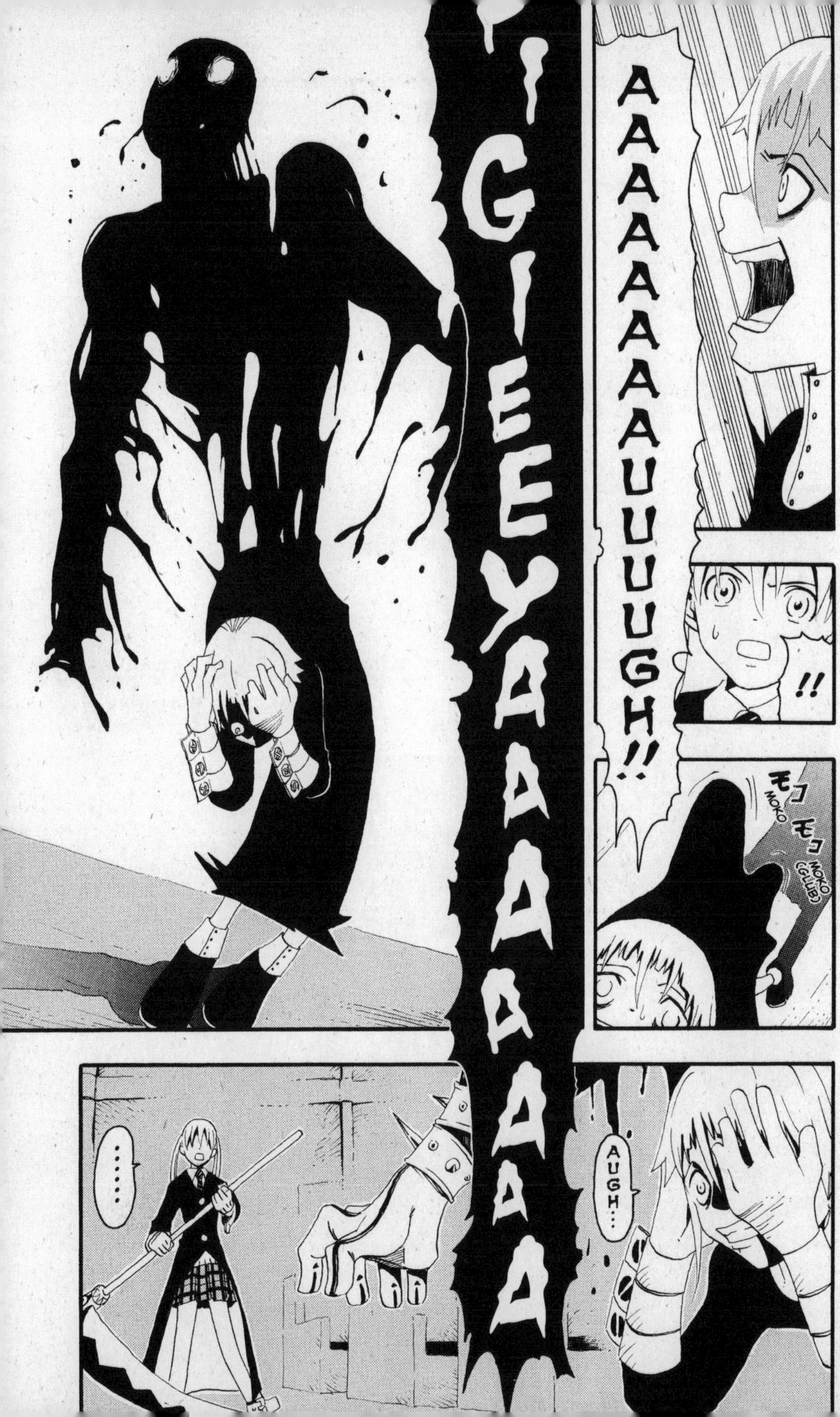

AAAAAAAAAUUUUGH!!
!!
モコ
MOKO
モコ
MOKO (GLUB)
GIEEYAAAAAAAAA
AUGH...
......

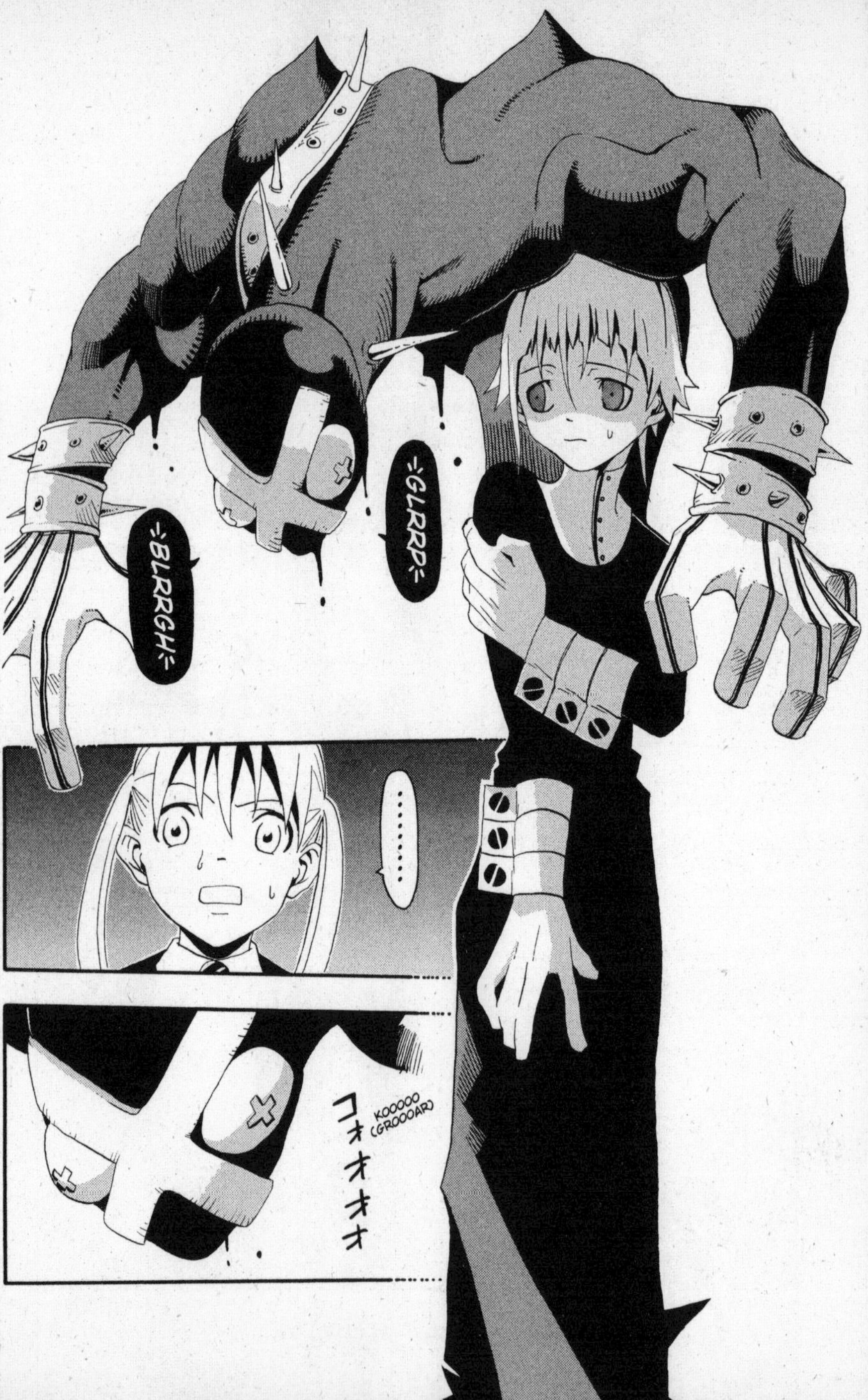
GLRRP
BLRRGH
......
コォオオオ
KOOOOO (GROOOAR)

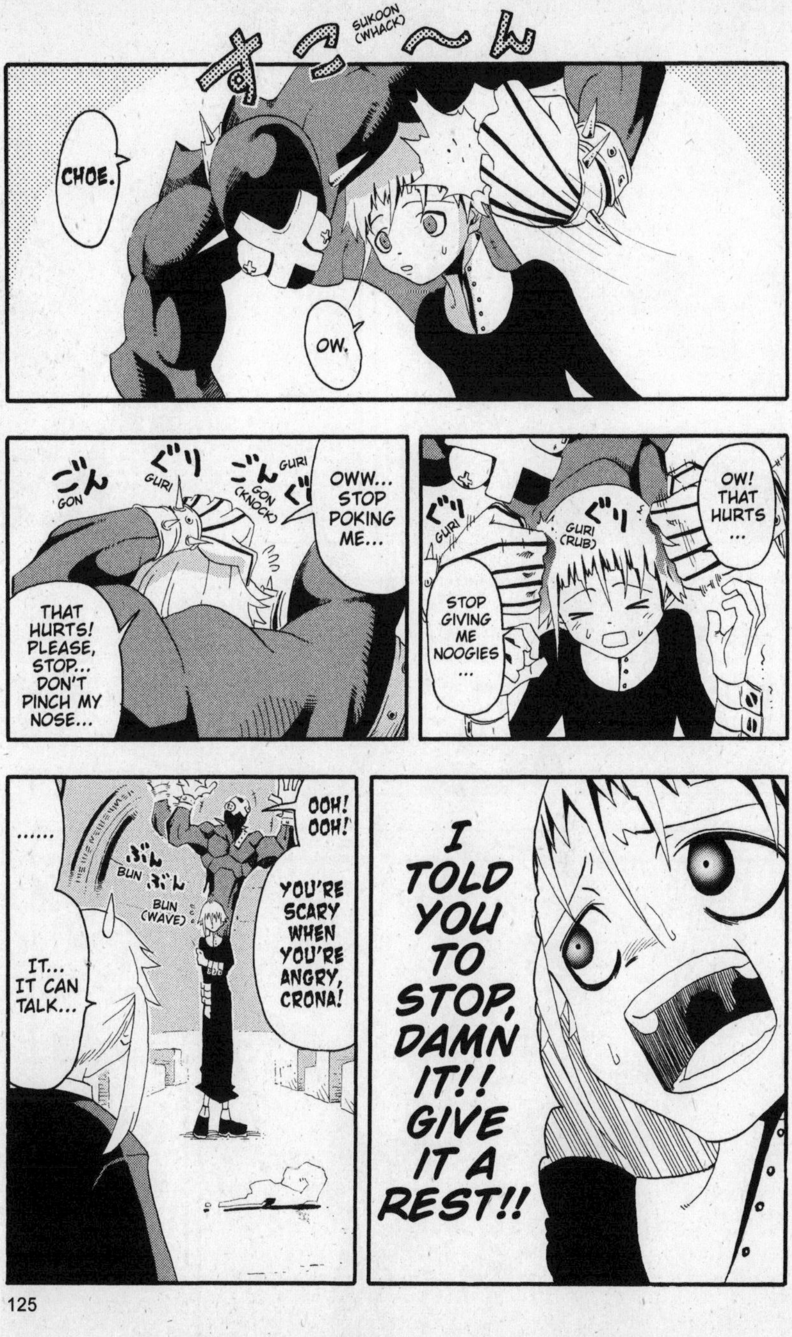
すこ〜ん
SUKOON (WHACK)
CHOE.
OW.
OW! THAT HURTS...
ぐり
GURI (RUB)
ぐり
GURI
STOP GIVING ME NOOGIES...
OWW... STOP POKING ME...
ぐり
GURI
ごん
GON (KNOCK)
ぐり
GURI
ごん
GON
THAT HURTS! PLEASE, STOP... DON'T PINCH MY NOSE...
I TOLD YOU TO STOP, DAMN IT!! GIVE IT A REST!!
OOH! OOH!
YOU'RE SCARY WHEN YOU'RE ANGRY, CRONA!
ぶん
BUN
ぶん
BUN (WAVE)
......
IT... IT CAN TALK...

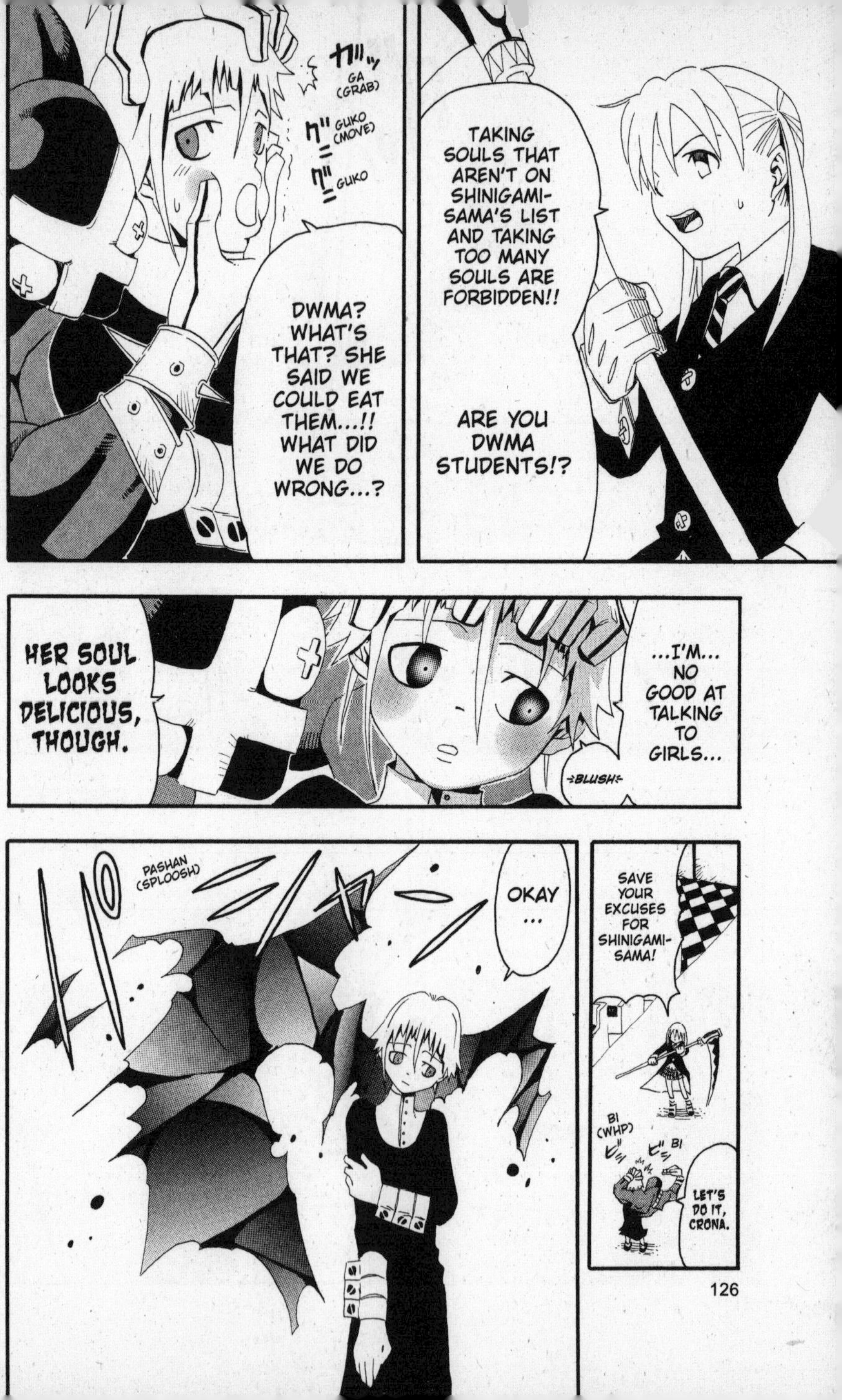
TAKING SOULS THAT AREN'T ON SHINIGAMI-SAMA'S LIST AND TAKING TOO MANY SOULS ARE FORBIDDEN!!
ARE YOU DWMA STUDENTS!?
GA (GRAB)
GUKO (MOVE)
GUKO
DWMA? WHAT'S THAT? SHE SAID WE COULD EAT THEM...!! WHAT DID WE DO WRONG...?
...I'M... NO GOOD AT TALKING TO GIRLS...
BLUSH
HER SOUL LOOKS DELICIOUS, THOUGH.
SAVE YOUR EXCUSES FOR SHINIGAMI-SAMA!
BI (WHP)
BI
LET'S DO IT, CRONA.
OKAY...
PASHAN (SPLOOSH)

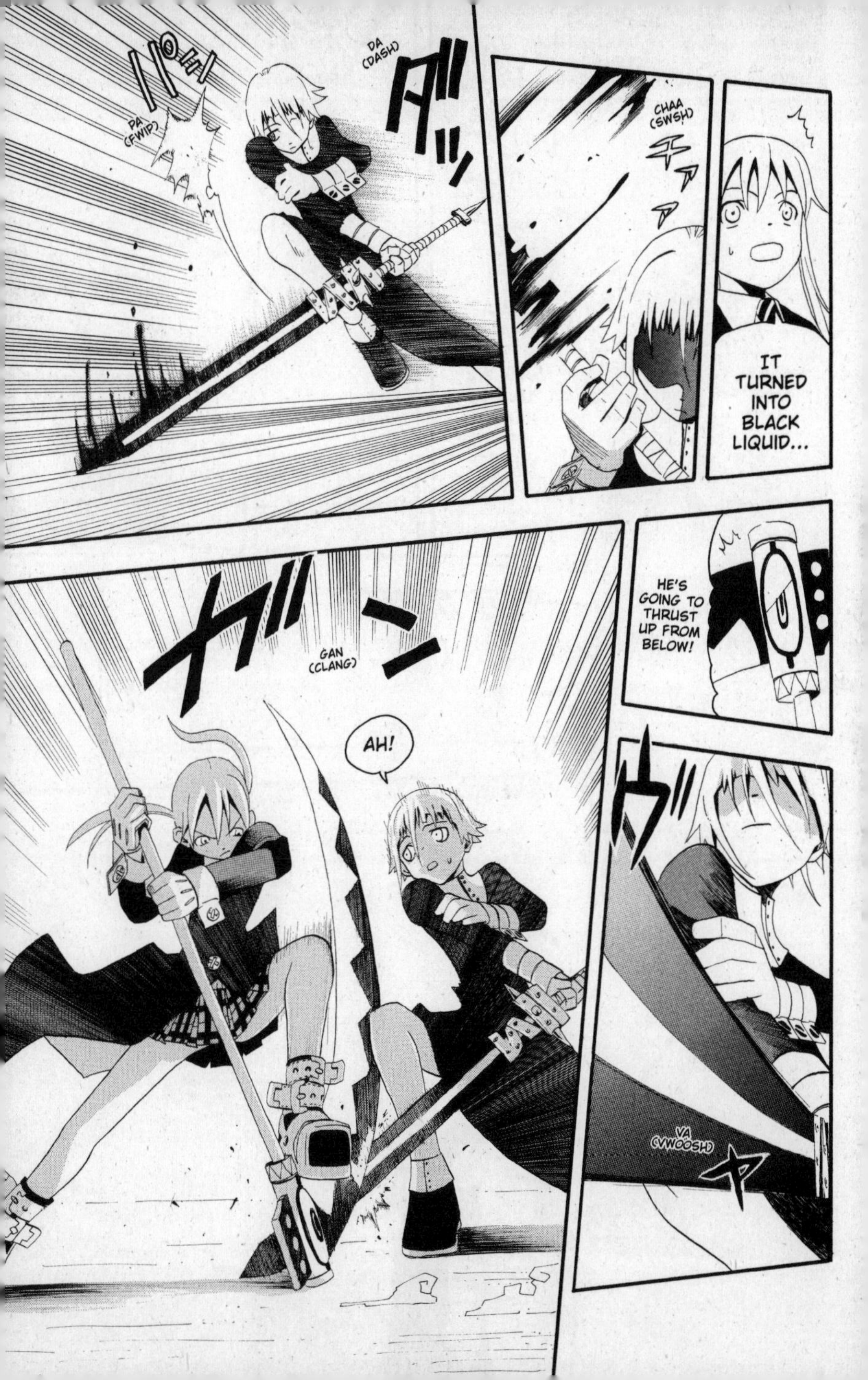
IT TURNED INTO BLACK LIQUID...
CHAA (SWSH)
DA (DASH)
PA (FWIP)
HE'S GOING TO THRUST UP FROM BELOW!
VA (VWOOSH)
GAN (CLANG)
AH!

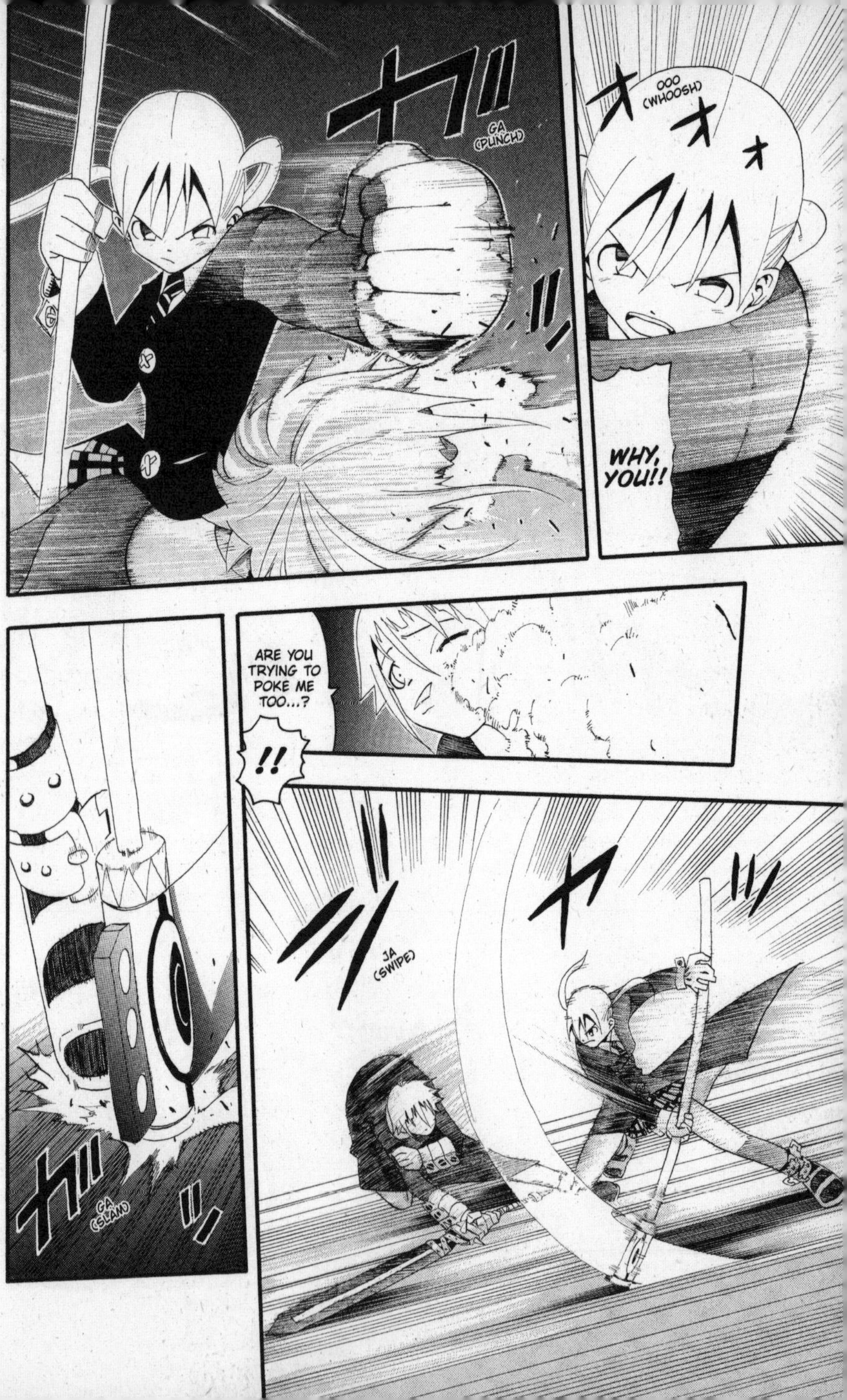
OOO (WHOOSH)
WHY, YOU!!
GA (PUNCH)
ARE YOU TRYING TO POKE ME TOO...?
!!
JA (SWIPE)
GA (SLAM)

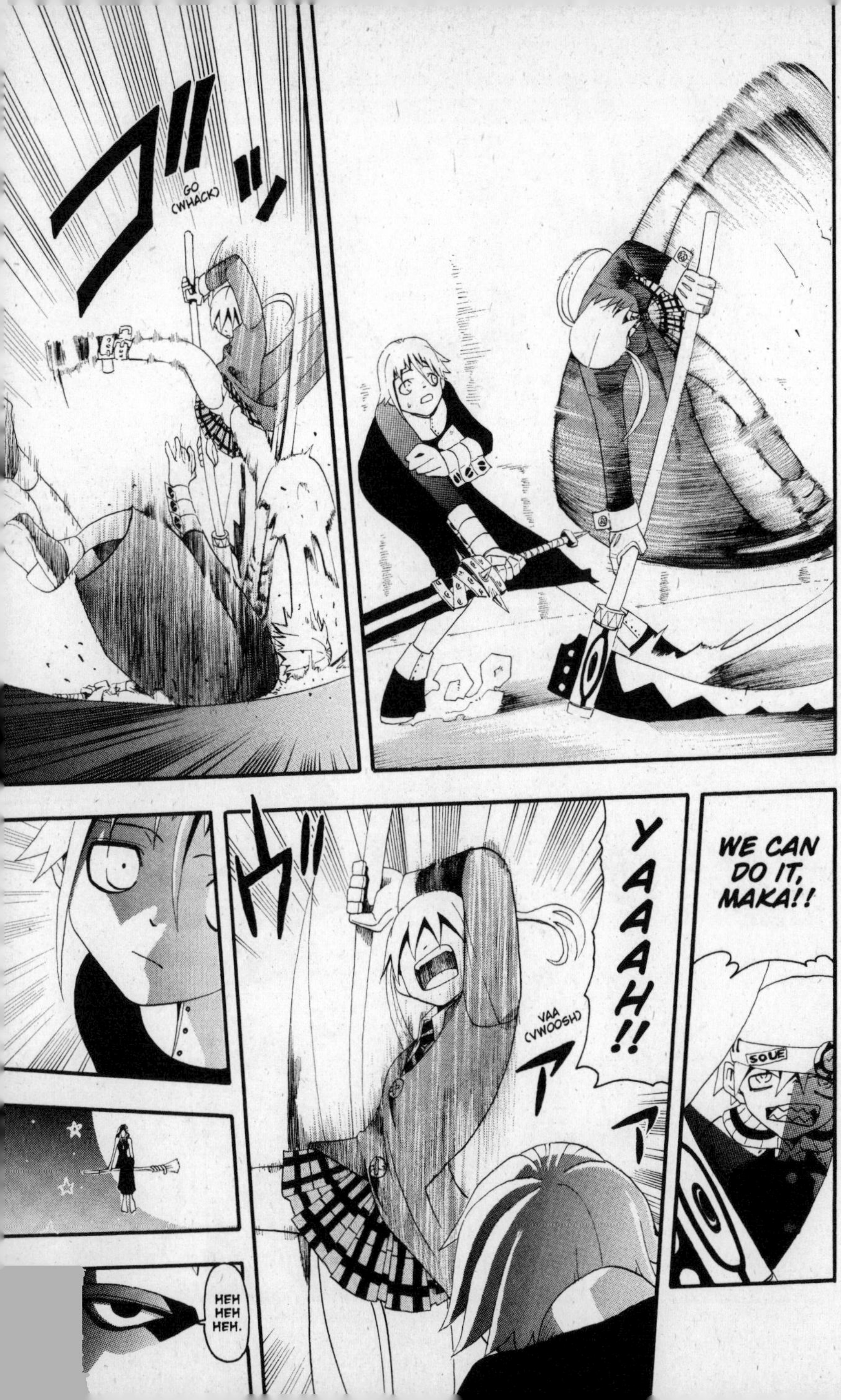
GO (WHACK)
WE CAN DO IT, MAKA!!
YAAAAH!!
VAA (VWOOSH)
HEH HEH HEH.

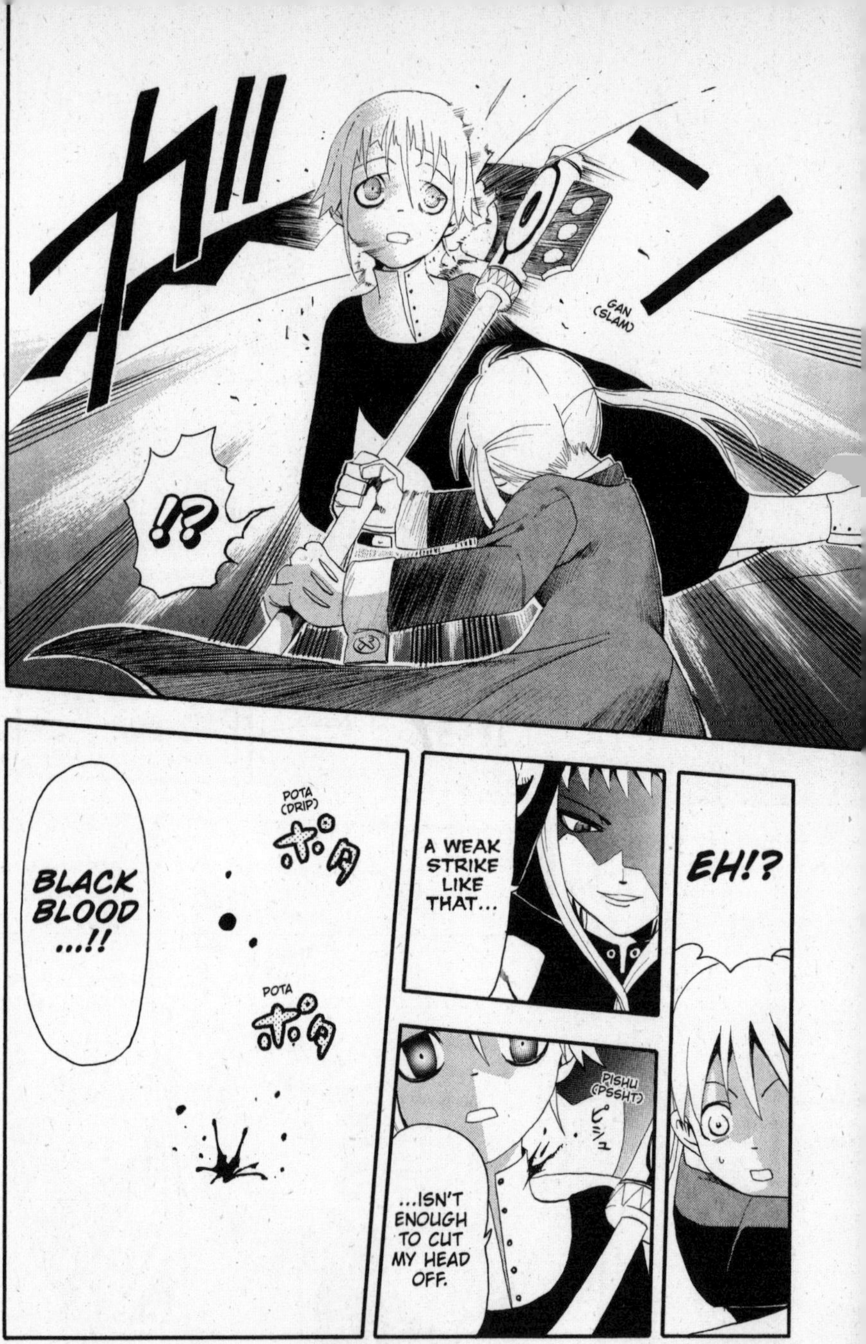
GAN (SLAM)
!?
EH!?
A WEAK STRIKE LIKE THAT...
PISHU (PSSHT)
...ISN'T ENOUGH TO CUT MY HEAD OFF.
POTA (DRIP)
POTA
BLACK BLOOD ...!!

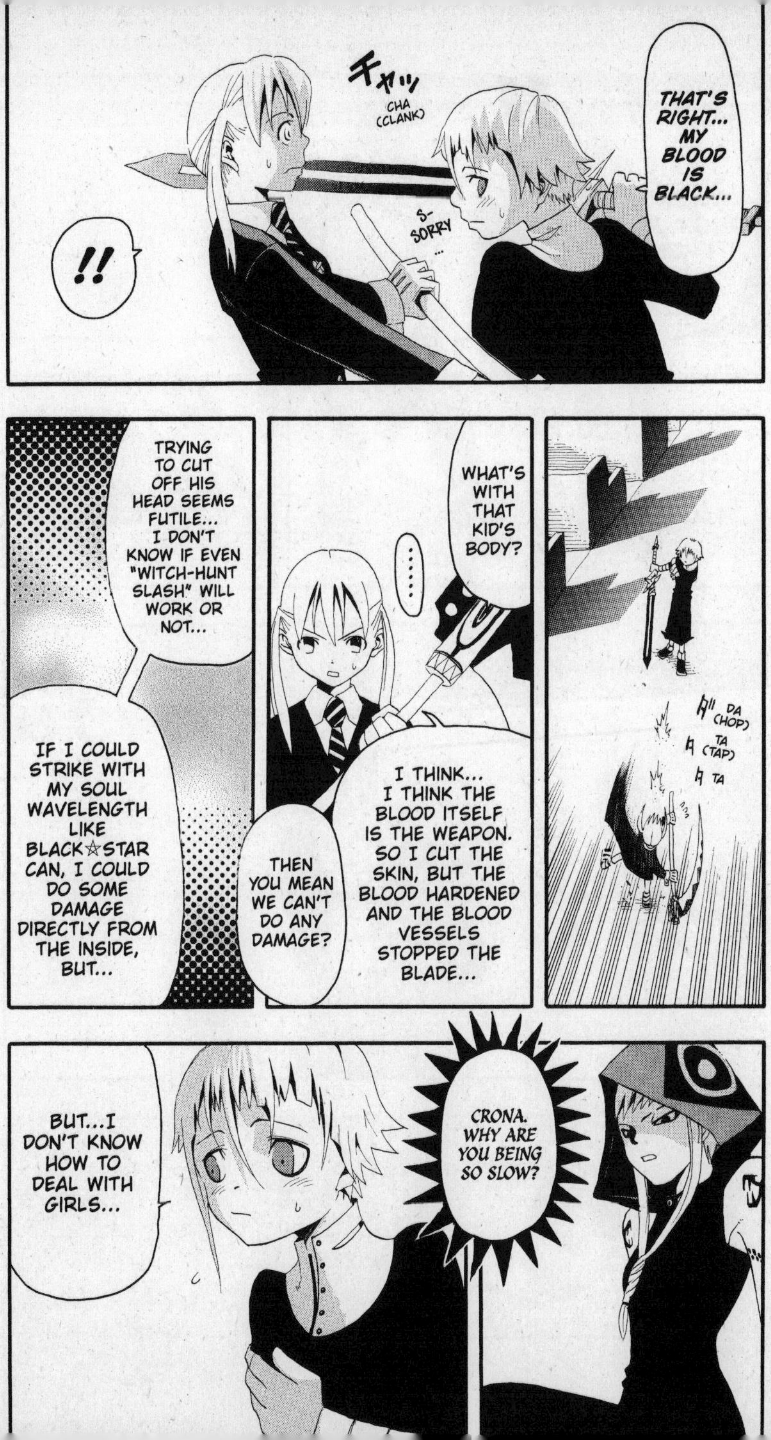
THAT'S RIGHT... MY BLOOD IS BLACK...
チャッ
CHA (CLANK)
S-SORRY ...
!!
DA (CHOP)
TA (TAP)
TA
WHAT'S WITH THAT KID'S BODY?
......
I THINK... I THINK THE BLOOD ITSELF IS THE WEAPON. SO I CUT THE SKIN, BUT THE BLOOD HARDENED AND THE BLOOD VESSELS STOPPED THE BLADE...
THEN YOU MEAN WE CAN'T DO ANY DAMAGE?
TRYING TO CUT OFF HIS HEAD SEEMS FUTILE... I DON'T KNOW IF EVEN "WITCH-HUNT SLASH" WILL WORK OR NOT...
IF I COULD STRIKE WITH MY SOUL WAVELENGTH LIKE BLACK☆STAR CAN, I COULD DO SOME DAMAGE DIRECTLY FROM THE INSIDE, BUT...
CRONA. WHY ARE YOU BEING SO SLOW?
BUT...I DON'T KNOW HOW TO DEAL WITH GIRLS...

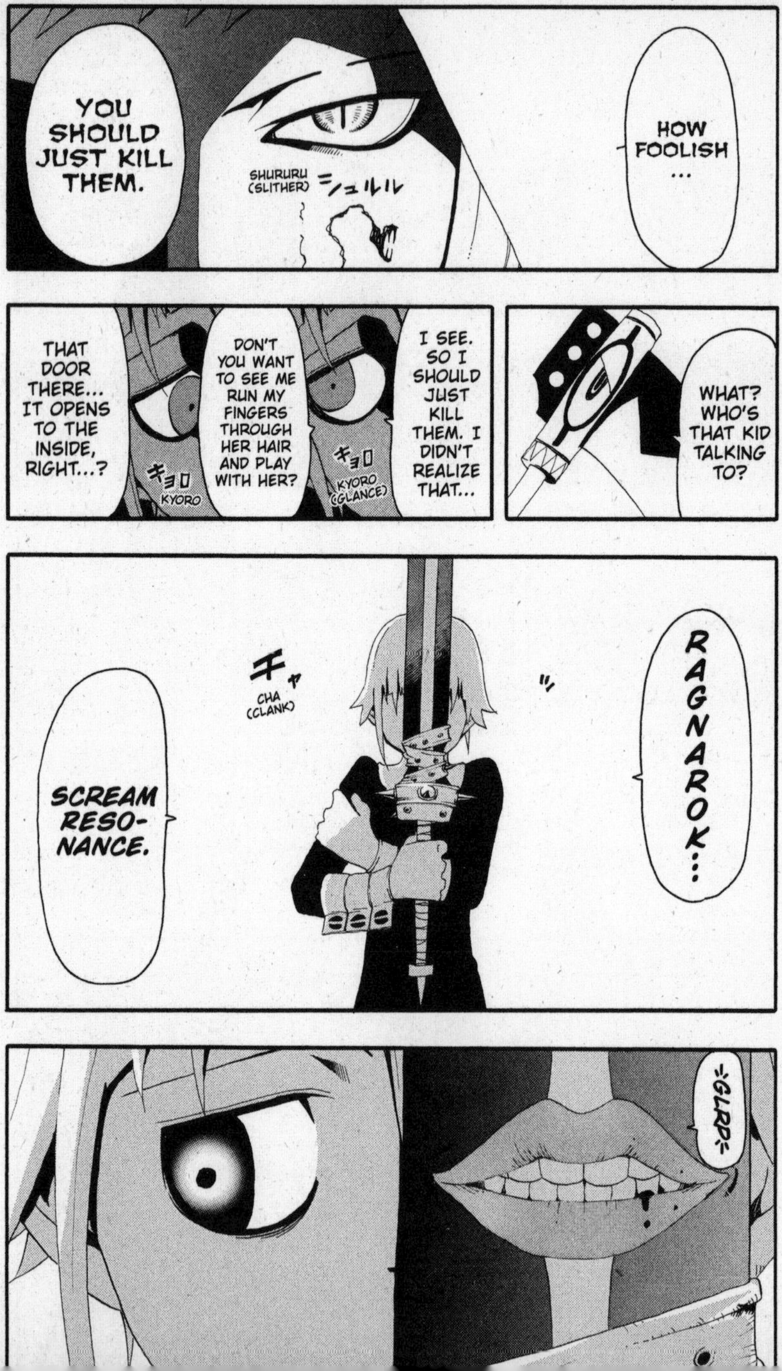
HOW FOOLISH ...
YOU SHOULD JUST KILL THEM.
SHURURU (SLITHER) シュルルル
WHAT? WHO'S THAT KID TALKING TO?
I SEE. SO I SHOULD JUST KILL THEM. I DIDN'T REALIZE THAT...
キョロ KYORO (GLANCE)
DON'T YOU WANT TO SEE ME RUN MY FINGERS THROUGH HER HAIR AND PLAY WITH HER?
THAT DOOR THERE... IT OPENS TO THE INSIDE, RIGHT...?
キョロ KYORO
RAGNAROK...
チャ CHA (CLANK)
SCREAM RESONANCE.
GLRP

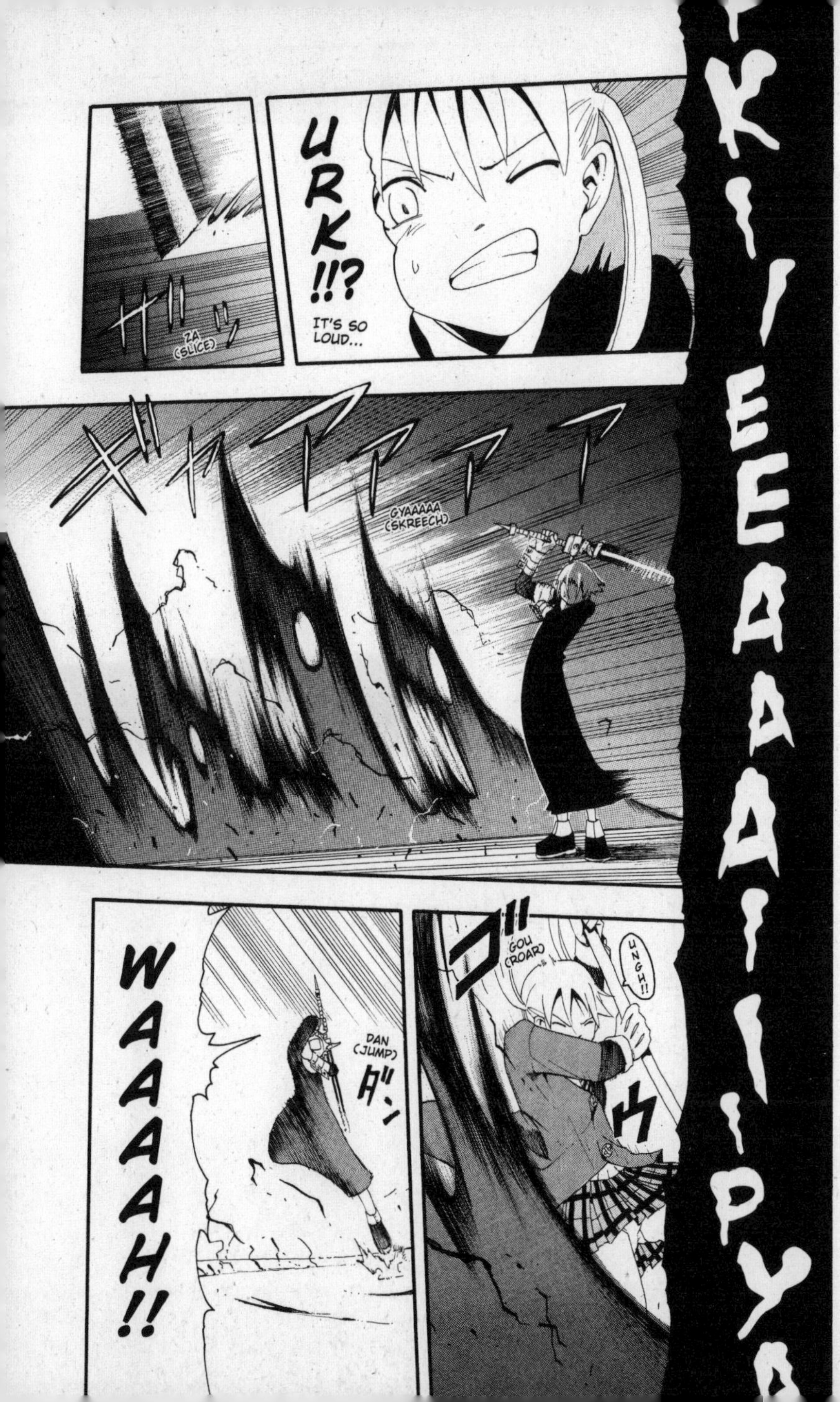
KIIEEAAIIIPYA
URK!!?
IT'S SO LOUD...
ZA (SLICE)
GYAAAAA (SKREECH)
GOU (ROAR)
UNGH!!
DAN (JUMP)
WAAAAAH!!

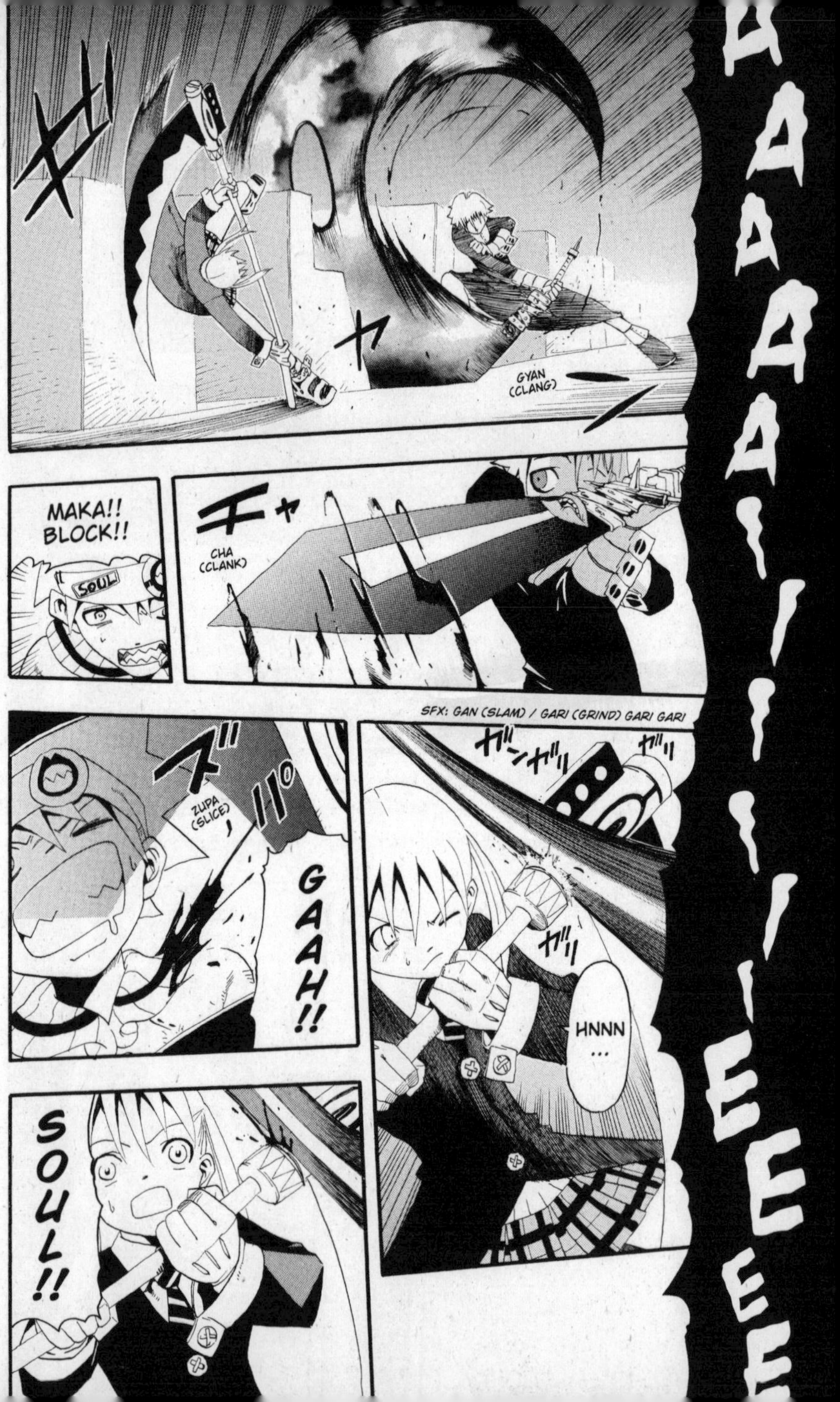
GYAN (CLANG)
CHA (CLANK)
MAKA!! BLOCK!!
SFX: GAN (SLAM) / GARI (GRIND) GARI GARI
HNNN ...
ZUPA (SLICE)
GAAAH!!
SOUL!!

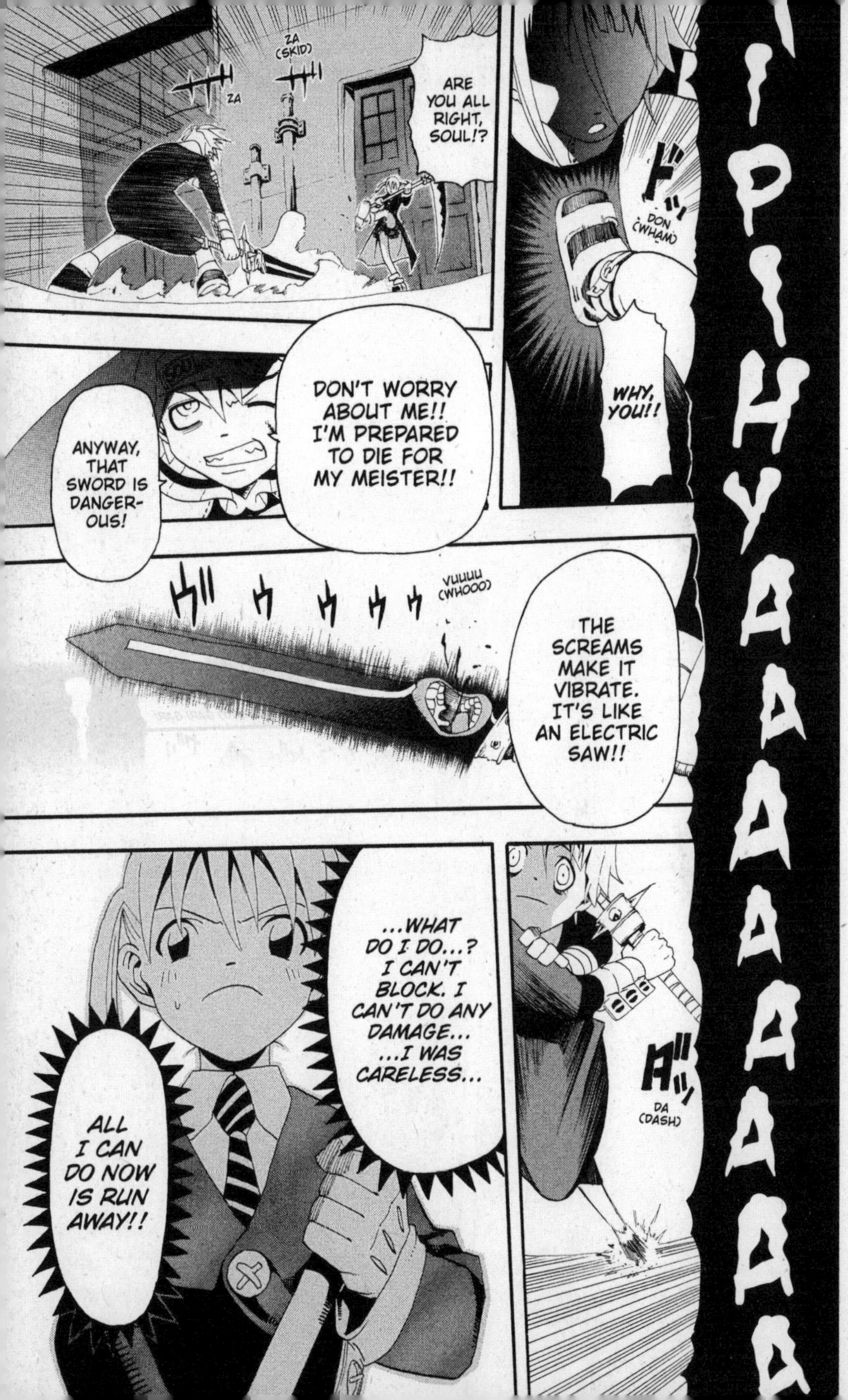
DON (WHAM)
WHY, YOU!!
ZA (SKID)
ZA
ARE YOU ALL RIGHT, SOUL!?
DON'T WORRY ABOUT ME!! I'M PREPARED TO DIE FOR MY MEISTER!!
ANYWAY, THAT SWORD IS DANGER-OUS!
VUUUU (WHOOO)
THE SCREAMS MAKE IT VIBRATE. IT'S LIKE AN ELECTRIC SAW!!
DA (DASH)
...WHAT DO I DO...? I CAN'T BLOCK. I CAN'T DO ANY DAMAGE... ...I WAS CARELESS...
ALL I CAN DO NOW IS RUN AWAY!!

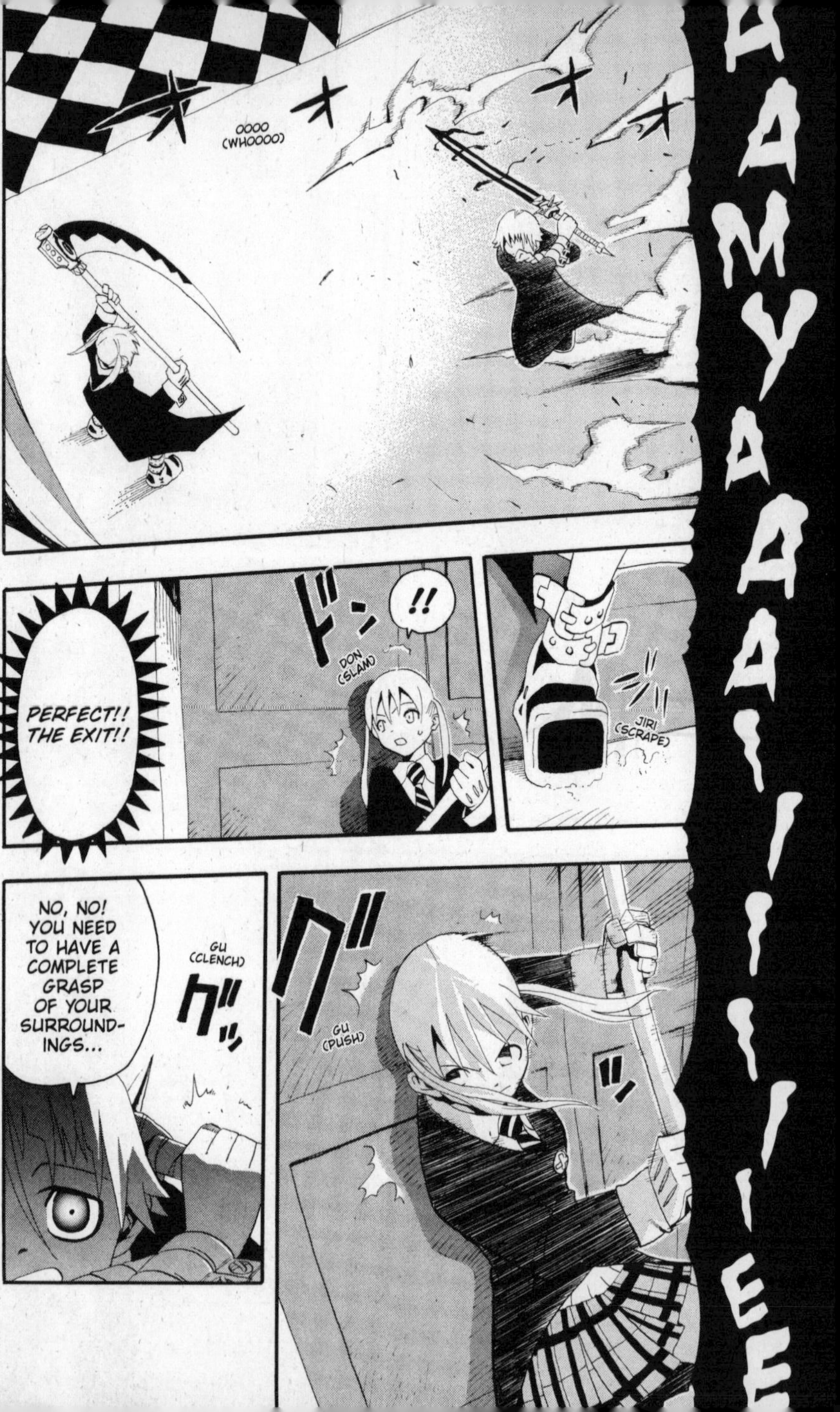
AAMYAAAIIIIIIEE
OOOO (WHOOOO)
JIRI (SCRAPE)
DON (SLAM)
!!
PERFECT!! THE EXIT!!
GU (CLENCH)
GU (PUSH)
NO, NO! YOU NEED TO HAVE A COMPLETE GRASP OF YOUR SURROUND-INGS...

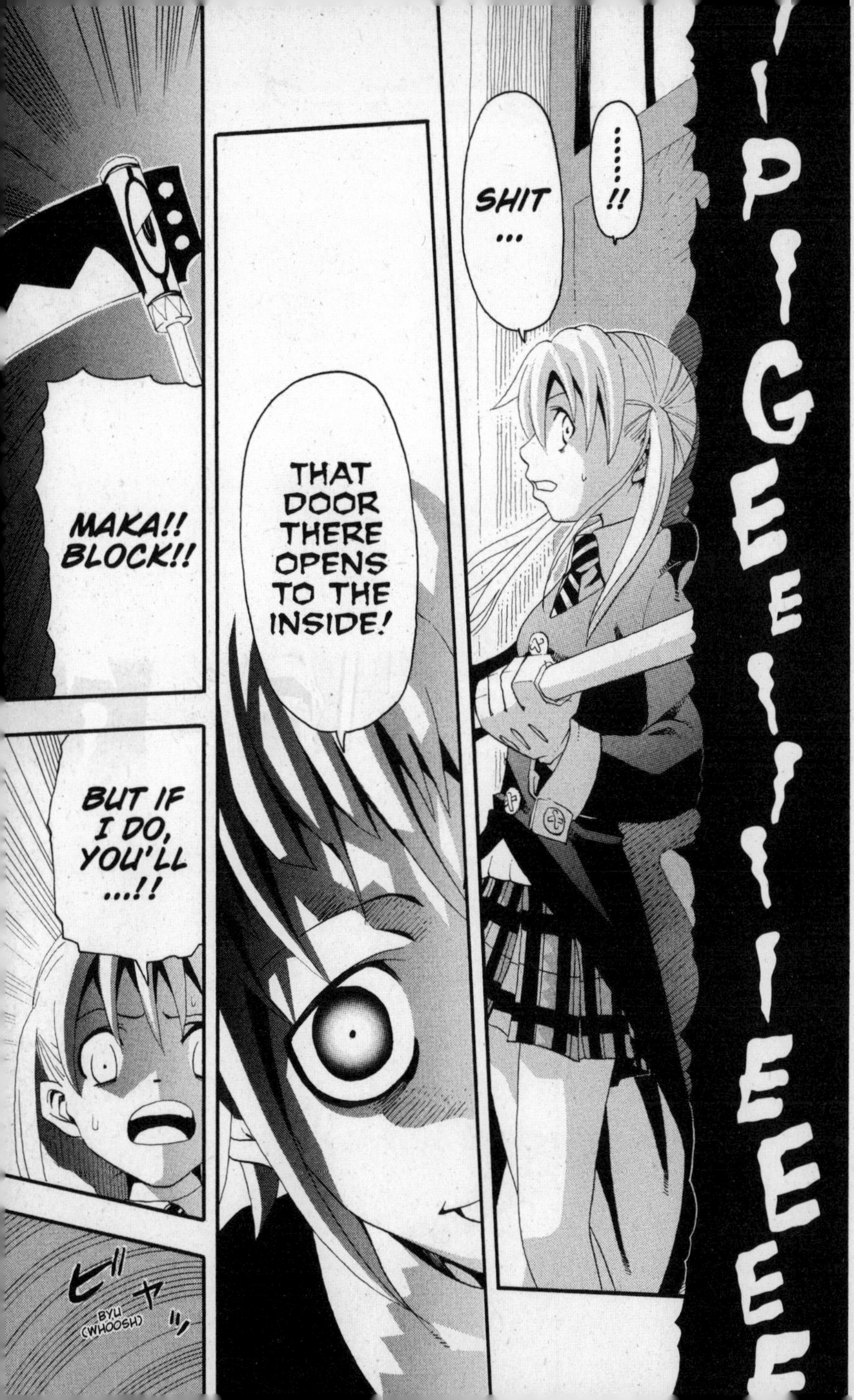
PIGEEEEEE
......!!
SHIT ...
THAT DOOR THERE OPENS TO THE INSIDE!
MAKA!! BLOCK!!
BUT IF I DO, YOU'LL ...!!
BYU (WHOOSH)

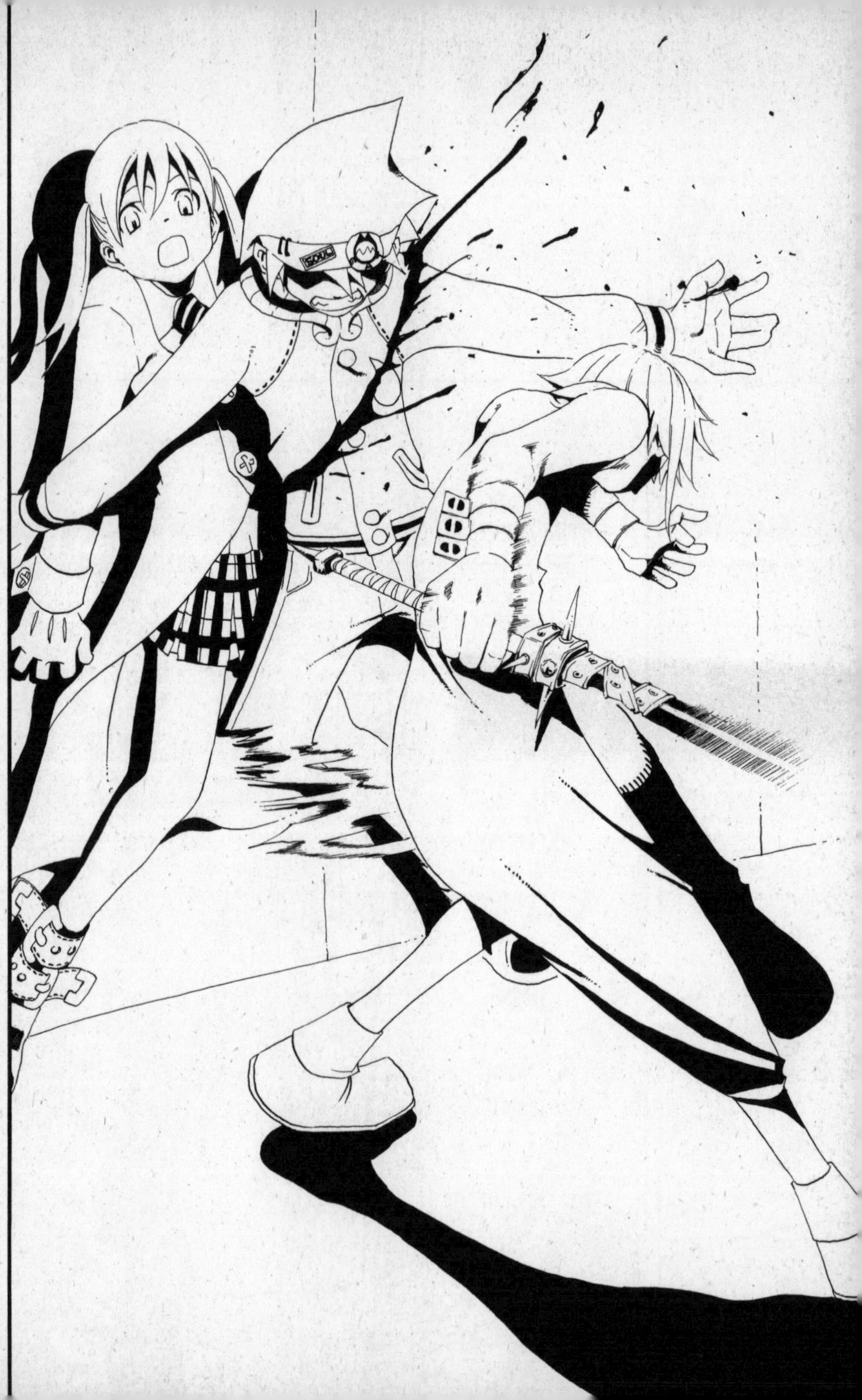
SOUL

SOUL EATER

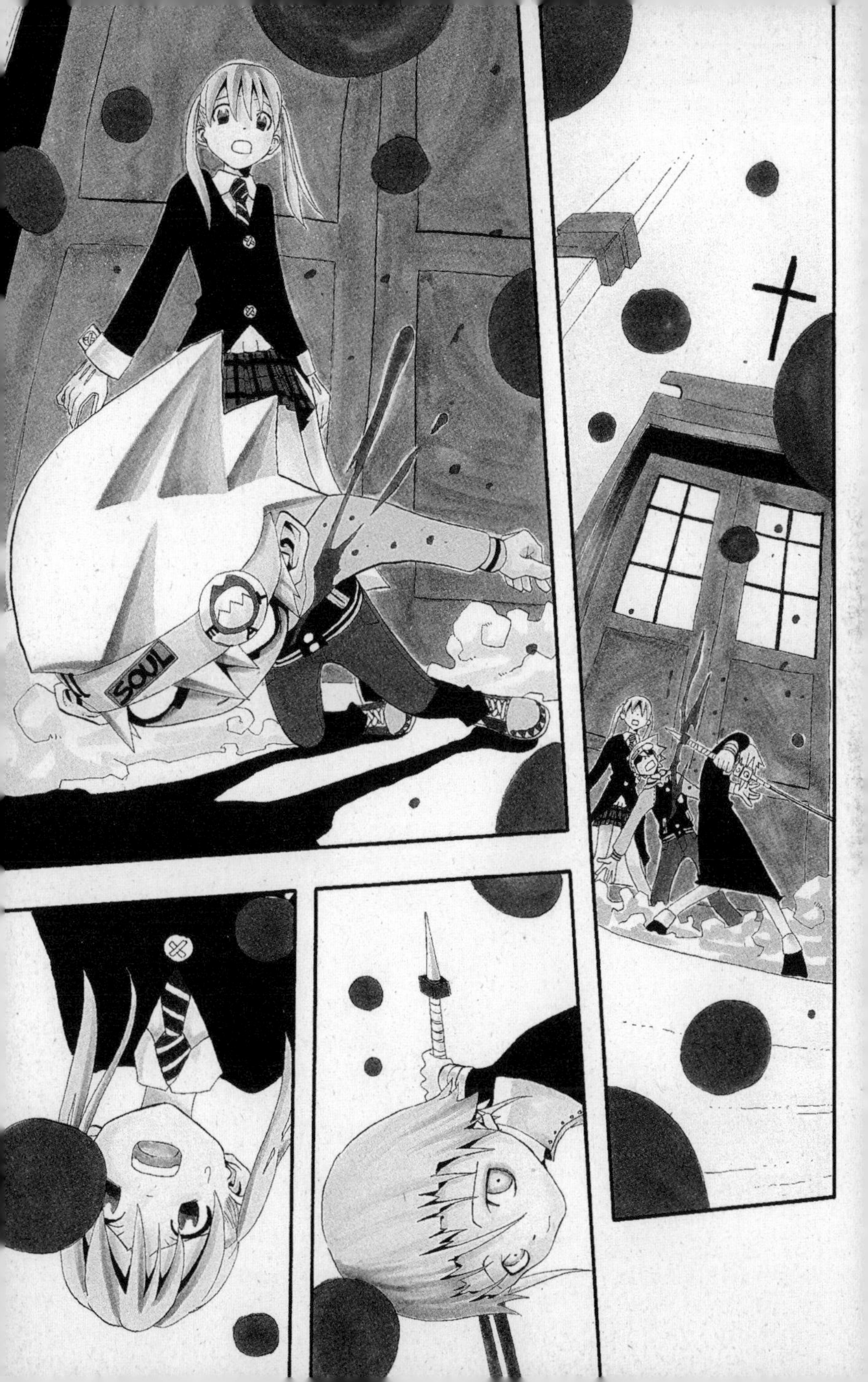
SOUL

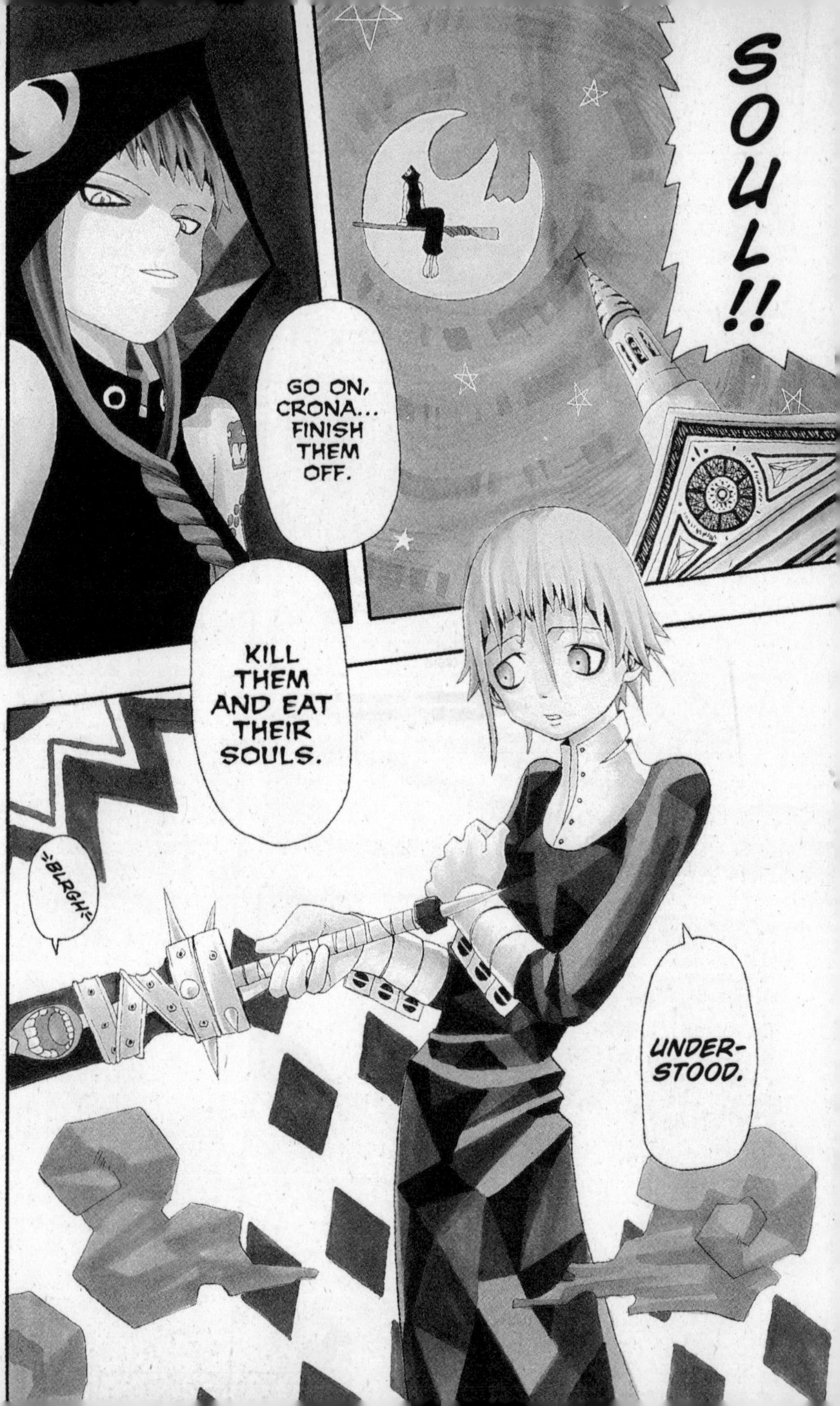
SOUL!!
GO ON, CRONA... FINISH THEM OFF.
KILL THEM AND EAT THEIR SOULS.
UNDER-STOOD.
BLRGH

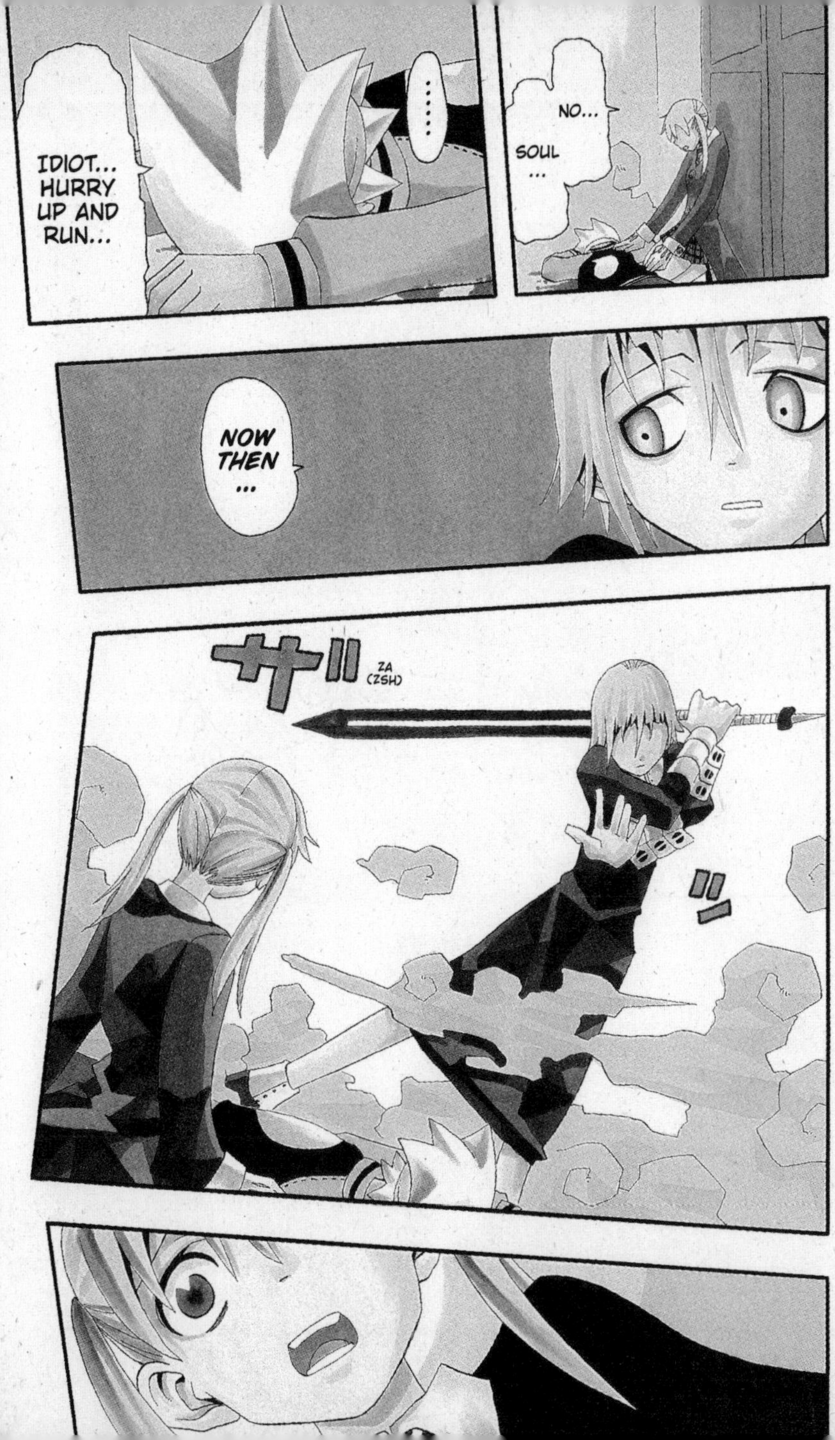
NO...
SOUL...
......
IDIOT... HURRY UP AND RUN...
NOW THEN...
ZA (ZSH)

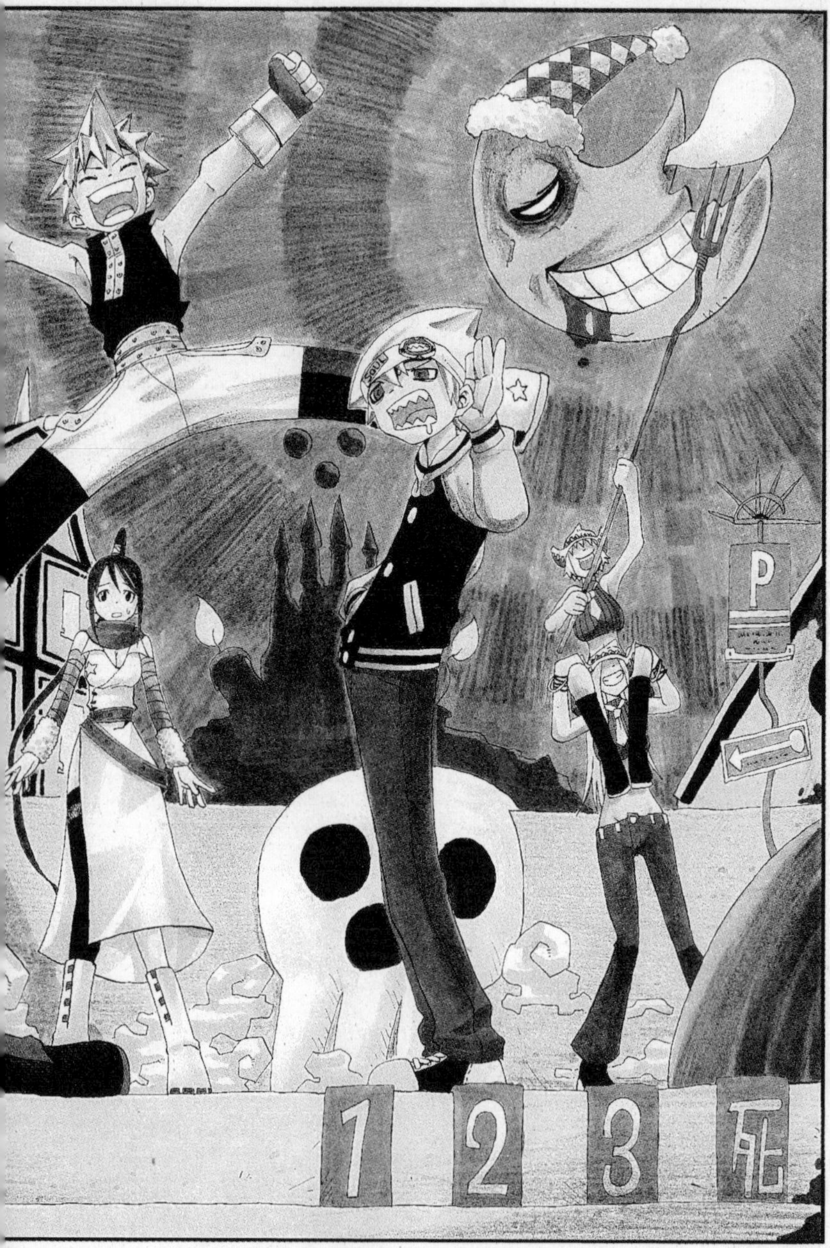
SOUL
P
1 2 3 死

CHAPTER 5: DEMON SWORD (PART 2)

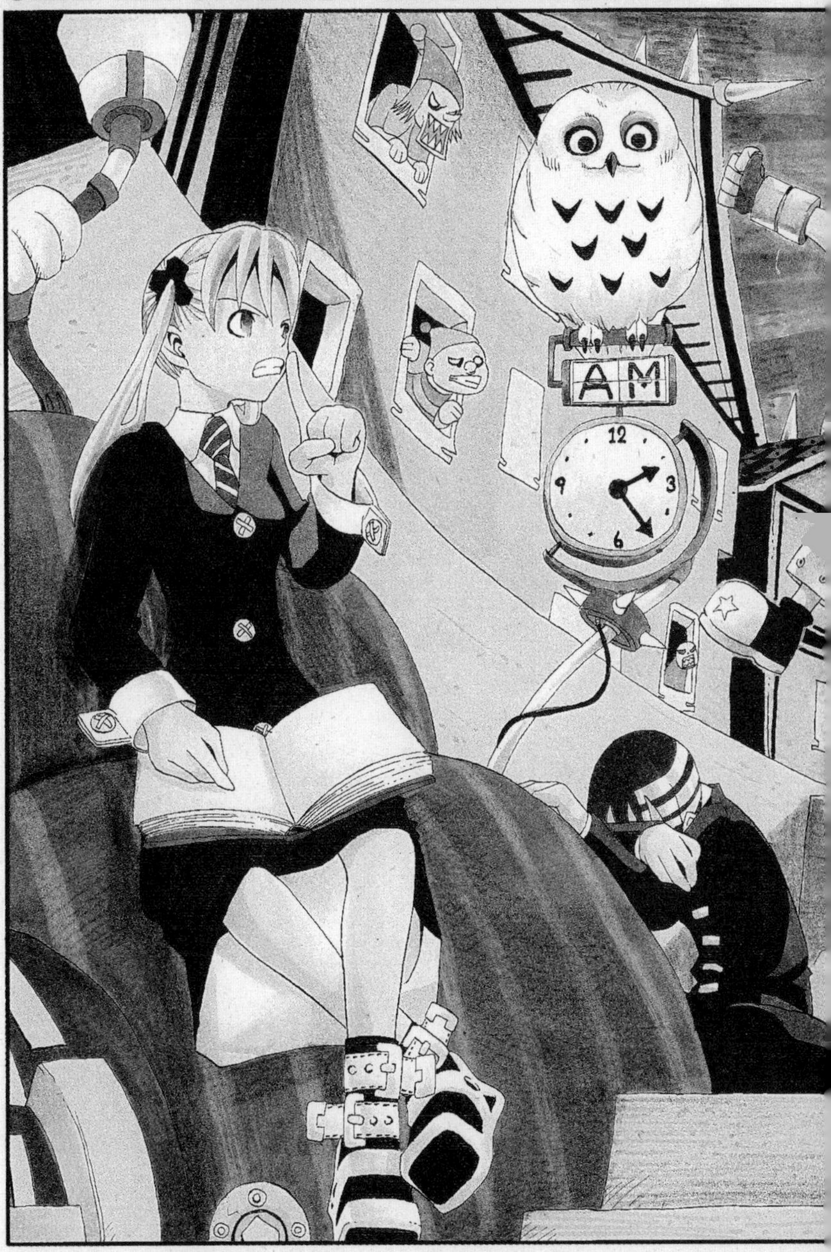
AM
12
9
3
6

SOUL EATER

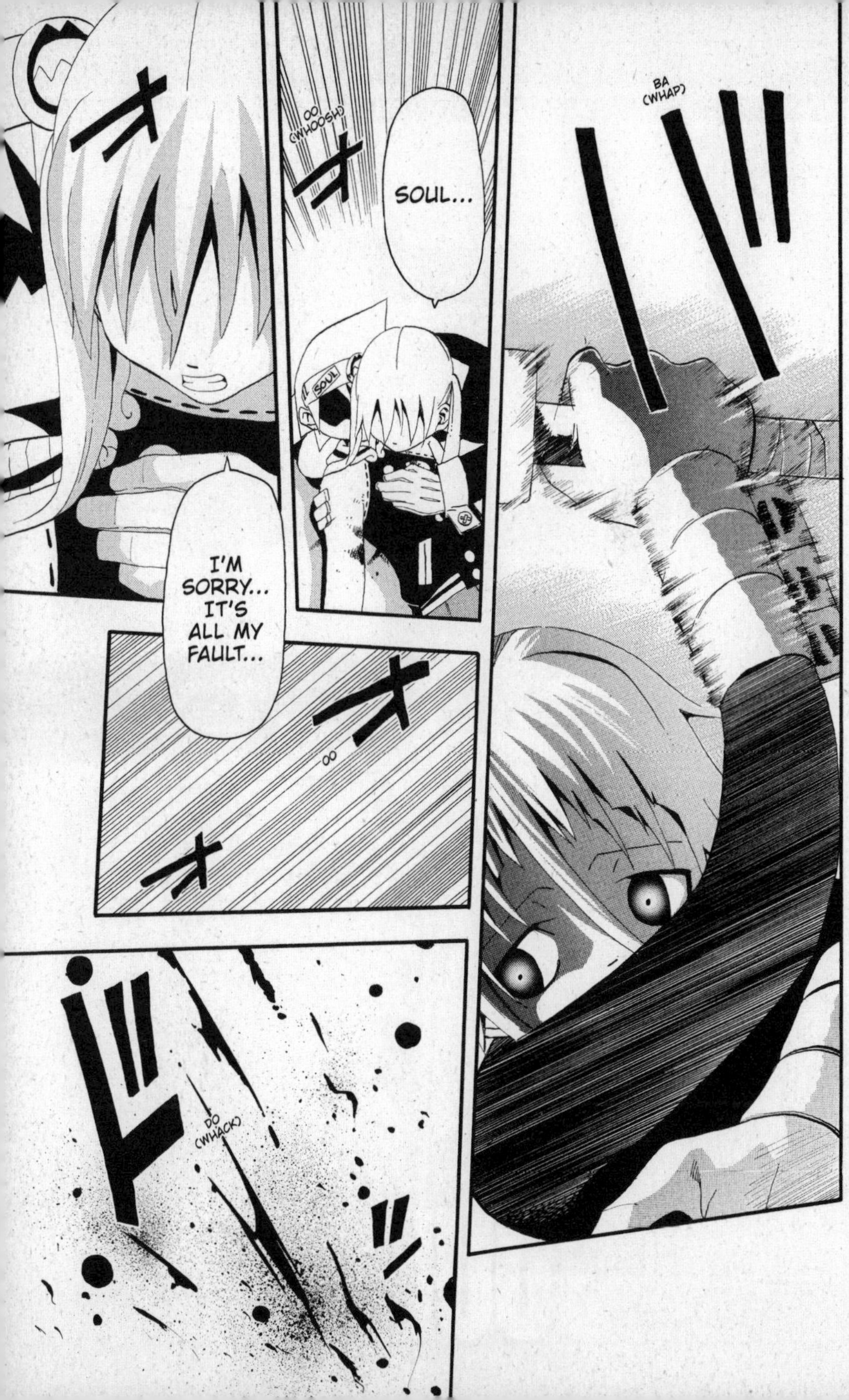
BA (WHAP)
OO (WHOOSH)
SOUL...
SOUL
I'M SORRY... IT'S ALL MY FAULT...
OO
DO (WHACK)

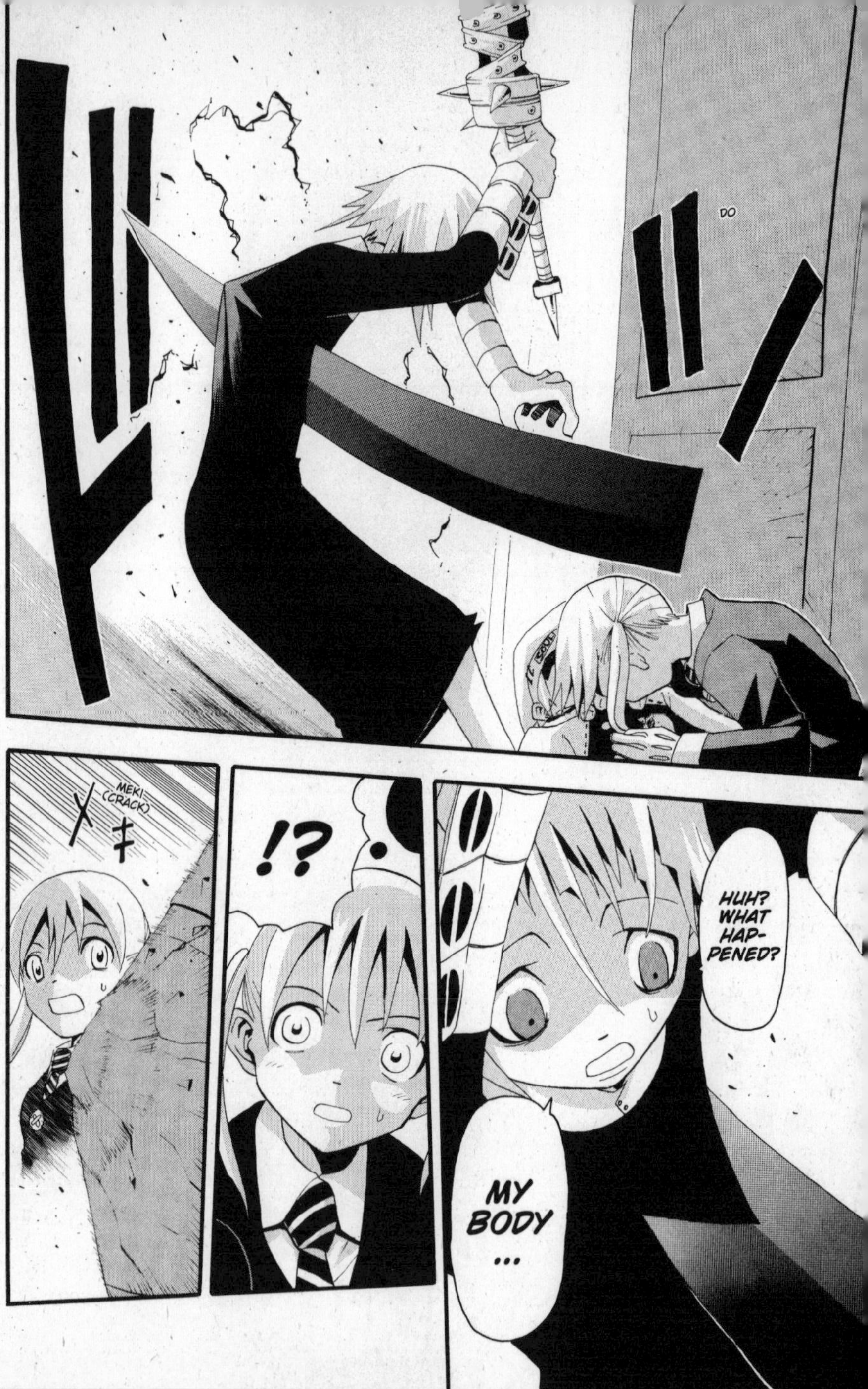
DO
HUH? WHAT HAP-PENED?
MY BODY ...
!?
MEKI (CRACK)

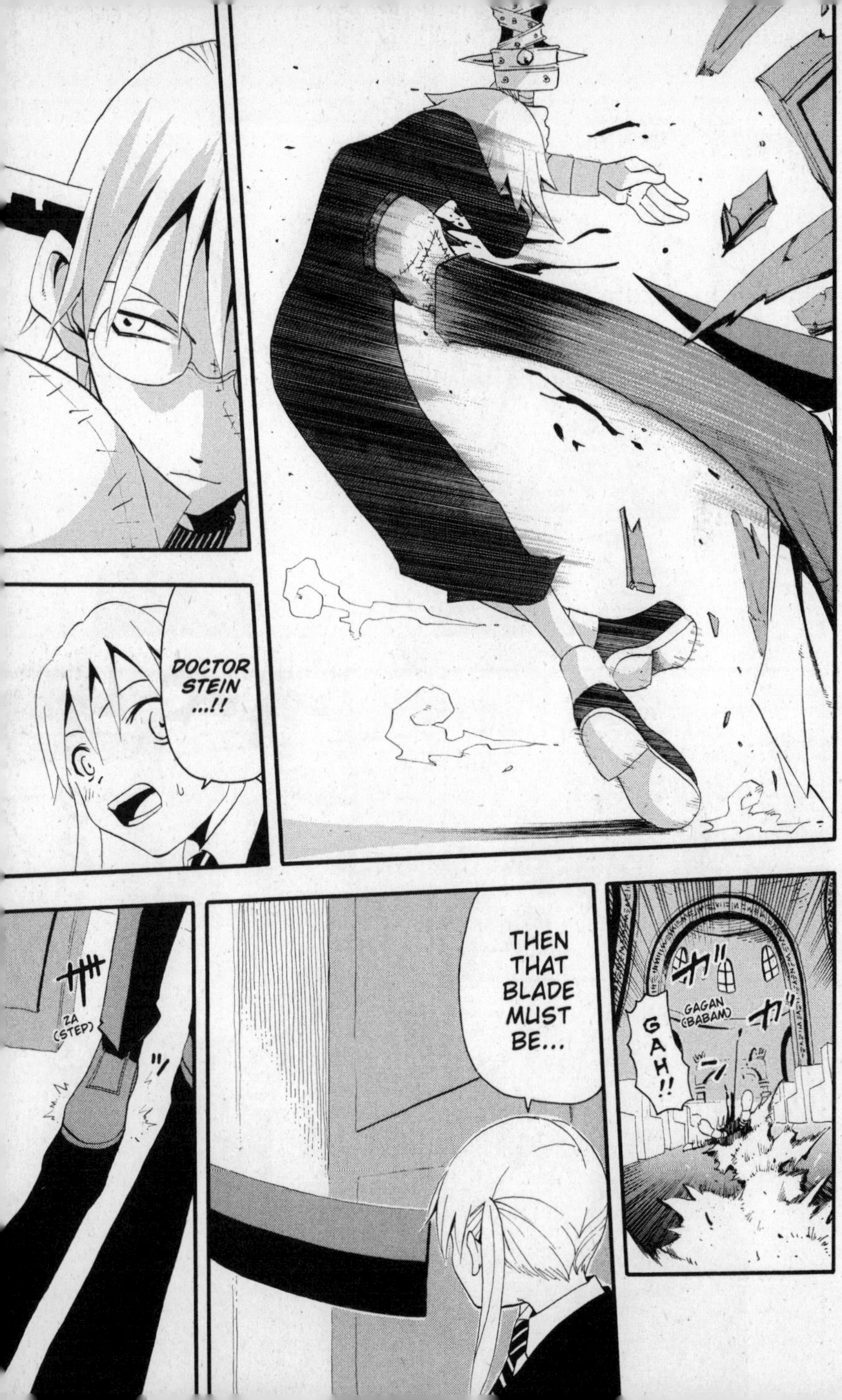
DOCTOR STEIN ...!!
GAH!!
GAGAN (BABAM)
THEN THAT BLADE MUST BE...
ZA (STEP)

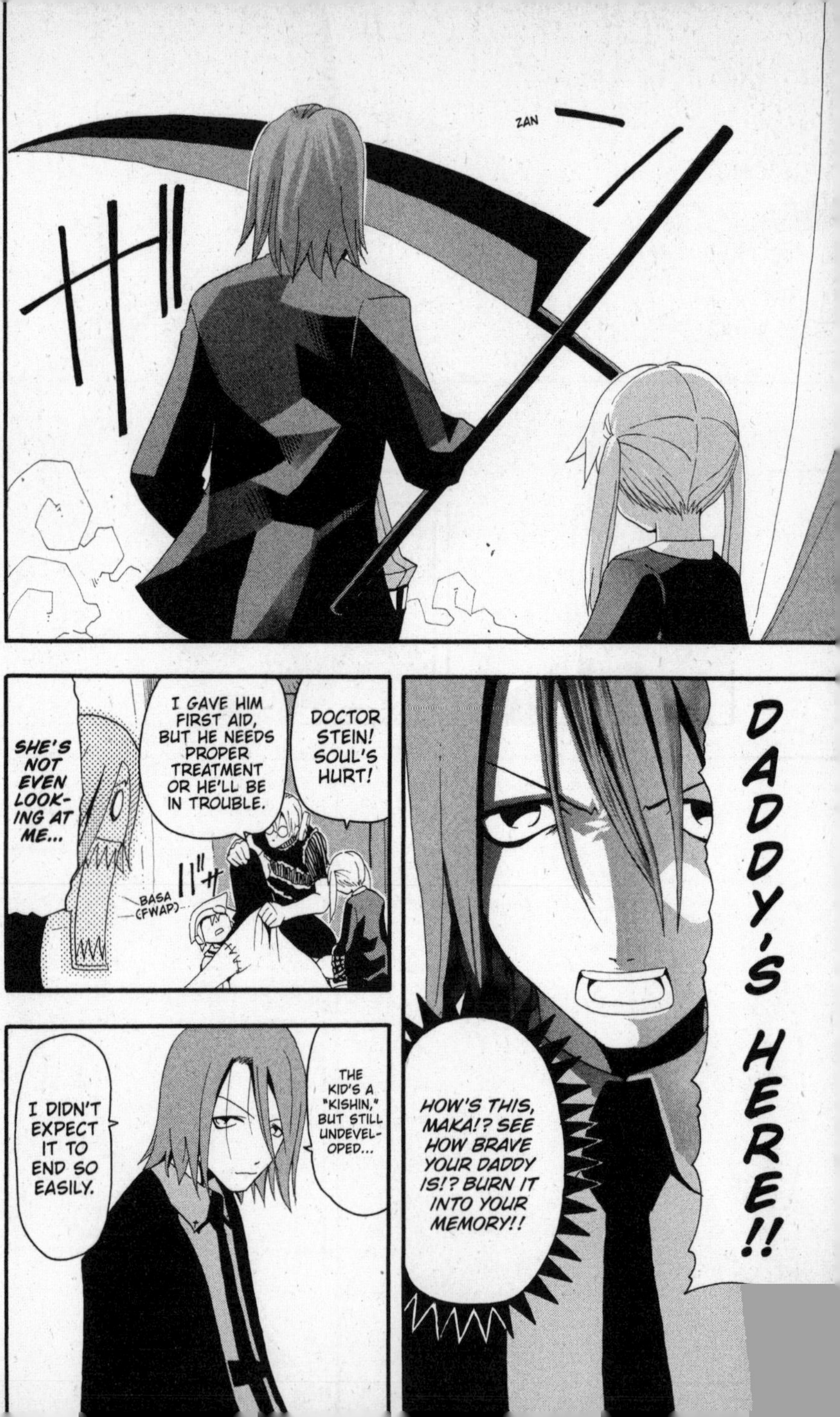
ZAN
DADDY'S HERE!!
HOW'S THIS, MAKA!? SEE HOW BRAVE YOUR DADDY IS!? BURN IT INTO YOUR MEMORY!!
DOCTOR STEIN! SOUL'S HURT!
I GAVE HIM FIRST AID, BUT HE NEEDS PROPER TREATMENT OR HE'LL BE IN TROUBLE.
BASA (FWAP)
SHE'S NOT EVEN LOOKING AT ME...
THE KID'S A "KISHIN," BUT STILL UNDEVELOPED...
I DIDN'T EXPECT IT TO END SO EASILY.

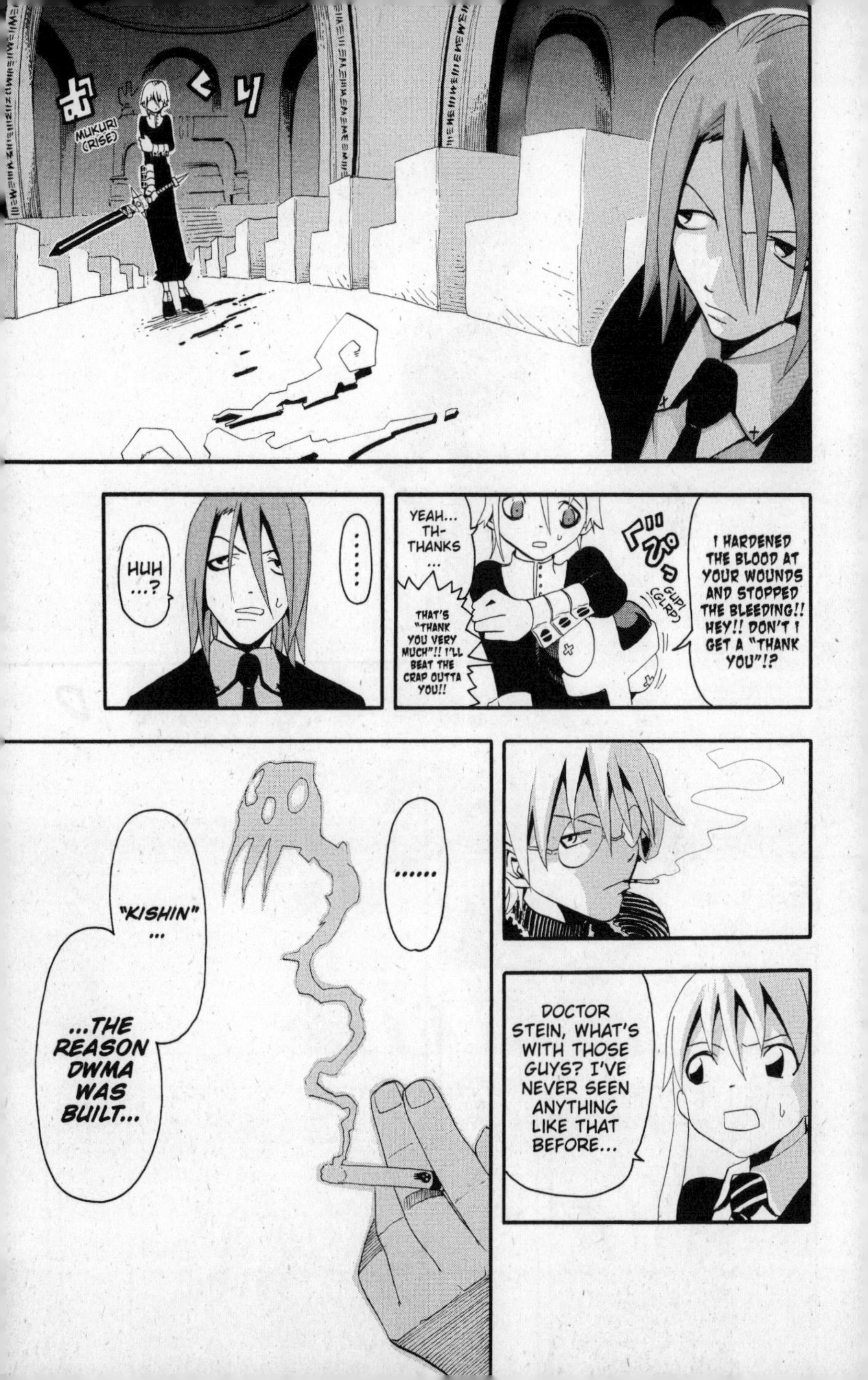
むくり
MUKURI (RISE)
I HARDENED THE BLOOD AT YOUR WOUNDS AND STOPPED THE BLEEDING!! HEY!! DON'T I GET A "THANK YOU"!?
ぐぴっ
GUP! (GLRP)
YEAH... TH-THANKS...
THAT'S "THANK YOU VERY MUCH"!! I'LL BEAT THE CRAP OUTTA YOU!!
......
HUH...?
DOCTOR STEIN, WHAT'S WITH THOSE GUYS? I'VE NEVER SEEN ANYTHING LIKE THAT BEFORE...
......
"KISHIN"...
...THE REASON DWMA WAS BUILT...

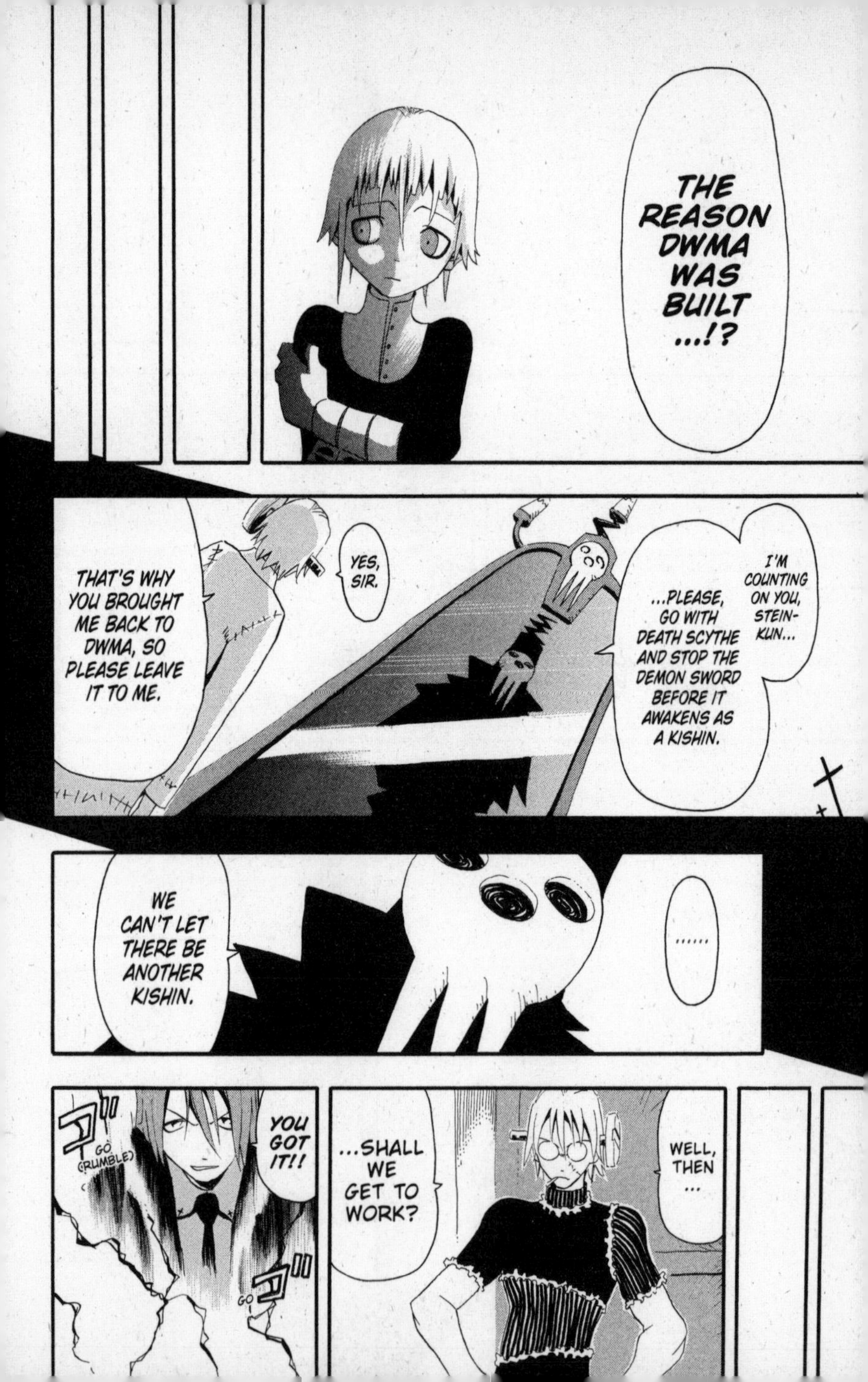
THE REASON DWMA WAS BUILT ...!?
I'M COUNTING ON YOU, STEIN-KUN...
...PLEASE, GO WITH DEATH SCYTHE AND STOP THE DEMON SWORD BEFORE IT AWAKENS AS A KISHIN.
YES, SIR.
THAT'S WHY YOU BROUGHT ME BACK TO DWMA, SO PLEASE LEAVE IT TO ME.
......
WE CAN'T LET THERE BE ANOTHER KISHIN.
WELL, THEN ...
...SHALL WE GET TO WORK?
YOU GOT IT!!
GO (RUMBLE)
GO

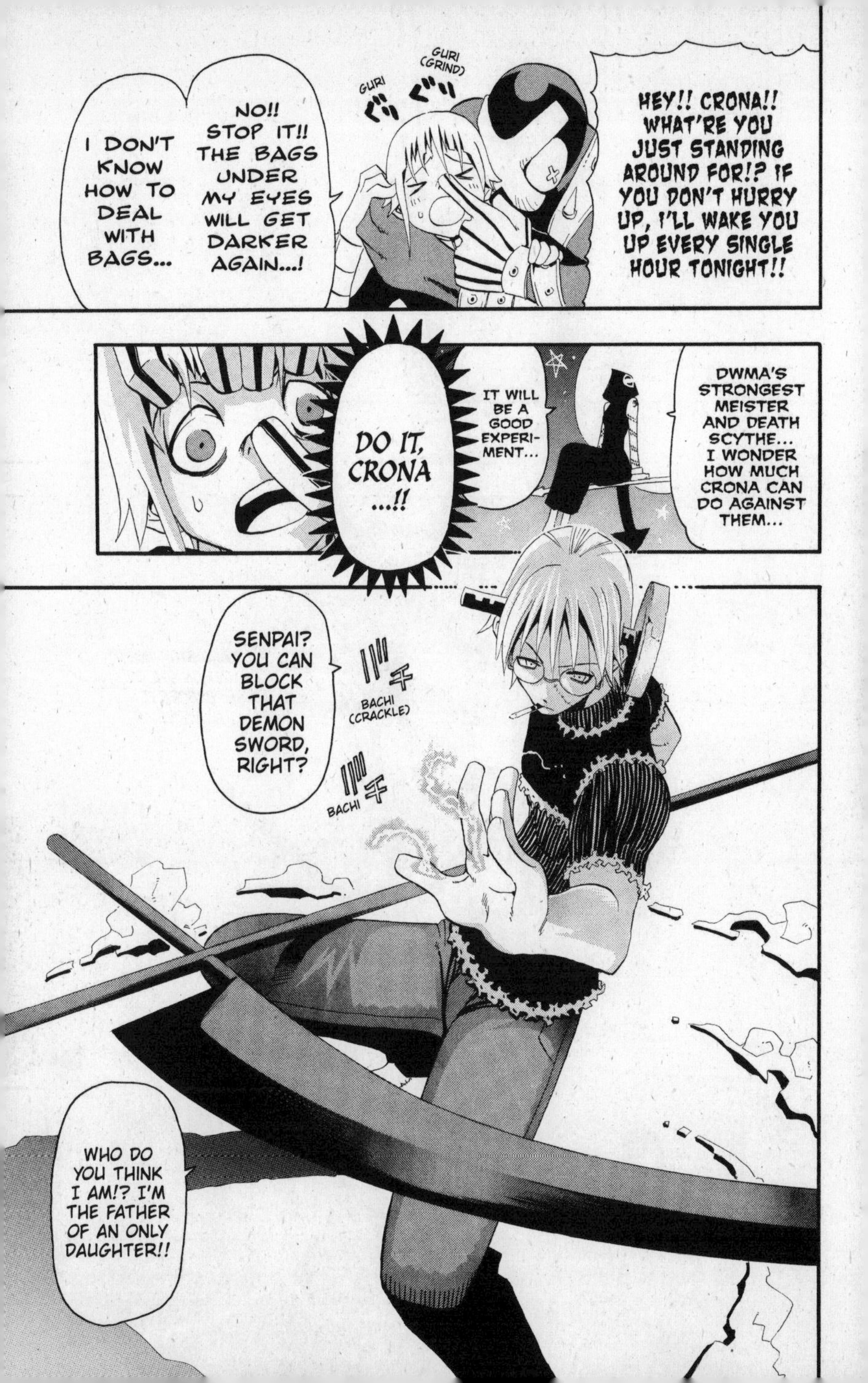
HEY!! CRONA!! WHAT'RE YOU JUST STANDING AROUND FOR!? IF YOU DON'T HURRY UP, I'LL WAKE YOU UP EVERY SINGLE HOUR TONIGHT!!
GURI (GRIND)
GURI
NO!! STOP IT!! THE BAGS UNDER MY EYES WILL GET DARKER AGAIN...!
I DON'T KNOW HOW TO DEAL WITH BAGS...
DWMA'S STRONGEST MEISTER AND DEATH SCYTHE... I WONDER HOW MUCH CRONA CAN DO AGAINST THEM...
IT WILL BE A GOOD EXPERIMENT...
DO IT, CRONA ...!!
SENPAI? YOU CAN BLOCK THAT DEMON SWORD, RIGHT?
BACHI (CRACKLE)
BACHI
WHO DO YOU THINK I AM!? I'M THE FATHER OF AN ONLY DAUGHTER!!

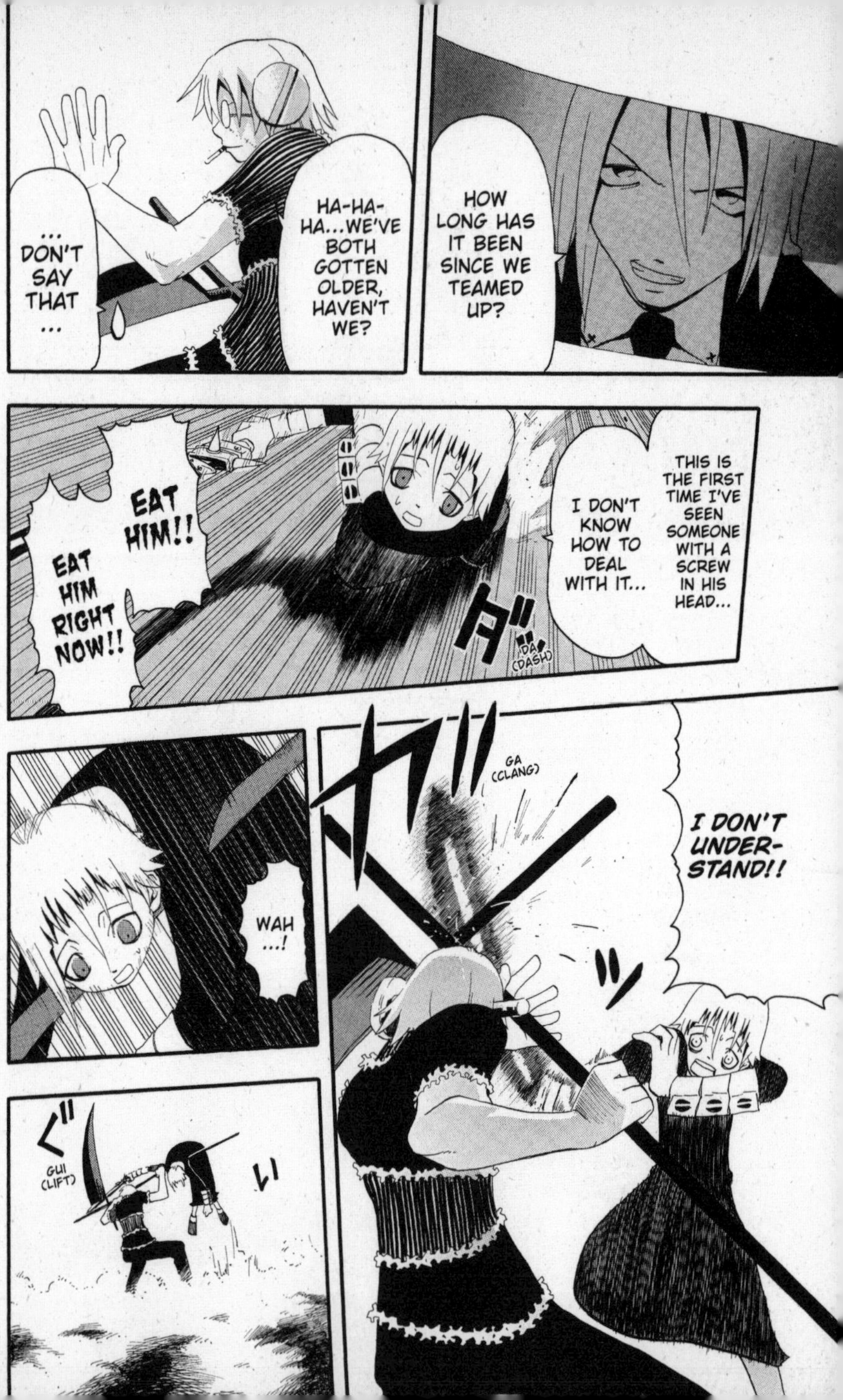
HOW LONG HAS IT BEEN SINCE WE TEAMED UP?
HA-HA-HA...WE'VE BOTH GOTTEN OLDER, HAVEN'T WE?
...DON'T SAY THAT...
THIS IS THE FIRST TIME I'VE SEEN SOMEONE WITH A SCREW IN HIS HEAD...
I DON'T KNOW HOW TO DEAL WITH IT...
DA (DASH)
EAT HIM!!
EAT HIM RIGHT NOW!!
I DON'T UNDER-STAND!!
GA (CLANG)
WAH ...!
GUI (LIFT)

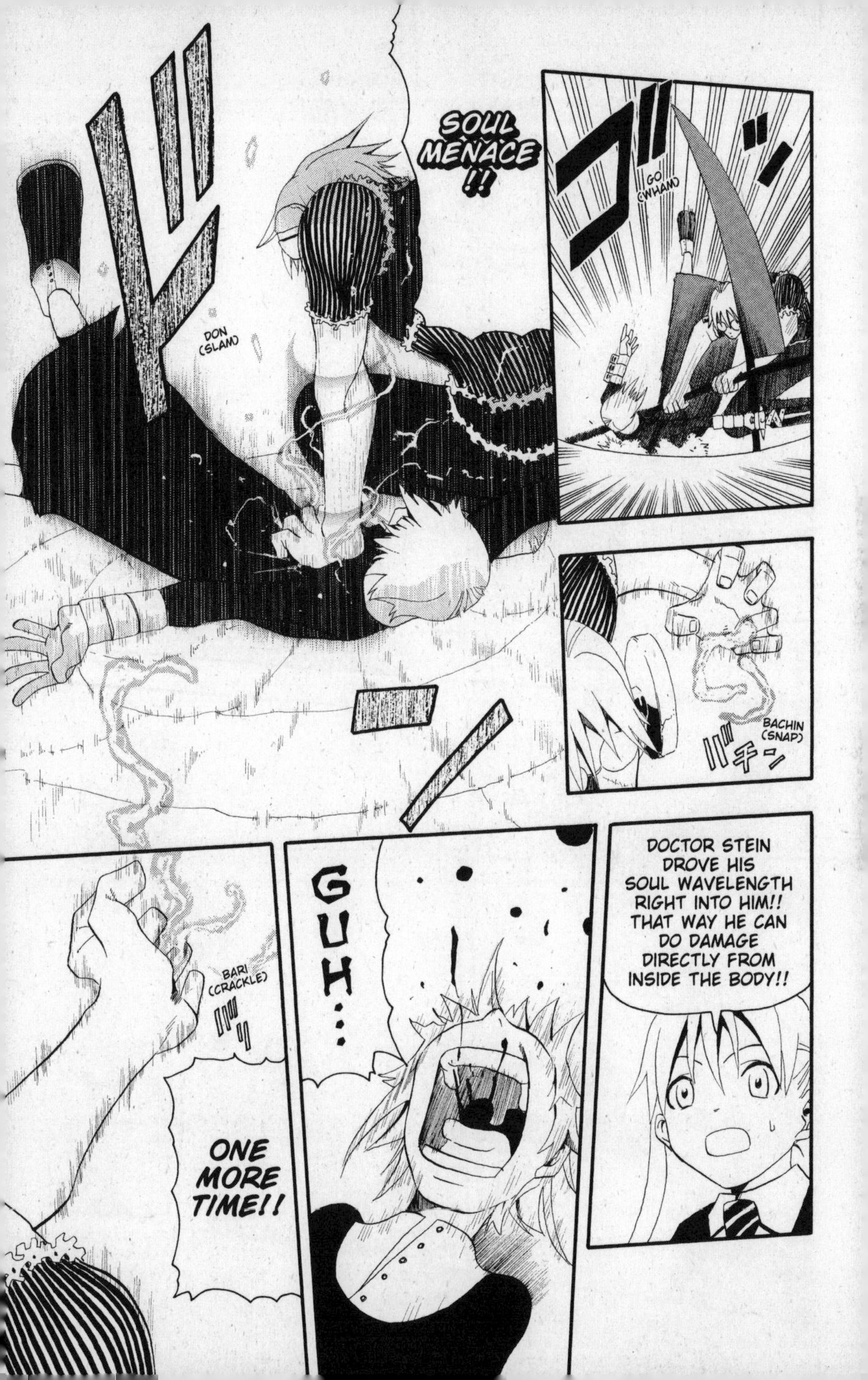
GO (WHAM)
BACHIN (SNAP)
SOUL MENACE!!
DON (SLAM)
DOCTOR STEIN DROVE HIS SOUL WAVELENGTH RIGHT INTO HIM!! THAT WAY HE CAN DO DAMAGE DIRECTLY FROM INSIDE THE BODY!!
GUH...
BARI (CRACKLE)
ONE MORE TIME!!

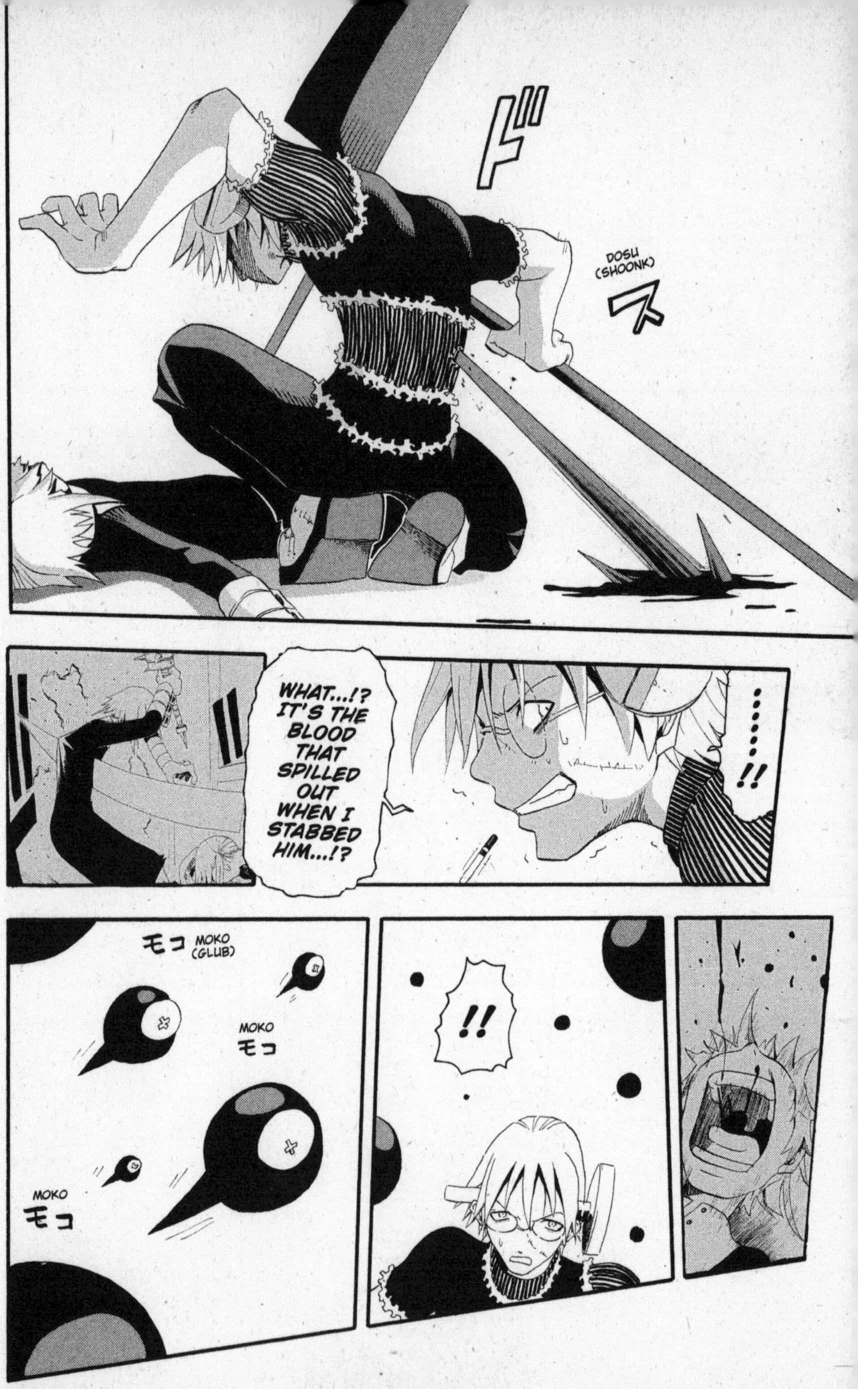
ド
DOSU (SHOONK)
ス
......!!
WHAT...!? IT'S THE BLOOD THAT SPILLED OUT WHEN I STABBED HIM...!?
!!
モコ MOKO (GLUB)
MOKO モコ
MOKO モコ

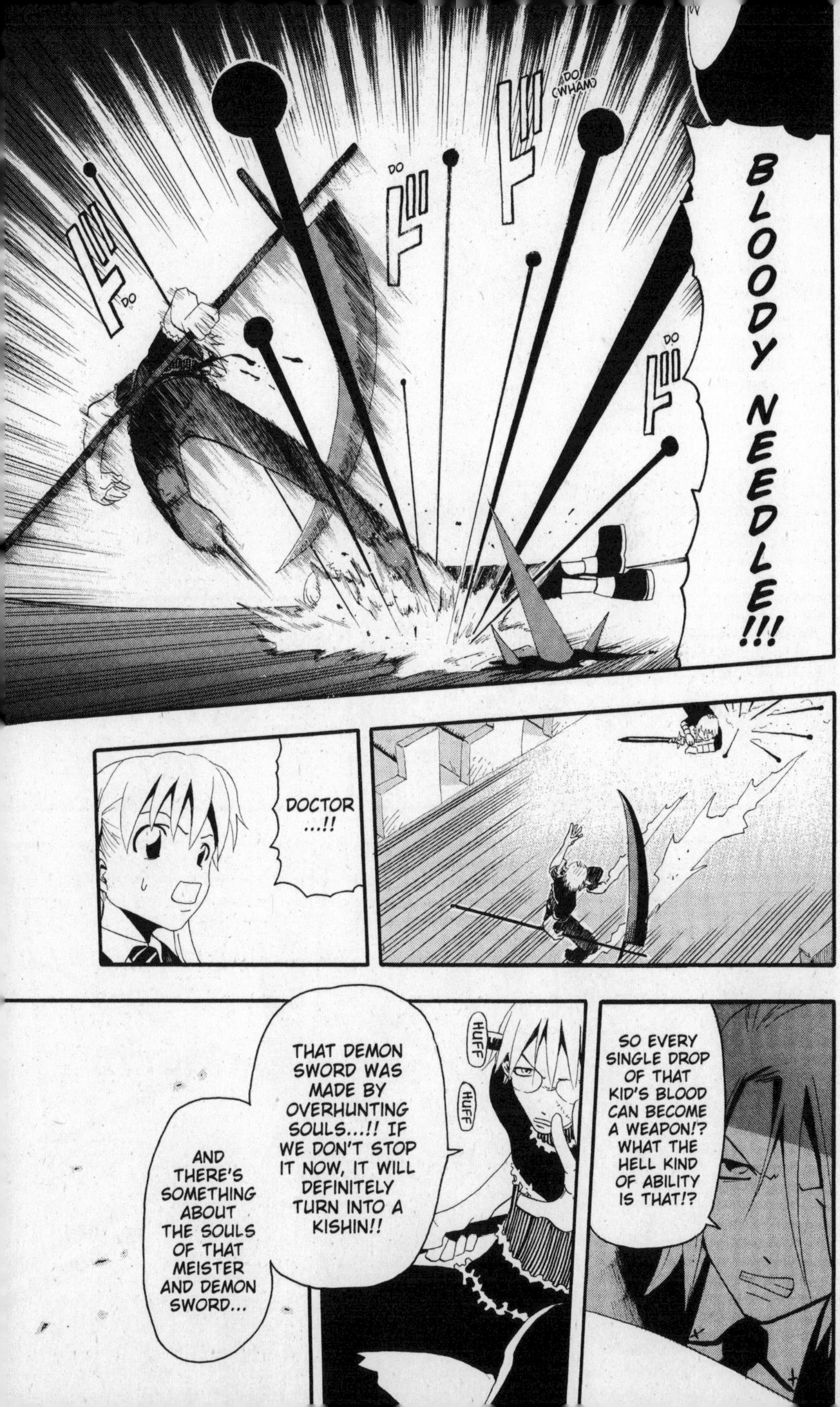
BLOODY NEEDLE!!!
DO
DO (WHAM)
DO
DO
DOCTOR ...!!
SO EVERY SINGLE DROP OF THAT KID'S BLOOD CAN BECOME A WEAPON!? WHAT THE HELL KIND OF ABILITY IS THAT!?
HUFF
HUFF
THAT DEMON SWORD WAS MADE BY OVERHUNTING SOULS...!! IF WE DON'T STOP IT NOW, IT WILL DEFINITELY TURN INTO A KISHIN!!
AND THERE'S SOMETHING ABOUT THE SOULS OF THAT MEISTER AND DEMON SWORD...

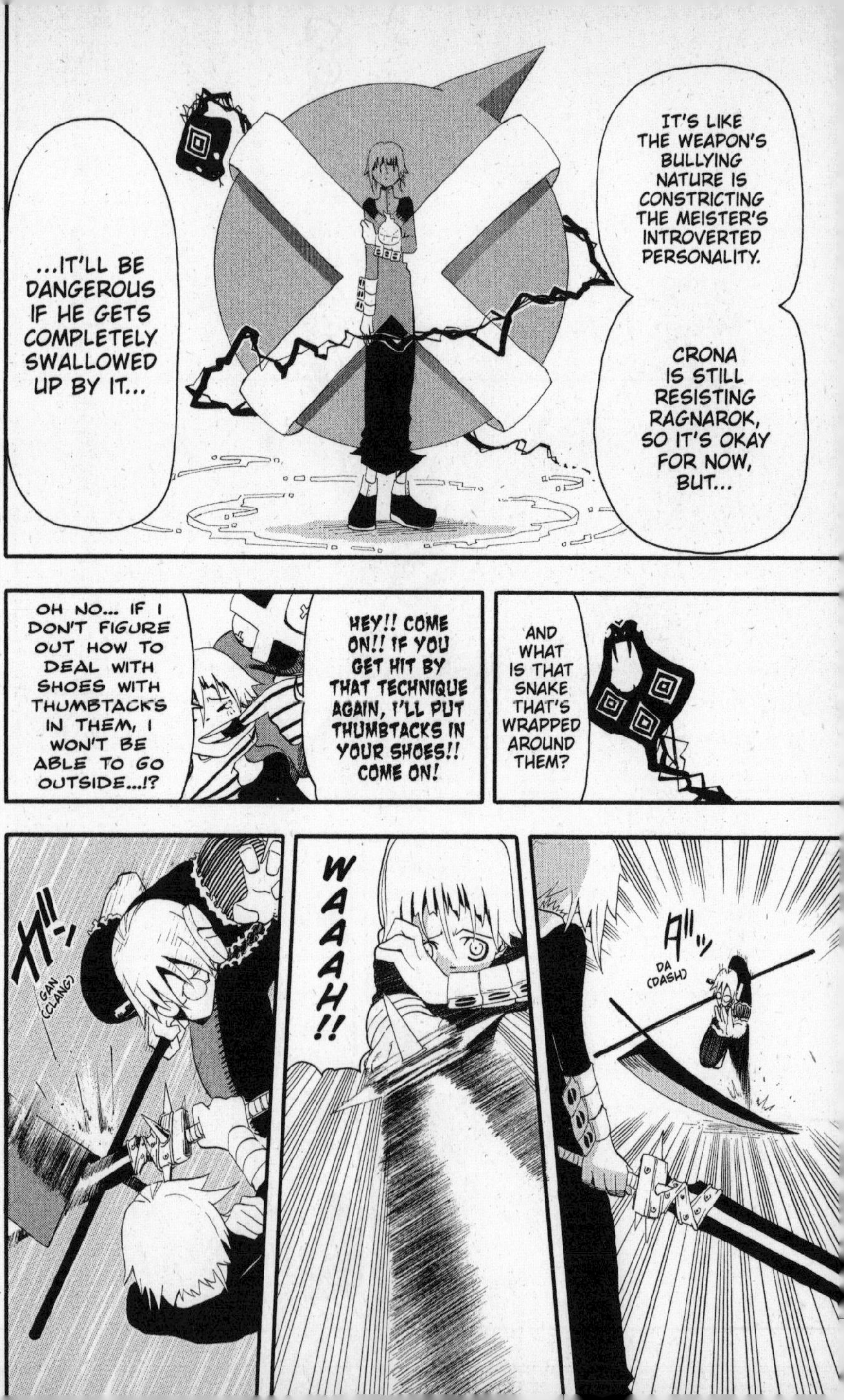
IT'S LIKE THE WEAPON'S BULLYING NATURE IS CONSTRICTING THE MEISTER'S INTROVERTED PERSONALITY.
CRONA IS STILL RESISTING RAGNAROK, SO IT'S OKAY FOR NOW, BUT...
...IT'LL BE DANGEROUS IF HE GETS COMPLETELY SWALLOWED UP BY IT...
AND WHAT IS THAT SNAKE THAT'S WRAPPED AROUND THEM?
HEY!! COME ON!! IF YOU GET HIT BY THAT TECHNIQUE AGAIN, I'LL PUT THUMBTACKS IN YOUR SHOES!! COME ON!
OH NO... IF I DON'T FIGURE OUT HOW TO DEAL WITH SHOES WITH THUMBTACKS IN THEM, I WON'T BE ABLE TO GO OUTSIDE...!?
DA (DASH)
WAAAAH!!
GAN (CLANG)

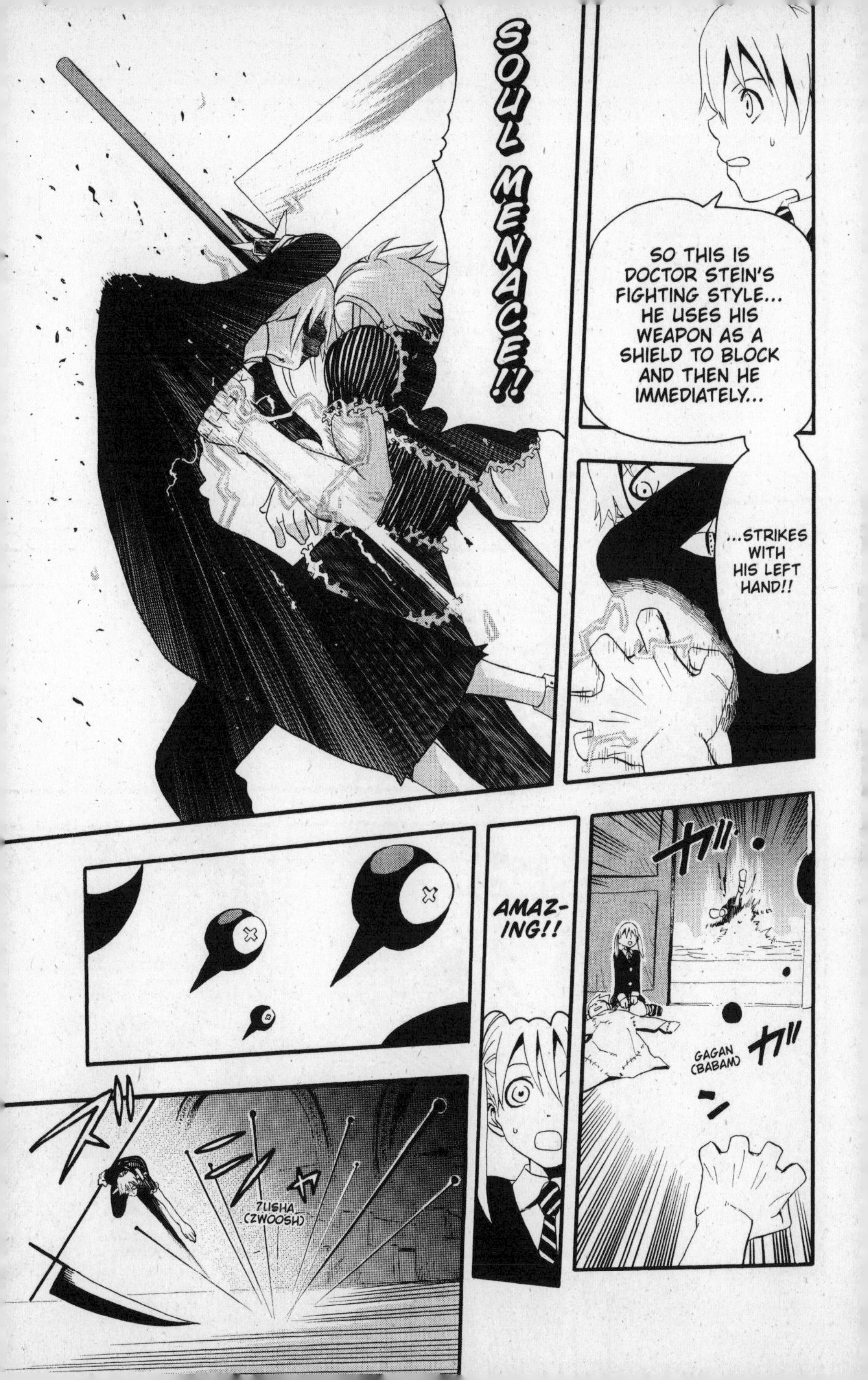
SO THIS IS DOCTOR STEIN'S FIGHTING STYLE... HE USES HIS WEAPON AS A SHIELD TO BLOCK AND THEN HE IMMEDIATELY...
...STRIKES WITH HIS LEFT HAND!!
SOUL MENACE!!
GAGAN (BABAM)
AMAZ-ING!!
ZUSHA (ZWOOSH)

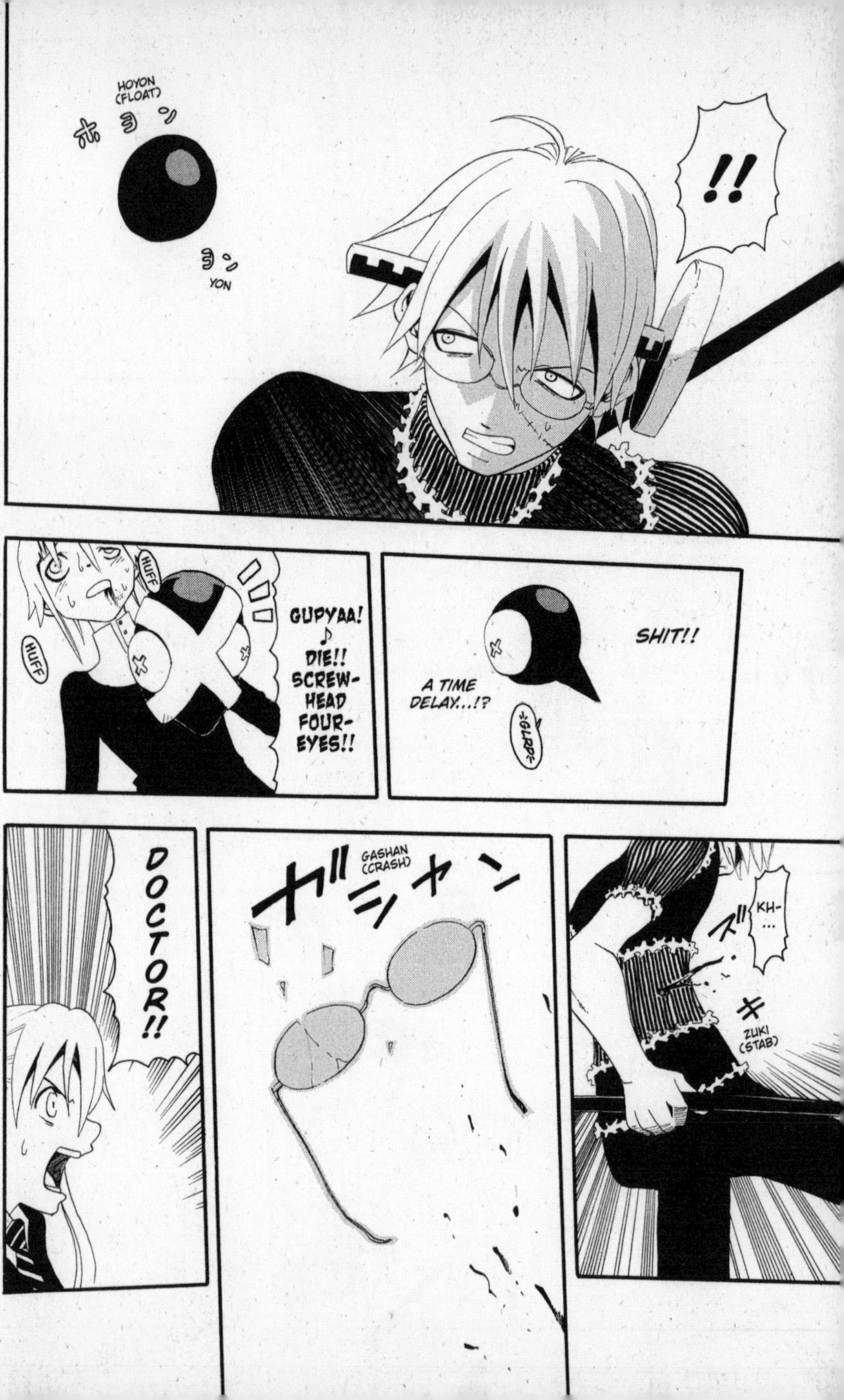
!!
HOYON (FLOAT)
ホヨン
ヨン
YON
SHIT!!
A TIME DELAY...!?
GLURP
GUPYAA! ♪ DIE!! SCREW-HEAD FOUR-EYES!!
HUFF
HUFF
KH-...
ズ
キ
ZUKI (STAB)
ガシャン
GASHAN (CRASH)
DOCTOR!!

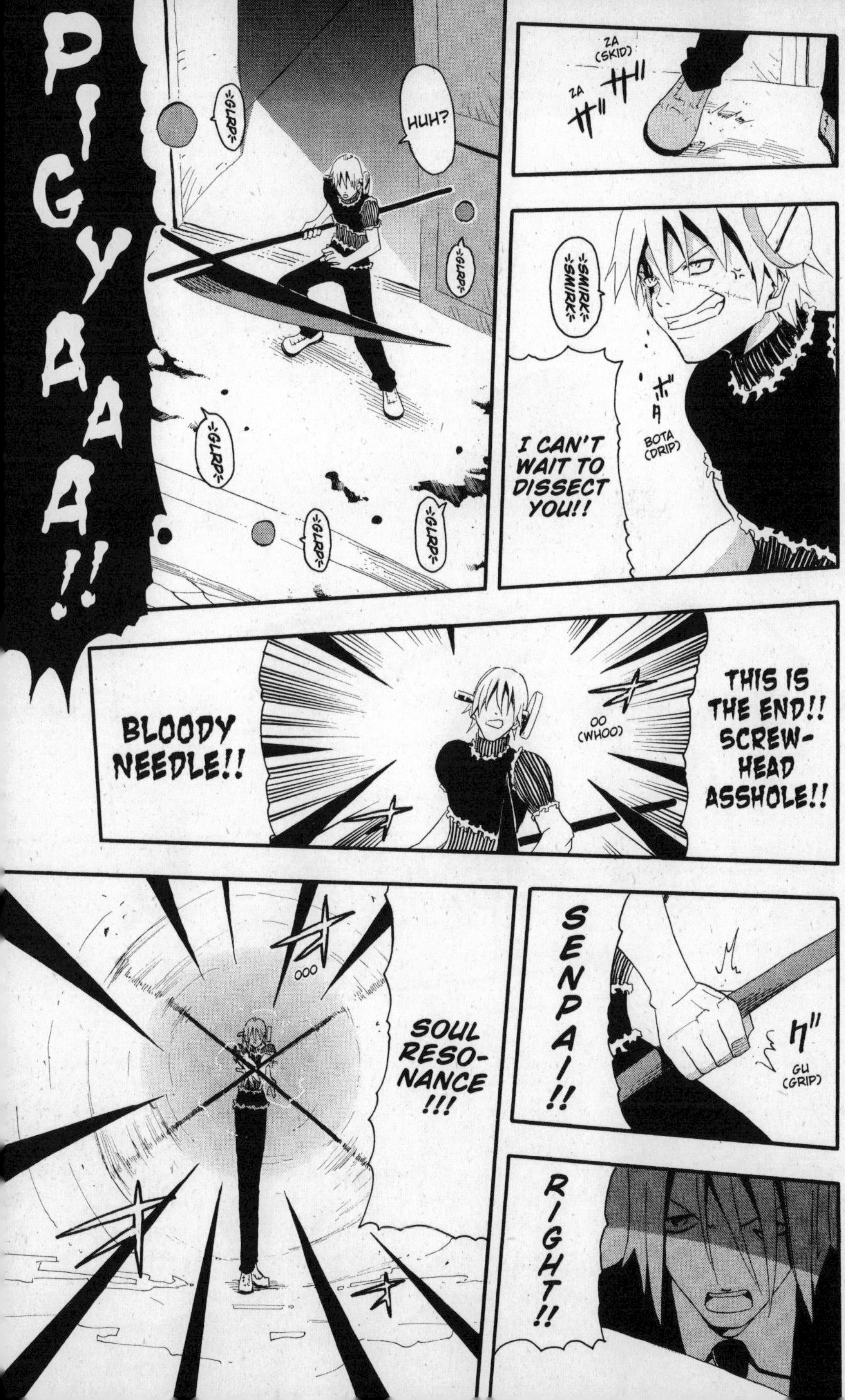
ZA (SKID)
ZA
-SMIRK- -SMIRK-
I CAN'T WAIT TO DISSECT YOU!!
BOTA (DRIP)
HUH?
-GLRP-
-GLRP-
-GLRP-
-GLRP-
-GLRP-
PIGYAAA!!
THIS IS THE END!! SCREW-HEAD ASSHOLE!!
OO (WHOO)
BLOODY NEEDLE!!
SENPAI!!
GU (GRIP)
RIGHT!!
SOUL RESO-NANCE!!!
OOO

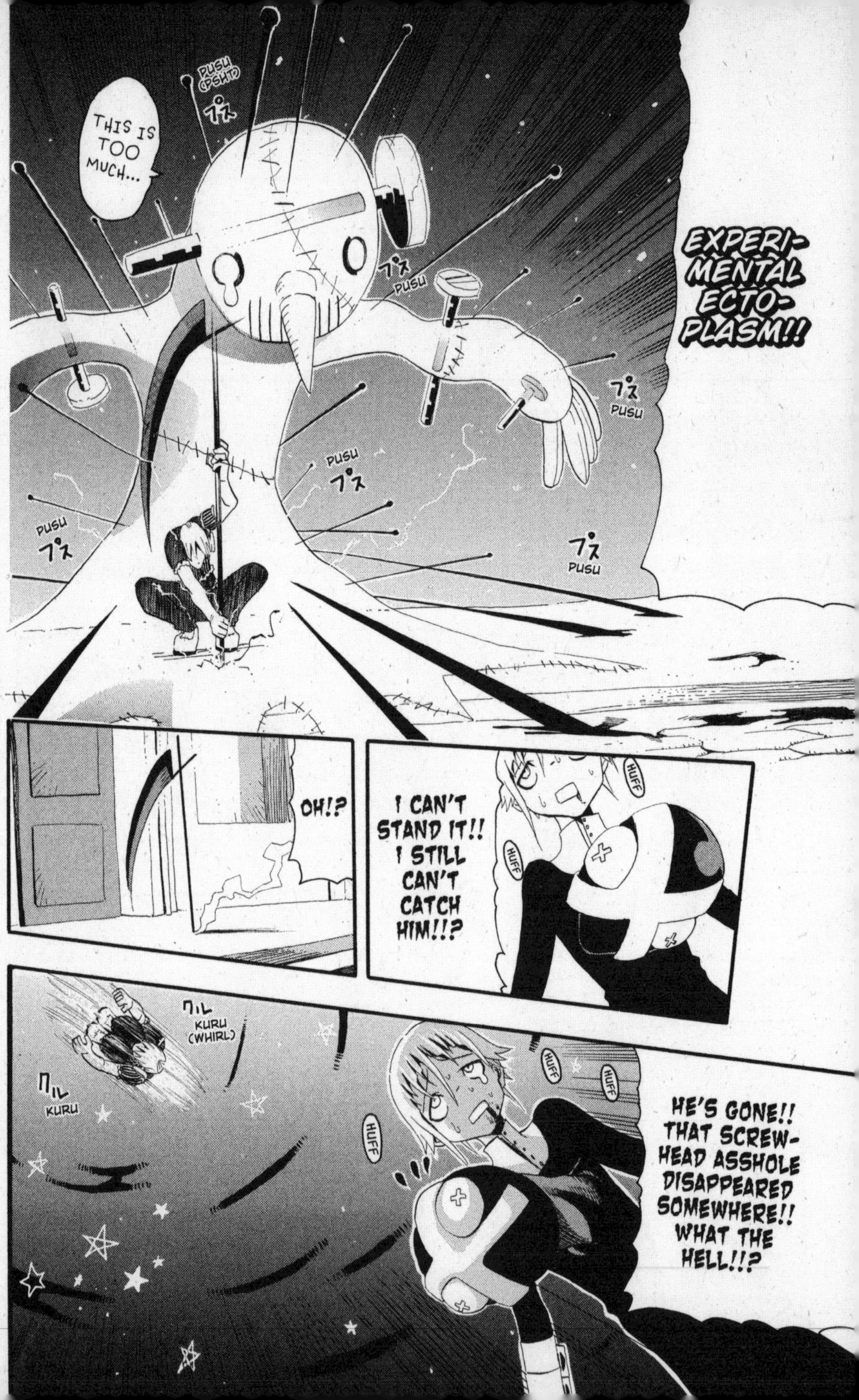

EXPERI-MENTAL ECTO-PLASM!!
PUSU (PSHT) プス
THIS IS TOO MUCH...
プス PUSU
プス PUSU
PUSU プス
PUSU プス
プス PUSU
HUFF
HUFF
I CAN'T STAND IT!! I STILL CAN'T CATCH HIM!!?
OH!?
HUFF
HUFF
HE'S GONE!! THAT SCREW-HEAD ASSHOLE DISAPPEARED SOMEWHERE!! WHAT THE HELL!!?
HUFF
クル KURU (WHIRL)
クル KURU

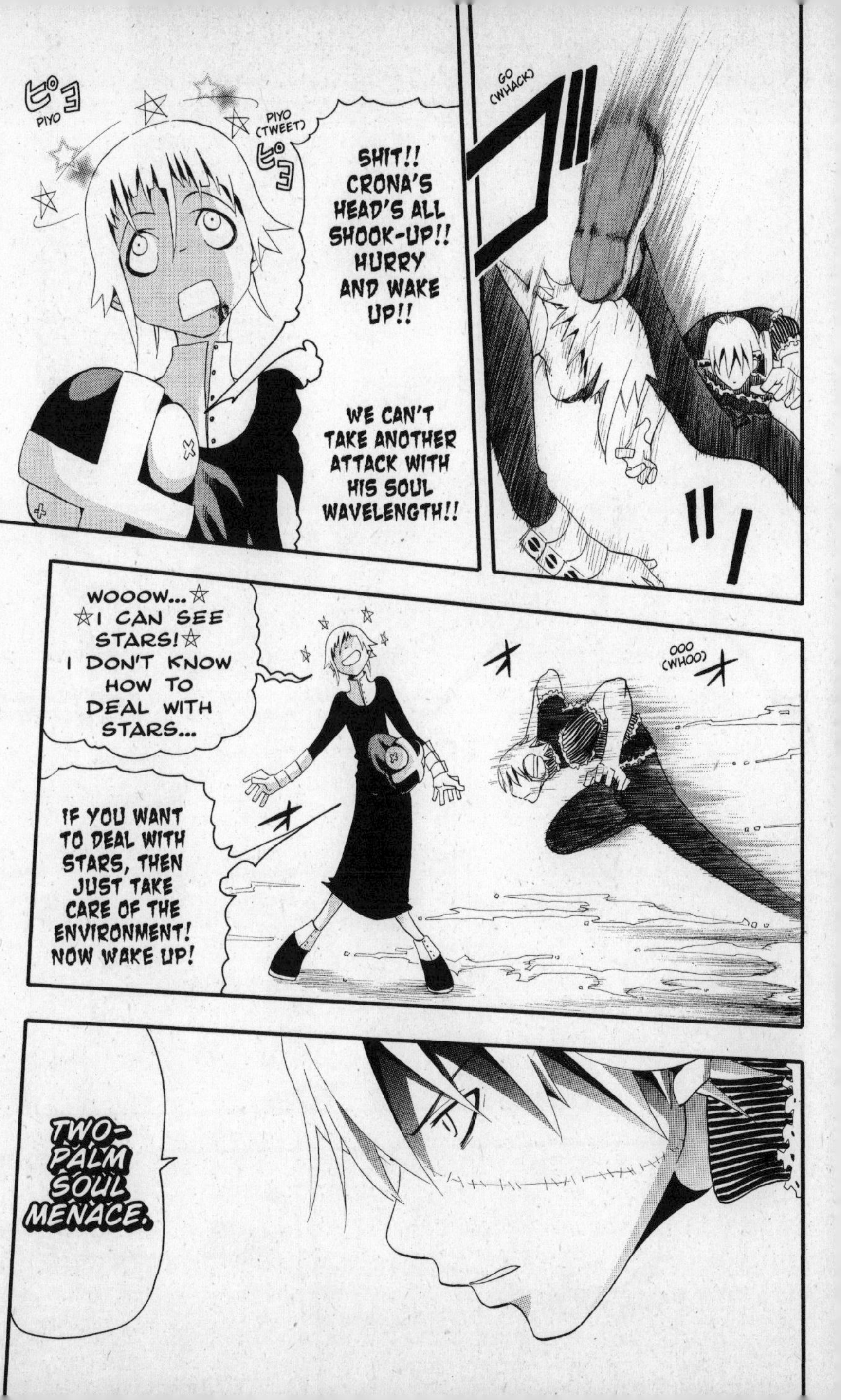
GO (WHACK)
PIYO (TWEET)
SHIT!! CRONA'S HEAD'S ALL SHOOK-UP!! HURRY AND WAKE UP!!
WE CAN'T TAKE ANOTHER ATTACK WITH HIS SOUL WAVELENGTH!!
PIYO
OOO (WHOO)
WOOOW...☆ ☆I CAN SEE STARS!☆ I DON'T KNOW HOW TO DEAL WITH STARS...
IF YOU WANT TO DEAL WITH STARS, THEN JUST TAKE CARE OF THE ENVIRONMENT! NOW WAKE UP!
TWO-PALM SOUL MENACE.

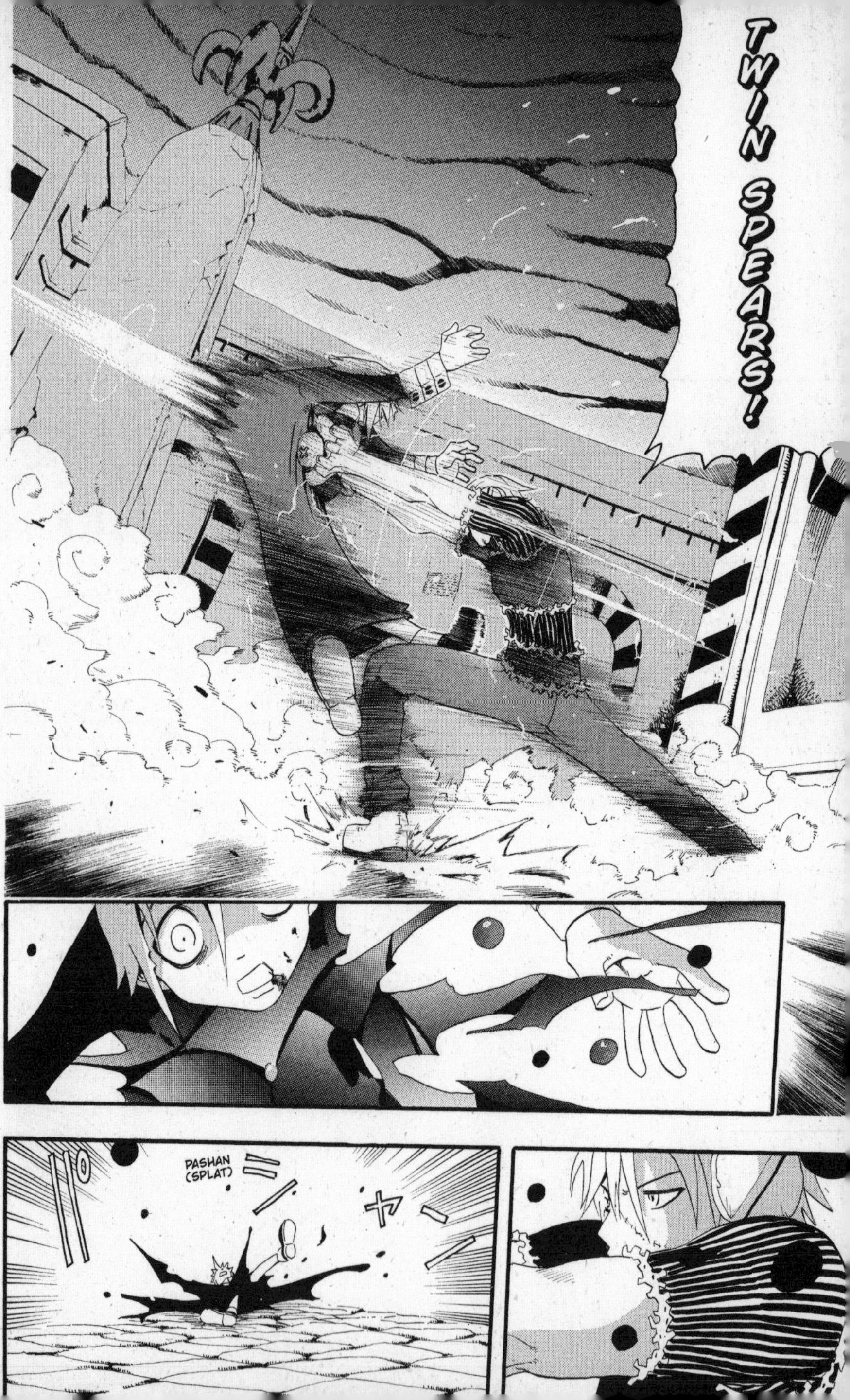
TWIN SPEARS!
PASHAN (SPLAT)

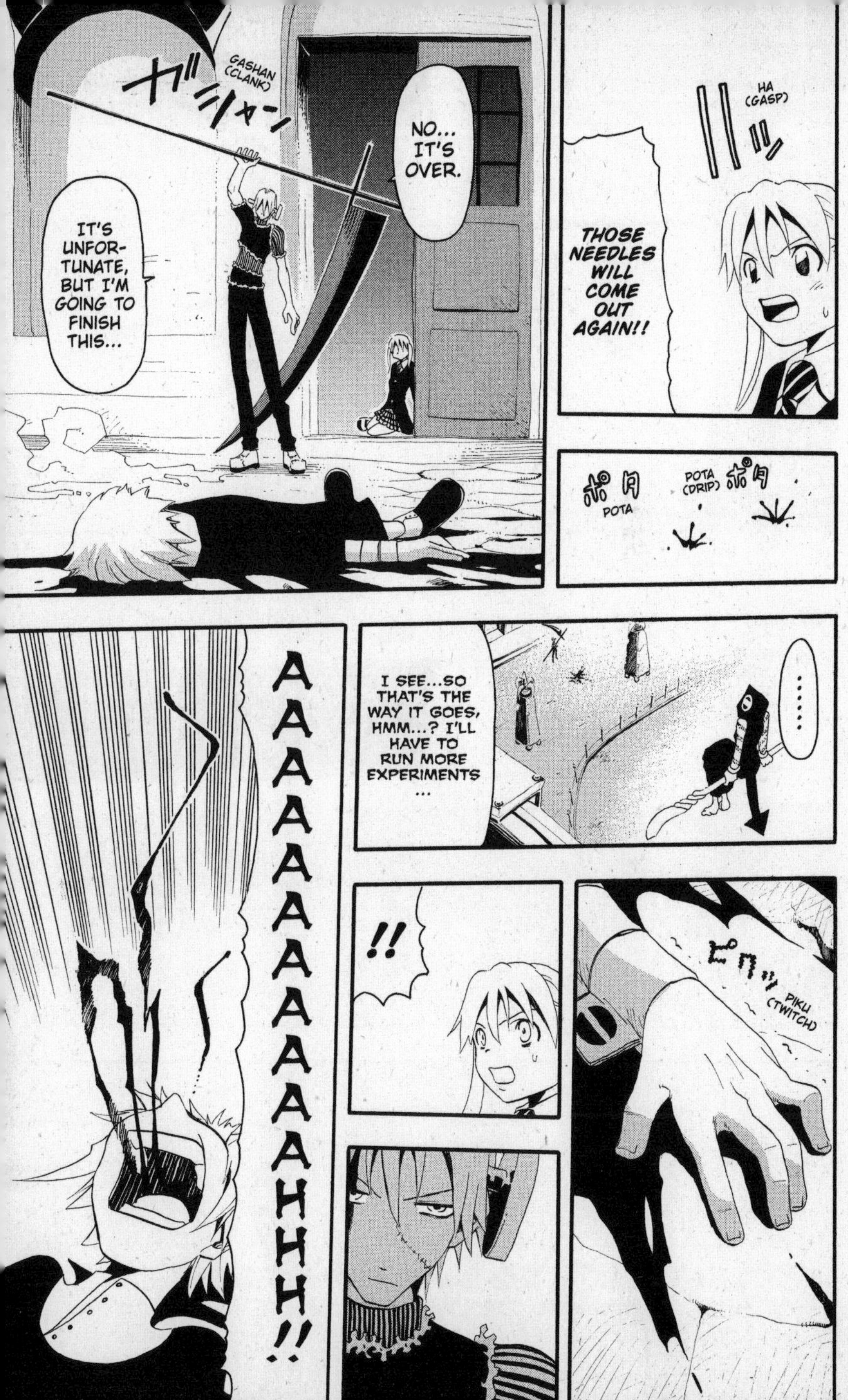
HA (GASP)
THOSE NEEDLES WILL COME OUT AGAIN!!
POTA (DRIP)
POTA
GASHAN (CLANK)
NO... IT'S OVER.
IT'S UNFORTUNATE, BUT I'M GOING TO FINISH THIS...
......
I SEE...SO THAT'S THE WAY IT GOES, HMM...? I'LL HAVE TO RUN MORE EXPERIMENTS ...
PIKU (TWITCH)
!!
AAAAAAAAAAAAAHHH!!

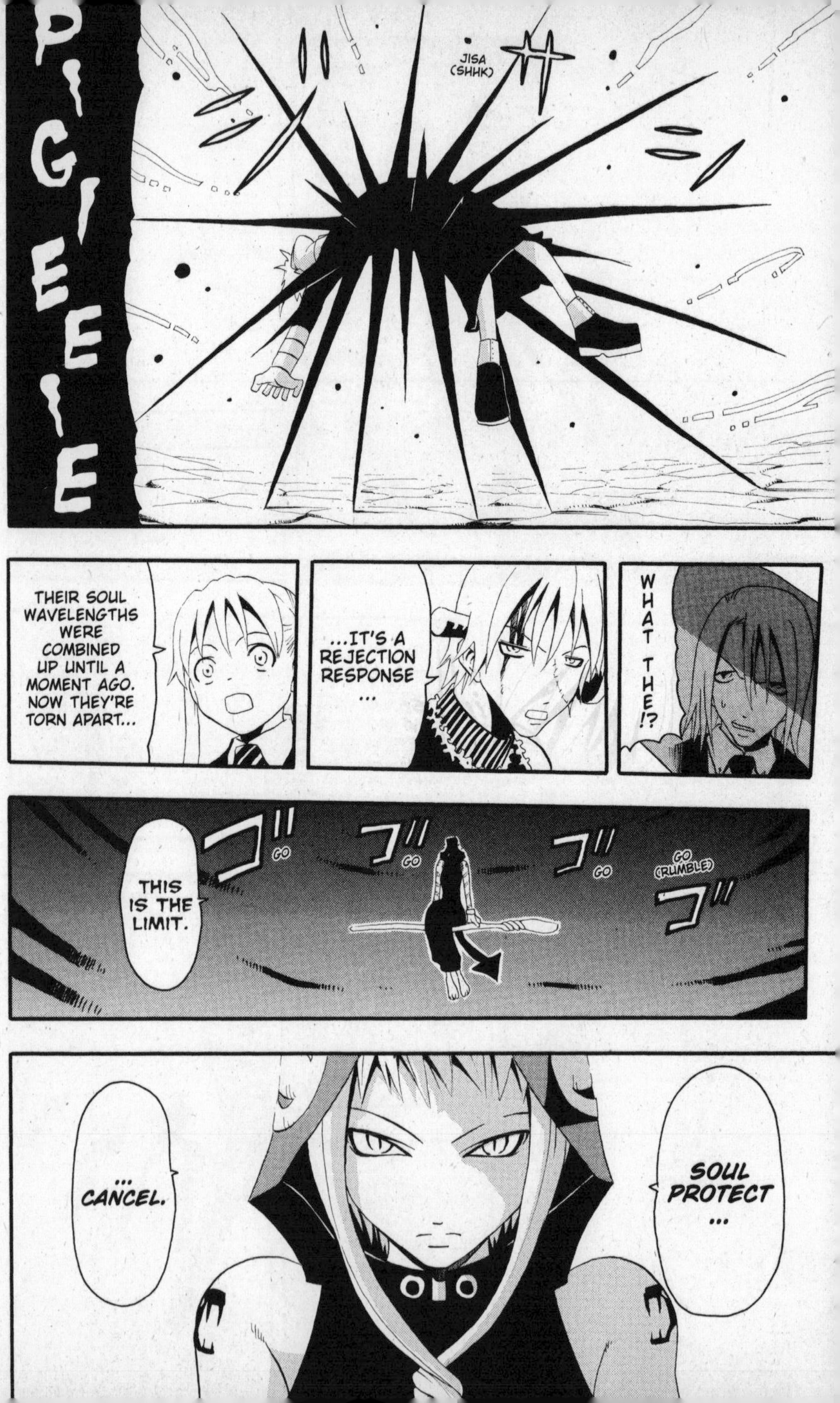
JISA (SHHK)
PGIEEE
WHAT THE!?
...IT'S A REJECTION RESPONSE ...
THEIR SOUL WAVELENGTHS WERE COMBINED UP UNTIL A MOMENT AGO. NOW THEY'RE TORN APART...
GO (RUMBLE)
GO
GO
GO
THIS IS THE LIMIT.
SOUL PROTECT ...
... CANCEL.

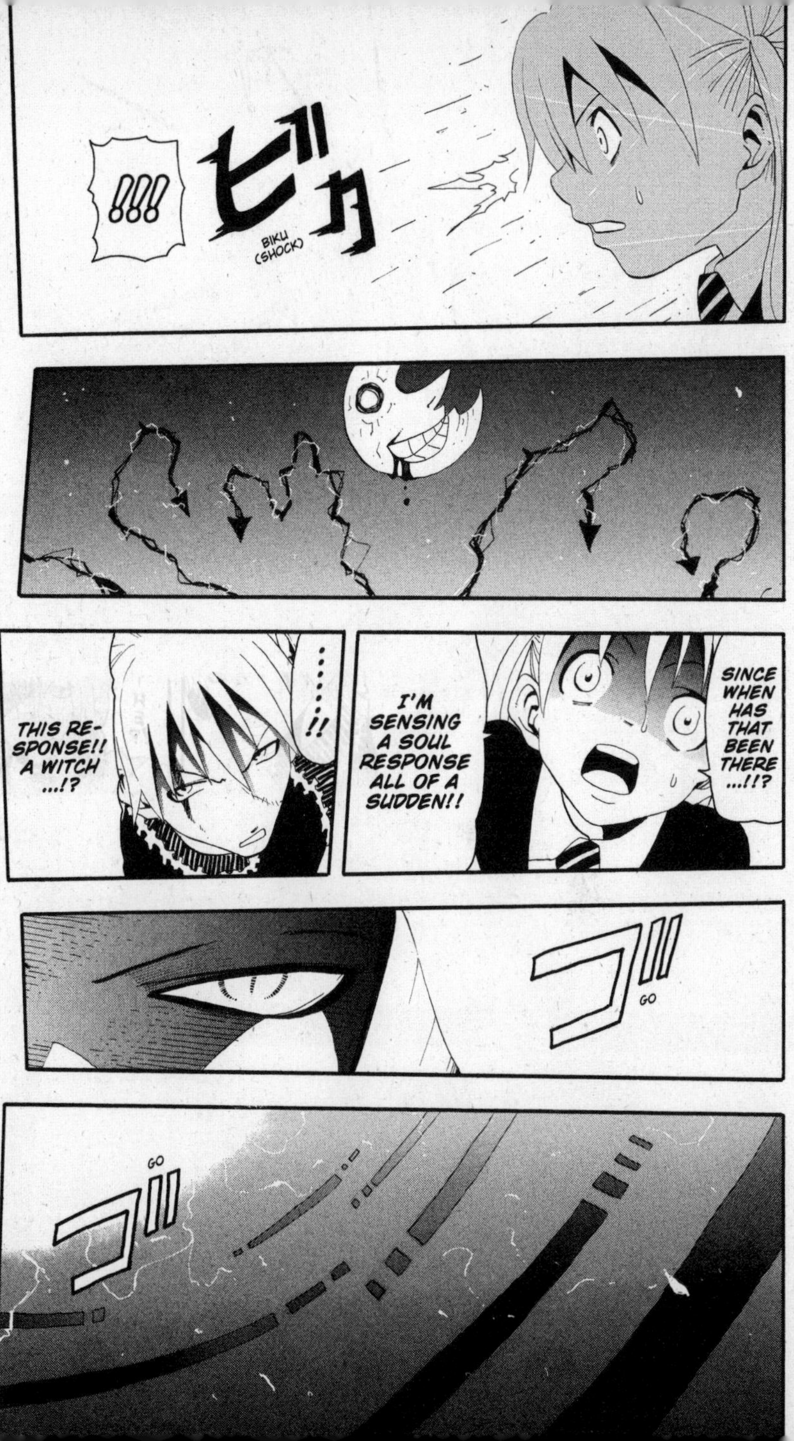
!!!!
ビク
BIKU (SHOCK)
SINCE WHEN HAS THAT BEEN THERE ...!!?
I'M SENSING A SOUL RESPONSE ALL OF A SUDDEN!!
......!!
THIS RE-SPONSE!! A WITCH ...!?
ゴ
GO
ゴ
GO

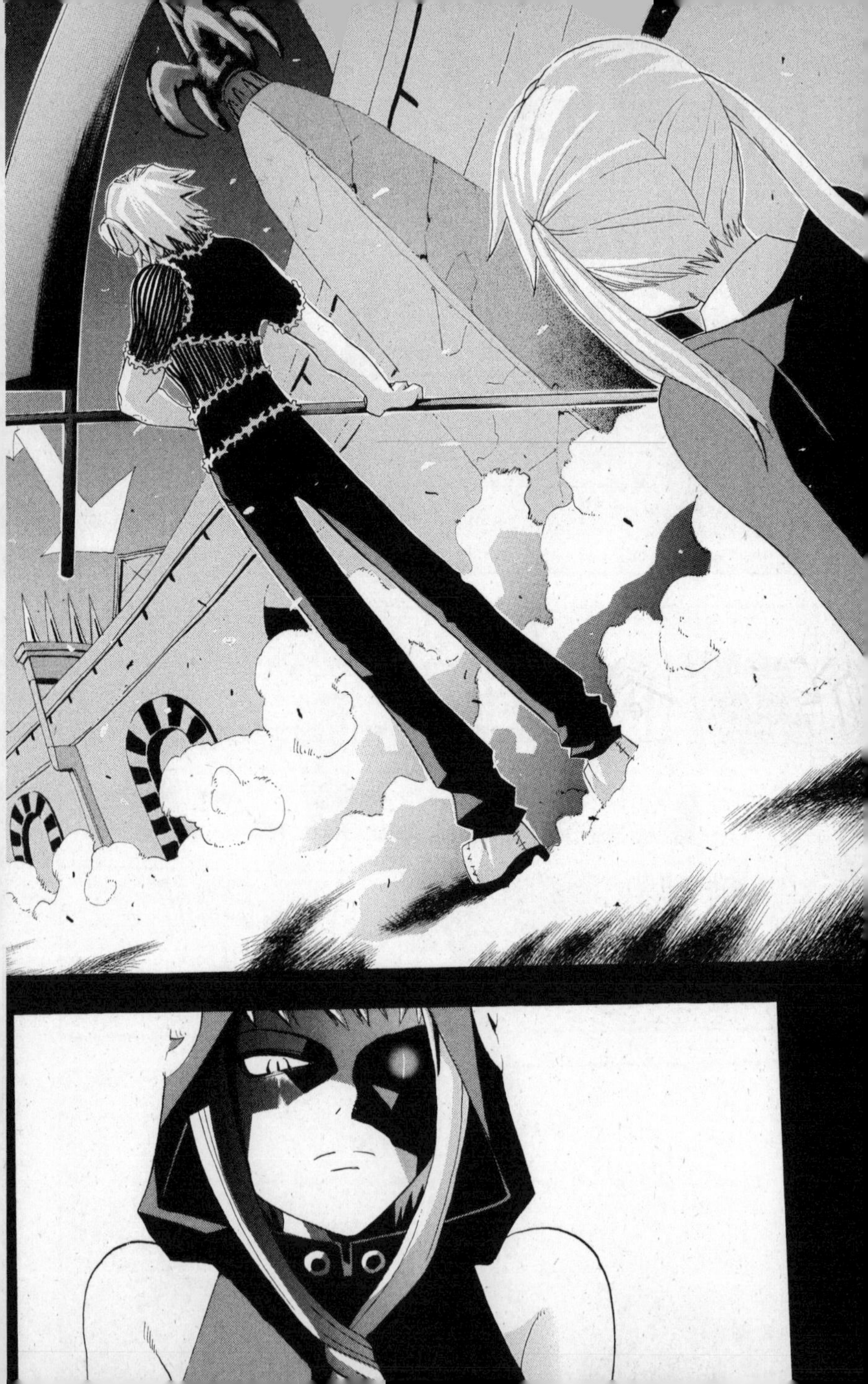

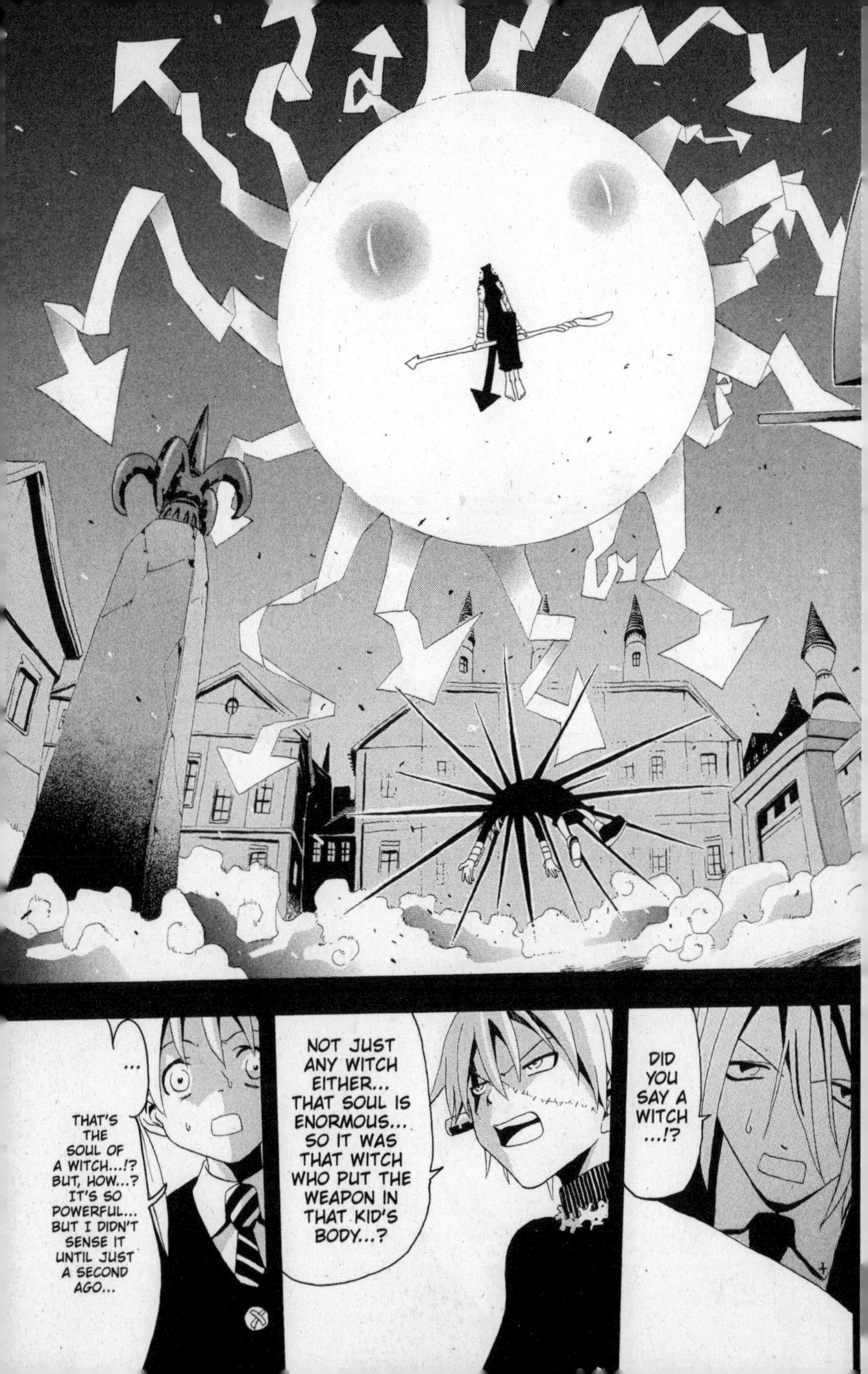
DID YOU SAY A WITCH ...!?
NOT JUST ANY WITCH EITHER... THAT SOUL IS ENORMOUS... SO IT WAS THAT WITCH WHO PUT THE WEAPON IN THAT KID'S BODY...?
...
THAT'S THE SOUL OF A WITCH...!? BUT, HOW...? IT'S SO POWERFUL... BUT I DIDN'T SENSE IT UNTIL JUST A SECOND AGO...

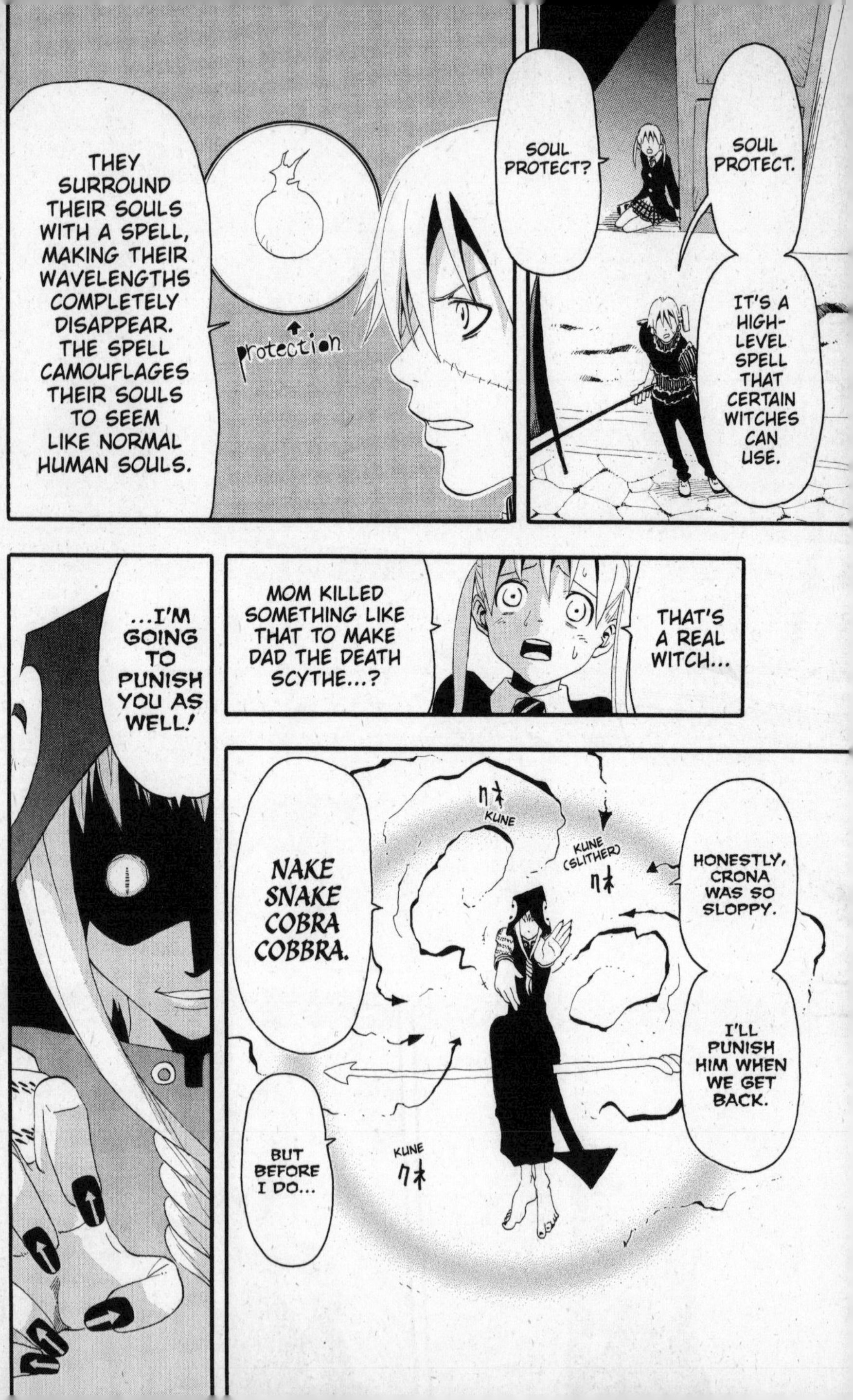
SOUL PROTECT.
SOUL PROTECT?
IT'S A HIGH-LEVEL SPELL THAT CERTAIN WITCHES CAN USE.
protection
THEY SURROUND THEIR SOULS WITH A SPELL, MAKING THEIR WAVELENGTHS COMPLETELY DISAPPEAR. THE SPELL CAMOUFLAGES THEIR SOULS TO SEEM LIKE NORMAL HUMAN SOULS.
THAT'S A REAL WITCH...
MOM KILLED SOMETHING LIKE THAT TO MAKE DAD THE DEATH SCYTHE...?
HONESTLY, CRONA WAS SO SLOPPY.
I'LL PUNISH HIM WHEN WE GET BACK.
クネ
KUNE (SLITHER)
クネ
KUNE
NAKE SNAKE COBRA COBBRA.
クネ
KUNE
BUT BEFORE I DO...
...I'M GOING TO PUNISH YOU AS WELL!

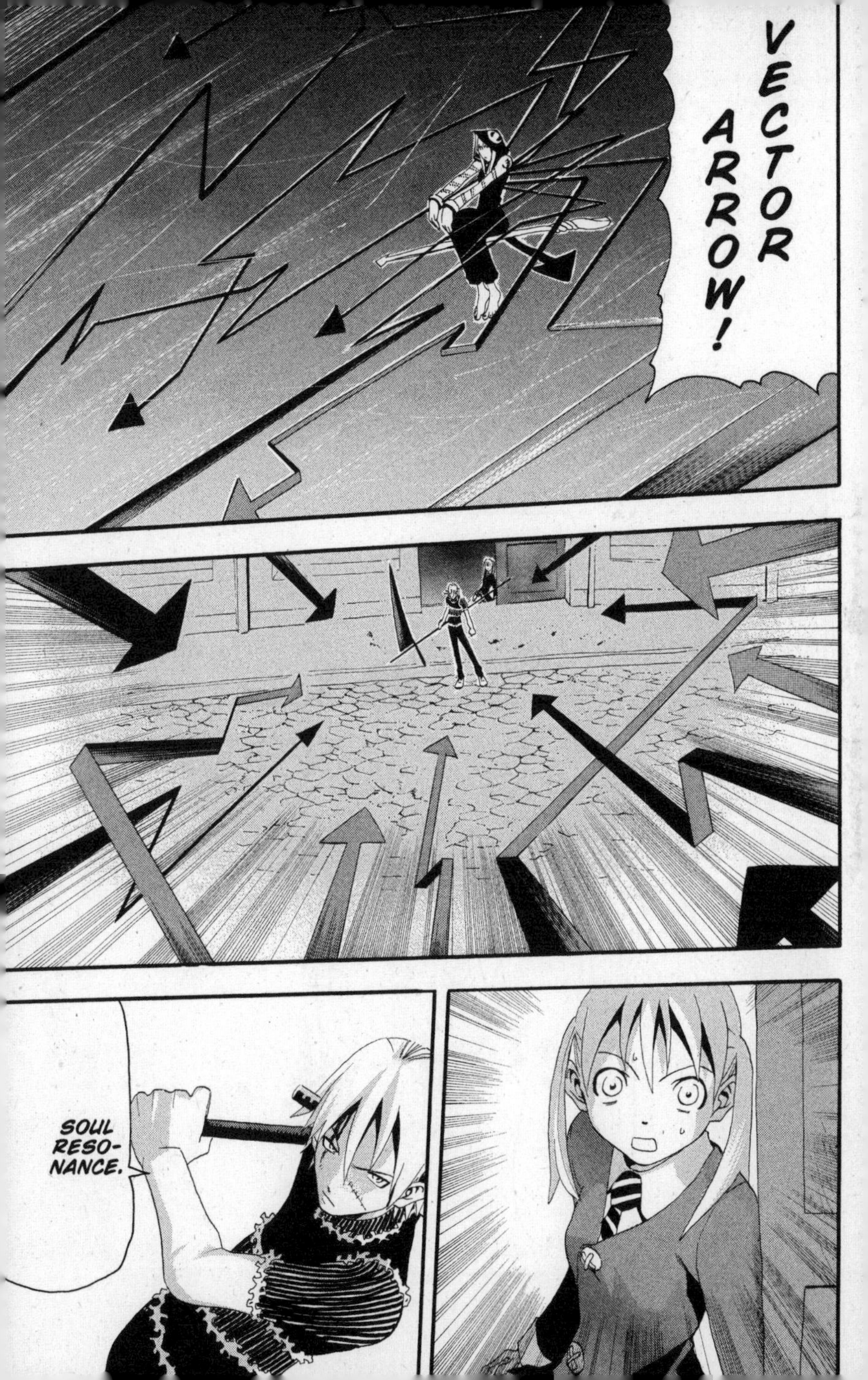
VECTOR ARROW!
SOUL RESO-NANCE.

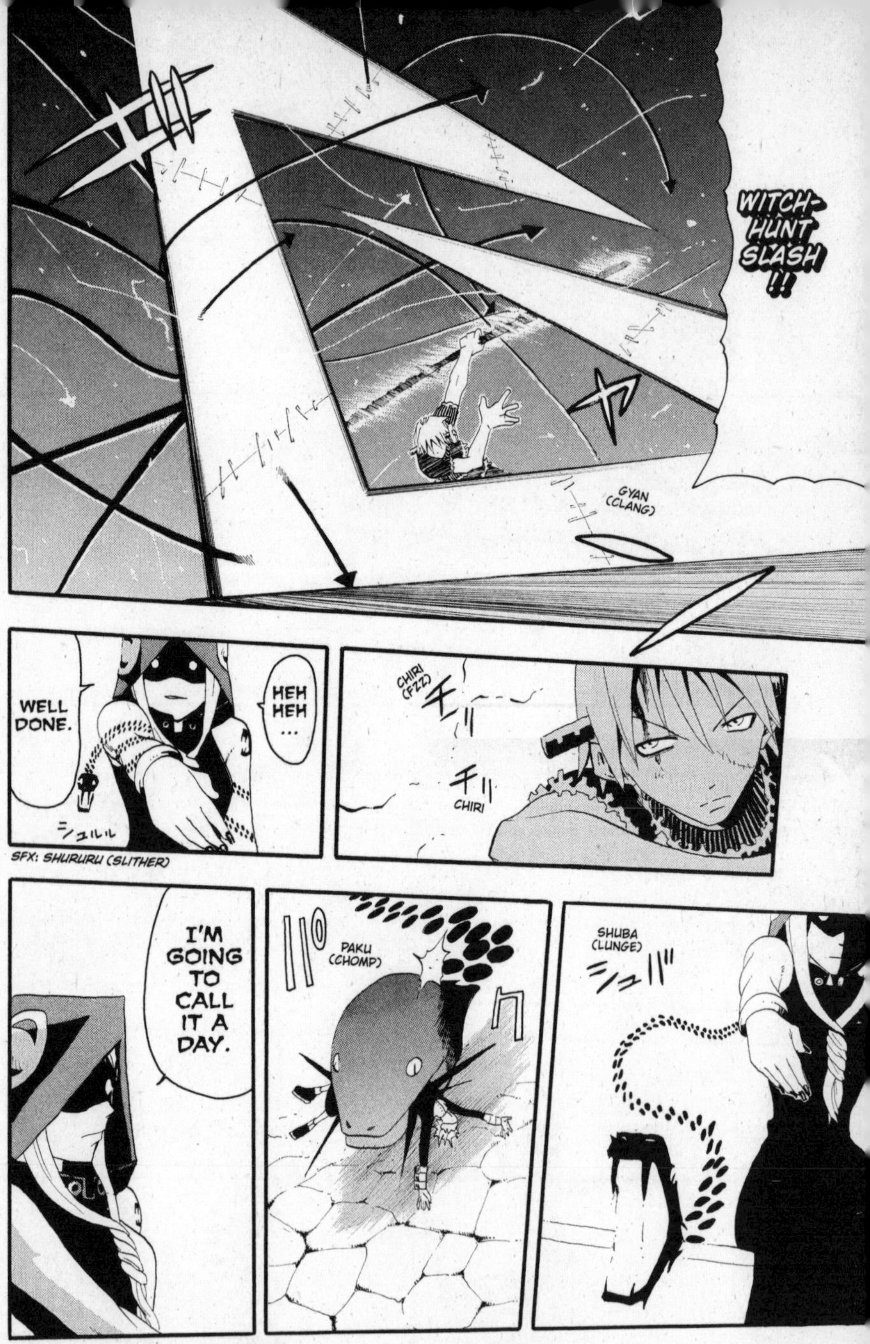
WITCH-HUNT SLASH !!
GYAN (CLANG)
CHIRI (FZZ)
CHIRI
HEH HEH ...
WELL DONE.
SFX: SHURURU (SLITHER)
SHUBA (LUNGE)
PAKU (CHOMP)
I'M GOING TO CALL IT A DAY.

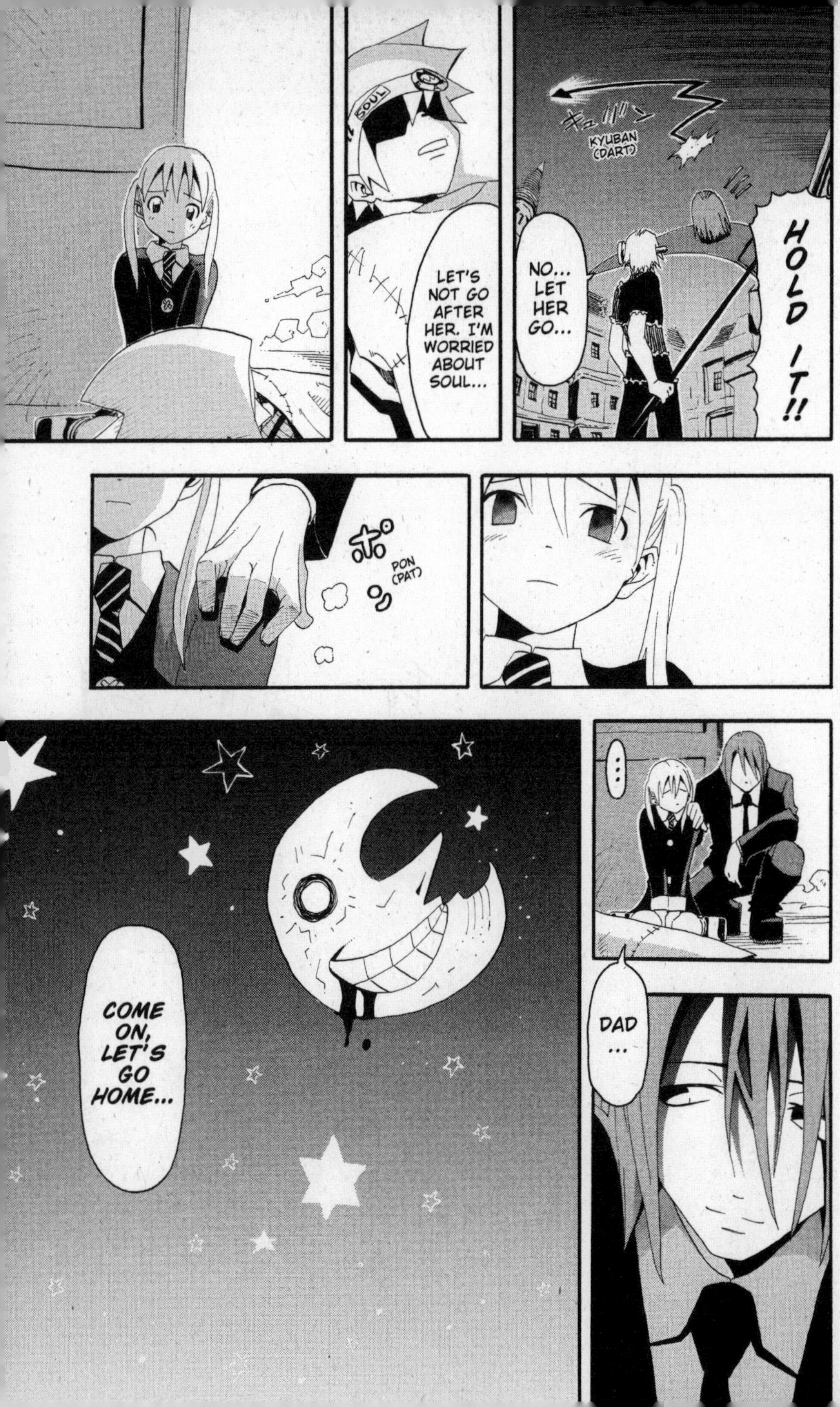
KYUBAN (DART)
HOLD IT!!
NO... LET HER GO...
LET'S NOT GO AFTER HER. I'M WORRIED ABOUT SOUL...
PON (PAT)
...
DAD ...
COME ON, LET'S GO HOME...

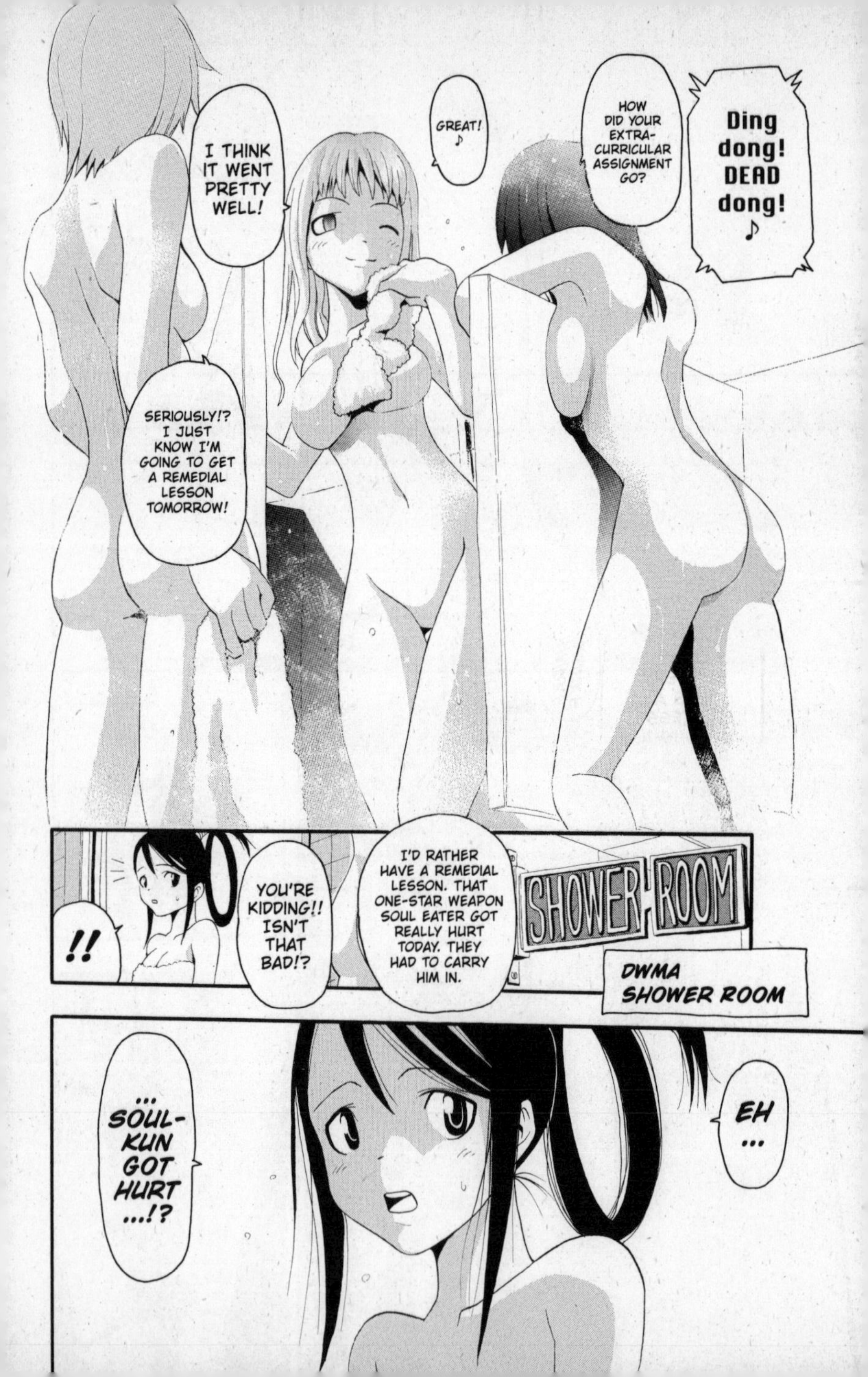
Ding dong! DEAD dong! ♪
HOW DID YOUR EXTRA-CURRICULAR ASSIGNMENT GO?
GREAT! ♪
I THINK IT WENT PRETTY WELL!
SERIOUSLY!? I JUST KNOW I'M GOING TO GET A REMEDIAL LESSON TOMORROW!
SHOWER ROOM
DWMA SHOWER ROOM
I'D RATHER HAVE A REMEDIAL LESSON. THAT ONE-STAR WEAPON SOUL EATER GOT REALLY HURT TODAY. THEY HAD TO CARRY HIM IN.
YOU'RE KIDDING!! ISN'T THAT BAD!?
!!
EH ...
... SOUL-KUN GOT HURT ...!?

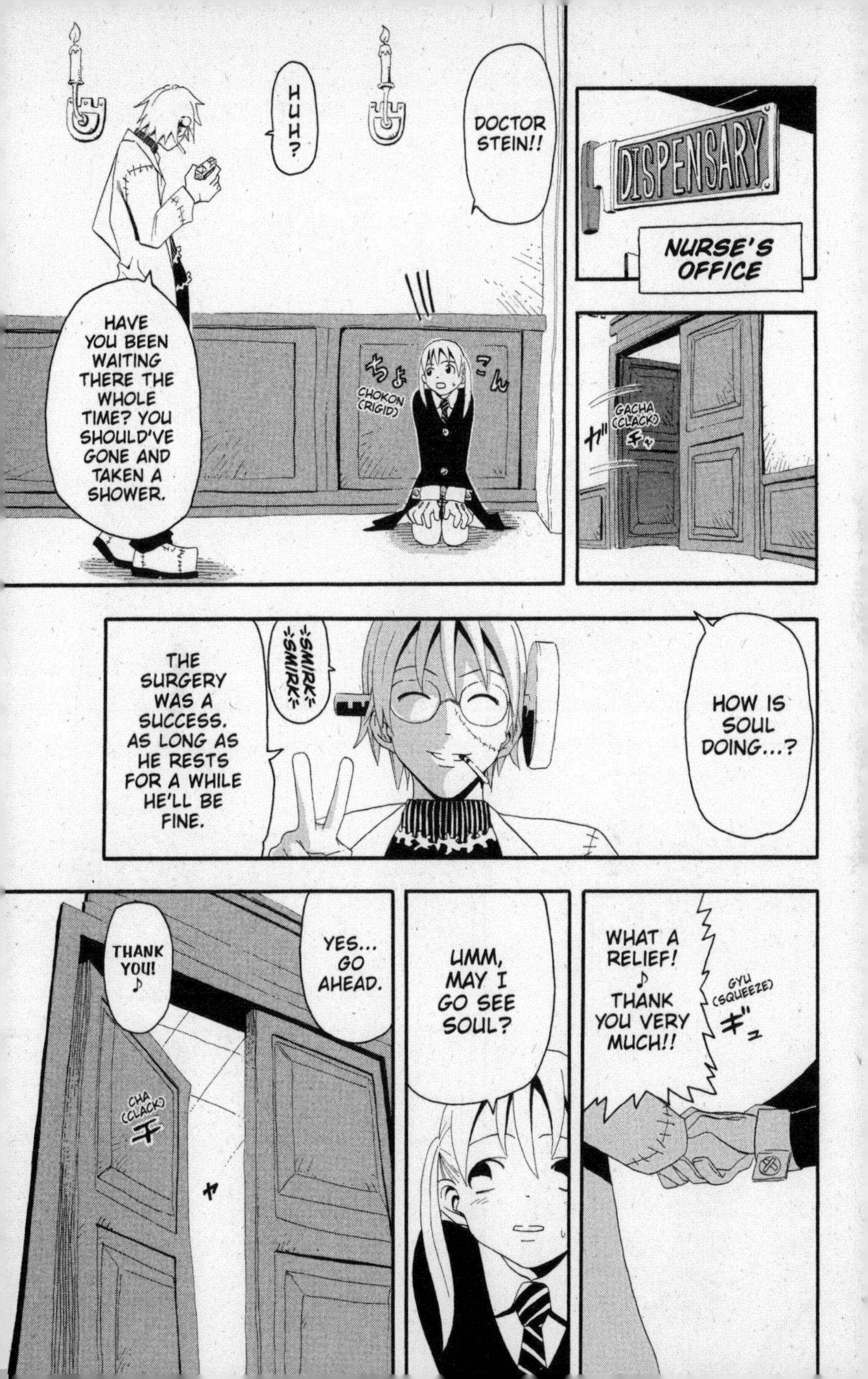
DISPENSARY
NURSE'S OFFICE
GACHA (CLACK)
DOCTOR STEIN!!
HUH?
HAVE YOU BEEN WAITING THERE THE WHOLE TIME? YOU SHOULD'VE GONE AND TAKEN A SHOWER.
CHOKON (RIGID)
HOW IS SOUL DOING...?
THE SURGERY WAS A SUCCESS. AS LONG AS HE RESTS FOR A WHILE HE'LL BE FINE.
SMIRK SMIRK
WHAT A RELIEF! ♪ THANK YOU VERY MUCH!!
GYU (SQUEEZE)
UMM, MAY I GO SEE SOUL?
YES... GO AHEAD.
THANK YOU! ♪
CHA (CLACK)

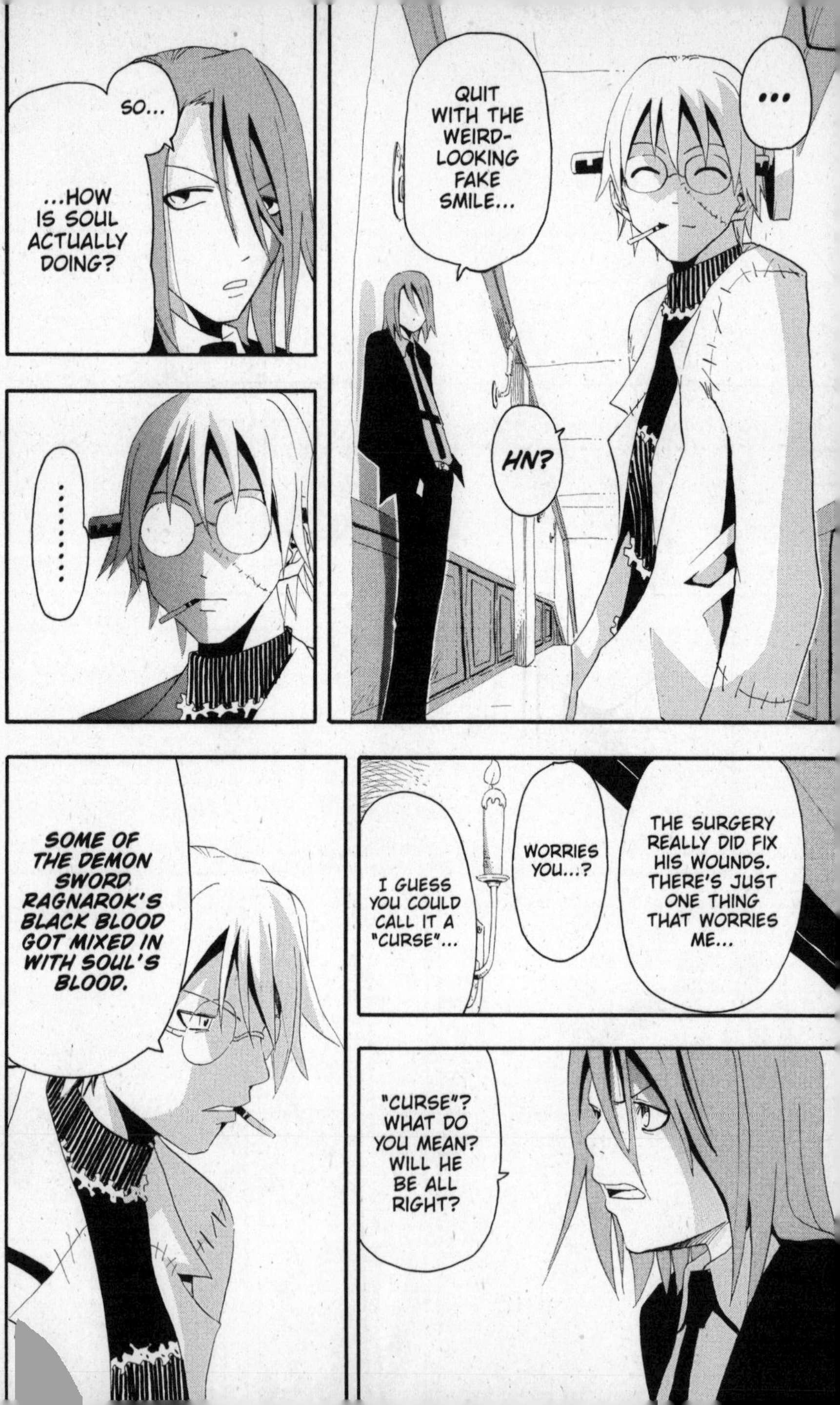
...
QUIT WITH THE WEIRD-LOOKING FAKE SMILE...
HN?
SO...
...HOW IS SOUL ACTUALLY DOING?
....
THE SURGERY REALLY DID FIX HIS WOUNDS. THERE'S JUST ONE THING THAT WORRIES ME...
WORRIES YOU...?
I GUESS YOU COULD CALL IT A "CURSE"...
"CURSE"? WHAT DO YOU MEAN? WILL HE BE ALL RIGHT?
SOME OF THE DEMON SWORD RAGNAROK'S BLACK BLOOD GOT MIXED IN WITH SOUL'S BLOOD.

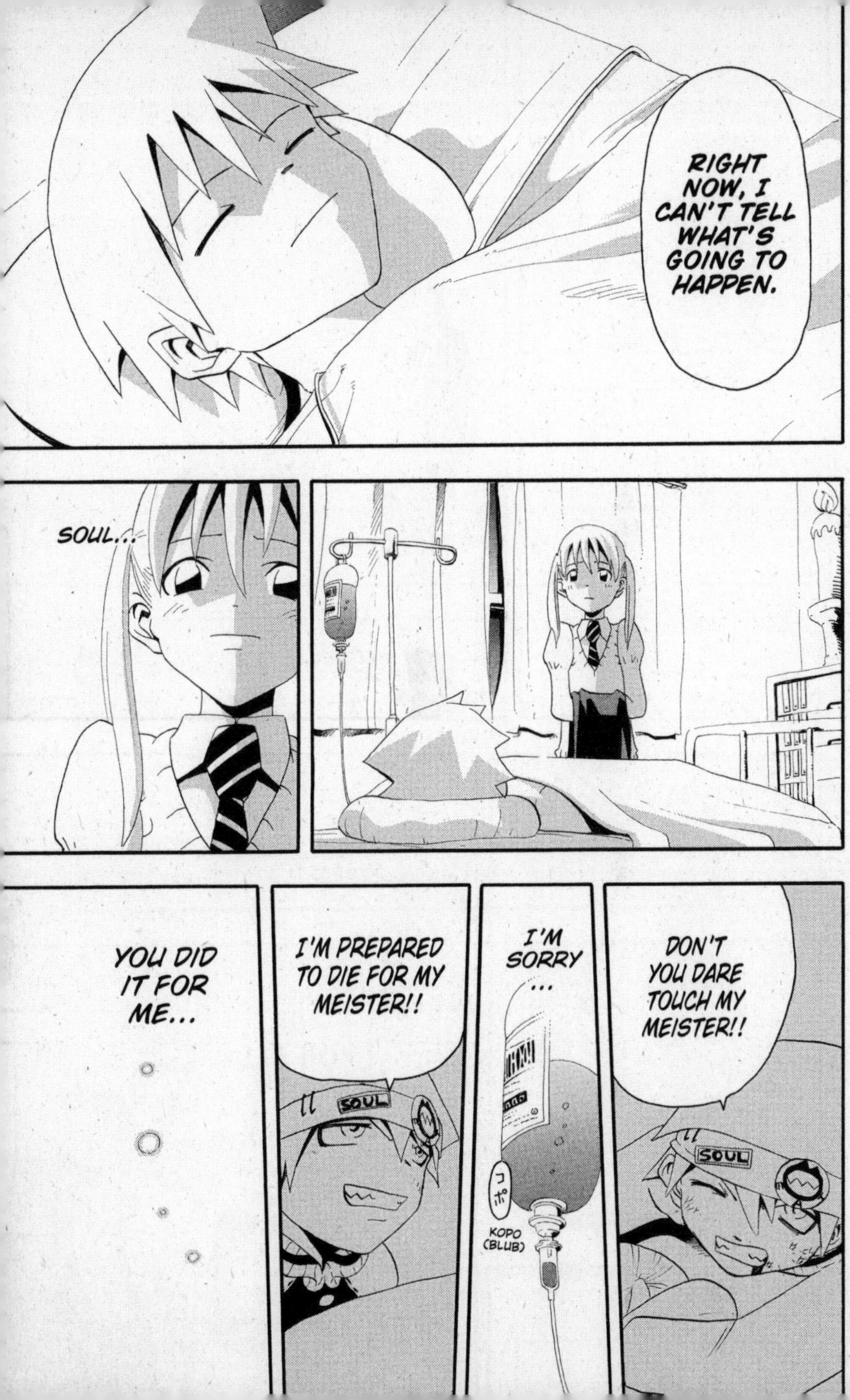
RIGHT NOW, I CAN'T TELL WHAT'S GOING TO HAPPEN.
SOUL...
DON'T YOU DARE TOUCH MY MEISTER!!
SOUL
I'M SORRY ...
コポ
KOPO (BLUB)
I'M PREPARED TO DIE FOR MY MEISTER!!
SOUL
YOU DID IT FOR ME...

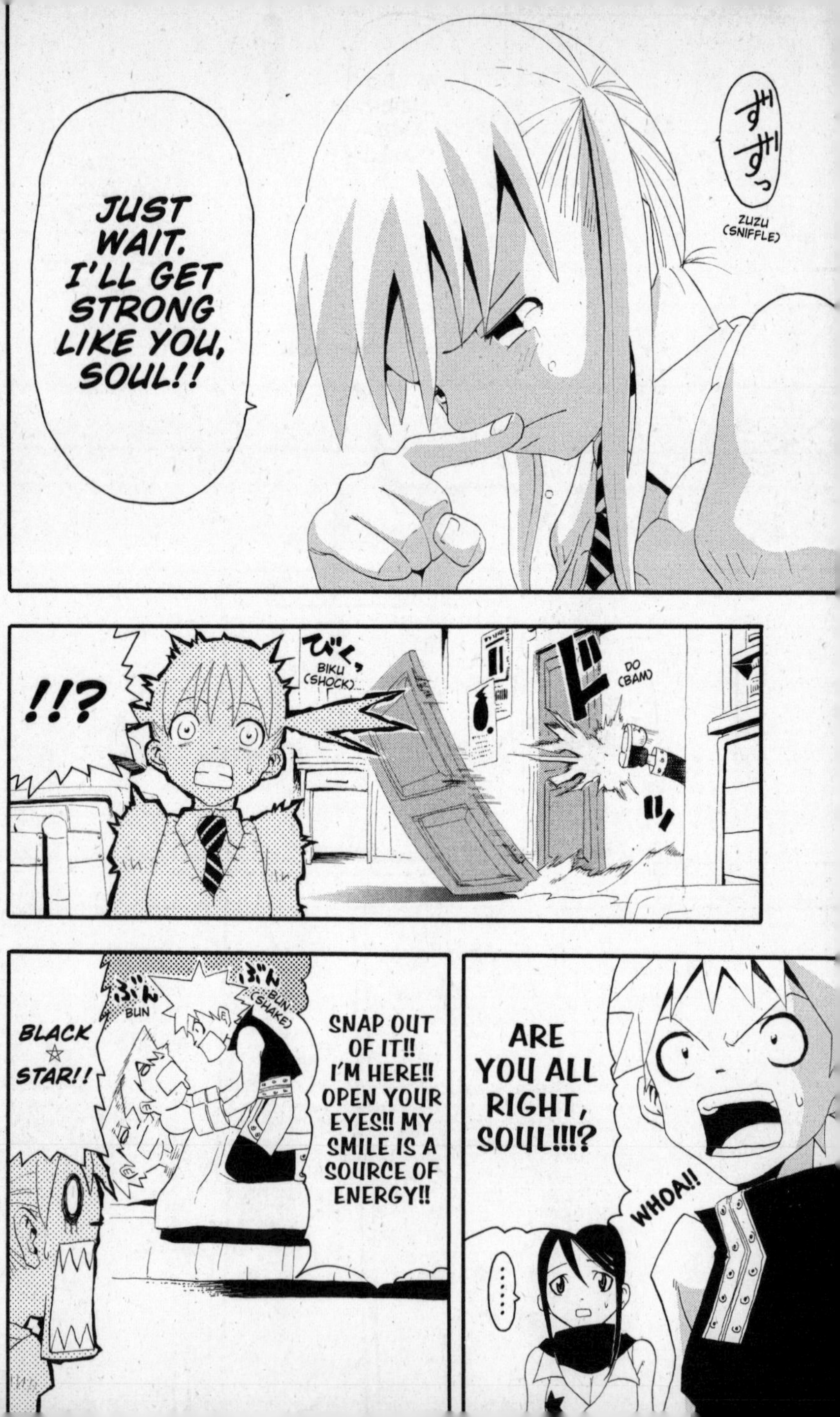
ずずっ
ZUZU (SNIFFLE)
JUST WAIT. I'LL GET STRONG LIKE YOU, SOUL!!
DO (BAM)
びくっ
BIKU (SHOCK)
!!?
ARE YOU ALL RIGHT, SOUL!!!?
WHOA!!
......
SNAP OUT OF IT!! I'M HERE!! OPEN YOUR EYES!! MY SMILE IS A SOURCE OF ENERGY!!
ぶん
BUN (SHAKE)
ぶん
BUN
BLACK☆STAR!!

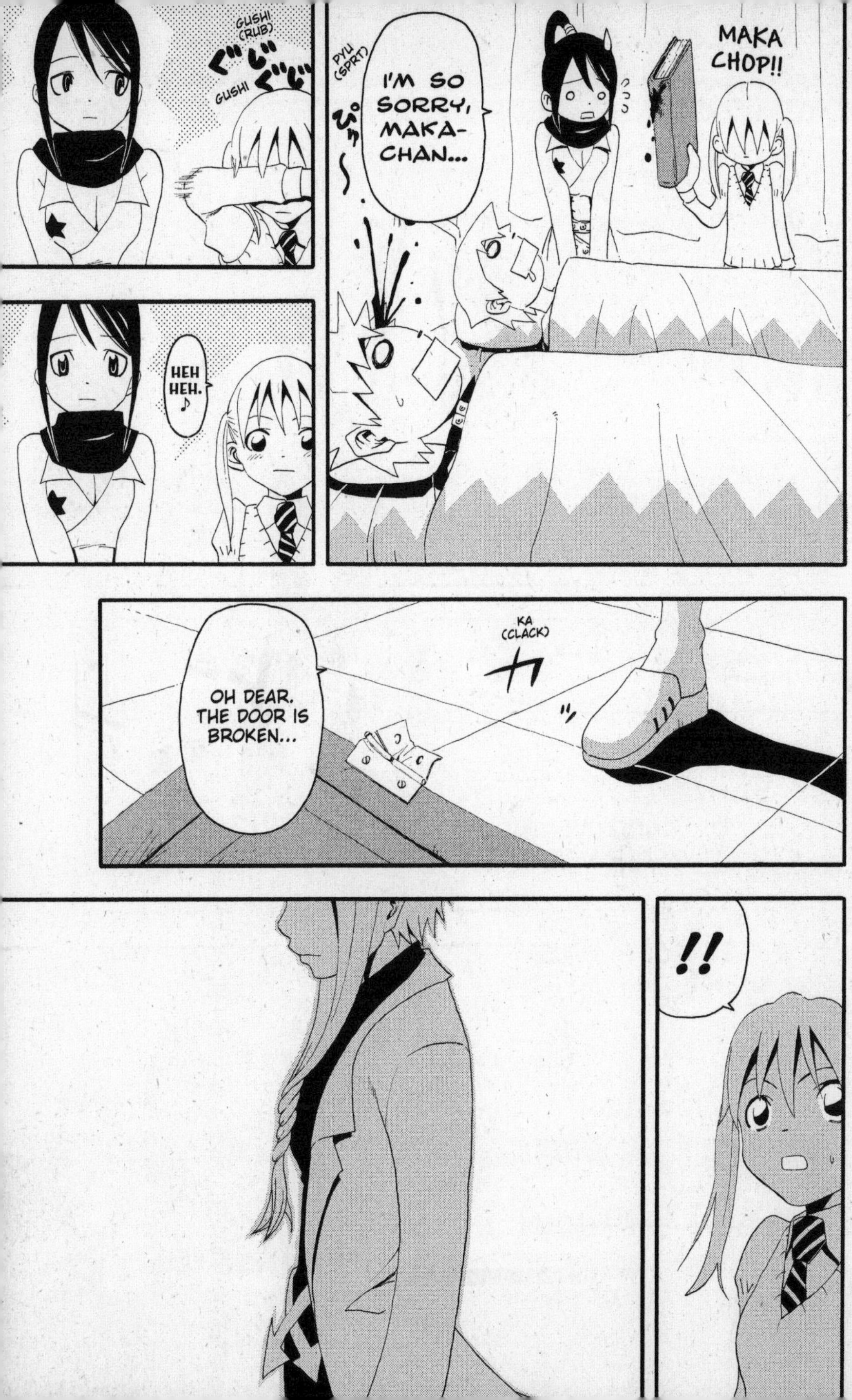
MAKA CHOP!!
I'M SO SORRY, MAKA-CHAN...
PYU (SPRT)
GUSHI (RUB)
GUSHI
HEH HEH. ♪
KA (CLACK)
OH DEAR. THE DOOR IS BROKEN...
!!

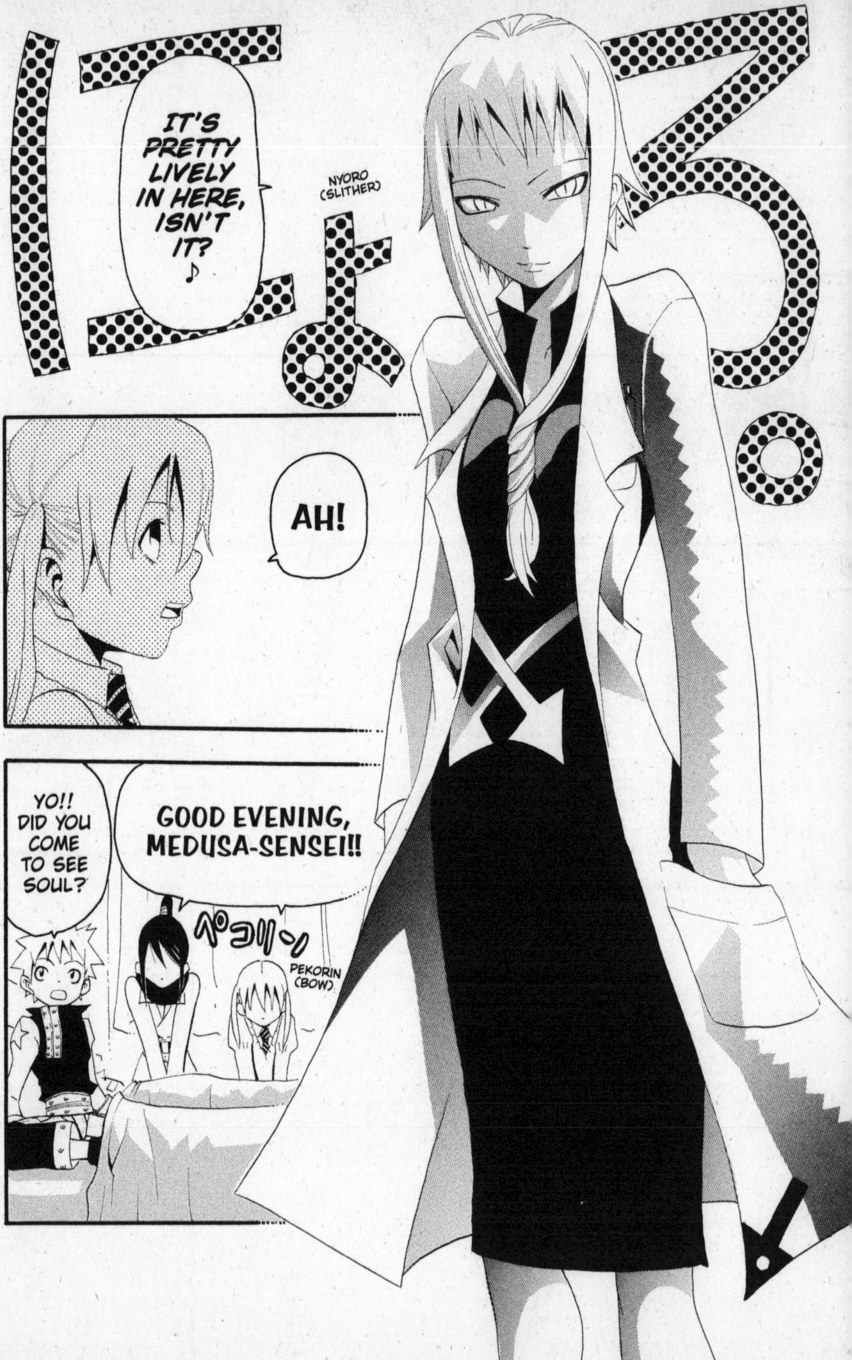
NYORO (SLITHER)
IT'S PRETTY LIVELY IN HERE, ISN'T IT? ♪
AH!
GOOD EVENING, MEDUSA-SENSEI!!
PEKORIN (BOW)
YO!! DID YOU COME TO SEE SOUL?

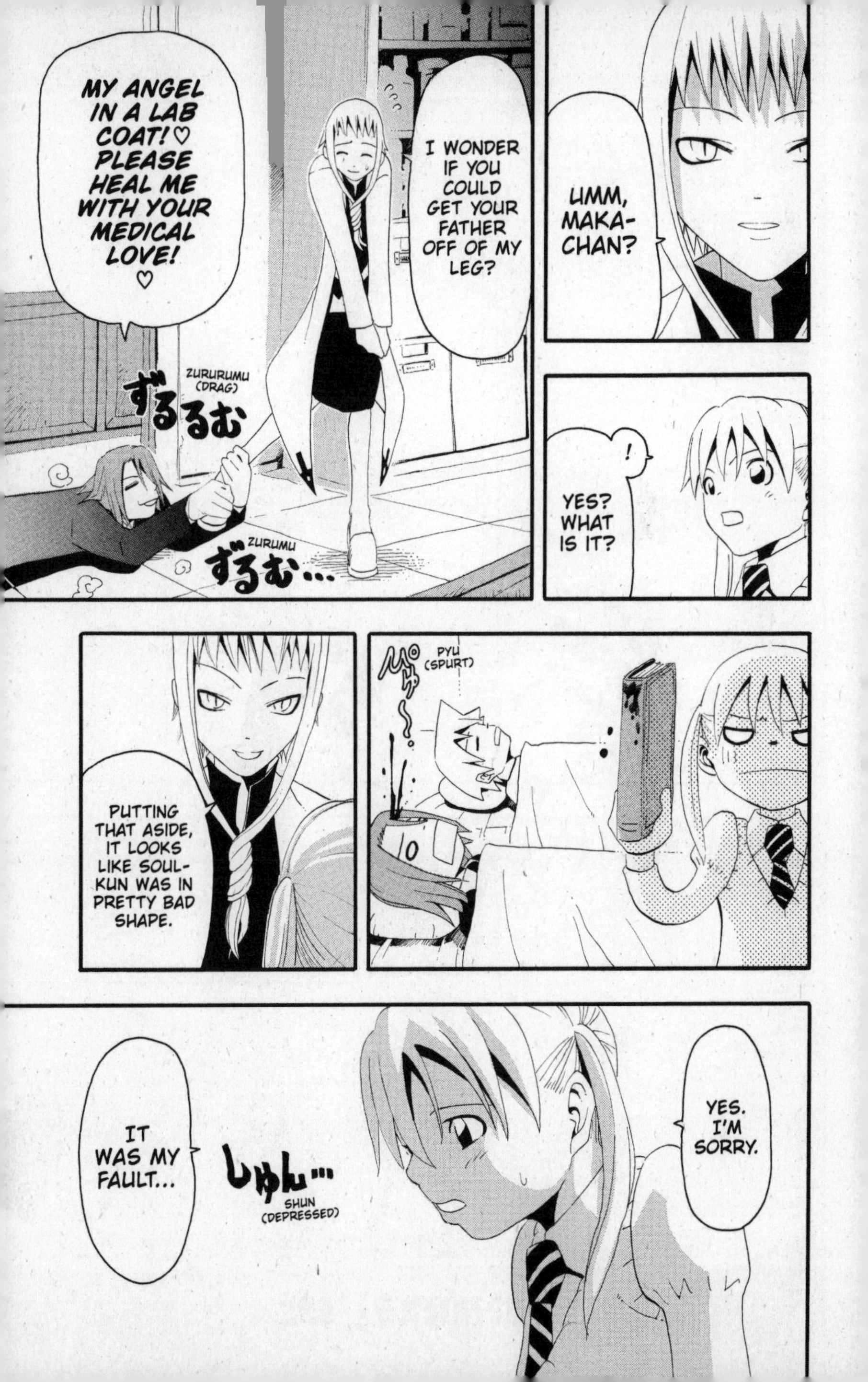
UMM, MAKA-CHAN?
YES? WHAT IS IT?
!
I WONDER IF YOU COULD GET YOUR FATHER OFF OF MY LEG?
MY ANGEL IN A LAB COAT! ♡ PLEASE HEAL ME WITH YOUR MEDICAL LOVE! ♡
ずるるむ
ZURURUMU (DRAG)
ずるむ…
ZURUMU
ぴゅ～
PYU (SPURT)
PUTTING THAT ASIDE, IT LOOKS LIKE SOUL-KUN WAS IN PRETTY BAD SHAPE.
YES. I'M SORRY.
しゅん
SHUN (DEPRESSED)
IT WAS MY FAULT...

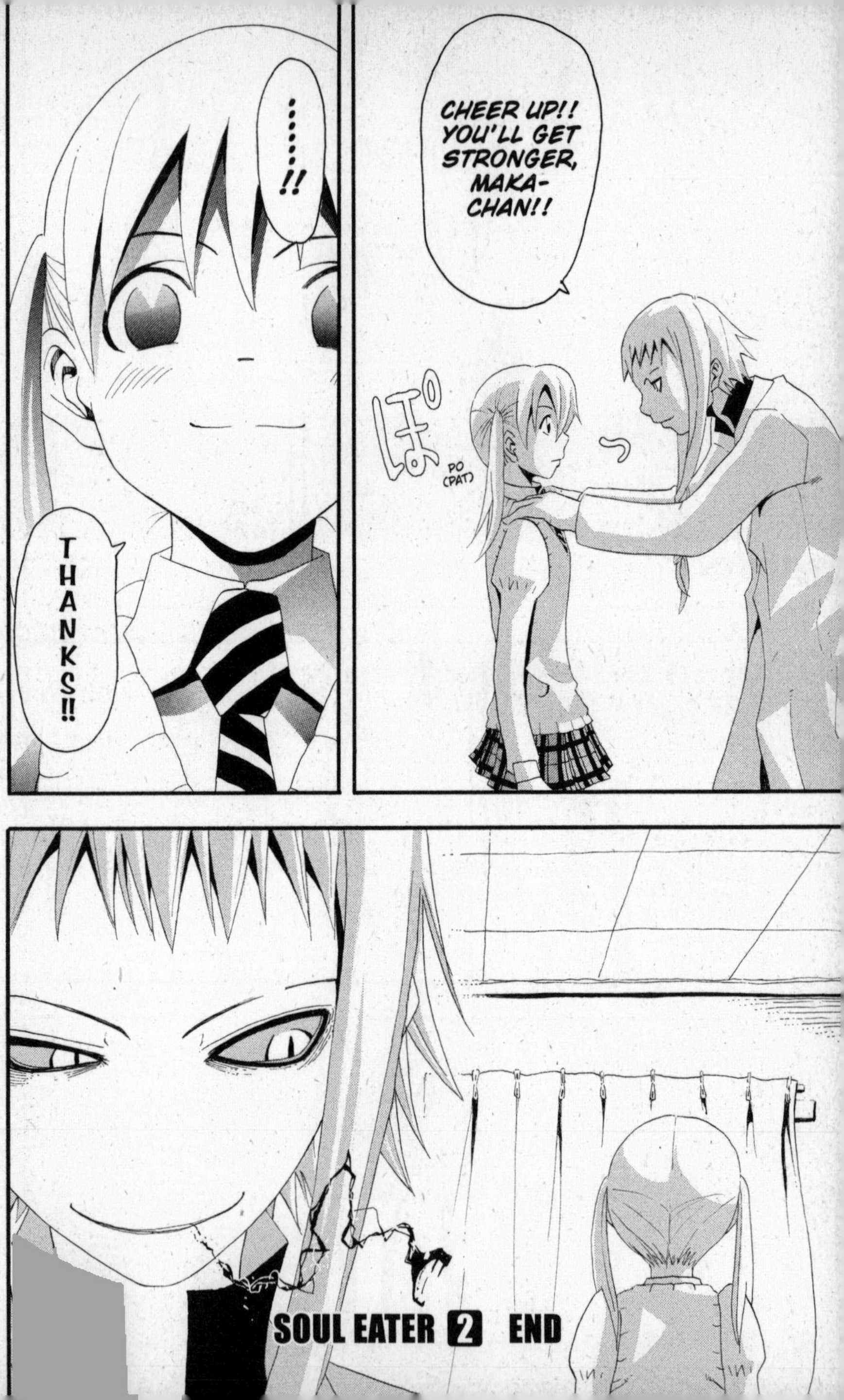
CHEER UP!! YOU'LL GET STRONGER, MAKA-CHAN!!
ぽ
PO (PAT)
......!!
THANKS!!
SOUL EATER 2 END

SOUL EATER

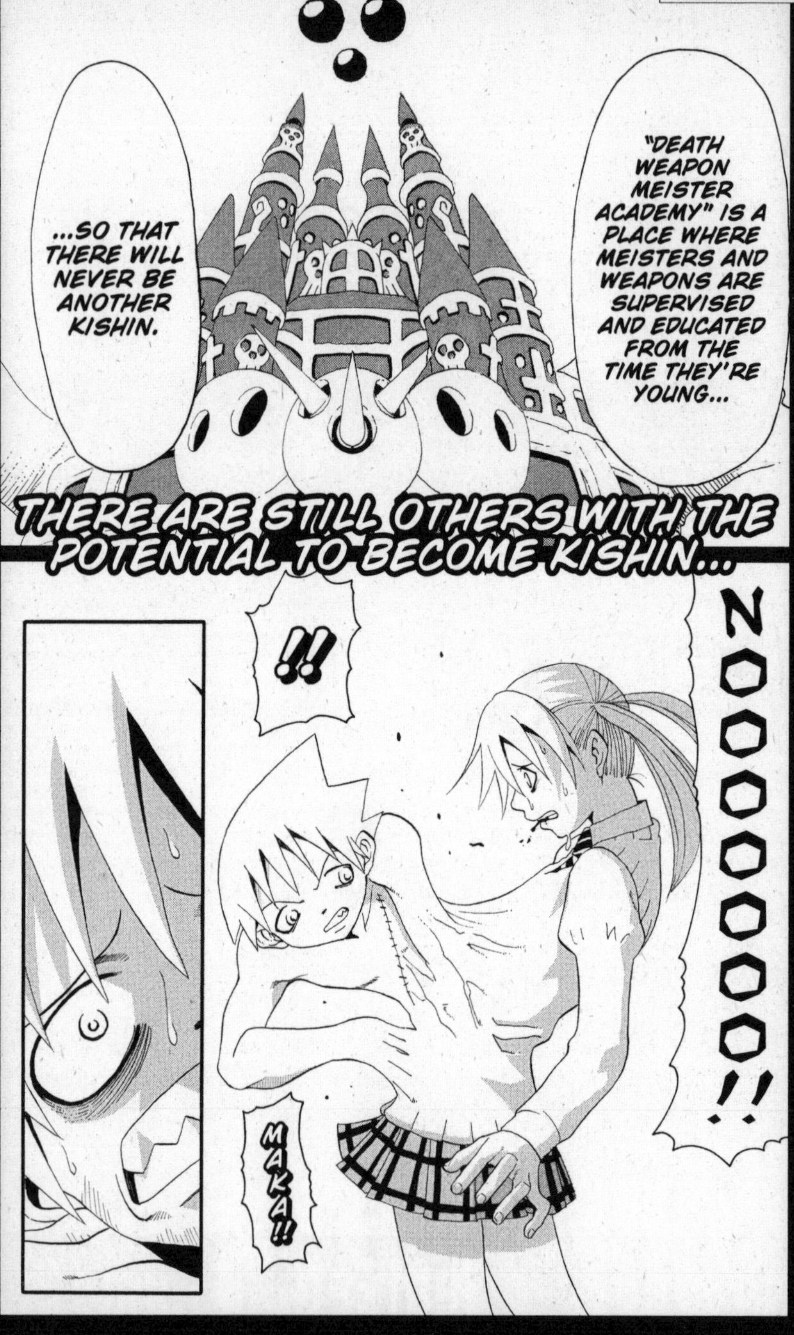
"DEATH WEAPON MEISTER ACADEMY" IS A PLACE WHERE MEISTERS AND WEAPONS ARE SUPERVISED AND EDUCATED FROM THE TIME THEY'RE YOUNG...
...SO THAT THERE WILL NEVER BE ANOTHER KISHIN.
THERE ARE STILL OTHERS WITH THE POTENTIAL TO BECOME KISHIN...
NOOOOOOOO!!
!!
MAKA!!

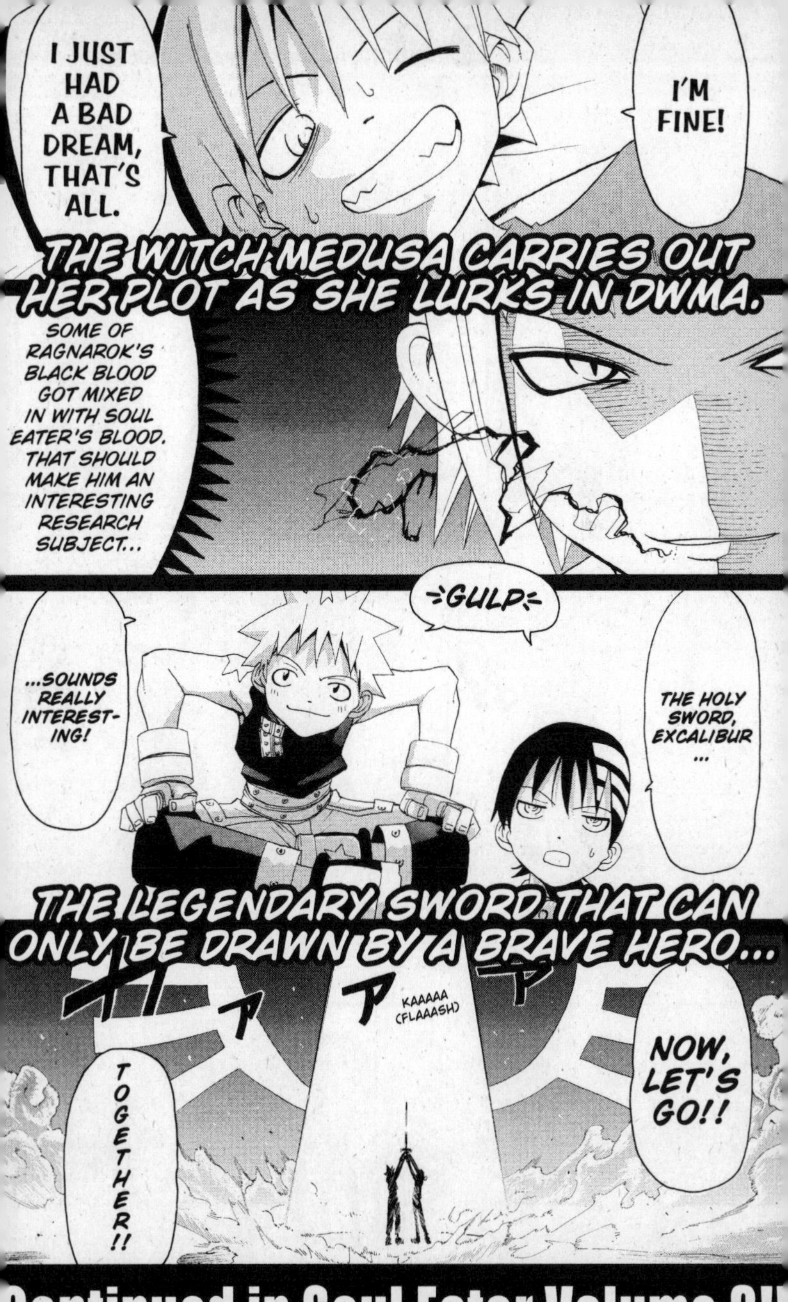
I'M FINE!
I JUST HAD A BAD DREAM, THAT'S ALL.
THE WITCH MEDUSA CARRIES OUT HER PLOT AS SHE LURKS IN DWMA.
SOME OF RAGNAROK'S BLACK BLOOD GOT MIXED IN WITH SOUL EATER'S BLOOD. THAT SHOULD MAKE HIM AN INTERESTING RESEARCH SUBJECT...
THE HOLY SWORD, EXCALIBUR...
GULP
...SOUNDS REALLY INTEREST-ING!
THE LEGENDARY SWORD THAT CAN ONLY BE DRAWN BY A BRAVE HERO...
NOW, LET'S GO!!
KAAAAA (FLAAASH)
TOGETHER!!

Continued in Soul Eater Volume 3!!

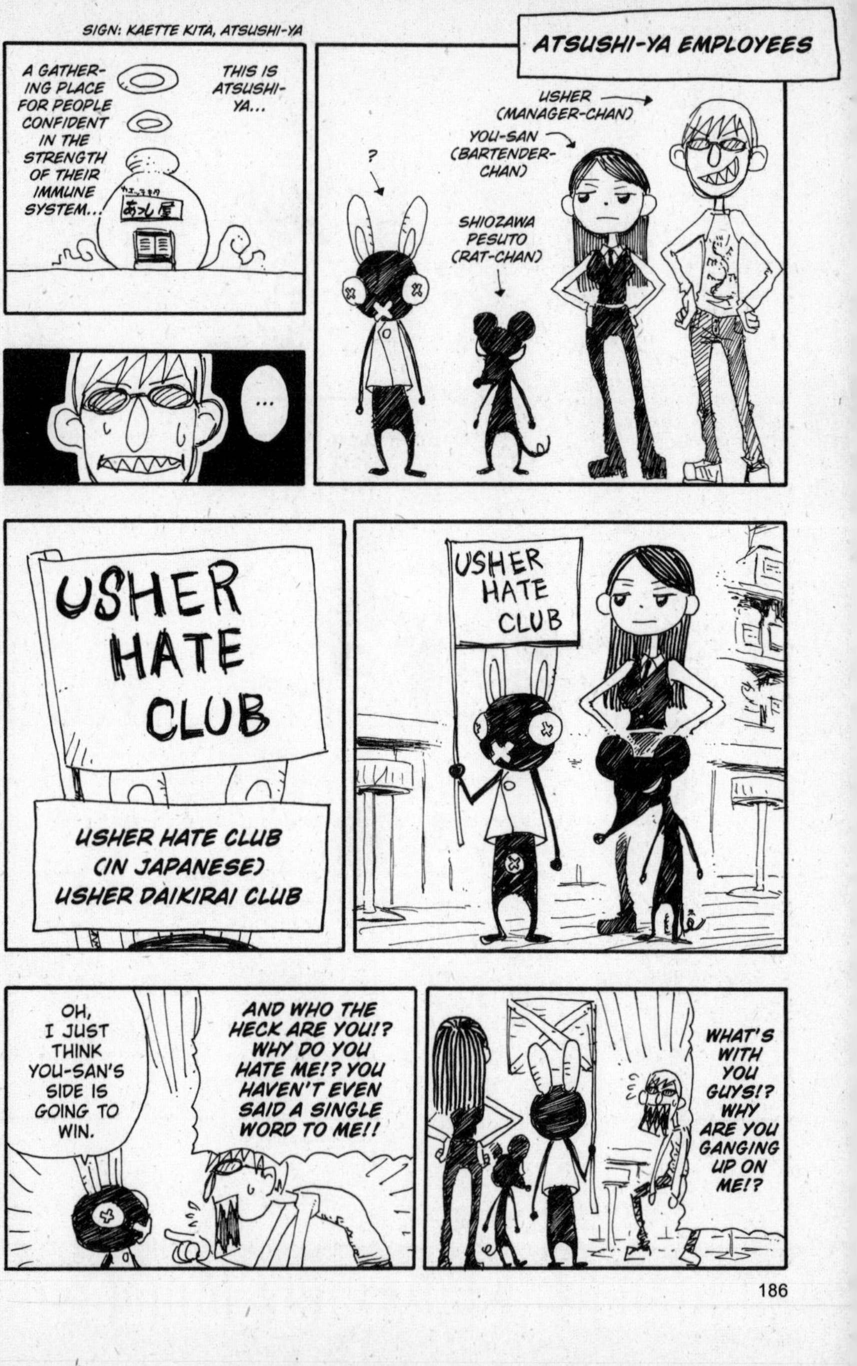
ATSUSHI-YA EMPLOYEES
USHER (MANAGER-CHAN)
YOU-SAN (BARTENDER-CHAN)
?
SHIOZAWA PESUTO (RAT-CHAN)
SIGN: KAETTE KITA, ATSUSHI-YA
THIS IS ATSUSHI-YA...
A GATHERING PLACE FOR PEOPLE CONFIDENT IN THE STRENGTH OF THEIR IMMUNE SYSTEM...
あっし屋
...
USHER HATE CLUB
USHER HATE CLUB
USHER HATE CLUB (IN JAPANESE) USHER DAIKIRAI CLUB
WHAT'S WITH YOU GUYS!? WHY ARE YOU GANGING UP ON ME!?
AND WHO THE HECK ARE YOU!? WHY DO YOU HATE ME!? YOU HAVEN'T EVEN SAID A SINGLE WORD TO ME!!
OH, I JUST THINK YOU-SAN'S SIDE IS GOING TO WIN.

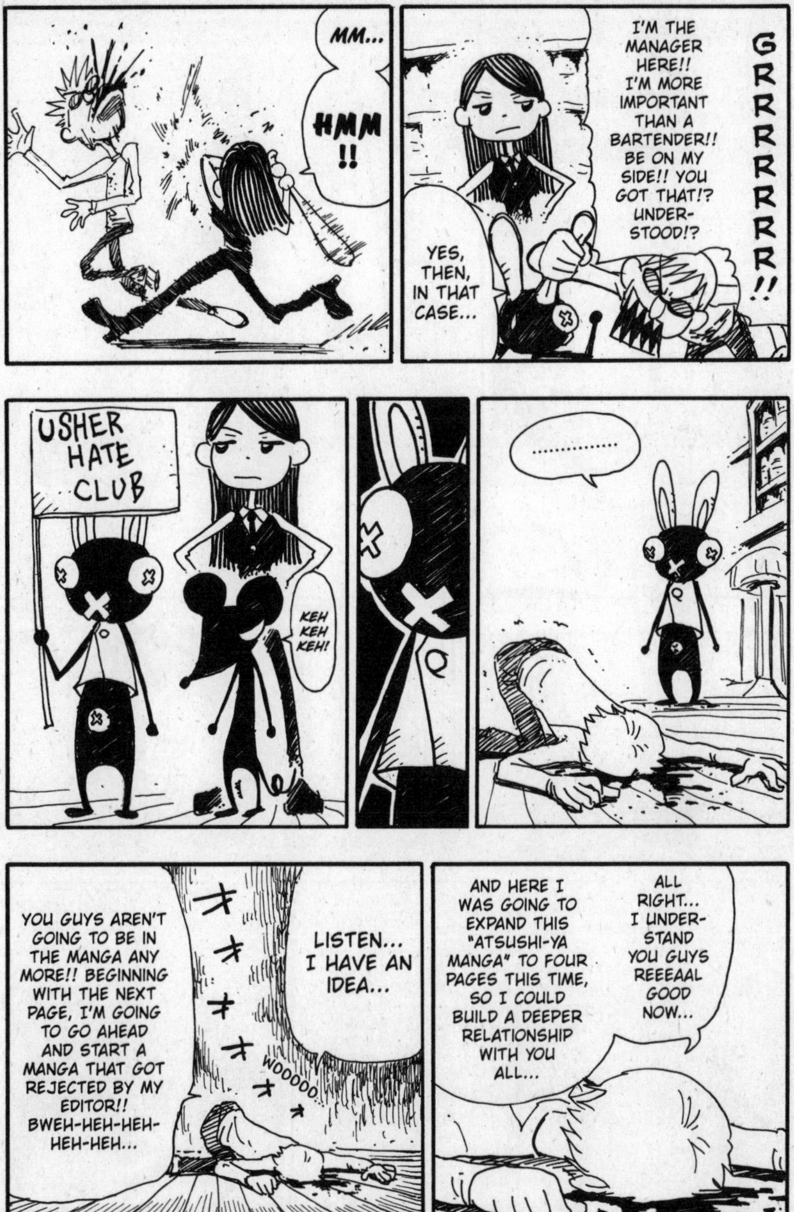
GRRRRRRR!!
I'M THE MANAGER HERE!! I'M MORE IMPORTANT THAN A BARTENDER!! BE ON MY SIDE!! YOU GOT THAT!? UNDER-STOOD!?
YES, THEN, IN THAT CASE...
MM...
HMM!!
....
KEH KEH KEH!
USHER HATE CLUB
ALL RIGHT... I UNDER-STAND YOU GUYS REEEAAL GOOD NOW...
AND HERE I WAS GOING TO EXPAND THIS "ATSUSHI-YA MANGA" TO FOUR PAGES THIS TIME, SO I COULD BUILD A DEEPER RELATIONSHIP WITH YOU ALL...
LISTEN... I HAVE AN IDEA...
WOOOOO...
YOU GUYS AREN'T GOING TO BE IN THE MANGA ANY MORE!! BEGINNING WITH THE NEXT PAGE, I'M GOING TO GO AHEAD AND START A MANGA THAT GOT REJECTED BY MY EDITOR!! BWEH-HEH-HEH-HEH-HEH...

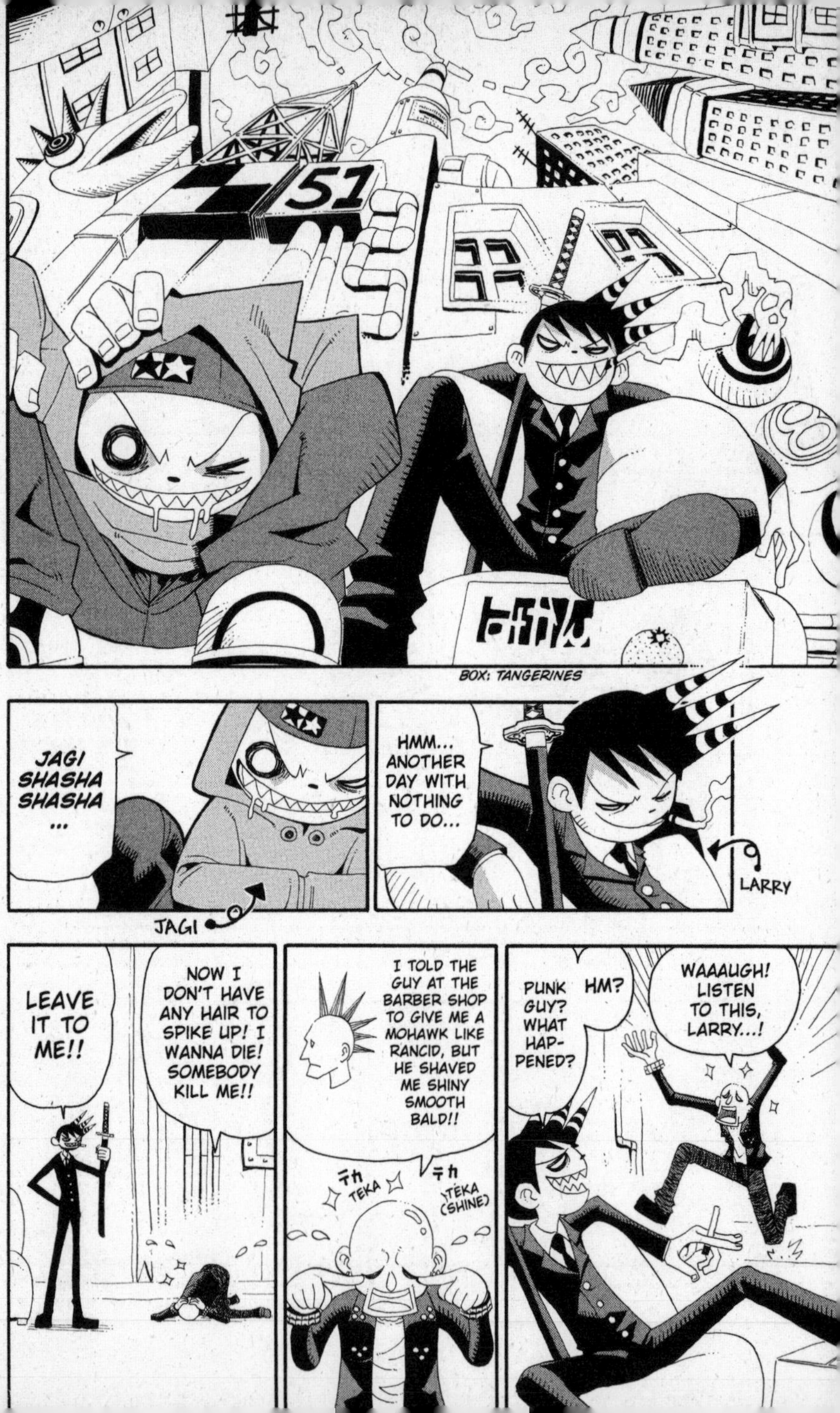
51
BOX: TANGERINES
HMM... ANOTHER DAY WITH NOTHING TO DO...
LARRY
JAGI SHASHA SHASHA ...
JAGI
WAAAUGH! LISTEN TO THIS, LARRY...!
HM?
PUNK GUY? WHAT HAP-PENED?
I TOLD THE GUY AT THE BARBER SHOP TO GIVE ME A MOHAWK LIKE RANCID, BUT HE SHAVED ME SHINY SMOOTH BALD!!
テカ TEKA
テカ TEKA (SHINE)
NOW I DON'T HAVE ANY HAIR TO SPIKE UP! I WANNA DIE! SOMEBODY KILL ME!!
LEAVE IT TO ME!!

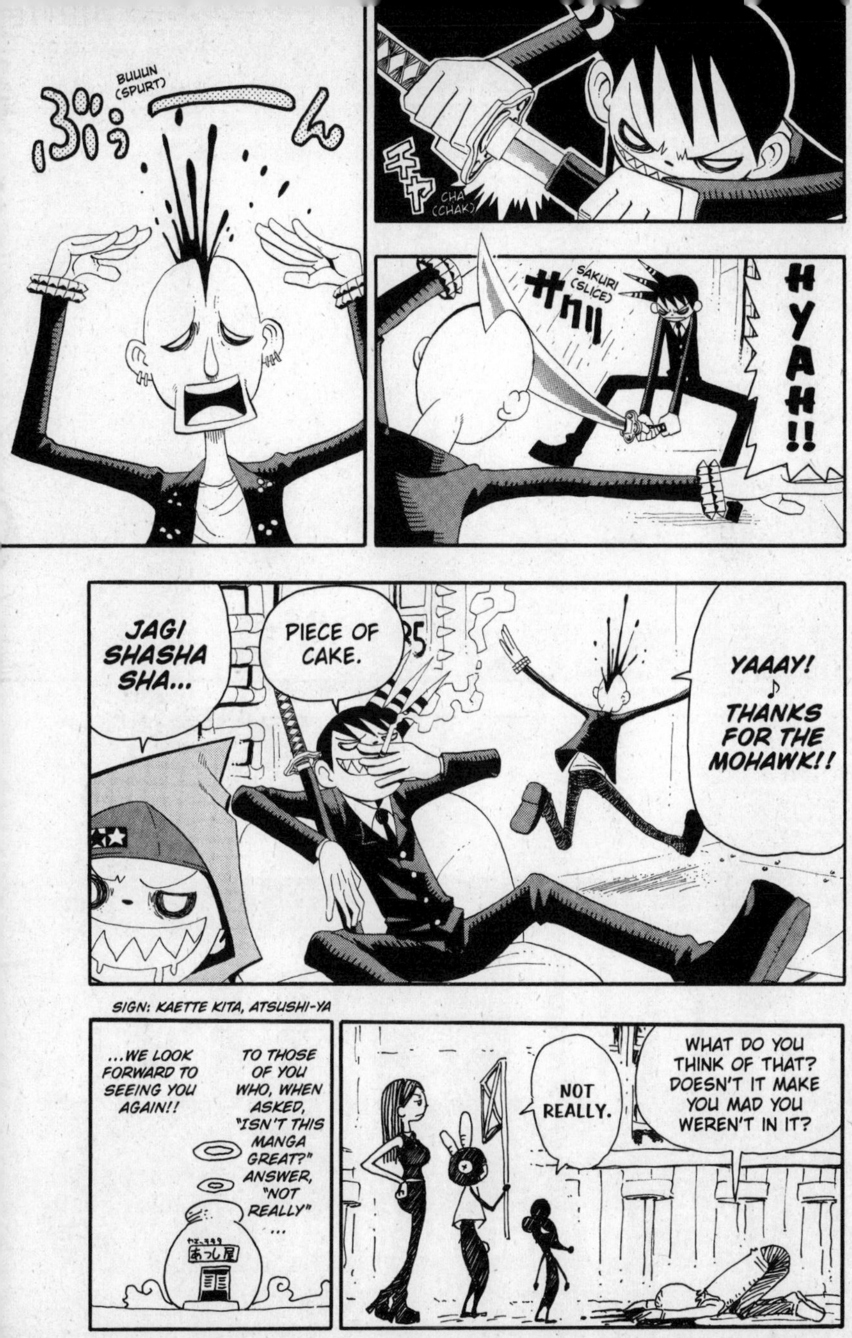
チャ
CHA (CHAK)
サクリ
SAKURI (SLICE)
HYAH!!
BUUUN (SPURT)
YAAAY! ♪ THANKS FOR THE MOHAWK!!
PIECE OF CAKE.
JAGI SHASHA SHA...
SIGN: KAETTE KITA, ATSUSHI-YA
WHAT DO YOU THINK OF THAT? DOESN'T IT MAKE YOU MAD YOU WEREN'T IN IT?
NOT REALLY.
TO THOSE OF YOU WHO, WHEN ASKED, "ISN'T THIS MANGA GREAT?" ANSWER, "NOT REALLY" ...
...WE LOOK FORWARD TO SEEING YOU AGAIN!!
あっし屋

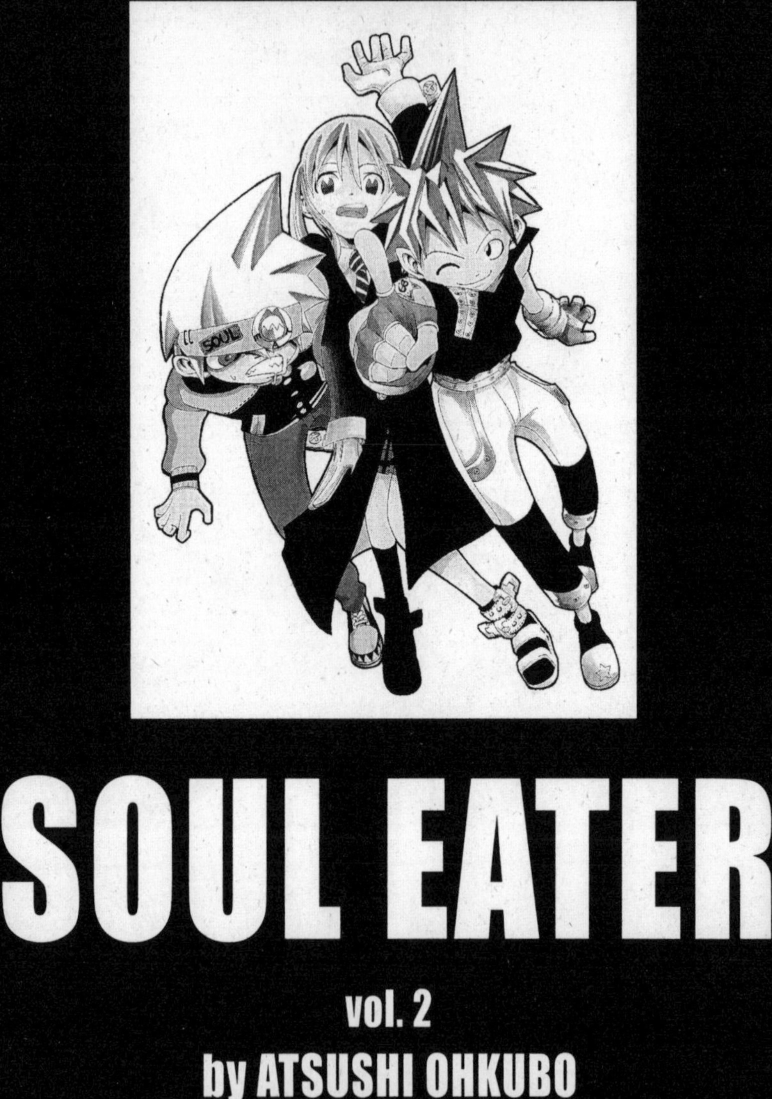
SOUL

SOUL EATER

vol. 2

by ATSUSHI OHKUBO

The jet-black SOUL,
Walk with me

Translation Notes

Common Honorifics

no honorific: Indicates familiarity or closeness; if used without permission or reason, addressing someone in this manner would constitute an insult.

-san: The Japanese equivalent of Mr./Mrs./Miss. If a situation calls for politeness, this is the fail-safe honorific.

-sama: Conveys great respect; may also indicate that the social status of the speaker is lower than that of the addressee.

-kun: Used most often when referring to boys, this indicates affection or familiarity. Occasionally used by older men among their peers, but it may also be used by anyone referring to a person of lower standing.

-chan: An affectionate honorific indicating familiarity used mostly in reference to girls; also used in reference to cute persons or animals of either gender.

-senpai: A suffix used to address upperclassmen or more experienced coworkers.

-sensei: A respectful term for teachers, artists, or high-level professionals.

Look for more Soul Eater in

YEN+ *Plus*

A monthly manga anthology from Yen Press!

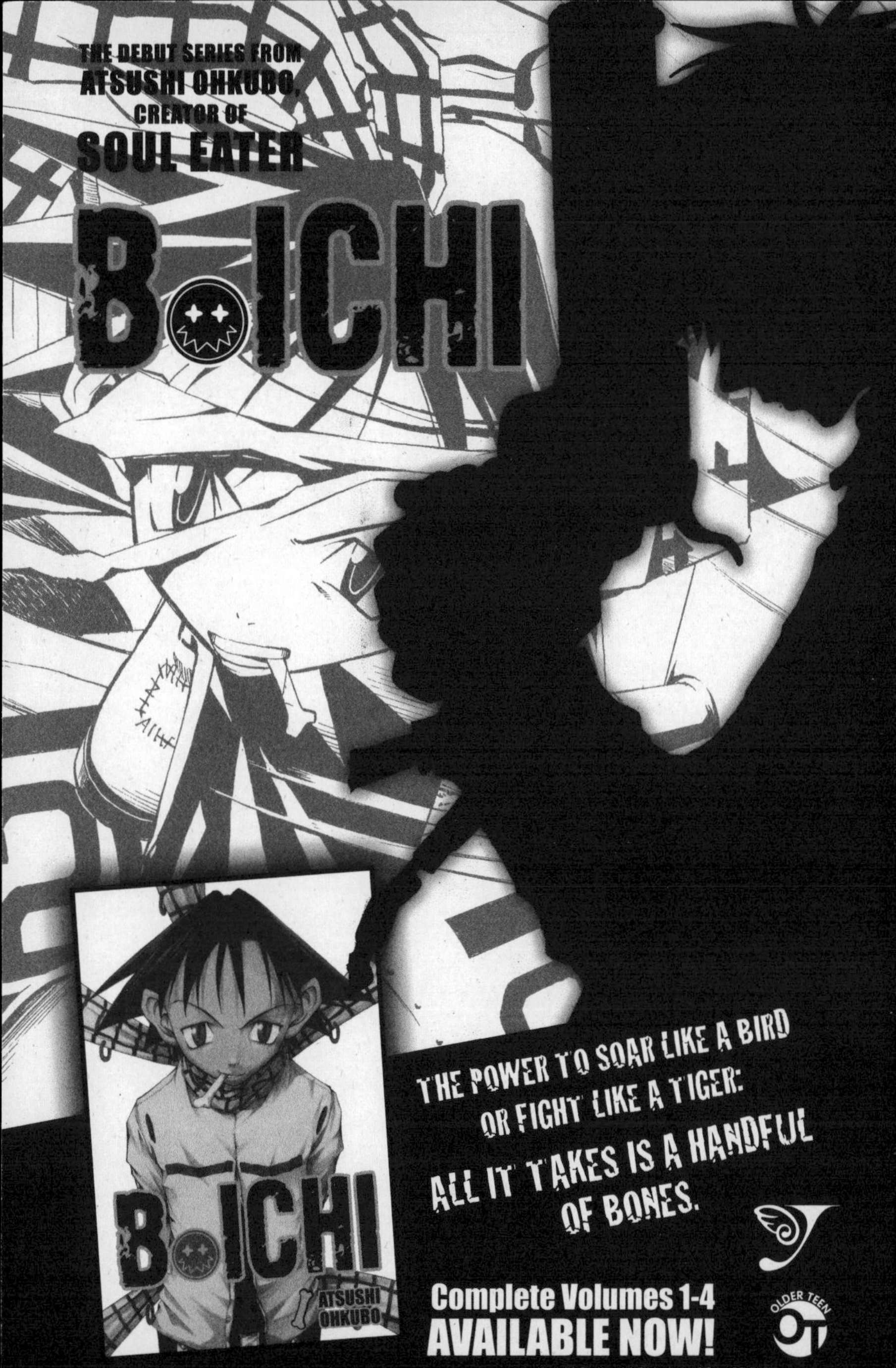

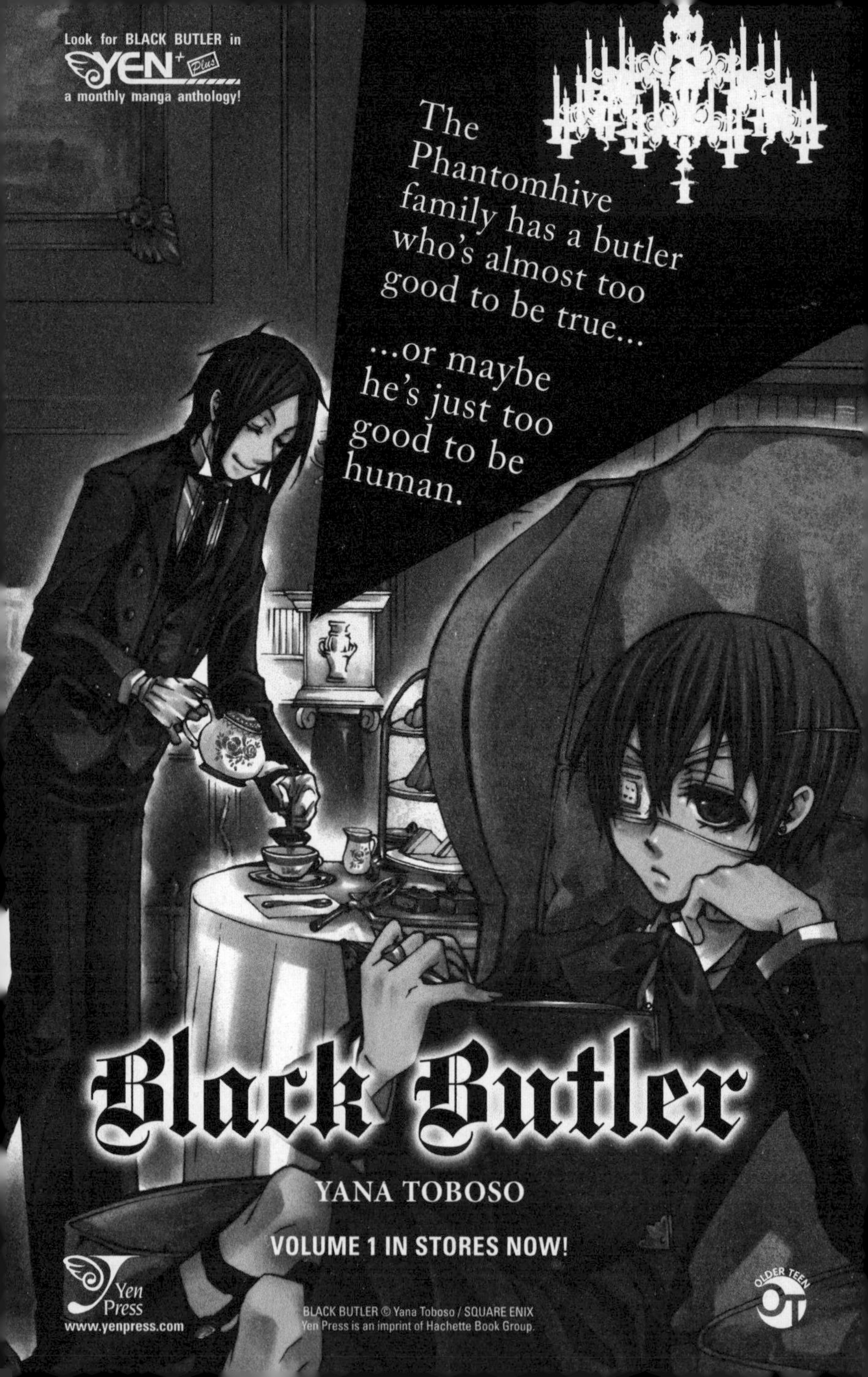
Look for BLACK BUTLER in
YEN+ Plus
a monthly manga anthology!
The Phantomhive family has a butler who's almost too good to be true...
...or maybe he's just too good to be human.
Black Butler
YANA TOBOSO
VOLUME 1 IN STORES NOW!
Yen Press
www.yenpress.com
BLACK BUTLER © Yana Toboso / SQUARE ENIX
Yen Press is an imprint of Hachette Book Group.
OLDER TEEN
OT

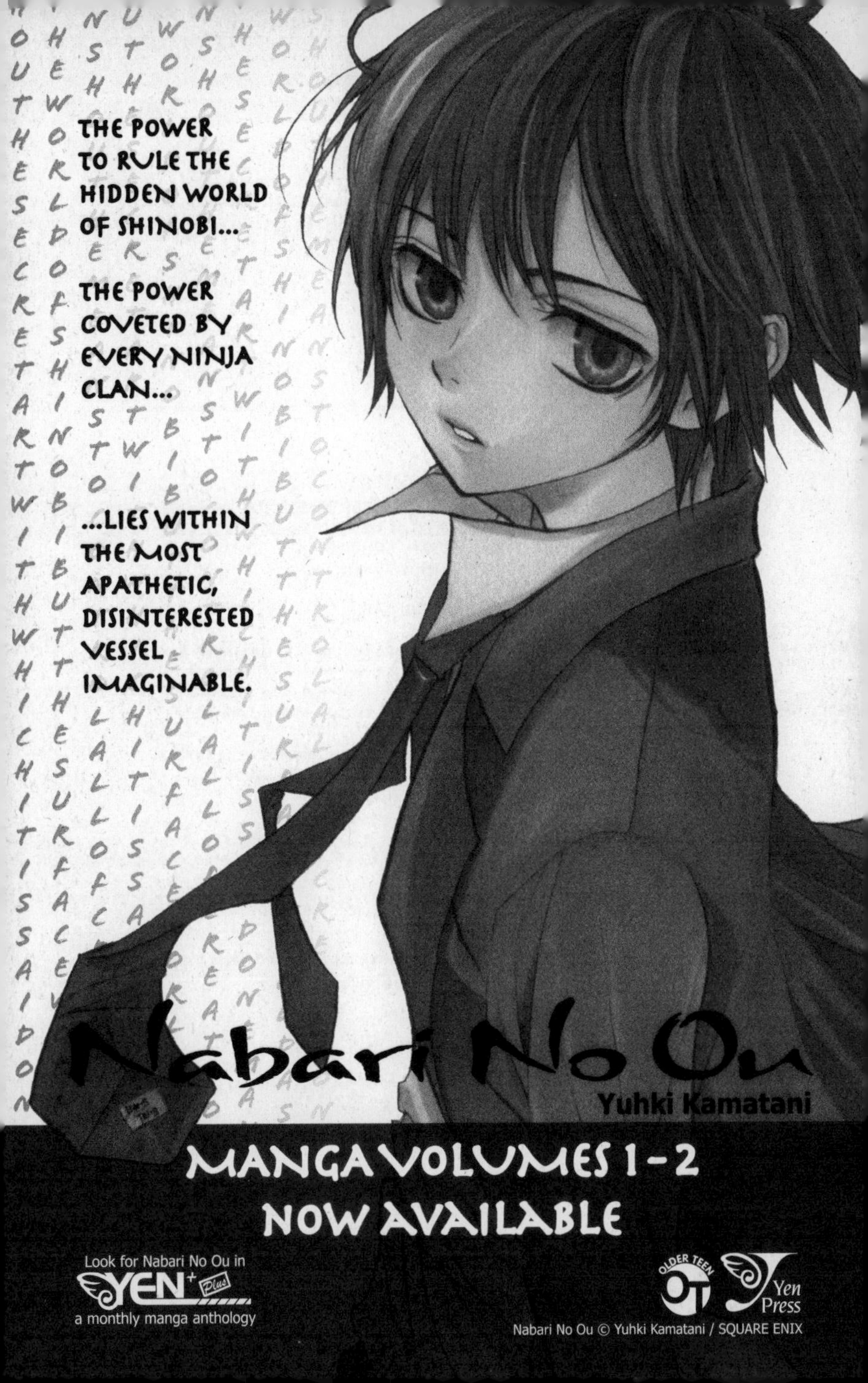

THE POWER TO RULE THE HIDDEN WORLD OF SHINOBI...
THE POWER COVETED BY EVERY NINJA CLAN...
...LIES WITHIN THE MOST APATHETIC, DISINTERESTED VESSEL IMAGINABLE.
Nabari No Ou
Yuhki Kamatani
MANGA VOLUMES 1-2 NOW AVAILABLE
Look for Nabari No Ou in YEN+ Plus
a monthly manga anthology
OLDER TEEN OT
Yen Press
Nabari No Ou © Yuhki Kamatani / SQUARE ENIX

SOUL EATER ②

ATSUSHI OHKUBO

Translation: Amy Forsyth

Lettering: Alexis Eckerman

SOUL EATER Vol. 2 © 2004 Atsushi Ohkubo / SQUARE ENIX. All rights reserved. First published in Japan in 2004 by SQUARE ENIX CO., LTD. English translation rights arranged with SQUARE ENIX CO., LTD. and Hachette Book Group through Tuttle-Mori Agency, Inc.

Translation © 2010 by SQUARE ENIX CO., LTD.

Yen Press
Hachette Book Group
237 Park Avenue, New York, NY 10017

www.HachetteBookGroup.com
www.YenPress.com

Yen Press is an imprint of Hachette Book Group, Inc. The Yen Press name and logo are trademarks of Hachette Book Group, Inc.

First Yen Press Edition: February 2010

ISBN: 978-0-7595-3048-5

10 9 8 7 6

BVG

Printed in the United States of America